Antithesis of Yoga

a non-fiction novel by

Jocelyn

First Edition 2003
Second Edition 2022

Antithesis of Yoga
Jocelyn

ISBN 978-93-95460-14-9 (print)
ISBN 978-93-95460-15-6 (ebook)

BISAC Code:
HIS062000, HISTORY / Asia / South / India
PHI034000, PHILOSOPHY / Social
BIO026000, BIOGRAPHY & AUTOBIOGRAPHY / Personal Memoirs

Thema Subject Category:
JBCC9, History of ideas
NH, History
NHF, Asian history
DNBX1, Autobiography: religious and spiritual

Printed and bound in India by:
PRISMA, Aurelec/ Prayogshala,
Auroville 605101, Tamil Nadu, India

Digital Editions produced by:
DMI Systems Pvt Ltd, Vishnupuri,
Aligarh 202001, Uttar Pradesh, India

Published by PRISMA, an imprint of Digital Media Initiatives
www.prisma.haus, www.dmi.systems

Dedicated to Binah

In the midst of time
there stands a citadel not of stone
but of mind and soul
that stands the test of time.

With thanks to The Mother and Sri Aurobindo for their inspiration. Thanks to John Kelly, Maggi Licchi Grazzi, Ananta, John Walker, Alain Bernard, Panditji, Kalya, John and Sunina Mandeen, Ellen, Gillian, John White, Michael Miovic, Verne, Kate, J.V. Ganeson, Otto, Anna Rivera, Otto and everyone else who has contributed to the story of Auroville.

And Special thanks to the Sri Aurobindo Ashram copywrite department Manoj Das Gupta for permission to use words of the Mother and Sri Aurobindo.

About the Author

Antithesis of Yoga is a nonfictional novel of the first 25 years of wonderful and terrible life in the City of the Future, written by Jocelyn. Auroville, The City Earth Needs, near Pondicherry India, is a global spiritual township started by The Mother in 1968. For those interested in learning about the history of Auroville, and would like to meet the fascinating people and hear the often amazing stories of the beginnings of this Utopian experiment they can find here a first hand account of the tumultuous years of Auroville's early development.

Roslyn, an American hippie single mother, had imagined she had had a vision calling her to India. She travelled to Pondicherry overland across Europe and Asia, not knowing her destination was Pondicherry. She arrived with her eight month old daughter Bliss in August 1969. She thought she had found Shangri la. Pondicherry was nothing like anywhere she had been. It sparkled.

She soon met many interesting, exotic people, John Kelly, a New York City fireman who had had visions of Mother and Sri Aurobindo in the trenches in WWII; and Ananta. a Boston Brahmin sadhu who had built a temple to Zeus on the island Mother had given him; the Countess de B, a hero of the French Resistance; the tantric guru, Panditji; and many others. But Roslyn was completely captivated by The Mother and Her vision and ideals for Auroville.

Roslyn's first glimpse of Auroville was a red eroded plain, pockmarked with impoverished villages. There was not a tree to be seen. There was no electricity in the area. There was 100% illiteracy among the villagers. But that was not what Roslyn saw. She saw a place where a utopia would be built by sun eyed children of a new dawn.

There were many adventures, misadventures and challenges along the way.

This book tells some of the story of the great adventure of the beginning of the town. Auroville today is a town in South India visited by VIP's, students and people from all over the world, the home of people from more than 30 countries, the winner of a Green Oscar, the site of the Matrimandir, and has applied for World Heritage status. It is a successful experiment in developing a spiritual global community.

Table of Contents

XII. *"Nobleness and generosity are the soul's real firmament; without them, one looks at an insect in a dungeon."**

XIII. *"Not to cull the praises of men as God made thee His own, but to do fearlessly His bidding."**

XIV. *"Care not for time and success. Act out thy part, whether it be to fail or to prosper."**

XV. *"Turn all things to honey; this is the law of divine living."**

XVI. *"The medieval ascetics hated women and thought they were created by God for the temptation of monks. One may be allowed to think more nobly both of God and of woman."**

XVII. *"Distrust the man who has never failed and suffered; follow not his fortunes, fight not under his banner."**

XVIII. *"Imperfect capacity and effect in the work that is mean for thee is better than an artificial competency and a borrowed perfection."**

XIX. *"It is easy to distinguish the evil worked by sin and vice, but the trained eye sees also the evil done by self-righteous or self-regarding virtue."**

XX. *"To commit adultery with God is the perfect experience for which the world was created."**

XXI. *"God took a child to fondle him in His bosom of delight, but the mother wept and would not be consoled because her child no longer existed."**

XXII. *"Love of man, love of woman, love of things, love of thy neighbor, love of thy country, love of animals, love of humanity, are all the love of God reflected in these living images. So love and grow mighty to enjoy all, to help all and to love for ever."**

XXIII. *"Our Evil is to God not evil, but ignorance and imperfection, our good a lesser imperfection."**

from Sri Aurobindo's 'Thoughts and Aphorisms.'

List of Illustrations

A Dream

There should be somewhere upon earth a place that no nation could claim as its sole property, a place where all human beings of good will, sincere in their aspiration, could live freely as citizens of the world, obeying one single authority, that of the supreme Truth; a place of peace, concord, harmony, where all the fighting instincts of man would be used exclusively to conquer the causes of his suffering and misery, to surmount his weakness and ignorance, to triumph over his limitations and incapacities; a place where the needs of the spirit and the care for progress would get precedence over the satisfaction of desires and passions, the seeking for pleasures and material enjoyment.

In this place, children would be able to grow and develop integrally without losing contact with their soul. Education would be given, not with a view to passing examinations and getting certificates and posts, but for enriching the existing faculties and bringing forth new ones. In this place, titles and positions would be supplanted by opportunities to serve and organise.

The needs of the body will be provided for equally in the case of each and every one. In the general organisation intellectual, moral and spiritual superiority will find expression not in the enhancement of the pleasures and powers of life but in the increase of duties and responsibilities. Artistic beauty in all forms, painting, sculpture, music, literature, will be available equally to all, the opportunity to share in the joys they bring being limited solely by each one's capacities and not by one's social or financial position.

For in this ideal place money would be no more the sovereign lord. Individual merit will have a greater importance than the value due to material wealth and social position. Work would not be there as the means of gaining one's livehood, it would be the means whereby to express oneself, develop one's capacities and possibilities, while doing at the same time service to the whole group, which on its side would provide for each one's subsistence and for the field of his work.

In brief, it would be a place where relations between human beings, usually based almost exclusively upon competition and strife, would be replaced by relations of emulation for doing better, for collaboration, relations of real brotherhood.

– The Mother

Chapter I

Dharshan

A deathbound littleness is not all we are;
Immortal, our forgotten vastnesses
Await discovery in our summit selves
Unmeasured breadths and depths of being are ours.
Deep in us a forgotten kinship points,
And a faint voice of ecstasy and prayer
Calls to those lucent lost immensities,
Even when we fail to look into our souls,
Or life embedded in earthly consciousness,
Still have we parts that grow towards the light.

Sri Aurobindo, Savitri

Our path is towards a threefold union. First, on the path of integral yoga is the yoga of knowledge, in spiritual essence by identity. Second is the yoga of devotion, to liberation from the ignorance and identification with the real and eternal. Third is the yoga of will in union by indwelling of our soul in the highest being, consciousness, dynamic union of likeness or oneness of nature between that and our instrumental being.

Knowledge is the growing consciousness of a consciousness above deciding the movements of mind. The sign of transformation of the mind is experienced with a controlled change of consciousness, with a growing direct experience, vision, feeling of the Supreme; a growing recognition of the Divine in itself, in all things. The mind is taken into a growing preoccupation and will feel itself widening into a more illumined means of expression of the one fundamental knowledge. The central consciousness will take up more and more the outer mental activities of knowledge and turn them into more and more spiritualised mind, an instrument on the surface as well as in its own deeper spiritual empire.

Love is the deepest and most intense knowledge, the highest luminous cave of nature. The dynamic process is the development of the true soul to take the place of the false soul of desire, the sublimation of human into divine love, and the elevation of the consciousness from its mental to its spiritual and Supramental plane, where power has both the soul and life force and can be utterly separate from the veils and prevarication of the ego.

The psychic has a flame of will insistent on perfection, on an alchemic transmutation of nature. The most intimate character of the psychic is pressure towards the Divine through joy, love and oneness.

(from Jim Bean's Journal exrtracts from Sri Aurobindo's Synthesis of Yoga.)

As the sun sets over the Pacific Ocean along the California coast of the United States of America, it is rising over the Bay of Bengal in India, heralding a new day in Auroville, "The City of Dawn."

Nothing belongs to anybody in particular in Auroville. Roslyn had lived in Auroville for twenty years. Then she had lived for two years in California. Because nothing belongs to anybody in particular in Auroville when she returned in 1990 she could not reclaim the house she had been living in when she left.

The only empty house she could find was the house built by Jim Bean. He had been her "true love." He had stopped talking to her nine years before he died. He had promised Dhyan, who had fallen off the Matrimandir - the Sanctuary of Truth in the center of Auroville - and broken her back, that until she could walk he would not talk to Roslyn.

In 1986 Jim Bean died and Dhyan committed sati. They had been in the process of building the house. Nobody could figure out what to do with the house when they died. It became a guesthouse. It was oppressively gloomy and dirty, so it was empty when Roslyn returned to Auroville. She moved in because she had no other place to stay. She had not wanted to come back to Auroville.

She had gone to the house only once before, to pay last respects to Jim Bean's body the morning after he'd died, before he was buried. That day the house was entirely gray, the place was unplastered cement and stone, it looked like Gormenghast.

Jim Bean's body was laid out on a table, cushioned on ice, wrapped in a white sheet surrounded with baskets of jasmine. When Roslyn looked at his face she was overwhelmed by the expression she saw there. He had been the most gentle and sweetest person in the world. There was a rictus of rage on his dear beautiful beloved face that nearly knocked her over. She laid the orchid she had brought him over his heart symbolizing eternal love for The Divine, and left. The only things in the place that were not horrible were the flowers filling the center courtyard, bright pink, Sri Aurobindo's compassion, a rich carpet of them. It was the only thing that made it bearable. She hated the place and never wanted to see it again in her life. Her best friend had moved into the caretaker's house next to Jim Bean's house a few months later, and Roslyn had told her, "I will never visit you there. I hate that place. If you ever want to see me you will have to come here to the forest." And there she was in that house, and not at all happy. The caretaker, Heinie, asked her if she wanted to live in the house before he left for Germany, and she very truthfully replied, "No!"

The house was an amazingly beautiful space, and as the grime slowly dissolved with Vim powder and elbow grease, the memories of the good old days surfaced. Sometimes she felt Jim Bean and Dhyan were there with her in the house.

Roslyn had been fleeing from her memories, had escaped to California. The time had come for her to face the memories, and she felt fate's irony that she was in that house which was the symbol of the story. The house rises lonely and majestic at the edge of a canyon, at the end of a road, in the middle of a forest. There, one could transcend loneliness; the peace of solitude is possible. The house is built into the land in harmony with the movements of the sun and moon. It is exquisite. In the summer the front of the house receives and absorbs the sun and acts as an umbrella to shade the terrace. In the winter the sun shines on the terrace, so it is never unpleasantly cold: unless it rains for too many days in a row. But Roslyn had to face the shockingly tragic deaths of Jim Bean and Dhyan to find the beauty in the house, because the whole place seemed covered with a gray miasma of nobody-cares-enough.

Her days of returning to Auroville became days of pain, exhaustion, and helplessness, and she felt as if they would again overwhelm her. She wept and wept and wept, as though the tears could change the past, or even assuage the anguish. Even five years after the deaths of Jim Bean and Dhyan the loss was not any less. They were part of Auroville. Part of the great exciting adventure that Auroville promised to be from the beginning. They were so completely committed to Auroville that they would not live anywhere else. They died leaving the house unfinished. Having no other place to go, Roslyn had gone there and found herself in the abandoned monument which Jim and Dhyan had built in wood and stone.

She entered as a guest, and was given a room upstairs on the terrace that was worse than bleak. It was grim. It was a cell. The mattress was hopeless. It was okay. There were cupboards for her clothes and cosmetics. The bathroom was grim. The kitchen was filthy. The white walls were overlaid with a patina of grime. The cupboards were full of ants. The house was full of flies during the day and mosquitoes and bats at night, and occupied by a fleet of frogs. It was being looked after by a caretaker, Heinie, who had been given the house to look after by Dhyan's daughter's father.

Heinie was on his way to Germany, and his significant other was looking after the house. When Roslyn mentioned it was very dirty, she was told to leave if she did not like it.

She had nowhere to go, so she shut up.   But every morning, as a type of spiritual practice and a gesture of respect to Jim Bean, she spent twenty minutes scrubbing a bit of the house with a brush and soap and Vim powder. She went around the house opening the windows, which at once transformed the gloomy cavern into a box of light. She felt that Jim Bean and Dhyan were alive in a spiritual dimension in the house, as friendly spirits.

Once upon a time Roslyn had been very very young, in the star shower of laughing gas, during the era of strawberry fields forever. Her parents had given her every comfort, care and advantage they could imagine. They were sadly disappointed with how she used those gifts.

She found herself on a rainbow bridge between the past and the future.

In 1969 Roslyn had been twenty-five years old, and she had a little baby. She had been wandering around the planet for years. At sixteen, she had graduated from high school. At 17, she had been suspended from college because she had hardly attended any classes, having fallen in love with canasta, broken her leg, and failed nearly all her courses. She worked and traveled for a couple of years, and went back to college. She wandered in Mexico during vacations, finally dropping out. She lived in Mexico in a tent of orange and white parachute silk with a person who had gone swimming often in the evening with Paramahamsa Yogananda as a child near his home in Encinitas. She spent some time with her sister in New York working for an advertising agency. Then, again back to school. She met and joined a tribe of hippies with a bus full of peyote, who were looking for The City of God. She lived with them on a mountain near a canyon and became pregnant. Sitting in a friend's house, looking at a painting, she had a vision that told her to go to India. She had planned to travel to the East Coast anyhow for her sister's wedding, but first she had to see San Francisco, the Mecca of hippiedom. After a few weeks in San Francisco she flew to New York. She worked for a few weeks in New York, and bought a ticket on a freighter to Antwerp. Her father, Bernie, drove into New York to say goodbye, and assured her that he would send her $100 a month regularly as long as she wrote to him regularly.

The boat docked at Antwerp. It was a heavenly crossing. She did not really meet or speak to anyone else on the boat, but sat on the deck watching the sky and sea, and enjoying the breeze. From Antwerp she went to Paris, and then the Baleares and Morocco. Bliss was born in Berlin a few days before Christmas. Roslyn's father, Bernie, flew to Berlin a few days after the baby was born. Roslyn had not told him she was pregnant, and he was slightly surprised that his little girl had a little baby. Bernie flew East with Roslyn and Bliss to Crete, and left them there promising Roslyn $100 a month for a year, even though he thought she was crazy to take a baby to India. She felt that she had been called to India by some far-out guru.* She was not thinking about what she was doing. Her intuition agreed with what she wanted to do: go to India with the baby. Bernie did not expect the baby to survive. He did not expect Roslyn to survive; but, he knew if he sent money regularly he would hear from them regularly.

From Greece, Roslyn traveled with her baby Bliss to Turkey, Afghanistan, Pakistan, Kashmir, Nepal, and finally South India to another ashram.* Tired, dispirited, disillusioned, carrying eight months old Bliss, she was feeling there was no place in the world she wanted to live with Bliss, so she might as well go back to the USA.

She entered the Sri Aurobindo Ashram for the first time at about 11:30 in the morning on August 7th, 1969, with Bliss on one arm and a carpetbag containing all her worldly possessions on the other arm. It was a hot sunny morning.

She had been traveling around India and Nepal with Baby Bliss for months, and was ready to write her father and ask him to send her a ticket back to the USA.

Sitting in a big comfortable chair in a friend's house in Arizona, two days pregnant, Roslyn had had a vision. She was looking at a painting on a wall directly in front of her, and the painting disappeared, the wall disappeared, the house disappeared, and there appeared two eyes and a face that spoke to her... "Come to India now."

She felt her heart beating, but she did not know where she was in relation to her body. It was as though she had moved into another dimension, and there was someone else out there in that dimension calling her to India. She still had her mental ego, which was able to reply to the invisible being she was looking at, and said, "No! I am two days pregnant, I don't have any money."

The being in the vision seemed to have heard and understood her, but replied to her, unequivocally, as though pregnancy and no money were bagatelles, "Come to India now!!!"

And she had gone to India believing that some far-out guru had called her and would find her. She didn't know the name or address of the guru, but she had had enough faith in the vision to leave where she was, and travel over land and by sea to India. Bliss had been traveling

East towards the rising sun her whole life. By the time Bliss was five months old they were in India. They had traveled across snow-covered mountains and parched deserts, through exotic towns and the Hindu Kush, and finally arrived in India by bus from Lahore. Roslyn had no idea where to go. The vision had said, "Come to India." She was in India, but did not know how to find the mighty guru of the vision. She hoped that there was truth in the saying she had heard, "When the seeker is ready the guru will find him."

After roaming around India and Nepal for months, she was wondering if she had really had a vision, or a vivid fantasy daydream.

She was tired. She had ventured far and wide searching for wisdom, understanding and truth, and had found nothing. It did not matter where she was; it was always the same. She was beginning to feel that she and Bliss were alone against the world.

She was really tired of people asking her, "Where is your native place?" or "Where is your husband?"

She felt that men, hotelkeepers, shopkeepers, were all trying to take advantage of her, a young foreign woman, alone with a baby.

She had met some gurus, but noone who resonated with the vision, if it was a vision. She decided in Katmandu, after meeting another disappointing guru; go to Ceylon to buy gems with what little money she had, and then go back to the States. Money seemed to be the one thing that had universal respect. Spirituality seemed to be an illusive fiction.

She had traveled to India on a psychedelic magic carpet. Wrenched from a cramped world where she felt she was dying of psychic asphyxiation to another dimension where she had to take a lot of deep breaths, for the world was constantly revealing itself as nothing like what she had always imagined it to be. She wanted to write, but even more than that, she wanted to live, to know, to experience this world, and understand some of its mysteries.

As Roslyn was leaving Katmandu, another traveler mentioned to her, "There is an ashram like a country club a hundred miles south of Madras, in Pondicherry, on the way to Ceylon. It is on the coast, with excellent guesthouses and beautiful white sandy beaches."

She decided she would perhaps break the long journey by bus, train and boat to Ceylon in Pondicherry. She had loved the white sandy beaches in Mexico, the long tropical days, warm nights and clear sky.

By the time Roslyn had gotten to Madras, after days of travel from Katmandu by bus to Patna, then by third class train to Calcutta and then another third class train to Madras, she could not bear the thought of another two days on the boat train to Colombo. She took a bus to Pondicherry.

She got off the bus in the Pondicherry bus stand, and into a cycle rickshaw.* She got into one of the less rickety looking of the rickshaws. There was even some tread on the tires, and the driver looked younger, stronger and healthier than most of the other rickshaw men. Some of the rickshaw men looked as if they were in a bad way. One had a terrible leg, swollen grotesquely with elephantiasis, another had leprous stumps instead of fingers on one hand.

She seemed to be the only white face in the crowded bus stand, barefooted, with Bliss on one hip and her Afghani carpet bag over her other shoulder, wearing bright red cotton pajamas. Many women covered in white sheetlike cloths, bourkas, stopped to look at her, as she negotiated with her rickshaw driver how much she would pay for a ride to The Ashram. The women would stop and stare and draw the slightly dirty white cloth more tightly over their faces. Local Muslim women, their heads and bodies covered with white cloth, under which a lovely skirt, or a ragged skirt, or an ankle bracelet flashed, or a glimpse of a nose ring, with a child on one hip and another by the hand. Women and men carrying children, bags and chickens walked together in groups of twos or threes. Roslyn sat in the rickshaw and her driver slowly pedaled through the throng in the bus station. The women seemed to be giggling beneath their veils. Roslyn sat in her rickshaw moving slowly among the sweet sellers and flower vendors trying to press their wares on her. She had asked the driver of the rickshaw to take her to The Ashram, but she could not remember the name of The Ashram. "Ashram" was enough for the scruffy driver to set off past the police officer with a whistle in the little kiosk in the middle of the street, and into the stream of bicycles riding west.

They rode slowly past people balancing baskets on their hips or heads, beggars, children, and a flock of ugly gray dirty buffalo. Little shops made from palm leaves lined the edge of the crowded bus stand. They rode through teeming streets with pigs eating offal, and smartly clad men and brightly clad women in pretty saris with bright bangles. The streets were full of bicycles and rickshaws, people and animals. There were not many motor vehicles in the town. The shops were full of saris, sweets and brassware. Policemen with whistles directed the thronging traffic at the crowded corners near the bazaar.

They passed through a charming small park, and through quiet streets where all the walls seemed to be painted the same gray/blue/white color.

There were not many people on the street at that hour in that part of town, and the few Roslyn saw seemed to be wearing white and looked a bit ethereal, walking or cycling on the streets where the walls on both sides were a soothing gray/blue/white color. The people were all in spotless gleaming white clothes, moving quietly and purposefully along the streets with the gray/white/blue walls, in a different rhythm to the people they had passed on the street in the bus stand and bazaar. There were gates, doorways, trees along the streets, and flowers peeping over the walls. It was certainly cleaner and quieter than any place Roslyn had seen in India.

The rickshaw stopped in front of an open door in the gray/blue/white walls.

"Ashram?" she asked him.

He wagged his head, and asked her for ten rupees.

He had agreed at the bus station to take her to The Ashram for five rupees, but it had been a very long ride, so she gave him six rupees, and he smiled. She took Bliss and her bag and entered the gate, barefoot, wearing her bright red pajamas, her dark hair standing out several inches from her head in every direction.

She walked through the gate. There were flowers to her right and left. In front of her were steps leading to a porch where several men wearing white were sitting on chairs.

A short man in a powder blue turban stood up, and asked with a friendly smile, "May I help you?"

"I am looking for a place to stay for a few days." Roslyn replied.

"This is the Sri Aurobindo Ashram," he replied.

"Yes. I had heard The Ashram has guesthouses."

"Guesthouses. Yes, would you like to put your bag down?" he asked kindly.

"Yes," she said with relief, and let the bag drop from her shoulder to the floor.

"You may leave it here," he said, pointing to an empty space next to an umbrella stand to the left of the steps.

"Here, take your seat," one of the other gentlemen in white said, pointing to an empty chair.

"I would like to have a room in a guesthouse for a few days, if that is possible," she said.

"Yes, but unfortunately the gentleman who handles that matter has gone for lunch, and will not be back before 3:30 this afternoon."

"Would you like to sit here and wait for him?" The man in the blue turban asked.

"No, I think I will go find a place to eat in town," she replied.

"May I show you around The Ashram?" he asked.

She had read Hesse's "Journey to The East", and thought it would be bad form to refuse, so she accepted his offer to show her The Ashram.

Carrying Bliss, Roslyn followed her gracious guide along the path through the flowers into the central courtyard of The Ashram. He pointed across the courtyard to the windows on the third floor, and told her, "The Mother has been The Master of this ashram since Sri Aurobindo died in 1950. She lives there. She comes out of Her room only four times a year to give Darshan to Her devotees. There will be Darshan next week for Sri Aurobindo's birthday anniversary, August 15th. Will you be here?"

"I don't know," she replied. She had planned to stop for only three days. Her money was running out, and she needed to write to her father for more. She had been planning to ask him to send the money and the ticket to Colombo, but she could stay in Pondicherry and wait for more money and then write for the ticket from Colombo.

Her guide led her across the courtyard into a smaller courtyard, and pointed to the door of the office that would be open in the afternoon, where she could get permission to stay in a guesthouse. Then they went through one of the graceful concrete arches at the end of the little courtyard into a great entry hall with marble floors.

"This is the meditation hall," the guide said softly. He pointed with his finger to the ceiling. "The Mother is sitting upstairs."

There was a marvelous staircase with a green carpet disappearing around a bend into a higher realm. They walked in through the hall to the part of the room where the ceiling looks like a vaulted silver dome. On one side of the room was a painting of The Mother and Sri Aurobindo. Mother, pale and dramatic, was swathed in gold silk draped sari fashion covering Her head, and held there with a golden crown. She sat regally, silently, looking within and without, Her hand casually resting next to Sri Aurobindo's hand. He sat next to Her on the tiger throne. The golden light of Her aura in the painting delicately merged with the blue white light emanating from the powerful silent sage wearing a white string, a white towel and a longi, amazingly luminous, as though lit from within by a powerful light, motionless but dynamic. The devotee who had done the painting had somehow captured the tranquillity and joy, magic and mystery which Mother and Sri Aurobindo had inspired in him.

Roslyn's guide explained to her, "They sit in the painting as they had sat four times each year, giving Darshan* to all their disciples, devotees and guests."

On the other side of the hall was a photo of Sri Aurobindo, set in the center of his symbol, a six-pointed star with a square in the middle, water in the square, and in the center, Sri Aurobindo.

Roslyn looked at that photo and it was as though little bells went off all through her body. She quickly turned away. She had come to India on a spiritual quest, but was not even interested any longer. If there was something there, she did not want to know about it.

Her guide led her back through the little courtyard, and into the central courtyard of The Ashram. He led her towards the big tree in the center of the courtyard, and told her that Mother had named that tree "The Happiness Tree." He pointed to the flower-covered marble slab in front of the tree and told her that was where Sri Aurobindo was buried.

Again, the little bells. She tried to ignore them and keep walking, back through the garden to the porch. She thanked her guide, and asked him if he knew of a good non-vegetarian restaurant.

"I do not know," he replied regretfully.

"You may leave your bag here," he offered.

All the rules of the road told her to take her bag, but she did not want to pick it up. She was carrying her passport and money, and Bliss. She left everything else next to the umbrella stand, and went out into the street, where she asked a rickshaw man to take her to a "meals hotel."

Roslyn had lunch in a place that had a separate eating room for ladies. It was pleasant and private, and she ate heartily, fed Bliss, and went back in the rickshaw - which had waited for her - to The Ashram.

Her bag was still sitting next to the umbrella stand. Her friend in the blue turban greeted her.

"Have you taken food?"

"Yes."

"He is in the office now. "

She thanked him and went with Bliss to the office.

The French doors were open, and there was a very big desk surrounded by bookcases full of books facing the doors, but no one was sitting at the desk.

She took another step into the room, and heard a voice on her right, "Can I help you?"

She turned her head and saw a large man wearing thick glasses peering over the top of his glasses at her.

"I am looking for a room in a guesthouse," she replied.

"I am in charge of The Ashram guesthouses."

"I need a room."

"For how many days?"

"I would like to stay for Darshan."

"All right, I will give you a room in Castelini Guesthouse."

He sat down and gestured to the chair opposite him, "Please take your seat."

She was very tired, and was happy to sit down. He set aside the book in front of him to speak with her.

He put another paper in front of him and picked up his pen. He asked her for all the details on her passport. She responded without going into her bag and getting her passport, because she had memorized all the numbers; she had been asked for them so often.

After she had given him the details he asked for the passport and checked it against what she had told him. He double-checked everything, then handed back the passport and gave her a form to sign.

He handed her a little green card that was a guest pass to admit her to all The Ashram facilities. He told her it would cost her 10 rupees a night, including three meals a day at the dining room, and that the times when the Dining Room was open were printed on the guest card. In bold letters on the bottom of the green card it said, "No smoking, drinking, or sex."

She was glad to agree to anything. She offered to pay in advance.

"That's all right, please come here to return the guest card and to check out after Darshan."

"Thank you very much" she said, taking the card and going out to collect her bag from the porch. She asked a rickshaw driver to take her to Castelini.

The Dining Room was on one side of the park, and the guesthouse was several blocks into the town on the other side of the park.

There was a wall in the glowing gray/blue/white tone of The Ashram, and an elegant polished open carved teakwood gate. She paid the rickshaw man and he handed her her bag at the gate. Barefoot in her red pajamas, she walked into the garden. She carried Bliss in her right arm, her bag on her left shoulder, up the wide steps through the pillars onto the marble verandah. It was an inviting place, but utterly silent. She felt like Alice in the rabbit hole.

The French doors on the left led to a staircase, and the French doors in front of her led to a huge living room with beautiful oriental rugs on the floor and Victorian furniture with antimacassars.

She walked into the room, saying, "Hello," but there was no-one there.

The ceiling was at least fifteen feet high. As there was no-one in the room, she walked through to another set of doors, out onto another verandah, where she found a very quiet man dressed in starched and ironed white shorts and shirt. She had not washed her feet since Calcutta.

"May I help you," he asked her very quietly.

She showed him her little green card which said that she, Roslyn, was a guest of the Sri Aurobindo Ashram at Castelini Guesthouse.

He took the card without looking directly at her. He was very shy. Finally, after studying the card for a long time, he introduced himself as the manager of Castilini Guesthouse, and asked her to follow him to her room. He took her upstairs and showed her a very clean and pleasant room, off a large sitting room. It was a large corner room, full of light, with fresh flowers on the dresser under a photo of The Mother and Sri Aurobindo.

"Thank you very much. What should I do with all my dirty clothes?" she asked.

He assured her that a servant would be along to fetch the dirty laundry in the morning, and would bring her back clean clothes in the evening. The servant would also put up her mosquito net in the evening and take it down in the morning and make up the room. Would she like bed tea or coffee?

"Tea," she replied, because she never drank coffee; but then she had never been offered 'bed tea' before.

"What time?"

"I don't understand."

"What time would you like tea in your room in the morning?"

"As early as possible."

"Four o'clock?"

"Six thirty?"

"Fine." He pointed down the hallway next to the door to her room, off the upstairs sitting room. "The bathroom is there."

She thanked him and he left her.

Roslyn and Bliss seemed to be the only people around. They had not seen or heard anyone else in the enormous house except the manager. Their room was off a large sitting room full of oriental rugs, Victorian sofas and love-seats with antimacassars artfully arranged, but looking as though no-one ever sat in that room. There was not even a speck of dust on the polished end tables. There were two sets of open French doors, one leading onto the front verandah in the front of the house, and the other leading out onto the back verandah. The room was full of the fading light of late afternoon, and there were two silent ceiling fans painted the same color as the trim on the walls. The room and the house were painted in delicate shades of the gray/blue white color of The Ashram buildings; it had a very pristine and safe atmosphere. There were doors against the far wall of the large sitting room leading to other guestrooms, but these doors were closed, and the curtains outside the open doorway were tied back. There was no evidence of other guests.

It was very silent. It was completely different from anything Roslyn had experienced in her travels. There did not appear to be other guests in the guesthouse. Roslyn figured that if she got too bored she could leave after two or three days as she had originally planned, but first she needed to wash and change and rest.

The bathroom was great, all white tile, and had endlessly abundant running water. The grime of days of travel was quickly dissolved, and after a few minutes even her feet were clean. She did not have any shoes. All of Bliss's things needed washing, so she washed a couple of things, and as it was very warm Roslyn felt it was okay for Bliss to be naked. Roslyn had taken off her dirty red cotton pajamas and put on her clean orange pajamas. Her hair was clean, but it still stood straight out from her head.

They were clean and ready to go, but she had no watch and did not know what time it was. Roslyn was thinking about walking towards the Dining Room. She really wondered what time it was. She still had not seen anyone else in the guesthouse. She walked over to the French doors to the back verandah, and saw someone sitting there, a big man, with red hair and beard, wearing mauve pajamas.

He was sitting on a blue rattan chair next to a blue round table. There were several empty blue chairs around the table. She walked out onto the verandah with Bliss in her arms and looked out onto a splendid rose garden.

Roslyn turned to the red headed man in the mauve pajamas and asked him what time it was.

He reached down and picked up a beer bottle, filling the empty glass in front of him on the table. She was surprised to see a person drinking beer in the guesthouse. On her little green card it stated clearly,

"No smoking, alcohol, or sex."

The red headed man was looking at her, but did not seem to have heard her. Then he asked her if she would like some beer.

"No thank you. I don't drink beer."

"What the hell do you drink?" he asked.

"Coca-Cola with ice," she replied.

Mother's visit to Ananta's Island

ii

A shapeless memory lingers in us still,
And sometimes, when our sight is turned within,
Earth's ignorant veil is lifted from our eye;
There is a short miraculous escape...

Our souls can visit, in great lonely hours,
Still regions of imperishable Light,
All-seeing eagle-peaks of silent Power,
And moon-flame oceans of swift fathomless Bliss,
And calm immensities of spirit Space.

Sri Aurobindo, Savitri

The psychic being is leader and priest in the sacrifice. All things become bodies, and all movements the play of the divine Beloved. Who gives with a heart of adoration a leaf, a flower, a fruit, a cup of water, the Lord takes and enjoys that offering of devotion. A psychic fire within must be lit into which all is thrown with the Divine Name upon it.

Spontaneous, self determining action. The heart senses the personal will is occasionally or frequently enlightened or moved by the illumined will. Human intelligence is more and more replaced by a high and intuitive spiritualized mind, the external human heart by the inner psychic heart, the vital becomes purified and selfless. Then we aspire to the Supramental levels above spiritualized mind. Our human will is a misled and wandering ray that has parted from the supreme puissance. The period of the slow emergence out of this lower working into a higher light and purer force in the valley of the shadow of death leaves nothing but the manifestation and play of the Divine spirit in life.

(from Jim Bean's journal extracts from Sri Aurobindo's Synthesis of Yoga.)

The person in mauve pajamas stood up and made a gallant bow, introducing himself as "John Kelly from Brooklyn."

Roslyn introduced herself and Bliss.

Then he said, "Excuse me for staring at you, but I have been dreaming about you, except you were wearing red pajamas."

Roslyn had no idea how to respond to that. She had been wearing her red pajamas for days, but she had just changed into her clean orange pajamas.

He turned away and called softly at the curtained doorway behind him, "Gabriel!"

From the curtained doorway at the end of the verandah a very wizened, very dark man dressed in slightly crumpled white clothes appeared.

"Gabriel, the lady wants a Coca-Cola with ice and I want another beer."

"All beer finished," the little dark man replied.

"Then go get some more and some Coca-Cola with ice. Put it on the tab at Magrees'."

"Very good, and dinner?"

"Will you join me for dinner here?" Kelly asked.

Roslyn was very pleased with the option of not having to walk to the Dining Room. But, she replied to the invitation, "I thought I would go to the Dining Room." She was dreading the long walk, carrying Bliss.

"I am having steak. I am sure you would prefer a steak dinner to Dining Room food. Gabriel, steak and finger chips for two and four bottles of beer, and one Coca-Cola with ice, and you better get a bottle of brandy."

"Yes, very good," the little dark man said, looking at Roslyn and Bliss and grinning.

"Will you join me?" Kelly asked, indicating a chair across the table.

Roslyn put Bliss in one of the empty chairs and sat down, quite enchanted by the whole scene.

It was a balmy tropical early evening. There were probably parrots and possibly even nightingales singing in the trees in the courtyard. It was a very 'at ease' moment, on the quiet verandah, in the big quiet house, on a beautiful evening, with an interesting new companion and dinner to be served, and all felt all right with the world.

There was a bit of desultory conversation, and the kind of questions she always found difficult, like, "Where are you from?"

Gabriel re-entered from the curtained doorway carrying white cotton bags full of empty beer bottles, and a long silver container with a handle. He turned and chuckled shyly at them as he disappeared through the curtains into the sitting room.

"Where was I born? Where do I live? Where am I going? I guess I have to answer that I am from Hazleton, Pennsylvania, but I haven't been there for years, and I don't know if I will ever go there again."

"Why are you here?"

"I don't know. I am here."

"Did you plan to stay for a while?"

"I don't know. I'm thinking about going back to the USA. How long have you been here?"

"Four years."

"You have been in this guesthouse for four years?"

"I have been here for six months. I have been in India for four years."

"Why did you come to India?"

"That's a long story."

"What did you do in Brooklyn?"

"I was a fireman."

"I never met a fireman before."

"I spent fifteen years with the New York City Fire Department."

"And then you came to India?"

"And then I came to India."

"Why did you come to India?"

"Do you really want to know?"

She had nothing else to do and nowhere else to go and it was very pleasant sitting there on the verandah, so she let him tell her his story.

They sat there for three days and nights, with Gabriel punctuating the stories with non-vegetarian South Indian cuisine three times a day, and beers for Kelly, and Coca-Colas without ice all day long from 7 a.m. to 10 p.m. for Roslyn. She offered to pay for her meals, but Kelly was magnanimous and said it was his pleasure, and they were both laughing so much she was happy to let him pay for the food, because she was very low on money, and needed some new clothes.

John Thomas Kelly was an amazing first contact for Roslyn with The Mother and Sri Aurobindo. It was the most unconventional and irreligious initiation imaginable, but it was a delightful initiation, into a world where ananda* is the purpose of existence.

Kelly told her to leave her mind as blank as the sky on a cloudless summer day, without prejudice or preference, incorporating the grace of the moment of the invisible glyph of time in space.

Kelly took her back in time with him to the time when he was a baby, maybe as big as Bliss. He was in his crib in Brooklyn. The people who thought they were his parents stood next to the crib bidding him good night. When they left him alone in the room his celestial parents, who were much larger and more beautiful than his human parents, filled the room and his heart with ineffable joy and his life with a little bit of radiance. Kelly sang in a sweet tenor voice, "A little bit of heaven fell from out of the sky one day," and he picked up baby Bliss and sang to her carefully offering his glass of beer to her. He was perhaps half leprechaun, and Roslyn had first fallen in love with a leprechaun when she was four years old and her parents took her to see "Finian`s Rainbow" on Broadway. Kelly was a bit of an old Atlantean, Irish, Druid, child, mystic, and fun. She did not think a little beer would hurt Bliss, and Bliss seemed blissed out as the amusing red haired man with the big red nose crooned sloppy sentimental tunes.

He continued his reminiscences, trying to explain to Roslyn how he got to be sitting on that terrace that evening. "As I grew older I could no longer see the magical beings who had watched over me as an infant, or even remember them.

"I was an ordinary American male from Brooklyn who had quit high school in his second year after the football season to earn money. The family was poor and I had two younger brothers. On my eighteenth birthday I was drafted into the army and after basic training shipped to France in the infantry."

At this point Gabriel arrived with his clanging bags, which looked very promising to Roslyn who always had a hearty appetite.

Roslyn was laughing at Kelly. "You are telling me about your magical parents who you could see standing next to your crib, thinking that they were your real parents and your natural parents were strangers? And then you forgot your magical parents, but you remember them this evening. I hope you are not going to sing, "Some enchanted evening" to me."

Kelly replied by singing, "Make believe," from "Showboat"."

Gabriel rescued the evening by appearing with a glass of Coca-Cola and a bottle of brandy, a bottle of beer, and glass for Kelly, and then two plates heaped with steak and French fries.

"This is wonderful, but do you have to tell me what happened to you as an American soldier in France to explain to me how you got to this house in Pondicherry?"

"Well, if you want to know how I came to be here, you have to listen to my story, because if it hadn't happened like that I probably wouldn't be here."

They were eating and drinking. Roslyn was smoking. Bliss was sitting in the chair next to Roslyn, like a doll just watching her mama laughing and the big red headed man blustering.

"I don't remember World War II at all," Roslyn said. "And I cannot imagine how anything from that other age could be relevant to us meeting here now, except that you were there, and now you are here."

"Would you like to talk or listen?" Kelly asked, offering his glass of beer to Bliss who took a few delicate sips.

Roslyn was laughing and chewing steak, and assured Kelly that she was fascinated by his story, or at least his absurd mauve pajamas. His red gold hair was nearly as luminous as his red nose.

"I was shipped to France and right to the front, and I was terrified and horrified. The first time I went into battle was on The Mother's birthday, 1945. These were the closing months of W.W.II and France was still occupied by Germany. I was part of the new bunch of GI's who had been sent in to replace some of the soldiers who had fallen in the Battle of the Bulge and Bastogne. We had been sent into a town called Faubourg. I don't know for how many hours or days I was in the midst of that battle, constantly under bombardment by rockets from the Germans, called 'screaming meemies'...terrible noise! I saw people hit by those rockets and flipped into the air like a flapjack. I guess maybe that changed my mind about a lot of things and opened me to something else.

"We were in a zigzag trench on a mountain in a graveyard from W.W.I. It had been a graveyard even before that. There were old crosses and grave markers, and we had dug our trenches in this graveyard like a great mass grave. The original company had been wiped out completely, to the last man. We had been sent in as replacements. There were unburied bodies of German and American soldiers sprawled on the ground all over. The world looked like a jungle of torn-up trees, earth and graves. Grotesque!!!

"They say, there's no atheist in a foxhole. I had been raised a Catholic. I thought I was almost dead anyway, and was probably going to be struck dead momentarily, so I tried to imagine what it is like to be dead. It was as though for a moment I was again an infant and had the sense of my glorious celestial parents nearby. Most of the guys who had gone into that cemetery with me were already dead, and I wondered why I was still living, and if I was not still alive in the morning where would I be? Was there anything left of all those dead bodies apart from the unburied corpses?

"It was freezing cold, February 21st, mid-winter in France. I had been in that graveyard forever, a sitting duck target for the German 'screaming meemies' and living in this great pit of death more horrific than the hells of Dante. It was late night. All my companions were dead. I was alone. I did not know if there was anyone else alive. I saw a wisp of white smoke, like cigarette smoke, but there was not anyone there to smoke a cigarette. The wisp of smoke began to glow with little sparks of light and I hoped it was an angel come to grab me before the next 'screaming meemie' landed in my foxhole, flipped me into the air, and blew me to bits. There must have been some other people around somewhere, there was so goddam much noise, but I could not see anyone but dead bodies and bits of unburied bodies. The sparkling wisp of smoke expanded like a foggy haze. The dazzling sparks were enormous but not threatening like rocket flashes, and then I heard a bubbling gentle laughter, laughter from the sparkling mist in the middle of this valley of death, and it was not a harsh laugh, but a compassionate sigh of a wise old man. It was captivating,, and something of a different order emerged from the dark chaos surrounding me. I saw, in the haze, a face, a human being with long white hair and a beard, smiling gently, drawing me away from the pain and horror and fear into profound peace. His eyes sent out a look, which would have knocked me down if I had not been lying wedged against the bottom side of the trench, and I was sure I was dead and looking at God.

"No. I wasn't dead. I could move my head and hands and legs. The charnel house atmosphere had disappeared, and although I was still in the middle of that graveyard full of unburied bodies there was something else there with me, or someone else, who seemed to have little to do with life or death, but was an emanation of the realm beyond.

"The vision spoke. 'If my help you choose, then your religion you will lose.' I understood immediately, 'I've got the devil!' But I didn't give a damn. I replied, "I don't have a religion, you have to give it to me," but silently I was saying the rosary.

"He laughed at me as if he knew I was trying to protect myself from the devil by calling Hail Mary! The Mother. Suddenly it was no longer a mist, eyes, a face, a voice, laughter, but a noble looking man with flowing white hair and beard, standing in the middle of the stinking battlefield emanating life, surrounded by a tranquil blue white light, like the sky on a summer day or an impossibly clear lake. His white clothes looked like a Roman toga, but he was more august than any Caesar.

"I was filled with his love and compassion for me, and vaguely recognized him as the celestial father who had hovered near me when I was a baby. Where was Mother?

"There was a flash, and next to him there was a building that looked like a small Greek temple. There was a wonderful luminescence. I could see a lady in a velvet housecoat in the temple. She looked like a Greek goddess of wisdom."

Kelly looked at Roslyn. "You have to remember I was in a filthy foxhole on a stinking battlefield, in a graveyard in France, and I was like in my crib with my lovely wonderful ethereal parents there visiting me as though nothing was happening. I was right in the middle of a goddam war! Guns were going bang, bang, and men were dying, and suddenly everything was okay. Except I did not know what was happening. Did I fall asleep and get hit by a 'screaming meemie' and go to heaven? Noone had ever even suggested to me that anywhere there would be anything as wonderful and beautiful as that woman in her temple. But She did not belong on that battlefield, so I told Her, 'Listen, sweetheart, you should get out of here, because we are having a hell of a time here, and if you do not leave now I will soon be insane with delight.'

"She smiled at me, and faded with Her temple into the night, and I felt so good."

"The next thing I recall is a soldier waking me. `Kelly, get up. We are going off this hill! We have been relieved!'"

"The place was always overhung with clouds and I could never tell what time it was. We were walking down the hill and I was trying to figure out what happened when I overheard two guys behind me talking. 'Did you see the beautiful light on the hill last night?' 'Yeah, wasn't that something!' They had seen something too!

"But then I figured that it was a dream or it never happened, and forgot it."

Roslyn thoroughly enjoyed listening to this incredible story. It was a completely different type of experience than anything she had known. She went to bed replete with good stories and good food. In the morning, she woke hearing a soft knock on the door to her room. The servant was there with the tea tray.

She took the tray out onto the verandah. Kelly was already sitting there at the little blue table with a pot of coffee and a newspaper.

There was only one table so she had to sit with him. It was such a beautiful morning, still slightly cool from the night. She had slept with the fan, but under a mosquito net, comfortable, safe, and secure after four nights on trains in third class compartments.

Kelly looked up over the top of his newspaper, "Good morning, my dear. Did you sleep well?"

"Like a top," she replied smiling at him.

"Would you like some coffee?"

"No, thank you. I am having tea."

"Gabriel should be here soon with breakfast."

That sounded wonderful to Roslyn. She was not eager to walk across town to the Dining Room for breakfast. She was delighted that she could sit and be served food and great stories, take baths all day long, change her clothes several times a day, and give all the dirty clothes to the servant and get them back clean and ironed in the evening. She could sleep as much as she wanted to, and when she wanted.   Food, drink, and Kelly were sitting there on the verandah. Kelly was seemingly always happy to entertain her with more stories, and she could not remember feeling more cozy or comfortable.

It was more than entertaining, it was something new, something unlike anything old-world-wise and world-weary Roslyn had come across. Exoterically Kelly's story was the story of a GI in W.W. II, but it was like a wonderful lyric ballad of the affection between this big red headed person in mauve pajamas and his celestial parents, his inner life distinctly as real - or more real - than his external life. He sat there, happy, calm, contented, radiating inner peace on the verandah of Castilini, with a glass of beer in hand, friendly, open-hearted, openhanded. Roslyn did not even go downstairs in the guesthouse for three days.

He went on, "I thought I was going crazy, which is reputed to be a bad thing in American Irish Catholic society, but I wanted to see the lady again, and the man who I began to address internally as 'Great Sir.' In the army everybody is called Sir, and I was in the army. Seeing that godlike man emerging from a wisp of smoke on the battlefield and surviving that battle gave me a different relationship to my mortality and immortality.

"Great Sir was my invisible companion as I marched with the liberating army through Europe. I have a lovely friend I want you to meet, here in Pondicherry, a French Countess who had fought in the Resistance and is living here now. She had similar experiences during the war."

"I`d love to meet a Countess!" Roslyn exclaimed.

"I will send her a chit* and invite her to dinner with us at Magree`s on Friday. Gabriel!!"

Gabriel came out through the curtains, bent over, in a servile posture.

Kelly turned to him, "Paper, pen."

"Yes, yes, I bringing master."

Kelly spent ages composing the note. Roslyn went to her room for a nap and when she got up it was noon.

She went out to the terrace. Kelly was sitting there. There was an empty glass on the table, but he refilled the glass from the bottle on the floor next to his chair.

"I really think I should go to the Dining Room for lunch."

"Don't be silly, Gabriel should be here any minute with lunch," Kelly replied. Bliss started screaming from the bedroom. Roslyn had to go and feed her and bathe her and dress her. When she got back to the table there were plates heaped with chicken curry and bottles of Coca-Cola and cold beer on the table.

While they were eating Kelly told her more stories about the New York City Fire Department, and about living in Nainital with the Himalayan saddhus.*

She listened and laughed and ate and slept.

There was a picture of The Mother carrying a basket of flowers on the wall over the table, and a big portrait of Sri Aurobindo on the front verandah. There was a calendar with Mother's photo in her room.

Bliss sat in the chair next to her, or on her lap, while she was eating, drinking, laughing and listening. Even if Bliss was only eight months old she seemed to travel with Roslyn on Kelly's pilgrimage through the horror and terror of the war and liberation of the concentration camps. Roslyn could feel how the compassion of his celestial parents comforted him and gave him wisdom and strength. Kelly was not talking from his mouth, but from his heart. He was recounting the story that had led him to be sitting on that verandah.

Roslyn realized that one thing that had been lacking in her life was someone to tell her entertaining stories all day long.

Kelly went on, "Finally they made me a sergeant because everyone else was sick or wounded or dead except for the new recruits. We were walking down a country road in France, and suddenly Great Sir appeared next to me and said, 'That underpass is going to be hit.' There was a train overpass in front of us we were heading for, so I ran down the road and caught up with the lieutenant leading us, and asked, 'Where are we going?' I tried to convince him to go another way, but he wouldn't listen.

"I went back to my men and Great Sir told me, 'Take your men and go first.'

"I was tired, exhausted, scared, but even though I had chosen the name Thomas because I was a doubter, I did not have much hope to make old bones, and I had no pride about doing anything to increase my chances of survival for another day. I told my men to follow me, and ran like hell down the hill, through the underpass and to the old farmhouse half way up the hill on the other side. They shot at us. We shot at them, but we did not stop until we were in that building and we were lucky there were not any Germans there when we got there. My company just made it. As the last man staggered through the door the explosions started. We slammed the door and hugged the walls, and after a few minutes it was quiet again.

I opened the door. When the smoke cleared I could see that the underpass and everything around it had been blown to bits, and the rest of the platoon was gone.

"You know, once I did not listen to Him. I was rather annoyed with Him floating in and out of my life. He looked usually as if He was sitting in a big gray chair, and He would sail in front of me at any moment, and tell me what to do. I was pissed off with Him, because if He was so smart, why didn't He do something about the mess the world was in instead of sailing around in an armchair. So He appeared to me one day and said, go right, and I went left, and a piece of shrapnel hit my shoulder. I was so happy. I hoped they would send me home. I immediately turned back, and was headed for the nearest field hospital, but The Old Man, Great Sir, appeared again, laughing at me. I saw that the wound was only a scratch with a lot of blood. I did not want to go forward, it was a good excuse to go back, but no, He prodded me on, and we found a German munitions supply dump, full of guns, bombs, every goddam thing.

"But I hated the war, and I was angry with Great Sir because I was always in the front line. I had gotten into arguing with Him when He would sail in on His armchair. Finally He told me, 'Don't worry, I'm working with the General'.

"'Ours or theirs?'

"He laughed at me and sailed away on that chair, and I didn't want to see Him anymore. He was part of my war and I was sick of war. I wanted to see Her again. What I really wanted to do was go back to Brooklyn and forget what I had seen in Europe, but I could not forget it. It was part of my life but the horror and callousness made me ashamed of my humanity.

"I could not stand thinking of myself as the same kind of creature, human being, who had created the concentration camps. Liberating those camps was worse than the battlefield for me. Humanity reduced to such a terrible state by inhuman treatment. Drinking, dancing, whoring, were the only escape from all the suffering and death.

"One night in a brothel in Germany, I had been drinking for I do not know how many days, and then I was puking for what seemed like half the night. I thought the women had poisoned me, the conquering invader; one of those fat goddam German bitches. The Germans were making lampshades out of human skin in those camps. I did not care if she had poisoned me. I wanted to die. I locked the door of the room from the inside because I did not want any of those German bitches to disturb me while I died. I took off all my clothes, and laid myself down between the dirty covers on the bed, crossed my hands on my chest, as if an undertaker might have done, and said to myself, 'Now I am going to die.'

"I said to the throbbing pain in my head, 'I cannot feel anything, I am dead!'

"I could not feel anything. I had a floating sensation as though I was a body of light floating above the tired, aching, sick body on the bed. Maybe I really was dead. I do not know. It was so peaceful; perhaps it was the realm where Great Sir rode around in His armchair. It was certainly different from anything I had known in Brooklyn or in the army. The body was lying naked on the bed with its arms crossed on its chest. I was somewhere else. I was fully dressed; but, not in uniform. I was somewhere with two other men. One was a priest, a tough-looking guy with a big black beard, pirate eyebrows, but with a perceptive penetrating, although gentle expression. He drew me towards him and his friend, who was smoking a pipe and had a very serious and deliberate expression on his face with a gesture.

"'Excuse me,' I interjected, 'if you are from over there, you might know Her.'

"The man with the pipe looked at me, bemused."

"The priest said, 'Yes, we know Her.'

"'Do you think you could arrange for Her to come and see me again?'

"'I'll ask Her,' he said, fading with his friend into the night, and there was Great Sir in his armchair, laughing at me as if I was Bob Hope.

"'I didn't want to see you!' I exclaimed. 'I want to see Her.'

"My body was gone, I had become a smoky mist, and Great Sir dissolved into a great light. We were on a great beam of energy traveling in our etheric bodies, over Germany, Switzerland and Italy. I could see other vague shapes flying in the atmosphere that weren't airplanes.

"I could not think. It was total exhilaration to be moving faster than you could even imagine, much faster than anyone has ever flown on an airplane, but somehow we were still in the dimension of space even if I was no longer in the dimension of form.

"Night melted into dawn, into morning, and suddenly I was in a beautiful room. Great Sir was sitting there on a chair looking more real than I had ever seen Him. And me? I seemed to be just a small pink glow hovering over the bed. She walked in the door.

"She stood there, looking like a person, but the kind of person who could see and recognize the tiny wisp of pink smoke, as me, John Kelly, Sergeant, US Army.

"She not only saw me and recognized me, but traveled with me to other places and other ages - then, BANG! I was back in the body on the bed in the brothel and happier than I'd ever been in my life.

"I looked out the window and saw a drunken soldier coming up the road with a bottle of wine in his hand, and he looked so damn beautiful. He was somehow connected to the mysterious lady.

"Anyhow, I could go on and on, and I guess I do a bit sometimes, but, even on the battlefield, when She appeared it, was the most wonderful place.

"With my Catholic background, it was easy for me to imagine that I might be having visions like Joan of Arc.

"But I was not a saint, I was an American GI from Brooklyn.

"Finally I got back to New York, and I thought I was crazy, or somebody was crazy, because it seemed that to the people who had lived in New York through the war, the war never happened.

"I could not talk about it, but I couldn't think about anything else. I went to work for the City Fire Department. Everyone wanted to hire a veteran and I wanted to work in Manhattan, so I was stationed at the Fire Station in Central Park.

"I did not want to go to a psychiatrist, but I was worried about my mental health, so I decided to go to the library, the big library with the stone lions out front, and read some books about psychology.

"I did not know what to read, so I decided to start with A. The psychology books were on the philosophy shelf. I started with a book by Adler. Then I went onto the next author on the shelf, Sri Aurobindo.

"The words seemed to flow from the page to my soul and acted as a balm for all the wounds and scars. I could rejoice as the elixir of sacred words healed the conflicts in my heart and mind.

"I read every book in the library by or about Sri Aurobindo, and I finally felt compelled to try to contact this marvelous being. I decided to check the New York City phone book, and I found a Sri Aurobindo Association on Madison Avenue.

"I called the telephone number and made an appointment to visit the office. That afternoon I was walking down Madison Avenue to that office, and right there in the middle of Madison Avenue, in broad daylight, hundreds of other people around me, suddenly Great Sir, sitting on his armchair, materialized in front of me.

"I did not want to stop and talk to him. People would think I was crazy. I was somewhat certain noone else could see him, so I did not stop, but he had no trouble keeping pace with me: 'Where are you going?' he asked.

"'I am going to the Sri Aurobindo Association office.' I replied without moving my lips.

"He seemed to be laughing at me. I didn't want to have visions walking down Madison Avenue in the middle of the afternoon. Finally I snapped at him. 'At least Sri Aurobindo is real. He is here on this planet doing something, not like you floating around in an armchair anywhere you like in the middle of the afternoon!' I guess I was shouting. People were staring at me.

"He winked at me and disappeared. I went to the office. There wasn't much happening, but in spite of the fact that I had learned in the army to never volunteer, I volunteered to work there. I went there pretty regularly. I came in contact with the Pondicherry Ashram, and we were selling Sri Aurobindo's books. I met people who had been deeply moved by Sri Aurobindo and The Mother.

"A few months after I had started working there for a few hours several afternoons a week, we received word that Sri Aurobindo had passed away. I had been planning a trip to India to meet the Master. He had retired into his room in 1926, and never went out. His room was actually more like an apartment, or a small suite of several rooms, including a beautiful entry hall with a small cupboard-like room on one end where He and Mother would sit and give their blessings to their disciples, from their throne draped with tiger skins, four mornings a year. Darshan.

"There is Darshan next week at The Ashram. The Mother will come out on her balcony and give Her blessing to the people who will be standing below in the street."

"Sounds a bit like the Pope in Rome," Roslyn interjected.

"Well, it is not a bit like that. You will see."

"What did Sri Aurobindo do in his room?" she asked.

"Nobody knows what Sri Aurobindo was doing. He said that noone knew anything about his life, in spite of all his writing, because it was not on the surface for others to see.

"Let me tell you another story," Kelly went on.

"Sri Aurobindo passed away on December 5th, 1950. There had been no photos taken of Sri Aurobindo from November 1926 when he went into retirement. All the photos of Sri Aurobindo I had seen were of a thin, dark man, dark haired, dark-skinned.

"Cartier Bresson had asked Mother if they could take photos of Her and Sri Aurobindo. She and Sri Aurobindo agreed. The photos were taken on November 24th, 1950, only a couple of weeks before Sri Aurobindo passed away.

"In the office one afternoon a few months later I was given a check from The Mother and asked to go to the Cartier Bresson office to pick up the photos. I walked into the big, Fifth Avenue office, and asked the receptionist for the Sri Aurobindo photos. She handed me a big folder, opened it and took out a paper telling what was in the folder, and started reading it off to me. There in front of me was a photo of The Old Man in his armchair. Great Sir!"

Kelly poured the last bit of beer from the bottle into his glass.

"It's a great story," Roslyn said, and toasted him with the last bit of warm Coca-Cola in her glass.

"A friend of mine, Mari, wants to use it for a book. I usually work with her in the mornings, but she can't write it. Women cannot write about war. But you'd like her. She sees The Mother every day. Maybe I will take you to meet her. Would you like that?"

"Yes." Roslyn had not left the guesthouse for three days.

"Maybe tomorrow afternoon. Tomorrow evening we are having dinner with La Countess de B. at The Grand Hotel d'Europe. She was a great heroine of the French Resistance."

"I can hardly wait. I can wear my new red Chinese silk brocade dress from Katmandu."

Suddenly a wild looking person with peroxide blonde hair, dressed only in a thin piece of white cloth wrapped haphazardly around his waist, burst through the curtained French doors onto the verandah.

"Kelly, you are the only one who can save me," he exclaimed in a huge and very resonant voice.

The wild blonde man suddenly stopped ranting and raving and looked at Roslyn, then at Kelly, then spoke in a soft, gentle, sweet voice, "I'm so sorry. I had no idea you had company! Who is this lovely lady?"

"Gabriel," Kelly called to his Tamil friend who seemed to be always waiting just inside the curtained doorway to his room, when he was not out shopping for them: "Is there another beer for Ananta?"

"All beer finished," Gabriel said as he came out from behind the curtain.

"You go get more beer," Kelly said.

"How many bottles I buying?"

"Two," Kelly said.

"Four," Ananta interjected.

"Very good. I going." Gabriel grinned and disappeared into Kelly's room for a moment, and reappeared with cotton bags full of empty beer bottles.

"You going quickly coming, signing chit, I looking Magree tomorrow," Kelly said.

Suddenly Ananta interjected authoritatively, what sounded like, "Secrum po y va secrum varum."

"Yes, yes, very good, I going, quickly coming," Gabriel bobbed up and down in his dirty white clothes, carrying his little bags of empty beer bottles.

Roslyn had been watching this exchange for days. It was always the same. Once Gabriel went out she never knew how long it would take him to come back: fifteen minutes, one hour, two hours. She had not had to lift a finger, but she sometimes had to be patient for three days. Food and drink had been provided, as she sat and listened to Kelly's stories and brief conversations with Gabriel. Gabriel would disappear through the curtains and reappear sometime later with bulging bags that disappeared into Kelly's room to reappear as food and drink, inevitably served on porcelain plates, with cutlery and napkins! She had not seen napkins in years!

Ananta threw himself into the empty chair between Roslyn and Kelly and looked at Roslyn intently, then said to her, "Thank God. At last you've come!"

She had to crack up. She was sure she never laughed as much in her whole life as she laughed in those three days.

"Roslyn, meet Ananta," Kelly said.

The journey into Kelly's mad and mystic world had been smooth and slightly removed, like watching a movie. Ananta made the here-and-now appear to be the movie.

Ananta explained that his name meant 'infinity'.

"My name isn't simply Ananta, Ananta is a name given to me by my guru, Panditji in Rameshwaram. I was Frederic Fulsom Bushnell from Boston. My father, the Lieutenant Governor, took a gun and wanted to shoot me, Mother saved me. My mother, not The Mother.

"My sister, Priscilla - there has always been a Priscilla Alden in our family, ever since we came over on The Mayflower - lives in the most beautiful house in Hollywood, but I also have another name."

Kelly was grumbling into his beer. Roslyn was all eyes and ears for Ananta. "What is your other name?" she asked.

"I cannot tell you that tonight. Maybe tomorrow. Will you come to the island tomorrow?"

"I`d love to."

"Ananta what are you doing here dressed like that?" Kelly asked.

"I just escaped from the Jipmer. My mother and servants thought I had gone crazy so they took me there, took everything away from me, and locked me in a cell. I just escaped because I could speak Tamil. I am going to be thrown out of The Ashram. Only The Mother can save me. Thank god Mother and I are going to see Her the day after tomorrow. It will be my mother's birthday. We will meet The Mother in the morning, then have lunch at Magree`s; will you join us?" he turned again to Roslyn.

Roslyn was delighted to accept.

Gabriel arrived with his little white bags full of beer and Coca-Cola bottles.

Kelly turned to Roslyn and explained to her, "The yoga of Sri Aurobindo has been described as an experience and affirmation of the adventure which is living."

Ananta drank a whole glass of beer in one swallow, and refilled his glass and toasted Kelly, "Hear! Hear!"

"I have been a saddhu in India since 1950. I was so heart broken when my father died that the only thing I could think of doing was to come to India and look for God. I don't know why I came to India to look for God. I am not Indian, I am Greek."

"I arrived in Pondicherry in 1953 after having traveled as a saddhu in India and Ceylon for three years. I had received a 'Quit India Notice.'

"I was visiting my guru in Rameshwaram, and I got this piece of paper telling me to leave India in three days. It was during the season when there were no boats to Ceylon from Rameshwaram, so I came to Pondicherry which was still a French territory.

"I came to Pondicherry to get a boat to Ceylon. But I had to wait in

Pondicherry for a couple of days for the next boat. While I was waiting, I went to visit The Ashram. I demanded to be presented immediately to The Master, The Mother. An attendant went to Mother to ask Her what to do. She sent a message that she would meet me the next afternoon. I was supposed to leave for Ceylon the next morning, but I didn't go.

"I went to meet Her. She met me at The Ashram gate and took me in Her car out to a river. I was dressed in the orange robe I had been wearing for years, and was nearly overwhelmed with the honor of being taken for a drive with The Divine Mother. We got out of the car and walked to the edge of the river.

She turned to me and asked, "Do you swim?"

"I had been a champion athlete."

"I took off my robe and waded into the water, then swam across to the island and back. When I got out of the water Mother said, 'Very good. I want you to live there and build a temple.'"

"That was sixteen years ago. I am still here in Pondicherry, may I come and get you tomorrow morning and take you to the island?"

She was happy to accept.

 In the morning Kelly was very reserved. He appeared very late for coffee on the terrace, then he ignored Roslyn and opened his newspaper. Roslyn had already finished her tea so she got up and picked up Bliss.

Kelly looked up at her over the paper and asked, "Roslyn, will you be in for lunch?"

She replied, "I was thinking I might try having lunch in The Ashram Dining Room as I am going out for the morning, I will have a rickshaw, and I am paying for my meals in the Dining Room, it might be fun for a change."

He reminded her that they had a tea date that afternoon with his biographer, Mari, and they were dining with the Countess.

She felt like a character in a novel about the good old days, and went to dress for her outing. It was still very early when Ananta arrived on his bicycle with a rickshaw in tow for Roslyn and Bliss. The morning still was very new, the streets were clean and not crowded. Fresh chalk drawings, kolams,* glowed on washed pavements and doorsteps. Roslyn and Bliss got into the rickshaw and followed Ananta on his bicycle down the road and around the corner, across the railroad tracks and down a beautiful, quiet paved country lane. They rode past houses and bicycles and people, rice fields and factories, past houses made of brick and houses made of palm leaves. Many coconut trees were growing along the road, and there was no motor traffic at all.

It was a glorious sunny morning. After meandering down little roads for a long time, Roslyn saw a large bridge spanning a river. Just before the bridge Ananta turned off onto a little dirt road that led through a huge plantation that he told her belonged to The Mother. At the end of the path was the river, and a ghat where bodies are cremated.

Across the river one could see the island. It looked entirely wild, just a green wall with a little pier jutting out into the river. Ananta whistled and a little boat manned by a dark man with a pole left the pier and came across the river.

The man poling the boat was the most handsome and healthiest looking Tamil Roslyn had seen. Ananta told her that his name was Ramakrishna, which means god/god. He was wearing shining clean clothes, yellow trousers and a white shirt.

The bottom of the little blue boat was filled with dirty river water, and when they got in the boat Ananta gave Roslyn a tin and told her to bail. The rickshaw and rickshaw driver waited on the shore. Ramakrishna poled them across the river to the little rickety pier on the other side.

They got out of the little boat onto the shaky pier, and carrying Bliss Roslyn followed Ananta through the trees. Wow!

The wall of green opened onto a manicured garden with large closely trimmed lawns bordered with flowers and shrubs. There were a lot of coconut trees; oh what a lovely bunch of coconuts! Also a kitsch statue of Athena with an owl on her shoulder, and a broken right arm like Venus de Milo. There was a small temple. Ananta told her that before Mother retired to Her room in 1958, She would come to The Island every year on a beautiful boat for his birthday. There were photos of The Mother coming to The Island in Her special boat on the walls of the temple.

He told Roslyn that one year when The Mother gave him his birthday card with his name, Ananta, written on the envelope, he told Her, "I am not Indian, I am a Greek. Please put my real name on the envelope."

Mother took back the envelope and sent her attendant for a pen. Then She crossed off Ananta and wrote, "Zeus."

The path from the temple led to a big pillar with plaster cobras sculpted into it and a light on top representing the pillar of Zeus. Nearby was a huge cage with an enormous boa constrictor which Ananta said had not been fed for days. He thought Bliss was just the right tidbit for the boa. Bliss and Roslyn clung to one another. The attractive island had also a menacing aspect. Ananta led them to a grotto with lotus and lily ponds next to the house, a small pink cottage where several more of

Ananta's servants were waiting, all dressed in immaculate yellow trousers and white shirts. Ananta invited Roslyn to sit with him on the verandah and servants brought them green coconuts with lotus stems for straws. The cool, sweet coconut water was refreshing after the long rickshaw ride.

Ananta was terribly sorry he could not invite them to lunch. The stove was broken. He invited them to lunch with him the next day at the Grand Hotel d'Europe with his mother.

Roslyn was enchanted. She took Bliss and went back to Pondicherry in the rickshaw. They had lunch at The Indian Coffee House instead of the Dining Room.

That afternoon John Kelly took them to meet his friend Mari. Mari lived in a charming little house in the block next to The Ashram that had been given her by Mother. Mother also sent an absolutely wonderful, warm and charming Italian gentleman to live with Mari.

Mari and Bliss seemed to love each other at first sight. Mari asked Roslyn if she had come to live in Auroville. Roslyn had never heard of Auroville.

Mari gave them tea, and with her warm, shining, sweet smile, in her quiet voice with an indefinable accent, told them that a new order for old planet Earth had been born, the Supramental World. The future would be something entirely new and different, a new order in evolution. The Mother had chosen a site, ten miles north of Pondicherry, of about 60 square miles, where She planned to build an experimental town according to Her vision of the Supramental World. People from all over the world were coming to be part of the new world being born.

Roslyn told Mari that she had come to India because she had had a vision, and after traveling in India and Nepal for five months was thinking about going back to the USA. She wanted to be a writer, even though she had not published anything. She had been traveling for years, gathering material. She had been everywhere and done everything, and was on her way to Ceylon and then back to the USA.

They parted with affection. Mari lent Roslyn a copy of a book she had written which had been published in London.

Roslyn only had time to read the blurb on the book jacket before dinner. There was a quotation from one of her favorite authors, that he wished he had written that book. For Roslyn a good book was always exciting, and she was very interested to read Mari's book, but her life was so dynamic that she did not have any time to read. She was having so much fun!!

Roslyn only had one dress, but it was a magnificent creation made by the best tailor in Katmandu of red Chinese silk brocade, fully lined, beautifully tailored, perfectly fitting. The Countess de B. was wearing something wonderfully elegant and understated, and although she must have been much older than Roslyn, she was also more glamorous and attractive. Roslyn felt like a clown. An authentic American hippie with a baby, a primitive, unusual dinner companion for the Countess. The Countess was gracious and appeared to be interested in Roslyn and Bliss. It was a cameo evening, with John Kelly drawing tales of heroism out of the Countess, who had apologized that her charmingly accented English was not perfect. She had left France, an apartment in Paris, a house in the country, a house in Saint Tropez, a husband and daughter, for the South Indian backwater of Pondicherry, to be near the lady, The Mother, after having been an active member of the French Resistance in WW II, and living among the most fashionable people in Paris after the war.

Roslyn was meeting people who had all been drawn to Pondicherry by the presence of The Mother, and these were the most interesting and intelligent people she had ever met.

She was beginning to feel that it might be interesting to spend more time in Pondicherry, and was glad she had not written for a ticket to go back to the USA.

On August 15th she went to The Ashram because she had heard that everyone, the devotees and guests, would all meet around the Samadi, Sri Aurobindo's tomb, and meditate together. She was, as always, barefoot, which was absolutely de rigeur for that event, and wearing her red pajamas, carrying Bliss. At the gate of The Ashram they were stopped by a man in an immaculate white shirt and shorts, who informed Roslyn that no children were allowed in The Ashram during meditation. Roslyn felt insulted and was indignant, but he was adamant. She got into a rickshaw and went back to Castelini. She went and sat on the cool marble floor of the upstairs front verandah, and leaning back against the railing, Bliss nestled quietly in her lap, she looked up and saw the photo on the opposite wall of Sri Aurobindo looking exactly as Kelly had described him to her, white-haired, white-bearded, in a white toga-like garment. The porch was full of sunlight, and the scent of sweet frangipani hung lightly in the air. The face in the photo smiled benevolently at her. She collapsed rolling with laughter, imagining herself to be at least as crazy as Kelly.

In the late afternoon The Mother came out of Her room onto the balcony. Roslyn was one of thousands of people in the street looking up as the doors to Her room opened and She stepped out, swathed in silk that flapped in the wind like the soft plumage of a tiny bird. She walked to the edge of the balcony, and stood there with Her hand on the railing and looked at the crowd assembled in the streets below, in all the windows and on all the rooftops nearby.

There was a long moment of silence, and it was as though someone whispered in Roslyn's ear, "Just look after Bliss."

The lady, The Mother, standing at the railing of the balcony half a block away, three floors up seemed to be looking at Roslyn, and Roslyn felt and could see Her smile. Mother looked around at all the people who had assembled from all over the world to receive Her blessings that evening. Just as the sky turned pink and gold with the setting sun, She turned and walked back into Her room. Roslyn was amazed that she felt aglow with happiness from the benediction.

The next morning Kelly arranged a car and took Roslyn and Bliss out to Auroville.

Auroville was a great barren plain of red clay with a Banyan tree, a few huts, and an amphitheater carved from the earth itself at the center. There was a marble lotus in the center of the amphitheater, a great urn, containing a bit of earth from all the countries of the world and a bit of the earth of Auroville sealed with a plaque that had Mother's signature on it.

They walked around and met a Canadian woman living in a beautiful hut in a small fenced compound with a few small flowering shrubs and a mangy dog.

"Do you want to come and live in Auroville?" the Canadian lady, Jane, asked Roslyn.

"I don't know."

"It would be impossible for you to live alone with a baby in Auroville," Jane firmly stated.

They walked back to the car and drove to the other side of the proposed town, to an area overlooking the beach and the Bay of Bengal. There buildings were being constructed for the first settlers who were traveling together by caravan from Paris, and were expected to arrive that fall. It was utopia. It was the dream Roslyn had been seeking.

The whole place was vibrant with the promise of a great adventure in consciousness and joy. Roslyn wanted to stay and live in Auroville, but she was alone with Baby Bliss, and Auroville was a great idea projected on a vast barren landscape.

They went back to Castelini. When they got there Roslyn was given a note telling her to please meet with the man in charge of the guesthouses at her earliest convenience.

She went to see him that afternoon.

He invited her in and bid her to take her seat. She sat in the chair opposite him.

"When are you leaving?" he asked.

"I think I would like to stay," she replied.

"It is not possible. There is no place for you here."

"What about Auroville?"

"It is not for you."

"How do you know it is not for me?"

"This is not the appropriate path for everyone. Many times people would come and Sri Aurobindo would send them to Tiruvanamalai. Have you been to Tiruvanamalai? You can go there from here by bus."

"I don't want to go to Tiruvanamalai. I want to stay here."

"You cannot stay here."

"If She is The Divine Mother, then She is my mother too," Roslyn insisted.

"No She is not. It doesn't work like that. Please pay your bill and go."

"I have no money. I am waiting for some money from the USA," she replied.

"Then please vacate the guesthouse, and you may send me the money when you receive it."

"But I cannot vacate the guesthouse. I have no money and no place to go until I get some money."

"You will please be out of the guesthouse by tomorrow noon."

The only thing she could say was, "Yes. Very good."

She went back to Castelini. The manager who she had not seen since she checked in came out and asked her when she was leaving. She replied that she was leaving the next morning. Kelly wasn't there. She had hoped he might lend her some money, but he wasn't there, nor was Gabriel, to be seen that evening or the next morning.

The next morning she had to leave the guesthouse. She went to the hotel near the park, and arranged to stay there and take her meals there until the money she was waiting for arrived.

She was astonished when Mari visited her that afternoon in her room at the hotel. Roslyn had not told anyone where she was going when she left the guesthouse. Kelly and Gabriel were not there, and the manager was patently not interested.

"Mother sent me," Mari explained.

"She told me to tell you not to worry about money. She also said you may use all the facilities of The Ashram and Auroville."

"I will wait here until my money comes, and then I will go to Ceylon," Roslyn replied.

"Do you want to write a letter to Mother? I would take it to Her for you." Mari offered.

"No."

Roslyn spent more than a week in the hotel near the park. She made several more friends; an American who worked in the press; a Dutch lady with two little girls who lived near the bazaar; a Danish lady who was studying Sanskrit; an Italian lady with a little boy a bit older than Bliss; and the guy she had met in Katmandu. The weather was consistently beautiful. Roslyn would swim every morning and afternoon on The Ashram beach near the tennis courts, where Mother had played tennis in the afternoon until She was 80 years old.

She went to check the mail every day at The Ashram Post Office, and one morning the letter with money was there. Roslyn picked up the letter and ran into Mari.

Mari had another message for Roslyn from The Mother.

"Mother will meet you when you come back from Ceylon!"

She had not thought about coming back to Pondicherry from Ceylon. She was still thinking about flying back to the USA from Ceylon. But she was curious about The Mother, so because of the message from Mari she decided to leave most of her things in Pondicherry and visit Ceylon. She would write to her father and ask him to send her and Bliss tickets to fly to the USA from India after meeting Mother.

John Kelly with Gabriel and Gabriel's family

iii

An outstretched hand is felt upon our lives,
It is near us in unnumbered bodies and births;
In its unshaken grasp it keeps for us, safe,
The one inevitable supreme result
No-one can take away and no doom change,
The crown of conscious Immortality,
The godhead promised to our struggling souls
When first man's heart dared death and suffered life.

Sri Aurobindo, Savitri

Mental ideals and opinions and constructions are no more for the mind has fallen into silence. It is only a channel for the light, the truth of Divine Knowledge. Ideals are too narrow for the vastness of the spirit. It is the ocean of the infinite that flows through us moving us in time.

Life is the altar of this sacrifice: works are our offering to a transcendent and universal power and presence, as yet rather felt or glimpsed, than known or seen. The essence of the sacrifice is the surrender of all desire for the fruit.

(from Jim Bean's Journal extracts from Sri Aurobindo's Synthesis of Yoga.*)*

From the Post Office Roslyn went to the bank and then set about settling her bills. First she went to pay her bill for the guesthouse. The man in charge was sitting behind his desk and was very happy to hear that she was leaving Pondicherry. She told him that Mother had promised her a private Darshan when she returned from Ceylon.

He told her, "Sri Aurobindo's yoga is not for everyone."

She replied that she had understood that Sri Aurobindo had said, "All life is yoga."

He smiled thinly and asked if she was going to Rameshwaram.

"I have to go to Rameshwaram to catch the ferry."

He suggested that she visit the Sri Aurobindo Nilayam in Rameshwaram and meet the famous yogi, Panditji.

She was not going to stop in Rameshwaram to meet a yogi. She was only going to Rameshwaram to get a ferry to Ceylon. She had had a good time in Pondicherry, The Ashram was very delightful, but she was very confused.

She had finished Mari's book, that was about a Canadian on a spiritual quest in Ceylon who meets an eccentric Irish Swami living in a little ashram next to a big temple near Jaffna. Roslyn was more interested in comfortable hotels, good meals, and interesting books than yogis and swamis. She liked the Pondicherry Ashram because it was clean and modestly comfortable.   She was not interested in dragging Bliss from one hut to another through the Himalayas on a spiritual quest.

She slept with Bliss in the luggage rack in the third class ladies' compartment through most of the overnight train journey to Rameshwaram.

They woke up early, and the women on the seat let her sit by the window as the train rolled through the southernmost part of India. Even in the early morning it was hot. The land looked like hard sand. No green. The people in the stations were brightly clad. There were vendors of coffee, tea, sea-shell necklaces, baskets and biscuits at each of the little stations, and beggars. The train stopped at every little village. A few people would get off. A few people would get on.

Then they were on a very very long, and seemingly slightly shaky railroad bridge connecting the island of Rameshwaram to the subcontinent India. It is an incredibly long bridge connecting one strip of sand with another strip of sand. The sun sparkled on the ocean and the clack of the train and the sound of the surf held them suspended in time like the train over the water.

A toot of the train whistle. The train stopped in front of a tiny cement block building on a pile of sand. A few people got off. A few people got on. Then the train started up again, across the most barren landscape imaginable. It might have been the moon. They moved at a snail's pace across the ocean of sand; even the few bushes were the bleached bone white color of sand. Then a cement block building, and the train stopped and someone would get on or off, until the conductor blew his whistle, and slowly the train started up again, chugging slowly again across the sand until it finally reached a big station. The train pulled in to a big concrete slab platform under an asbestos roof and stopped.

There were several tracks, but only one platform in the station. It was as though the intense heat and bright sun made everything quieter. The atmosphere was so bright that everything seemed to pale in it. Roslyn felt very insignificant and alone in the mob of travelers, and didn't know where she was or where she was going. She had not seen any other European travelers on the train or in the station.

Everyone got off the train. She took Bliss and her bag and followed the crowd down the platform to the gate, where she handed her train ticket to the gate keeper. She was out of the gate and on the bright street. There were little wagons and horses with bells on their harness, and bicycle rickshaws. There was a well trod dusty road through the hot desert which seemed to begin at the station and go south.

"Ceylon boat?" she asked the rickshaw men.

"Ceylon boat already going. Ceylon boat three days coming."

She had missed the boat.

Roslyn decided to wait in Rameshwaram for the next boat. She didn't want to get back on the train and go back to Pondi, and her visa was expiring. She had to go to Ceylon to get a new visa. She asked the rickshaw wallahs, "Hotel?"

They wagged their heads. One of them pulled his rickshaw out of the line, and gestured that she should get in. She wouldn't get in until he agreed how much she would pay him to take her to a hotel.

They agreed on five rupees, and she got in the rickshaw with her bag and Bliss and started off in the parade of wagons and rickshaws going into Rameshwaram from the station.

Rameshwaram is one of the seven holy cities of India. Roslyn remembered reading in a book that every devout Hindu aspires to visit the seven holy cities in India during his lifetime. There is a great temple in Rameshwaram that had been built by devout Hindus on the exact site where Sri Ram did his puja before leaving India for Lanka and the great battle with Ravana. They rode down the hot dusty road to the little town that had grown up near the temple. They passed a Gandhi statue, so realistically rendered that it took a second glance to ascertain that it was a bronze statue, and not a man who looked like Gandhi standing in the middle of the road at the corner where the two square blocks which make up the town meet. The temple is near the beach. The rickshaw driver stopped in front of a building between the temple and the beach, with the words "Vivekananda Nilayam" over the door

"Hotel?" she asked.

He wagged his head, "Yes, yes."

At the entrance there was an office with a young English speaking Tamil man who greeted her and offered her a room, and a guide to show her Rameshwaram. He told her, "This island, only temple island. There is no food growing on the island. All the rice, everything is brought from the mainland by train or boat because there is no bridge for cars. The only work on the island is the temple and serving the pilgrims and priests."

Roslyn had passed the temple in the rickshaw on the way to the Rest House. The temple completely dominated the town. It was at least as big as a football field. It had enormous sculpted towers on the north and south that went up into the air some fourteen stories, amazing intricately carved edifices of myth. The entrances on each of the four sides were constructed of huge stones, many times the height of a man. The whole construction was essentially of huge stone slabs that had to have been brought to the island from the mainland before there was a railroad bridge.

She did not see a single motor vehicle in the town. It was the most quiet place she had ever been. There was a sense of quiet wellbeing of a different era before motor cars, etc. Everyone seemed happy and well as they walked along the dusty streets, every person a little speck in space compared to the vastness of the temple. It was as though she had traveled through time to a place where clearly everyone was a beggar before the Lord. Even Sri Ram begged the Lord's favor in Rameshwaram, and his victory was the grace of his divine benefactors.

Roslyn went to the temple. She was overwhelmed by the awesome size of it, enormous statues and carvings everywhere depicting scenes and characters from the Ramayana. Many of the statues were brightly painted. The ceiling over the huge main corridor was at least thirty feet high, and went all around the temple with a width of around thirty feet. The corridors were magnificent, and every inch different, carved, painted, with huge monoliths. Standing there in the vast cool silence, she felt very safe.

Halfway down the north corridor was a large cage. A young elephant walked back and forth, occasionally taking some straw in its trunk and putting it in its mouth. In the west corridor there were stands with postcards, statues, toys for children, puffed rice, seashell necklaces, ribbons, kum-kum, and many exotic inexpensive souvenirs for sale. There were even little tiny baby bangles for Bliss which Roslyn bought and put on her little chubby wrists. Bliss cooed with delight, at the tinkling jangle of the little glass bangles. Alert, looking at everything, the child seemed completely content in her mother's arms, enjoying the stroll through the ancient holy place. There were no foreign tourists there.

When she came out of the temple into the bright sunlight, Roslyn decided to go and look for the Sri Aurobindo Nilayam. The town was very small. She took a rickshaw because she did not know where she was going.

The rickshaw man pedaled slowly up the street from the main entrance, on the west side of the temple. The houses and buildings in the town were all nicely made of brick, wood and cement, no palm roofs. The houses were dwarfed by the mammoth temple. The town was only one block long. At the corner the buildings stopped and the paved street continued on to the right, where there were few buildings.

The rickshaw turned to the right, on to a little dusty lane, started up a little hill, and stopped in front of a genuine cement house on the edge of the dirt track through the sand. There was a strange looking person standing there at the door welcoming her, but she was so confused she could not understand him. "Sri Aurobindo Nilayam" was written above the door.

"I am looking for Panditji," she explained to the roundly shaped bald person with thick glasses who had been greeting her.

He grinned. She saw a gold tooth light up his smile, "I am Panditji."

If there is an edge she might have been a little bit over it at that point. She did not even know what she wanted to do, or be, or why she was where she was. She did not know what to think or say.

The person who was grinning at her, obviously welcoming her, was not like anyone she had ever seen, or even seen photos of. He was very round, and his skin was not white or brown, but a warm golden color. His head was shaved and his forehead and arms streaked with three broad white lines, and in the middle of his forehead there was a big red U. He was wearing a white longi, a white string, and there was a white towel on his shoulder.

He nodded his head and bid her, "Come, come."

She followed him into the house that was a large courtyard surrounded by terraces. There were rooms along the sides of the courtyard that opened into the front and back of the house. It was full of light, and a cool breeze. He offered her coffee.

She never drank coffee, but she accepted.

He clapped his hands and a woman appeared from the back of the house. She was very beautiful, very delicate of form and feature. She was wearing a bright sari wrapped differently to any Roslyn had seen; it went around her legs like a dhoti, a type of folded pant, then across her bosom. She was wearing gold chains and bangles and a wide grin. Her arms went out to Bliss and Bliss jumped into them.

"Coffee," Panditji said.

She wagged her head and disappeared with Bliss.

Roslyn sat there wondering what she was doing in a strange house near the southernmost tip of India. The human being in front of her was another stranger, but even though she had never met him or anyone even vaguely like him, he felt like an old friend.

"What do you want?" he asked.

"I am confused," was all she could say. She did not tell him that she was afraid she was losing her mind. She could barely stand to admit that to herself, but she was afraid that was the case.

"I do not speak English. Come back tomorrow afternoon and I will have someone here to translate for me," Panditji said.

They sat there not speaking. He was sitting in front of a door to a room where she could see many statues decorated with fresh flowers. Above the door to the room was a photo of a fat man wearing a longi and mala with a bright nimbus around his head, and photos of The Mother and Sri Aurobindo.

The woman reappeared with Bliss on one hip, and a tray with two cups of coffee and some sweets in the other hand. She gracefully put the tray on the floor between them and disappeared, with Bliss completely absorbed by her.

Panditji served Roslyn coffee and sweets. She did not know what to say, so she just sat there looking around at the sunlit space, enjoying the coffee and sweets.

When she finished her coffee she thanked him. He clapped his hands and his wife reappeared with Bliss, who jumped into Roslyn's arms as she stood up. The baby's hair had been combed, and she had black liner around her eyes and a black spot like a beauty mark on her cheek. With one arm around Bliss, Roslyn brought her hands together in front in a greeting everyone uses in India, palms together, fingers pointing towards the sky.

Panditji's wife smiled at them, returned the gesture, nodding her head. Panditji walked with them back out through the entry hall to the porch,

He reminded her, "Come tomorrow. I will have someone here to translate for us."

She thanked him and walked down the hill feeling she had just met someone she already knew. She had two more days before she could get a boat to Ceylon.

Roslyn stopped at a small cafe that emanated the redolent aroma of fresh sweets. She ate a plate of still warm jellybies and Mysorepack with several cups of tea, and then walked through the temple back to the hotel.

Although there were many people around she felt completely alone. The beggars around the temple seemed to be giving her a hard time, having singled her out for their attention, perhaps because of her white skin?

In Rameshwaram beggars line up from the little temple on the seashore, where devout pilgrims bathe, to the large temple. As the pilgrims walk from the large temple to the small temple, they give a coin to each beggar they pass. Roslyn did not have enough coins for all the beggars. When she passed them without giving them money they pressed her, and they got rowdy. She was terrified, a beggar herself. It was awful. Little girls with babies, old women with babies, lepers, people with huge gray limbs afflicted with elephantiasis. There was a crazy saddhu wearing orange, with his forehead and body streaked with the three white stripes of Shiva, who carried a big stick and spoke his version of Esperanto. He was particularly aggressive, and she was afraid he might hit her with his stick as he demanded her attention and donation. She tried to pretend he wasn't there. He was so frightening. The beggars were mostly only troublesome around the temple, and they did not go into the temple.

Roslyn always walked through the temple, as the hotel was near the beach on the opposite side of the temple from the town. She would walk through rather than around the temple because it was shaded and out of the sun. Alone in the long empty corridors she felt less frightened, less confused. She was there and helpless and there was nothing she could do. She had believed that she had had a true vision. She had traveled to India. She had wanted to find a true spiritual path but she had found only poverty and uncertainty, a never ending road, and strangers who might become friends for a moment. She was alone with Bliss. They had been traveling since Bliss was born. Roslyn knew there were people who would think that she was running away from herself because she had had a baby without being married. She might have agreed with them if it had not been for the vision, but maybe it was not a vision, maybe it was just a hallucination, or a device created by her imagination.

Bliss was the only stable thing in her life, and even though she was only a baby she had helped Roslyn get to India. Bliss was two months old when they were in Turkey. They were staying in a small hotel near the Blue Mosque and had taken a bus to the Hilton to check at American Express for mail.

Roslyn was expecting money from her father, Bernie, and a letter from a friend who had promised to travel overland with her and Bliss to India.

Roslyn got a postcard from Bernie, "In the Caribbean, having a wonderful time. Should I send money to Istanbul? Love, Dad."

She was absolutely broke. It would take at least a week for him to receive her reply, and then it would be at least another week until she'd get any money. Two weeks with no money, living on credit in the sleazy hotel, eating at the small cafe which offered credit, was not an appealing prospect. The letter from her friend told her she'd fallen in love and was staying in Germany. Roslyn collapsed into a puddle of tears. She had no money at all, and to travel overland alone with an infant to India even for her was nearly unthinkable. Bliss looked at her as though the whole thing was a joke and she entirely understood it, and there was nothing to worry about. She reached out her little baby hand and patted Roslyn's cheek. Roslyn stopped crying. She suddenly felt everything was okay.

It didn't make any sense, but it was okay. Months later, and she still did not know anything. She was alone with Bliss, even though she could not imagine how they had survived. They had made it to India. They had had a fantastic trip; but she was still wandering around not knowing where she was going. The vision had simply called her to India.

She had traveled to New York from Arizona, then by boat to Europe, by train and boat around Europe and North Africa, then went back to Europe. Bliss had been born in West Germany, and they had flown to Greece when she was only three weeks old. When Bliss was two months old they flew to Istanbul, where they were stranded for a couple of weeks without any money. Then they started out overland on the old silk road, across Turkey, Iran, Afghanistan, Pakistan. It had taken her more than a year from the day she had had the vision to get to India. She had never had enough money together at the same time to buy a plane ticket to India. She had spent four months in India and Nepal and had many wonderful experiences, but had found no place for her and Bliss to live. Roslyn did not know what to do next. She was going to Ceylon, then she was going back to Pondicherry to meet Mother. Then what?

She was in Rameshwaram, and it was exotic and tropical. The ocean was warm. The water on the beach was very shallow, and the waves more gentle than any she'd ever seen. It was a superlative place to play with Bliss, except people gathered to stare at them. Roslyn swam in the sea in her pajamas, which had a Nehru collar, sleeves down to her wrists, and pants down to her ankles. She hoped not to give all the people who were staring at her too much of her to stare at. Even though the boat to Ceylon leaves India from Rameshwaram there seemed to be very few foreigners who visited Rameshwaram.

She woke up at four in the morning to the sound of singing from the loudspeakers of the temple. Bliss and Roslyn went out onto the balcony in front of their room and looked out over the dusty road between the big temple and the small temple on the beach at sunrise. Below them on the street there were musicians playing the South Indian horn, the chenai, and beating drums in front of priests with shaven heads wearing white longis and white strings. They carried strange things, and were followed by the elephant from the temple, caparisoned with a golden howdah and guided by a mahout wearing a loincloth. Pilgrims followed the swaying elephant and noisy musicians towards the shore, and then the beggars lined up on the side of the street. Roslyn watched the musicians and elephant and some of the priests coming back from the beach and continuing the procession around the temple, followed by children and pilgrims. Then from the beach the devout pilgrims returned, their clothes soaked, even their hair soaked with sea water. As they walked back to the great temple they gave all the money they were carrying to the beggars quietly lining the streets with their outstretched bowls. This procession seemed to be going on all morning and it was breakfast time, so Roslyn decided to brave the street and the crowds again. She went out and through the temple to the satisfactory cafe she had found the day before for breakfast.

She did not really have anything to do but eat and sleep and look after Bliss. Rameshwaram was so peaceful it seemed to be profoundly boring. She was happy to visit Panditji again that afternoon.

He was there to greet them when she walked up the hill carrying Bliss. He was with another man, a short, dark man whom he introduced as the local English teacher. Panditji clapped his hands and a young woman appeared. He introduced his daughter. She took Bliss from Roslyn. Panditji, the interpreter and Roslyn sat on mats on the terrace looking into the bright courtyard.

Panditji showed Roslyn a card he had been given by The Mother in Pondicherry. On the front there was a very beautiful, very mysterious photo of Mother swathed in a sari that looked as if it were gossamer veils flowing gracefully around her luminous presence, as She stood at the top of a staircase which was nearly completely overgrown with flowers. Her eyes were nearly as large as Her face, and seemed to be the center of the exquisite picture. He opened the card and showed Roslyn what The Mother had written, in English. "Thank you for your help. Thank you for helping me overcome the force which was paralyzing me." It was dated 1958 and signed, "With love and blessings M."

Then He looked at Roslyn and asked her, "What do you want?"

"I am confused," was all she could reply.

He said something to the translator. The translator said something to Him. Then He looked at Roslyn and said very simply, "Confusion is ego."

"Yes, but what am I supposed to do?"

"Yes, yes. Have some tea. These sweets are very nice." Panditji's wife had unobtrusively brought tea and sweets for them. His daughter gave Bliss back to Roslyn.

Roslyn did not want tea. She wanted answers; but she drank tea and ate the sweet.

After tea Panditji told her to come back the next afternoon, and he would give her something.

She went back out to the street, and to the temple where she sat in the courtyard and watched the elephant and musicians, pilgrims, children, vendors and beggars. It was Ganesh Puja, the sacred day of Lord Ganesh, the elephant-headed god, son of Shiva and Parvati, who broke off a tusk for a pen to write the Mahabharata and is 'the remover of obstacles.'

The horns blared very loudly. There were fireworks. The elephant carried the god.

They went back to their hotel room and to sleep, listening to the loud speaker of the temple blaring traditional chants and carnatic music in the night.

Roslyn was awakened again the next morning by the sound of chanting voices blaring from the loud speaker at the temple. She got up with Bliss, and then walked to the sea and watched the sun rise over the ocean and fill the air and water with all the colors imaginable. It was a quiet, peaceful and holy moment. She nearly forgot herself and her confusion. She was simply there with Bliss at the edge of the warm and gentle sea watching the sunlight color the night sea and sky until it became a glorious blaze in that moment before morning.

The priests had lit a small fire in the temple near the beach, and the air was sweet with incense and the chanting of ancient sacred mantras.

There was nothing to do all day long, and she was happy that she would be able to leave for Ceylon the next day.

On her way to Panditji's house that afternoon she stopped and bought him some flowers. She had seen many flowers in his house, fresh garlands around the photo of his Guru, garlands around photos of Mother and Sri Aurobindo, mountains of fresh flowers in his meditation room. She walked with Bliss up the little hill from the town to Panditji's house. His daughter was there to meet them. She took Bliss and disappeared into the back of the house.

The translator was with Panditji, and asked Roslyn, "Would you come for a walk?"

She agreed, and followed him and Panditji out of the house and up the hill away from the town.

"Panditji likes to go for a walk every afternoon," the translator explained.

She walked with them on the hot dry road. Panditji's house was nearly at the edge of town. There were two or three huts after that, and then just a road across the sand. There were a few goats and cows grazing on the sand accompanied by ragged children. The animals were very thin. They passed some pilgrims walking in the other direction. Finally on the horizon they could see another temple. It was a very enchanting small-scale temple out at the edge of the island. There was no one and nothing around it. It just rose on white cement steps going round the pink building, sitting solidly and silently there in the gentle breeze in the sunny afternoon, a place where a man has built a monument to his aspiration for God.

The translator turned to Roslyn and told her that Panditji had lived alone in the temple for twelve years doing tapasya. The priests in his family for seven generations had looked after this temple as well as having been in charge of the great temple.

A few pilgrims passed them with a priest in a white longi with a shaved head. They walked around the temple on the steps, and then entered the building from one side and came out another. They came back down the steps. It was so quiet. The sea barely licked the sand near the base of the temple steps, the surf was gentle, the sea was calm and clear and there was not a cloud in the late afternoon sky. The warm breeze was more like a gentle breath than a wind.

Panditji turned and looked at Roslyn, and said to the translator, "Chello," with a shake of his head.

They started walking back towards town. Roslyn took a long look at the beatifically peaceful place. They walked back to Panditji's house. Panditji invited them in for tea. They sat on straw mats on the shaded terrace next to the sunlit courtyard.

Panditji told the translator to tell Roslyn, "The Mother sent Her contractor to Rameshwaram with train-loads of materials and a crew, and they rebuilt this house, which had been in his family for many generations. Mother always keeps a house for Him near The Ashram in Pondicherry even though He only goes there two or three times a year, whenever She calls."

Roslyn sipped her tea, not understanding.

After tea Panditji asked the translator to ask her, "Would you do some practice?"

She said, "I would be willing to do some spiritual practice, but I have a baby."

Panditji clapped his hands and his daughter came running to his side. He said something to her in a language Roslyn did not understand. The daughter disappeared into a room and reappeared a moment later with a pencil and a small pad of paper.

Panditji tore a little piece of paper off the pad, wrote something on it and handed it to Roslyn. Then he turned to the translator and explained.

The translator turned to her and told her to write on a small piece of paper exactly what Panditji had written three times every morning for 34 days.

It was simple, so she agreed.

Then the translator said, "Bring that piece of paper back to Panditji tomorrow morning."

"I am going to Ceylon tomorrow," she said.

"Yes, but the boat does not leave until noon. Panditji wants you to come here tomorrow morning at nine. Roslyn agreed. Panditji clapped his hands and his daughter brought Bliss from the back of the house, followed by her mother, who greeted Roslyn with a friendly grin. Bliss's hair was tied together on the top of her head. There was eyeliner on her eyes, a black spot between her brows, and another on her cheek. She seemed very happy with her new friends.

The translator explained: "The spot on the forehead is a bindi for her third eye. The spot on her cheek is to keep away the evil eye."

Roslyn took the baby and Bliss gave everyone a big smile. They walked into the street and down the hill for another meal of fresh sweets, savories, and tea.

They walked back to the hotel through the temple to the lodge for their last night under the whirring fan in the fine gauze mosquito net tent.

They were packed and ready to check out of the lodge before they went to visit Panditji in the morning. It was another halcyon day. Roslyn picked up some more flowers for Panditji, and some sweets for his daughter and his wife in the bazaar. When she got to the house his wife and daughter were on the porch to greet them. Bliss gave them a big cooing bouncing smile. Roslyn gave them the sweets. Panditji's daughter seemed very pleased and took Bliss and disappeared with her. Panditji's wife beckoned Roslyn into the house, but gestured that she should be quiet. Panditji was sitting in his meditation room. There was a glow of ghee lamps and the smell of incense. His back was facing the open door to the terrace. There was a small bamboo mat next to one of the big pillars on the terrace. She gestured that Roslyn should sit, so she sat cross-legged on the mat.

Roslyn sat there, leaning against the pillar wondering what she was doing there, but it was a pleasant enough place. There was a large photo of The Mother on one side of the door to the room where Panditji was sitting, and a large photo of Sri Aurobindo was on the other side of the doorway. Above the doorway was a photo of Panditji's guru, a very fat swami-type who had a glowing nimbus that somehow the photographer had gotten in the photo. Apart from the light that seemed to emanate from Him into the photo, Panditji's guru looked fatter than any Indian Roslyn had ever seen. Each of these photos had fresh flowers every day. Panditji seemed to be taking flowers from the pile of flowers on his right, and after removing the flowers from the day before from each of the objects he would say a mantra and put fresh flowers. Then he poured water on things all the time chanting mantras that were nearly inaudible, like the low murmur of running water, except occasionally, like when he would ring a bell, he would say a mantra so Roslyn could nearly hear him, and then the murmur again.

She was really bored with sitting there. She did not want to be impolite, so she stayed where she was. There was really nothing else she could think of doing at that moment anyway. It was very quiet and peaceful and the courtyard was full of sunlight. Suddenly it was as though a cloud or a limitation within her melted like ice in the sun; her whole being felt suddenly freed, and waves of bliss as gentle as the warm surf on the beach filled her.

She felt more confused than ever. Panditji got up from his meditation and came out of the meditation room. He put some powder on her forehead, and then gestured that she should make a cup of her palm. He poured some water into that leaky cup and she drank it. It was sweet with spices and herbs. He explained, "This water was used in the ritual to symbolically wash the feet of The Divine Mother. The Goddess."

He went back into the room where he practiced his worship and brought her two bananas, one for her and one for Bliss.

She thanked him and went on to tell him that she had had some experience sitting there.

He looked at her smiling. "Yes, yes, I know. You do not have to do the work I gave you. I will do it for you. Do you have the piece of paper?"

She gave him the piece of paper.

He invited her to visit when she returned from Ceylon.

She looked forward to seeing him again.

She took Bliss, and went to collect their bag and go to the pier for the boat.

The boat trip to Ceylon from Rameshwaram only takes about an hour and a half, however the Customs and Immigration process on both sides takes at least four hours, with endless chaotic queues as every bag, basket and letter is carefully perused by conscientious officials.

Roslyn was completely exhausted when she finally finished with Ceylonese Customs and Immigration late that evening. She dragged herself and Bliss and their bag across the sand from the pier to the train station. There was an overnight train leaving for Anaradapura. That was the only train. She had no idea at all where that was. Someone explained to her it was in the middle of Ceylon, and filled with ancient palaces and temples. She bought a ticket in a reserved third class car, found her seat was the top tier of a three tier sleeper, and tried to go to sleep.

Vendors were shouting to sell their wares in the bedlam of the little station full of tired people who had gotten off the boat from Rameshwaram. Children were screaming, women chattering, men shouting, everyone dragging bags, suitcases, or boxes. There were a few red turbaned porters with piles of bags and boxes on their head. The vendors even came into the railway car, and the train that was supposed to leave at 10 p.m. sat there until every last passenger had gone through Customs and Immigration and the Customs House was closed and the officials got on the train. They sat in the station most of the night. Nearly everyone was asleep by the time the train started. Roslyn finally slept when the train started, and woke a couple of hours later because the train had slowed down. The whistle tooted. She tried to look out the window. There was a woman with about eight children on the seats below.

They were coming into a station. It was cooler than anywhere she had been in months. Even around the station everything was very green. The train stopped and they got out. They followed the crowd into the station. Roslyn felt completely lost in the crowd of people moving in every direction. She had had to go to Anaradapura to catch a train to Colombo. Roslyn was tired, but she was not in a hurry because she didn't know where she was going. She decided it would be better to stop and rest for a day before going on to Colombo. Instead of joining a queue to buy another ticket she headed for the exit and the sunny street. There were rickshaws and even a few taxis lined up outside the station.

She went to a rickshaw man. "Hotel?" she asked.

"Government Guesthouse," he replied.

"Nice?" she asked.

He wagged his head.

"How many rupees?" she asked.

"Five rupees," he replied, reasserting the figure by putting up his right palm and showing her his five fingers.

She agreed. She put her bag in the corner of the seat, got in, and settled herself. They pulled out of the station, around the corner, and into a driveway in front of a big new white cement building. The driver stopped in front of the entrance. Roslyn paid the rickshaw man reluctantly.

Such a short ride should have been only one or two rupees. But she had agreed to five, and so she paid him five rupees.

She went through the entrance into the lobby. There was a man standing behind a counter with a sign, "Reception."

"Hello," she said. "May I have a room?"

"Yes. Single or double?"

"Single," she replied.

"What about the baby?" he asked.

"She sleeps with me, a single room is fine."

"No, impossible, two people double room."

"How much?" she asked.

"Double room 200rs."

"Single room?"

"Single room, 100rs., but two people double room."

She was really upset. Even a single room was too expensive, and she was dirty and uncomfortable and did not know how to find another place to stay in Anaradapura. She started crying.

A barefooted, white skinned elderly man dressed in the white longi and towel of a swami interrupted them. He asked her what was the problem, and since she was nearly hysterical, suggested that she join him and his friends for a drink first, then explain her problem.

She started to argue with him, but he calmed her and assured her she would feel better after a drink.

Roslyn followed him out onto a terrace. He introduced her to his friends who were the only people sitting there, Ceylonese men in Western suits with white shirts and ties.

They greeted her gently and asked her what she would like to drink. Although it was before noon they were already drinking whiskey. She asked for a Coca-Cola with ice.

Everyone spoke English. The Swami had an accent. They asked her where she was from, and she told them she was an American traveling in India and had been in Pondicherry and Rameshwaram.

The swami asked if she had met Mari in Pondicherry.

She replied that she had.

Then he introduced himself as 'German Swami,' the person whom Mari had depicted as her character, 'Irish Swami' in her book.

It was the only book Roslyn had read in months. She was overwhelmed at the serendipity that the first person to talk to her in Ceylon was a devotee of Mother, and a friend of Mari, and the person she was slightly curious about meeting in Ceylon.

His friends worked for the government in archaeology and tourism. They were all staying in the other guesthouse, The Old Guesthouse, which was much nicer. They invited her to lunch with them there, and offered to take her around the ancient temples afterwards to see wonderful ancient sculptures, sacred to Buddhists and Hindus. German Swami told her that if she would wait at The Old Guesthouse for two days he would take her to visit his ashram in Jaffna.

She told him she wanted to go to Colombo.

He replied that there was a direct train from Jaffna to Colombo. Both his friends insisted that she visit them in Colombo.

It seemed that her Ceylon tour was set. Roslyn and Bliss joined their new acquaintances as they left the New Government Guesthouse and went in their car to the Old Government Guesthouse in Anaradapura.

They drove through the stone fence at the large ornate rod iron gates, which were opened for them by a uniformed gateman who saluted the car as they passed down a graveled divided road, through a vast park, with manicured flower beds along the center of the drive. The car stopped at an entrance, under a portico, supported with big columns. A man wearing white gloves and a turban opened the car doors for them. After they all got down the driver parked the car next to the glorious huge sprawling colonial building.

Scarlet O'Hara would have felt right at home walking up those broad front steps onto that verandah with huge white Corinthian pillars. Roslyn was barefoot in her red pajamas with Bliss on one arm, her carpet bag over her shoulder, and accompanied by two very respectably dressed Ceylonese men in suits and leather shoes, and an old bare footed European swami.

The entry hall was a large room full of Victorian furniture, and there were some people sitting there reading newspapers. She checked into a single room for two nights and bid her friends au revoir until lunch.

She followed a boy in a clean white jacket and trousers from the desk to her room. The man at the desk had given him the key.

They entered the room from a verandah overlooking the gardens. There was a huge frangipani tree near the verandah filling the air with the sweet scent of its white blossoms. It was a large room with high ceilings. The boy put her bag down on a wooden stand next to a cupboard. He turned on the fan and showed her the glamorous attached bath that even had a huge bathtub in it. It was the first bathtub she had seen since Greece.

She bathed Bliss and herself, put on fresh clothes, and went back down to meet their new friends. They were drinking whisky in the lobby and offered her a drink. She had another Coca-Cola with ice.

A few minutes later a man dressed in an immaculate white jacket and pants, barefooted, wearing a turban and white gloves came over and bowed, "Lunch is ready."

He went over to other guests. They finished their drinks and went into the dining room.

The dining room was a long room. All the French doors along the back wall were opened to the terrace during lunch. Ceiling fans whirred overhead and there was a huge buffet table along one wall. There were starched and ironed white linen table-cloths and napkins, and a flower in a vase on each table. The waiters all wore white uniforms, gloves and turbans.

They were served soup at the table and then had to help themselves at the buffet. Roslyn had Bliss on her hip and her empty plate in one hand. One of the waiters rushed up to help carry her plate. She had only to point to what she wanted. Gingerly, without getting a splash on his immaculate white gloves, the waiter filled her plate, and even before they were halfway down the length of the table her plate was heaped with salads, vegetables, curried chicken, thick slices of ham and roast beef. The potato puffs were rolling off the edge of the plate and towards the floor. She finally had to say "enough." The waiter carried her plate back to her place at the table.

German Swami and his friends were very jolly. The Swami started drinking whiskey in the morning but did not eat meat. Roslyn noticed some curried prawns on the archaeologist's plate, and dove into her plateful of food, determined to go back to the buffet table for seconds. They ate heartily. The men drank wine with their meal. Roslyn drank Coca-Cola with ice. Bliss watched everything with detached bemusement. The Swami told stories about living in Tibet until the Second World War, when the German Army threatened to invade that region. He hightailed it to India, traveling as a saddhu. He was suspected as a spy in British India, and was fortunate to get away from Pondicherry to Ceylon by boat. He met an old swami near the temple in Jaffna who was willing to let him stay as a disciple in a small ashram near the temple. It is a temple where many miraculous remissions of psychological and emotional illness had occurred. Crazy people from all over India and Ceylon would visit this temple hoping for a miracle. "It is very difficult to tell the difference between people who are crazy and people who are not crazy," the Swami said.

Roslyn laughed at that, not knowing if she was crazy or dreaming as she stuffed herself with ghee rice and curried fish. She really had too much food on her plate, but there was the dessert table beckoning her. Everybody needed a cigarette break before dessert. Roslyn was thoroughly enjoying herself. She had not a word to say, could barely hear the conversation at the table, she was so completely absorbed in the marvelous food. After several days of steamed rice cakes, sweets, bananas and tea in Rameshwaram, she was in ecstasy. She felt a little bit awkward. The only other women in the room were wearing lovely saris, and were very discreet. The table they had been given seemed to be in the middle of all the other tables, and she felt like the cynosure of every eye, in her slightly tattered pajamas, with her baby on her lap, inhaling huge quantities of food. The Swami in his white longi was not more badly dressed than Roslyn in her orange pajamas, but she decided she had better dig out a sari she had bought in Pondicherry from her bag for dinner. She hoped she would be able to find a servant to iron it.

They all got up to go to the dessert table. There was an entire table covered with puddings, pastries, fresh fruit, tinned fruit, and a big silver thermos full of ice cream. She took a little bit of nearly everything and by the time she was half way through picking at the delectable goodies on the plate, she knew she could not finish it. She felt drunk with too much food.

She rolled into bed and slept until tea time. When she woke up, she found German Swami and his friends were waiting for her at a table on the verandah with tea and cakes. After tea they got into the car and rode and walked to beautiful old temples, and a current archaeological excavation. It was like paradise on those cool green hills in the late afternoon. The stones of the old temples seemed to be nearly as old as the hillside. The place was aglow in the colors of the setting sun. At one of the excavations they had just found statues of Buddha in pure gold, and a beautiful, thin dancing Ganesh made out of gold, painted black.

The big trees, the beautiful birds, the glamorous guesthouse, all declaimed to Roslyn that she was in a very special place, and had for some reason received an unexpected and very wonderful, very special day.

By the next evening she was a bit bored by it all, except for the amusing conversation of the Swami. She had had enough to eat. She had had too much to eat. All her clothes were clean. The conversation between Swami and his friends consisted mainly of, "Would you like another beer?" "Is it too early to start drinking scotch?" (This at 9 a.m.).

"Let's go for another round." Swami would occasionally drop a pearl of wisdom, "This bottle is empty." She was relieved to hear that he did not drink in his ashram.

She was happy to set off with him on the train to Jaffna, in a first class car with tickets provided by their friends from Colombo. The train was very comfortable. The day did not seem to be too hot, because the train was moving and the journey only took a few hours. As they came down from the hills to sea level it got hotter and less green.

Jaffna was at the end of the line and seemed nearly as parched as Rameshwaram, though it was much bigger. It was perched on the sand at the edge of the sea and the smell of the sea hung in the air. It was a very quiet town.

The Swami refused to get into a rickshaw, so they took a taxi from the station to the temple.

German Swami directed the taxi driver to a little dusty path off the end of the little dusty road past a large temple with a big open well under a large tree, just as it was described in Mari's book.

The taxi stopped. There was a scraggly thorny fence around a little piece of land on which were two small huts; actually one small hut and one very small hut.

The large hut was German Swami's house, and it had a broad cement bench that filled the back half of the room where there was a straw mat and a thin cotton mattress. There was no other furniture, except a water pot and a cup, and another bamboo mat.

The guest hut had a bed made from a bamboo frame strung with rope, a water pot and cup. The water came from the well near the temple, and meals arrived in a stainless steel tiffin* from the temple kitchen.

It was very exotic, very quiet, and very peaceful. There was not even a cushion to sit on. Roslyn would sit for hours on the floor on the thin bamboo mat, while Bliss cooed and squealed and German Swami shared his pearls of wisdom of a Western traveler who had lived in the East for over thirty years.

He had no money at all. He had two or three longis and towels he carried in a cloth bag, a bowl, a spoon, a water pot and a cup. He had a place to sleep that was given him by the temple. He had nothing at all and he did not want anything. Roslyn asked him about his dogma regarding money, and he told her, "My Guru told me it is all right to have money, but not to keep it overnight."

A redheaded Irish Canadian, Austin, had spent a couple of years living in the guest hut as German Swami's disciple, and then went to Pondicherry and became a disciple of The Mother. Austin invited German Swami to visit Pondicherry and there he had met The Mother and Mari. When Mari was working on her book she visited the little hut and stayed overnight in the little guest hut.

Roslyn put on a sari and took a bath by dumping forty buckets of water over herself, which was how Swamaji and the other men at the temple bathed. It was not satisfactory. She sat on the hard floor, sometimes leaning against the wall. Bliss was made much of by the women, in the neighborhood, who brought food. The food was very simple vegetarian food. It was too spicy for Roslyn. They used coconut oil for cooking oil and she did not like it, so she ate mostly plain white rice. Sometimes there were sweets, or fruit. The chappatis had a coating of coconut oil, so she would not eat them.

The women would take Bliss and she would come back to Roslyn with a big black spot on her forehead and on her cheek, a ribbon in her hair, eyeliner around her eyes, and bangles on her wrists.

Bliss seemed to love it. There was a little girl who used to carry Bliss on one hip and a little black haired Tamil baby boy on the other hip. The little girl had a friendly smile, and neatly combed and braided hair. Roslyn visited the child's family's hut where a family of seven people lived. It was a tiny coconut palm hut, and the child's mother welcomed her and insisted she take tea. Roslyn sat on the ground outside the hut drinking tea from a glass. Many children stood around staring at her.

It was all very interesting, but she was happy to leave after three days and continue her tour of Ceylon.

German Swami and Roslyn bid one another fond farewell and she was off in a rickshaw to the railroad station.

She took a train to Trincomalee and found a room there in a small hotel run by a Chinese man who served wonderful Chinese food. It was pleasant, although boring to be alone near the sea with Bliss. She did not know anyone, and noone knew her. She found a good book in English that some other traveler had left behind and spent a few days enjoying the good food, balmy weather, and a novel.

Then she went to Kandy that is in the hills surrounded by tea plantations. It is exceptional lush jungle. All kinds of tropical fruit are abundant there.

Finally she went to Colombo.

Roslyn did not feel like contacting German Swami's friends. She stayed in the Youth Hostel for a few days, walked around the town, looked at jewelry and gems, and bought some jewelry and gems to resell in the USA. She took the boat train back to the northern part of the island for the boat to Rameshwaram, India. She bought a pineapple for Panditji before getting on the queue at the customs shed. Several hours later they were finally on the boat back to India.

Then there were the hours of standing in line to get through customs and immigration in India, and finally she was back in Rameshwaram.

She went to the resthouse where they had stayed before and slept. In the morning Roslyn woke blazing to see Panditji again. She waited until 9 o'clock to approach his house.

There was noone on the steps to meet her, and noone on the porch. She stepped inside calling softly, "Hello."

The door to the meditation room was closed and there were no fresh flowers around the photos of Panditji's Guru, Sri Aurobindo and The Mother.

There was a woman whom Roslyn had seen before around the house. She wore such huge gold earrings for such a long time they had made huge holes in her ear lobes and the earrings nearly touched her shoulders. Roslyn had noticed her because of the big holes in her earlobes and the big hunks of gold hanging from them. The old woman said something to Roslyn, which Roslyn could not understand.

"Panditji?" Roslyn asked.

The old woman with the big gold earrings repeated what she had said, several times before Roslyn understood she was saying, "Pondicherry."

She gave the old woman the pineapple, and went back to the hotel to get her things together, and get the next train to Pondicherry.

Aspiration 1970

A greater vision meets us on the heights
In the luminous wideness of the spirit's gaze.
At last there wakes in us a witness soul
That looks at truths unseen, and scans the Unknown;
Then, all assumes a new and marvellous face.
...Life's borders crumble and join infinity.

Sri Aurobindo Savitri

There is first a period of endurance in which it is learned to confront, to assimilate to suffer all contacts. In the unstirred seas of our spirit are all the things that can possibly come to us down the ways of the soul's infinite experience. The gain of this period of resignation and endurance is the soul's strength becomes equal to all shocks and contacts.

Then there is a period of high seated impartiality and indifference. All is regarded from above by the spirit undisturbed. The gain of this period is the soul's peace.

Through the joy of a total giving to the Divine and Universal Mother strength is crowned by peace deepening to bliss. The possession of the Divine calm uplifts and makes ground for the possession of Divine movement, enters into the sea of a supreme and all embracing ecstasy of eternal beatitude.

'I' is replaced by a luminous formation of the consciousness, a pure channel and instrument. All can be transformed by a higher power into its divine equivalent, supreme repose, calm, divine illumination and bliss. The will of the mental and psychic can unify with the eternal divine dynamic by the grace of the transforming power.

(from Jim Bean's Journal extracts from Sri Aurobindo's Synthesis of Yoga.*)*

The train rolled into Pondicherry at 5:45 in the morning, just as the sun was rising and the dawn sky filled the morning with the promise of a new day.

It felt auspicious to be back in Pondicherry. Roslyn had been traveling for four days from Colombo, and for weeks before that; since she had left Pondicherry in fact. She was looking forward to seeing Panditji, Kelly, Ananta, Mari, her other friends, and, The Mother.

She did not want to go back to the hotel on the park. She wanted to stay in one of The Mother's guesthouses, but she did not want to see the person who was in charge of The Ashram guesthouses.

She went to Mari's little house near The Ashram and rang the bell ...and rang and rang. There was a big sign on the gate, "Beware of Dog." She had not noticed any dog when she had visited Mari. She went on ringing the bell.

Finally the gate opened. Standing there, all dressed in white, with his white hair softly curling down over his collar, was the Italian gentleman who lived with Mari.

It was only 6:30 in the morning. Roslyn hoped her behavior was not unforgivable, but she did not know where to go. Mari had brought her the messages from The Mother. She would tell her what to do.

The very distinguished looking gentleman, nodded his head, and said, "Bon giorno."

"I must see Mari."

"No, no. Impossible," he said very politely, very quietly, but very firmly.

"No, no. I must see Mari."

"Mari never sees anybody until after she visits The Mother in the afternoon. Mother told her not to," he said gently, not wanting to cause distress, but unwilling to allow her to disturb Mari.

"I don't know where to go. Are there any guesthouses that are not managed by that guy in The Ashram?"

"Yes, you can try Society House. They also have guesthouses. It is just down this street."

He led her away from the gate to the corner. "The big white house next to the Ganesh temple."

"Do you know where Panditji is?" Roslyn asked.

"Yes, he is in the big house on this side of the Ganesh temple," he replied, kind and helpful as well as gracious and distinguished.

She thanked him very much and he gave her a broad smile wishing her "Good luck!"

She started off down the street opposite the wall of The Ashram, Bliss on one arm, her Afghan carpetbag on the other, still barefooted, wearing her red pajamas. She passed people she had seen before in Pondicherry. They smiled at her. She had an impulse to go to The Mother's room and insist on seeing Mother immediately. Mother had said She would see her when she got back from Ceylon. She was back from Ceylon. She still did not know whether she was coming or going.

She was alone with a baby, and as good as she was, Bliss was still a human baby, and Roslyn could not imagine how, alone with a baby, she could live on the barren wasteland that was the proposed site for Auroville. For Roslyn the Charter of Auroville had resounded as a verbalization of the principles she believed in and wanted to live by:

> *"Auroville belongs to nobody in*
> *particular. Auroville belongs to humanity as*
> *a whole, but to live in Auroville one must be*
> *a willing servitor of the Divine*
> *Consciousness.*
>
> *"Auroville will be the place of an*
> *unending education, of constant progress,*
> *and a youth that never ages.*
>
> *"Auroville wants to be the bridge*
> *between the past and the future. Taking*
> *advantage of all discoveries from without*
> *and within, Auroville will boldly spring*
> *towards future realizations.*
>
> *"Auroville will be a site of material*
> *and spiritual researches for a living*
> *embodiment of an actual Human Unity."*
>
> *-The Mother*
> *February 28th, 1968*

Roslyn followed directions to the Sri Aurobindo Society House. The Sri Aurobindo Society, not The Sri Aurobindo Ashram, was the sponsor of Auroville.

She was surprised to find that she had been thinking about Auroville all the time she had been walking from Mari's gate to the gate in front of the Sri Aurobindo Society mansion, and often during her journey to Ceylon. She braved her way through the beggars gathered in front of the gate and opened it. Roslyn found herself in an exquisite little garden with a fountain in front of a huge old white colonial mansion. She was really tired, even though it was only seven in the morning. She needed a bath and bed.

An Indian lady in a white sari, with her long hair in a crown of braids around her head, wearing glasses, greeted Roslyn.

"I am looking for a room in a guesthouse," she explained.

"Please go to the office across from The Ashram, next to the school, after nine o'clock."

"Please. I'm very tired and very dirty. I have been traveling for days from Colombo. Please, don't make me wait."

The lady invited her into the parlor. There were great red plush sofas and chairs near the walls of the huge room. A large crystal chandelier hung from the high ceiling.

"Please take your seat," she said, indicating a chair near the door.

She disappeared for a moment through a curtained doorway, and came back carrying some papers and a pen.

She sat on the sofa.

"I am sorry to disturb you so early in the morning," Roslyn said.

"That is quite all right. How long will you be staying?"

"I don't know."

"Would you like to stay for more than a month?"

"I don't know."

"Would you like to pay a daily or monthly rate?"

"Is it cheaper by the month?"

"Slightly, but you must pay in advance."

"That's okay."

"Will you please fill in these forms."

They were the standard forms that Roslyn had had to fill in at every overnight stop for months. She had her baby on her lap. She was very tired, and dirty. She did not want to fill in forms. She wanted a bath and a bed.

"No, please. I am too tired and dirty. I have been traveling for days, from Colombo, please, could you give me a guestroom and let me come back later and fill in the forms."

The lady looked at her with great compassion. "Excuse me, a moment.

I must make a telephone call."

She disappeared through the curtained doorway again. After a few minutes she came back and said, "A room has been arranged at the Shelter Guesthouse just across the street. Please come back later in the day, and fill in the forms."

"Shall I come here or to the office?" Roslyn asked.

"Please come here."

Roslyn thanked her, and the lady guided her back to the street, past the line of beggars outside the gate. From the corner she pointed out an ugly green building across the street with shops downstairs and an innocuous row of doors in the green cement wall upstairs. She pointed upstairs. "That is Shelter Guesthouse."

Roslyn made her way across the street and found the door between the shops and went up the stairs, carrying Bliss and her bag. At the top of the stairs she was met by a young slender Indian man.

"I am the manager, please come into the office for a moment."

He led her into a dark and dingy office behind the stairs with iron bars on the window. There was a huge old wooden desk that nearly filled the room. He sat down in a chair behind the desk and pointed to an old rusty metal folding chair and said, "Please take your seat."

"Please, could you give me a room, and let me do the papers later."

"No, no. That is not possible. I cannot give you the room key until these papers are filled in and you give me your passport. It is against the law."

She put her bag on the floor and Bliss on her lap. She could not put the baby on the floor, it did not look very clean. She gave him her passport and filled in the forms.

He was looking in her passport.

"What were you doing in Ceylon?"

"Please, may I have a room. The lady across the street also wants me to fill in forms, but she said I could have a room and come back later."

"Yes, yes. Where is your husband."

"Please give me back my passport."

"No, no. Will you pay me for the room now?"

"I have to go to the bank. Please give me my passport."

"No, no. I must show Police then I give back."

"I need it for the bank," she said.

"Don't worry. I will give it back before lunch. You will take your meals in the Dining Room?"

"I don't know. How much does it cost?"

"Four rupees a day."

"And the room?"

"Five rupees a day. How many days will you stay?"

"I don't know."

"You must give me hundred rupees now and I give key."

"I don't have any money. I must go to the bank."

He handed her her passport, "You go bank, come back, you give money, I give key."

"Please, bank is not open, please, let me use the room and I will go to the bank when it opens."

"Give me the passport. I will show you room. I will give passport when you go bank."

Reluctantly she handed over her passport. He got up and she followed him down the narrow balcony that had an iron rail, past a row of indistinguishable doors that had barely discernible numbers written on them in pencil. Near the end of the row he stopped, unlocked a padlock, and opened the iron bolt on the door.

He handed her the key and the lock, and pointed out the cupboard, desk, chair, bed, sink, and tiny bathroom with a squat toilet and shower.

"You come office before you go outside," he said, holding her passport.

"Yes please, I am very tired."

"This Ashram house, please, very quiet."

"Is there someone to wash clothes."

"Yes. One piece, one rupee, one week come back. Urgent, one piece, two rupees, same day come back."

"One week to wash clothes?"

"Yes. Very good. Very clean. I send servant?"

"Okay."

She really wanted to throw him out of the room, and over the balcony onto the street!

Finally he left and she locked the door from inside. There were little windows on either side of the door. If they were open, anyone passing on the balcony could look into the room, and they were the only windows, except a vent above the door.

She closed the windows and the curtains and opened the vent. She felt as if she'd just checked into jail.

She opened her bag full of dirty things. She would have to go and get the things she had left with her Danish friend who lived near the beach. She had nothing clean to put on, so she looked for things that were less dirty than what she was wearing.

There was a knock at the door.

She opened the door. There was a man wearing a dirty white longi and shirt.

He bobbed his head, "Dhobi."

She looked at him. She knew that dhobi meant washerman, but his clothes were so dirty!

She looked at the pile of stuff on the bed.

He looked at it, and wagged his head, "Yes, yes, very good. How many pieces?"

She went and counted it. Twenty-six pieces, including Bliss's two diapers. She put her navy blue Tibetan dress on the floor and all the laundry on it and rolled it all up in a ball and handed it to the dhobi. "Urgent. Twenty six pieces."

He wagged his head, "Yes, yes. I give back tomorrow. He put the bundle under one arm and held out his palm, "Fifty two rupees please."

"No, no, you bring back today. You bring back twenty six pieces, I give money."

"Yes, sure. I bring back. Please give five rupees now. I must buy soap."

She gave him five rupees. "What time you come back?"

He wagged his head. "Yes yes. I come back five o'clock."

She shut the door and bolted it from the inside. She had some doubts about wanting to stay for a month. It was ugly and expensive. She thought about sending her father, Bernie, a telegram and telling him to send plane tickets. She had returned to Pondicherry to meet Mother. Kelly, Ananta, and other friends had told her that Mother usually would see devotees on their birthdays. Her birthday was coming; maybe she would see Mother twice, once now that she was back from Ceylon, and again on her birthday.

She washed, slept, put her less dirty clothes back on, and took Bliss out without any clothes on, rather than put on her dirty clothes. She went to pick up her passport to go to the bank.

The manager was out and the office locked. She waited, and waited, getting angrier and angrier. Finally he came back and gave her her passport.

She took Bliss to her Italian friend with a little boy. The friend was very friendly, happy to keep Bliss with her while Roslyn went to the bank. She invited Roslyn to come and have lunch when she returned for Bliss.

The guy at the guesthouse was a jerk. It was annoying to have to wait until late afternoon to see Mari, but Pondicherry was lovely that fall morning. The sky was perfectly clear. There were birds singing in all the trees around the park. The only traffic was bicycles and bicycle rickshaws. Familiar faces smiled back at her as they passed. Some acquaintances who passed her on their bicycles stopped to talk. "So you have come back."

"Yes," she replied, "Mother said She would see me when I came back from Ceylon."

Francis, who was from Auroville, replied to that: "You mean, you will see Her, She sees you all the time."

Others asked about Bliss.

The park was full of flowers, and there was a man with a little wagon on one corner where she could get a Coca-Cola with ice. The vendor offered to put a twist of lemon in the Coke.

Roslyn went to the bank. She went and filled in the forms at Society House and paid for her room and food at the Ashram Dining Room. She went to the Post Office: as she had written to Bernie that she was going back to Pondicherry, she hoped he had written and sent some more money, and she was not disappointed. She bought some garlands of jasmine.

She stopped at the house where Panditji was staying. She walked in the gate and through the garden. Panditji was sitting on a broad verandah surrounded by men in starched white clothes and women in white saris.

He saw her and gave her a big grin and said, "Yes, come."

She saw the man in charge of The Ashram guesthouses sitting there, and Ananta's friend Joe from California. She did not know any of the other people. She gave Panditji the jasmine garlands wrapped in leaves. He opened the fragile parcel, and took out the jasmine and shook his head, "Yes, yes. Very nice." He took the garland of jasmine and put it around the already garlanded photo of The Mother. He clapped his hands loudly. His wife appeared. "Where is Bliss?"

"She is with a friend."

"Please, you bring her this evening. I like her very much."

"You will take coffee?" Panditji asked her.

"No thank you."

He told his wife to bring coffee, then walked into his meditation room and brought her two bananas, one for her, and one for Bliss.

"Please take your seat," he said gesturing to an empty place on the mat next to Joe.

Panditji sat on a pile of cushions. He was speaking in some language Roslyn did not understand, but it was fun being there. Then Panditji asked one of the men to translate.

He said, pointing to another man, "He writes books and wants Panditji to write a book, but Panditji says what is the point to write more books when we already have the Vedas and the writing of Sri Aurobindo and The Mother?"

There was a radiant atmosphere on that bright sunlit verandah. Panditji excused himself for lunch. He invited Roslyn to come back at four in the afternoon to take a walk with him.

Roslyn put her palms together and left for her Italian friend's house for lunch and Bliss.

She visited Panditji in the afternoon. There were several disciples there, including Joe, and a young Frenchwoman working on drawing the mystical symbol, "Sri Chakra," according to the formula Panditji gave. He said none of the drawings were correct, and gave them the formula again. He looked at Roslyn and laughed. She could not understand how the formula he was giving them would result in the beautiful diagram of 36 interlocking triangles that is Sri Chakra, but it was very interested to listen to him explain the meaning of the point in the center and all the triangles and their relationship to one another. It was as if a cloud of intelligent energy hooked on to her intelligence, above her mind, like a gossamer mist above her head. Panditji glowed as he spoke. With words and with his graceful hands he explained to the disciples something about the esoteric tradition of Sri Chakra. Everyone was very quiet, happy, interested.

The triangles seem to be the invisible web that holds it all together. Roslyn could see that there are as many triangles in the Sri Chakra as there are branches on the Cabalistic Tree of Life.

After a while Panditji excused himself from the others and invited Roslyn and Joe for a short walk around The Ashram. They passed near Mari's house. Roslyn wanted to see Mari. Joe and Panditji left her there, and Panditji asked her to give his greetings to "The Mari."

Roslyn conveyed Panditji's greetings to Mari and asked her to tell Mother she was back from Ceylon and would like to meet Her. Mari told her to come back the next afternoon. Mari offered tea, but Roslyn had to go back to Panditji's for Bliss.

At Panditji's tea was being served. There were sweets and a few more people than had been there earlier in the afternoon.

Panditji sat in the middle of the people from The Ashram who had come to visit him. His wife and daughter served tea and sweets, and one of the young Indian guests helped them. There was fabled conversation. Roslyn could not think of a thing to say. She did not need to think of a thing to say. It was more fantastic than anything she had imagined. A group of sages sitting sharing stories of inspiration, and she was allowed to sit there and listen while being fed tea and sweets.

Panditji told a story about a Guru and his disciple. "The guru asked the disciple to fetch a bucket of water from the well. The disciple was not happy with the task. He went to the well with the bucket, but there was a long line of ladies with buckets in front of him, and he had come to learn yoga with the guru. It was hot in the sun, and he knew that if his guru wanted water there were other ways to get it than to send him to the well. He remembered very well seeing large full water pots in The Ashram. He wanted to be with the master, not standing in a slow moving queue to get a bucket of water that the master did not need, so he left the queue and went back to The Ashram. The master was sitting there and a king cobra suddenly appeared in front of him, coiled, ready to strike. The master looked at it, and it very gently uncoiled and slithered away. The disciple said with enthusiasm, `Master, I want to learn to do that.` The Master replied, `First you must learn to fetch a pail of water.`"

The moment was too short. The evening shadows crept onto the terrace and they all had to leave when Panditji said, "Now I take rest." Roslyn took Bliss back with her to the guesthouse, and dinner in the Dining Room.

In the morning she engaged a servant named Marie to look after Bliss. She left them at the guesthouse and went to Panditji's.

He was sitting in his meditation room chanting mantras, with the disciples sitting silently on the verandah. Some of the disciples had malas. Most of the people she had seen there the day before were there. She sat there daydreaming, enjoying the quiet morning and the sunlight on the garden.

She knew absolutely nothing about the strange ritual Panditji was performing. However, it was in no way threatening her to watch him sitting in the little room in a merry glow of ghee lamps and the smoky mist of incense, playing with water, flowers, his mala, statues of deities, symbols of deity, chanting mantras, ringing a bell. None of the people there stirred, even a little bit. Finally Panditji stood up and came out among them with a little pot and spoon. He stopped in front of each person and dipped a bit of the water, with which symbolically he had washed the feet of The Mother, into cupped palms. Then the disciples drank the water out of their palms and anointed their foreheads and eyes with their damp palms.

Roslyn tried just to do what the others had done. She had always wanted to take communion in a Catholic church. The water was fragrant with flowers and spices.

Panditji's wife and daughter served coffee. One of the disciples was a homeopathic doctor who generally did not allow himself or his patients to take coffee.

One of his patients was there, and declined to take coffee because his doctor had forbidden him coffee. The doctor smiled, and said, "You can drink this coffee. Anything Panditji gives you is better medicine than anything I could give you," and it was clear he meant it, because he also drank the coffee, even though as a homeopath he never drank it.

After coffee Panditji dismissed everyone and inviting them to return in the afternoon. As they were going out Roslyn had a moment to talk to Joe.

"Why isn't Ananta here?" she asked.

"He is in the hospital."

"What happened?"

"He took too many sleeping pills."

"I must go see him."

"He is at the Ashram Nursing Home."

She hurried off and got a rickshaw to the Ashram Nursing Home.

Ananta was there in a private room on the top floor shouting at a poor little frightened Tamil nurse in Tamil, when in Roslyn walked.

He seemed very pleased to see her.

"My dear, how are you. I need a barber." He was sitting on an unmade bed wearing only a white longi carelessly wrapped around his waist.

The door opened and two of the servants she had seen on the island came in. They were both wearing yellow trousers and white shirts.

The big one smiled at her, then turned to Ananta. "We go island."

Ananta looked at her, "Now?"

The smaller one said, "Yes, yes. We go island."

Ananta said, in his great booming voice, "What did the doctor say?"

"Doctor telling you America going. You no America going. You going island," the smaller, broader servant, Ramakrishna, insisted.

Ananta looked at Roslyn with a desperate expression on his face, "I knew it. They've kicked me out of The Ashram."

Just then someone else came into the room. A tall thin man wearing blue shorts and a white shirt whom she had seen around The Ashram.

He ignored her and the servants and greeted Ananta warmly. He had a card for Ananta from Mother. Ananta opened the card.

Ananta's whole face and bearing changed. He lit up. He sat up straight. He thanked the messenger, and hastily scrawled a reply to The Mother.

Ananta said something in Tamil to his servants. They looked very happy and left. The messenger took leave.

Ananta showed Roslyn the card, "My Dearest child," The Mother had written.

Roslyn left Ananta arguing with a nurse, and promised to come and visit again in the evening.

When she went that evening to the Nursing Home, he had already left.

The next morning she left Bliss screaming in Marie's arms and went off to Panditji's in her clean orange pajamas. He was sitting at his puja She joined the silent disciples sitting primly and unmoving.

Just as Panditji finished his puja and was sharing the theertham among his disciples, the gate to the garden burst open and Ananta entered, absolutely shining, his peroxide hair nearly platinum, clean shaven, wearing a yellow silk shirt and snug white trousers, followed by all nine of his servants in their white shirts and yellow pants. He ignored everyone else sitting there, just short of stepping on them, and threw himself on the floor in front of Panditji, as Panditji was walking among the quiet sober disciples with the little cup of sweet scented water. Panditji took the little spoon and eloquently dropped a drop of the theertham on the back of Ananta's head. Ananta's nose was on the floor next to Panditji's big toe.

Panditji had a huge smile on his face, and the mood had changed in moments from very lofty and sober to nearly hilarious. "Stand up, Ananta," Panditji said. Ananta stood up, next to Panditji, nearly stepping on Joe, who muttered under his breath as he was forced to move, "For God's sake, Ananta."

Ananta ignored him. The moment Ananta stood up his Number One Worker, the tall one, prostrated himself at Panditji's feet, then stood up and walked away, as the second, third, fourth, fifth, sixth, seventh, eighth and ninth man also prostrated themselves at Panditji's feet. The other friends and disciples sat there watching, for the most part rather disdainfully.

Panditji pointed to an empty mat, behind all the other disciples. "Take your seat, Ananta."

Ananta moved in the opposite direction, to the front of all the disciples, just in front of the door to Panditji's meditation room, under the garlanded photos of The Mother and Sri Aurobindo and Panditji's Guru, and went down again in a full prostration with his nose on the floor. Panditji continued his peregrination among the other disciples, giving each one, including each of Ananta's workers, some drops of the sacred water from his little bowl. Then Panditji went back into his meditation room. Ananta sat just in front of the door. Panditji came back out, carrying a tray of bananas, ignored Ananta, nearly stepping on him, and distributed the bananas among the other disciples, giving Roslyn two, one for Bliss and one for herself.

Panditji walked again through the disciples to the puja room. Ananta was sitting very quietly in front of the door. Panditji brought out again the little copper bowl and spoon and three times poured into Ananta's cupped palm the holy water that had washed the feet of The Divine Mother in the ritual, and Ananta put some in his mouth, and some on his forehead and on his eyes with exaggerated piety.

Then Panditji gave Ananta some bananas, and laughed at him.

Panditji went and sat on a pile of cushions between two doorways leading into the house. There were bamboo mats spread on the floor around the cushions. The disciples all moved from the mats in front of the meditation room, to the mats around the cushions.

The ensuing conversation was as esoteric and dramatic as one might wish. Everyone was trying to catch the golden wisdom; there was not a whisper while Panditji spoke or the interpreter translated Panditji's words into English.

A disciple would ask or make a comment, and Panditji would reply in English, Sanskrit or Hindi, often using fables from the Vedas as illustration, or from the shashtras or sutras or other traditional esoteric lore to explain the mundane.

Panditji's wife served coffee and the sparkling conversation complemented the sunlight on the flowers in the garden.

Panditji only came to Pondicherry for two or three weeks two or three times a year, whenever he was called by The Mother. She always kept this very beautiful house near The Ashram for Him, and always had Her gardeners maintain the gardens, and servants maintain the house and the special utensils She had provided for his use. It was Panditji's house in Pondicherry, and She maintained it so that it was always comfortable and ready for Him.

He was deeply devoted to Her. She respected and supported Him and His work as a yogi, and generously supported Him financially, in such a way that His financial responsibility towards His family was looked after largely by Her. This enabled Him to do the work He had always done for Her in comfort and security. The only purpose of the spiritual work Panditji did according to the tradition of his gurus was for the love and blessings of The Divine Mother. All the practices, tapas, sadhana, siddhis, disciplines, legends, all concurred that the aim of life is to attain the love and blessings of The Divine Mother.

The Mother felt that Panditji's prayers and occult work had been helpful in alleviating the paralysis which had beset her in 1958; at least that was what She had written on a card He had shown Roslyn in Rameshwaram.

Panditji's disciple, Sri Navajata, invited Him to visit the exhibition in the new offices for Auroville. Panditji invited Roslyn to join him in the afternoon.

Joe was also with them. Panditji had declined the use of a car. They walked past the Ganesh Temple. Usually the beggars mobbed Roslyn when she walked past that temple. Panditji had put on chappals* before he left his house, explaining to her, "Chappals are nice. You are not wearing chappals?"

Joe, a super clean-cut American, looked at her: "Panditji said you should wear chappals."

She was barefooted; she did not wear shoes because she did not have shoes. They were walking in the middle of the streets of Pondicherry, very straight, clean-cut Joe wearing a freshly starched and ironed shirt with a stiff collar, crisp clean shorts and very respectable chappals, looking like an 'A' student; then there was Panditji, a golden dumpling with a piece of white cloth around the middle, another piece of white cloth on his shoulder, a white string over his other shoulder, with vibhuti and kum-kum smeared on his face and body, glasses perched on his nose, shaved head, gleeful; and finally Roslyn, as tall as Joe and Panditji, but fatter than Panditji, and much fatter than Joe, with her hair standing straight up in the air, barefooted, with a cloth bag on one shoulder in her orange pajamas walking next to Joe and Panditji. She felt like a real princess from a far-off age.

Panditji stopped for a moment in front of the temple with its painted plaster images, brought his palms together, and mumbled a mantra.

Joe looked at him and asked, "Why did you do that?"

Panditji smiled, and pointing at the temple said, "It is very nice."

There was a hoard of the scraggiest beggars, scrawny bodies covered in tatters, hanging out in the sunny late afternoon on the quiet street. Little sleepy stalls sold flowers, incense, coconuts. Through the open door they could hear music and priests chanting mantras. They walked around the block. The whole area was the quiet blue/gray/white of The Ashram buildings. The streets were unbelievably clean and quiet, like something one might imagine in a surrealistic movie, not at all like overpopulated India's.

Walking with Panditji, the streets of Pondicherry seemed as warm and gentle as the surf on the beach at Rameshwaram.

They finally got to the corner across from The Ashram Post Office, where the Auroville Office was located. Sri Navajata was at the door to greet them.

They went in the white door of the white building across from The Sri Aurobindo Ashram. Panditji and Joe took off their chappals. The floors were white. Roslyn felt self conscious because her feet were dirty. There was an impressive exhibition about "The City Earth Needs," "The City of The Future," "The City of Dawn," "The Cradle of the Superman," "Auroville," a town to be built on the assumption that this time the collective evolutionary process would allow humanity to surpass what it has done, and become what it must be, to meet and survive in time and space despite having been given the power to destroy itself and Earth.

Auroville would be a place where all the fighting instincts of the people who would make up the community would be used to fight poverty, disease and ignorance, and not one another.

Panditji looked with great interest at the exhibition, and said, "It is a young man's dream."

The following afternoon Panditji told them a bit of the fable of Durga.

"The gods had been driven from their kingdom by the buffalo demon, Mahisha, and were on the brink of extinction. To save themselves they summoned The Divine Mother, who appeared to them as flaming, fierce, and beautiful Durga. The gods armed Her with all their weapons and symbols, and She was the epitome of cosmic force.

"For ten days, in ten aspects of shakti, she battled the demon who is sometimes described as a buffalo-headed incarnation of ignorance. Victorious, she restored the order in manifestation, the Great Mother's round of birth, death and rebirth."

The translator went on, "Panditji is leaving tomorrow. Durga puja is next week, and he would like to celebrate it in Rameshwaram."

Panditji looked at Roslyn, "You come to Rameshwaram for Durga puja."

She was honored by the invitation. Although there were many disciples and devotees sitting there, all known to Panditji for some time, he only invited her. She immediately said she would go to Rameshwaram for Durga Puja.

"What day?" she asked.

"It is beginning next Wednesday." he replied.

"That is my birthday, I am going to see Mother." She had been astonished when she received Mother's reply from Mari.

Mari had told Mother that Roslyn was back from Ceylon. Mother replied, "I will see her on her birthday." Roslyn had not told Mari it was her birthday soon.

"You see The Mother and then come to Rameshwaram," Panditji said.

She had liked Rameshwaram very much, and was excited about meeting The Divine Mother and then going to Rameshwaram to celebrate several days of the Durga celebration.

She was sorry that Panditji was leaving Pondicherry for Rameshwaram. She was delighting in being around Him and His disciples in the mornings and afternoons, drinking coffee and tea, meditating, and hearing wonderful stories. She looked forward to going to Rameshwaram after meeting The Mother. There were also so many likeable and interesting people in Pondicherry, and so much to do. She was walking on the softest clouds.

That was a time that redefined halcyon days. Each day dawned, with a glorious sunrise over the ocean. She would get up early, and by sunrise be walking on the Cours Chabrol, along the white beach, where the sun came up dramatically over the sea.

The street was very quiet, except there was one man on a bicycle with a big stainless steel urn roped to the carrier, who rode slowly down the street calling, "Coffee, Coffee."

In front of some houses she passed, walking from the beach to The Ashram, servant women would be sweeping and washing the pavement in front of the houses, and drawing with chalk dust the traditional Tamil designs called 'kolams' on the sidewalk in front of their front door. These drawings were renewed daily in front of many houses, and were very pretty when they were fresh in the morning. The ladies would wash the pavements in front of their houses, then draw a pattern of dots with white chalk, and then connect the dots in unusual harmonious geometric designs on the clean pavement in front of the house.

The 'kolams' are symbols of protection and good fortune that anything and anyone entering the house would have to cross.

Roslyn would go to The Ashram with Bliss and they would sit near The Samadhi, located uinder the Happiness Tree, watching the ladies in white saris arranging the flowers. A few minutes after dawn every morning two men would hang a painted silk canopy over the marble tomb of The Samadhi, which by then would be blanketed with exquisitely arranged, sweet smelling flowers. Great sticks of incense were burning there. In a corner of the courtyard there were two women, one with a big basket of flowers and one with a basket of incense, and anyone could take flowers and incense to offer at the tomb.

No-one spoke. It was a very quiet time of day, yet very dynamic. Just sitting there quietly, leaning against a wall of one of the rooms off the courtyard, Roslyn felt at peace with herself and the world. She could not think of why she was there, or what she was going to do. It was an irreproachable place to be, and she had nothing better to do. It felt so good to be there, that for a few minutes she would feel as if she could sit there all day in the delicate fragrant atmosphere with Bliss on her lap, quiet and content. They just sat there until the sky was blue white with the clear tropical early morning light, then Roslyn would feel her stomach grumbling and get up and go to The Indian Coffee Shop on Nehru Street for breakfast.

The Indian Coffee House was the only place open that early. The Ashram Dining Room did not open until seven, and they served porridge and chocolate milk and a banana for breakfast. Roslyn would usually have scrambled eggs and toast and coffee at The Coffee House, and several cigarettes. Sometimes she would meet an old acquaintance or a new acquaintance there.

There are Indian Coffee Houses all over India, and it is a traditional place where travelers from the West meet other travelers from the West.

After breakfast she would go visiting.

She had a friend, Lorelei, who had two little girls, one a few months older than Bliss, one a few months younger. She was from Holland. She and her husband had joined The Ashram. Her younger daughter had been born in the little community at Promesse, at the outer edge of Auroville that had been built by The Mother as a place for the children of Auroville to be born. When Lorelei and Roslyn were together all they could talk about, all they could think about, was Auroville. The three children played together, and they talked and talked about Auroville.

The Mother seemed to think that the children are the future, and prenatal care for mothers-to-be and child care and education were the priority for the Auroville community. Mother had said that children chose their parents. Every person, according to The Mother, has a psychic being, an immortal aspect. According to Sri Aurobindo "the psychic being lives in the heart." Babies are so beautiful because they are the naked psychic being, unclothed in ego.

The first child that had been born in the Auroville community had drowned when he was eight months old. That had been a terrible blow to the community.

Lorelei lived with her family in a little house near the bazaar that was given to them by The Ashram. She and her husband had given all their money to The Ashram when they arrived in Pondicherry. They were given a house, a servant, food, clothing and access to the facilities of The Ashram, including health and dental care and education. They had no money at all. Lorelei borrowed a few rupees from time to time, and bought some inexpensive shirts in the bazaar to embroider flowers around the neck and sell them for a small profit at Auroboutique.

She and Roslyn would dump the babies in little buckets of water in the tiny courtyard in Lorelei's house, and sit at a table, talking and dreaming about Auroville and embroidering. Roslyn was helping Lorelei to get the shirts ready to resell. Lorelei needed the extra rupees for little treats, like tea and oranges. She wanted a bicycle and a sewing machine very much. Her husband had left her once they got to The Ashram. He continued to live in the same house, but he never spoke to her or took meals with her or the children. He worked at The Ashram soda factory bottling "Sodalicious" soda. He would leave early in the morning, breakfast at The Dining Room, go to work, have lunch in The Dining Room, come back and rest in his room after lunch, then go back to work, have dinner in The Dining Room, and go to the playground to meditate or the library to listen to classical music in the evening.

Lorelei's servant brought her food from The Ashram dining room. She was lonely, and happy to have a friend; the children were a riot together.

After sitting and stitching and gossiping for a couple of hours, they would usually go out for tea and sweets or dosais, and then Roslyn would go back to the guesthouse, leave Bliss with Marie, and go to lunch.

The days were all sparkling sunny and clear. There was never a cloud in the sky. Everyone she met was full of devotion to The Mother, and enthusiasm about the future.

Sri Aurobindo had written in 1940 that humanity was on the verge of an evolutionary breakthrough, and that the world would be transformed by the Supramental Force. It seemed that all the bad things were going to evaporate like morning dew, and there would be roses without thorns everywhere as the laws of time and space change, and humanity goes forward to meet its neighbors among the stars.

The community around The Mother then was often referred to as "Mother's World." It was a very special place and time. It was clean and orderly, and there was profound goodwill and equality among all the members of the community. It was not simply that Mother saw to it that every member of the community was maintained at a decent standard of living, it was the understanding of everyone in the community that as a child of The Mother, even with more money, or more responsibility, one is no more important than any other child of The Mother. It was apparent that Her consciousness was radically different, and everyone else was approximately the same.

The Mother loved Her children unconditionally. She demanded an atmosphere of mutual goodwill and respect between Her children. She told people to meet one another every day - whatever the relationship - as though for the first time, with openness and trust.

People were sincere and friendly. It was a very quiet peaceful place where the emphasis was put on knowledge, self knowledge, and understanding the world, rather than acquiring possessions and power.

The Ashram was very powerful. There were 2000 resident members, and maybe as many guests. There was a school with a campus that extended for blocks in every direction around The Ashram, a bakery, Nursing Homes, factories, shops, guesthouses, a press, all managed by The Mother, all painted the same blue/gray/white color of The Ashram, a quiet color that glows softly in any light, even in darkest night. And then there was the Auroville project.

There were clean bathrooms and water filters everywhere in The Mother's world. The aesthetic and hygienic standards were amazing for planet Earth, unimaginable for India, yet they were scrupulously maintained, and the result was beautiful and harmonious, a place where an atmosphere of happy well-being prevailed.

Roslyn ran into John Kelly. He invited her to have dinner with him at Castelini after meeting The Mother on her birthday, before taking the train to Rameshwaram. She tried to borrow some money from him. She did not have enough money to go to Rameshwaram. He said he had not received his check.

She went to see Mari. Mari told her she had an appointment with The Mother at 2:30 in the afternoon on her birthday. She told Mari that Panditji had invited her to Rameshwaram for Durga puja, but that she did not have any money. Would Mari lend her some?

Mari lent her forty rupees: that was enough for the third class train fare both ways.

At last it was Roslyn's birthday.

That morning the sunrise seemed even more glorious than the daily beautiful mornings she had been having with Bliss in Pondicherry. The sky was more colorful than usual, and the light show of the sunrise on the waves was perhaps the most spectacular she had yet seen. There was a moment when the whole world suddenly became a dazzling pink, the pink of the hibiscus Mother had designated as the Auroville flower, the pink of the psychic being, which is more orange than blue. The sea wall and the sand and the blue/gray/white buildings, the pavement, Bliss and Roslyn were bathed in the pale salmon pink glow, just for an instant, and then like a turning kaleidoscope the brilliant purples, and every hue of pink, blue, yellow and white filled the sky. The day began as a bright orange gold disk rose shimmering over the ocean.

Bliss rode on Roslyn's hip. They were completely happy and in harmony with each other, walking on the cool pavement in the warm tropical light when the day was still filled with the resounding silence of early morning. The boy on his bicycle with the large stainless steel coffee urn rode past them singing, "Coffee, Coffee."

They walked down the little quiet street from the beach to The Ashram. On the corner near the sea there was a large, elegant white colonial mansion that was the French Consulate, according to a plaque on the gate. From there to The Ashram, and on for blocks in the other direction, the buildings were all the gray/blue/white color of Mother's world. Although it was painted the same color by the same painters who had painted all the other walls, the walls of The Ashram were somehow different. It was as though the very plaster of the building that housed The Mother was happier than the plaster of other buildings.

In the very sober blue/gray/white wall, above the beautiful long open wooden doors in the gate, was a "Mother's symbol," a twelve petaled lotus in red and blue neon light glowing in the silent street. Occasionally Roslyn would pass someone dressed in white walking to or from The Ashram, like a floating ghost flitting through the door under the psychedelic lotus. Bliss was wearing a black shirt embroidered with a gold dragon Roslyn had bought for her in Kashmir, and it seemed that everyone else was dressed in white. Inside The Ashram gate, there was peace and silence in the early morning, with warm lights, flowers, birds. Roslyn walked into the central courtyard. She looked up and saw the lights on the third floor, in Mother's room. There was a seemingly special stillness pregnant with the promise of a special day. There were many more people than usual at that hour of the morning in The Ashram, around the Samadhi and in the Meditation Hall, because it was also the first day of Durga puja, one of the special days when The Mother, before she retired to her room in 1958, would put Her chair downstairs in the meditation room and give Her blessings to Her disciples. Roslyn had never seen Her chair before. It was very special, delicately carved, with an exquisite footstool and delicate silk cushions. Fabulous flowers had been arranged around the chair and disciples were sitting silently in front of it with shining faces. Roslyn sat down with Bliss. She had nearly become accustomed to the wonderful little explosion like little bells she would experience whenever she went into that meditation room.

It was a release of energy, or an absorption of energy, that left her completely calm, tranquil, mindless, right there in the river of time near the now.

She was completely blissed out. Suddenly she realized that her nose was on the floor. She was almost asleep, she was so relaxed. She sat back up and picked up Bliss, who was sitting there next to her - ten months old, with her legs folded like an old yogi, or a traditional cherub with golden curls, dressed like an Asiatic goddess in black with gold embroidery, with bangles on her wrists and ankles. They went back out into the morning.

Roslyn had to get ready to leave for Rameshwaram; she had to get flowers to present to The Mother; she had to get herself ready to present to The Mother; she had to eat and feed Bliss and get Bliss ready to present to The Mother. She walked by the Ganesh temple and went inside. There were musicians playing long South Indian horns and drums, with priests chanting, and paintings of the Lord Ganesh, the son of Lord Shiva and the goddess Parvati, everywhere. There were pictures of Ganesh with Shiva and Parvati and his brother Murugan. There were pictures of Ganesh with his wife, the beautiful bountiful goddess Lakshmi, and with Lakshmi and Saraswati, the goddess of music. There were pictures of Ganesh with Vyasa, the sage, transcribing The Mahabharata with his tusk. There were pictures and statues of the god with the head of an elephant all around them. The morning was full of flowers and music, and little girls, and comely young women with flowers in their hair and jingling silver ankle bracelets. It was fun, standing there watching the ritual, the air fragrant with flowers and incense, vibhuti and kum-kum, everywhere, happy people in bright clothes remembering god, the friend, the child, the lover, the remover of obstacles. Roslyn accepted some kum-kum and vibhuti from a priest and smeared it on Bliss, and then another priest gave her a piece of fresh coconut. Some men were turning round and round in circles like ecstatic dervishes in front of the inner sanctum at the center of the temple courtyard. Finally she went back to the street, and around the corner to Shelter Guesthouse.

Her servant was there waiting for her. Roslyn left Bliss with her and went off on her errands.

She had a new white organdy sari with delicate mauve embroidery along the edge that she had bought to wear to meet Mother. Bliss had a white wool baby suit which was horribly inappropriate for the tropics, but the only white clothes she had, and Roslyn wanted Bliss to look like a lady when they went to meet The Mother. Bliss was 10 months old. It was Roslyn's twenty-sixth birthday.

Mari met them at the bottom of the green carpeted staircase in the Meditation Hall at 2:30p.m. with an enormous smile and a small parcel for Roslyn. They went upstairs. At the second landing Mari pointed to a door on the right and said in a hushed voice that inside that door was Sri Aurobindo's room. They went through an open doorway to their left, through a long room which had bookcases covered with dust sheets along all the walls and a big long table in the center which might have been a library table, out onto a little porch, and then up another, narrower green carpeted staircase and through an open doorway onto a large balcony.

There was another lady standing on the balcony. She was one of the most beautiful women Roslyn had ever seen. Her dark hair was in a chignon, and she had the posture and grace of a ballet dancer. Mari introduced her as "Poorna, Mother's granddaughter."

Just then the door to the room across from the door to the balcony opened. A man dressed in a longi and a white string over his shoulder, with long white hair and twinkling eyes, looked out and caught Poorna's eye. She followed him through the door and the door closed.

Mari looked at Roslyn, and said, "People usually kneel in front of The Mother. You go into the room and kneel in front of Her. She is very old, and can not look up at you if you are standing in front of Her."

Roslyn did not believe in kneeling in front of other people; maybe in front of God; but she would never meet God, and was not certain that she would even kneel then. Still, she did not argue with Mari; she just did not say anything.

Mari had a beatific smile on her face. She stood there, silent, as though in a rapturous trance. Roslyn walked over to the edge of the balcony and looked over the rail to the quiet Ashram courtyard, and across the courtyard to other rooms and terraces. Bliss was quiet as a doll, riding on her hip, smiling at her like a happy cherub in the gentle tropical afternoon. A sweet breeze from the sea caressed them. Roslyn opened the little package Mari had given her, a bar of Mysore Sandalwood Soap, just what she needed! She shoved it into her cloth shoulder-bag.

The door across the hall from the door to the balcony opened again and Poorna came out, looking even more beautiful, and walked down the stairs. The little man beckoned to Mari, who then beckoned to Roslyn, and they went into Mother's room.

Bliss was on one arm, and Roslyn had a bedraggled bouquet of flowers in the other hand, because someone had told her that it was a tradition to bring flowers to Mother.

The floor was thickly carpeted, and the only thing Roslyn could see in the room was The Mother sitting in her chair. They walked into Her room, and without thinking Roslyn's body sunk to its knees in front of Her. She was sitting on Her chair peering gently at them. Roslyn sat Bliss down on the carpet next to her.

Between The Mother and Bliss there was a beautiful straw basket. Bliss lunged for the basket. Mari said, "Stop her, it is a basketful of eggs."

Roslyn grabbed Bliss and sat her down. Again the baby lunged for the basket, and Roslyn grabbed her and sat her down; but, Bliss was clearly going to jump at the basket again. Roslyn was trying to hold onto Bliss with one hand, and still had the bedraggled bouquet in the other, when The Mother looked at Bliss, a powerful piercing look that made Bliss sit back and sit up straight, and look back at The Mother. Roslyn did not know what passed between them, but the forceful look Mother was giving Bliss was so strong, Roslyn was glad she was not the target of that penetrating gaze. Then The Mother's face dissolved into the sweetest smile, and Bliss was smiling at Her, and they looked as though they shared the most marvelous joke, perfect, clear, wordless communication. Mother was ninety years old. Some people had told Roslyn they thought, perhaps She was a senile figurehead. Seeing Her communicating with Bliss, Roslyn thought, perhaps She is senile. Mother seemed to understand

Bliss better than Roslyn did, so She had to have the consciousness of a baby.

Then Mother turned to her, and said, "Parlez-vous Francais?"

Bliss was sitting very quietly, smiling blissfully at Roslyn's side, paying no attention at all to the basket of eggs. Roslyn had not expected Mother to speak to her. Everyone had told her that Mother usually did not speak to people when they went to receive Her blessing. Roslyn was so spaced out she did not even feel able to speak English, or American, which she had been talking all her life. She just looked at Mother.

Mother said, in perfect, unaccented English, "Do you speak French?"

Roslyn could not reply. Her entire being seemed to be going through such a convulsion of bliss; but it was as smooth as silk, nothing was different, everything was different, she was utterly too blissed out to reply.

Mari replied for her, "Elle ne parle pas Francaise, Mere."

She couldn't speak, she couldn't move, she couldn't think, Mother looked at her and she was too happy to be laughing, but Mother seemed to be laughing at her. Because She kept asking her a string of questions, in English, knowing very well that for the first time in her life, the cat had got her tongue. Mari answered for her, things like, "Do you like Pondicherry?" "Have you visited Auroville," "Where was Bliss born?"

Roslyn felt very foolish, and Mari very graciously answered Mother's questions for her, as though she were an idiot child.

Mari told Mother Roslyn was going to Rameshwaram for Durga puja.

Mother gave Roslyn a long look. She turned to the table next to her chair and found a green fluffy flower with the most amazingly pungent and fragrant scent.

She handed Roslyn the flower and told her to give it to Panditji, because it was a special flower that signified the Supramental manifestation.

Roslyn slipped the flower into her cloth shoulder bag with the bar of soap and all the junk she always carried, and forgot it.

Mari finally asked her if she would like to give the poor wilted bouquet she had been holding to Mother. She handed the flowers to Mother. From the table next to her chair, The Mother picked up a beautiful fresh bouquet of flowers and handed them to Roslyn, with a card, and a single pink rose. She gave a little stuffed lamb with a little bell on it to Bliss.

Bliss took the lamb from The Mother's hand, and seemed enraptured with the simple toy. She reached out and took the flower Mother was also holding out to her in her other little baby hand, and waved her hands stuffed with the little lamb and flower at Mother, then brought them down into her lap and looked at the wonderful gifts Mother had given her. She looked up at The Mother again, holding the little treasures tightly against her body.

Mother looked at Roslyn and told her, "Bring Bliss to me again on her birthday."

She answered Roslyn's unspoken question. They would stay in Pondicherry at least until Bliss's birthday.

Then She gave them a huge smile, and Roslyn went down with her nose on the floor. She picked up Bliss and the gifts from Mother and walked out. The white haired attendant was holding the door for her, and she started down the green staircase. She had gone only a few steps, then she stopped. She did not want to go back down those stairs. She did not know what had happened in Mother's room, but whatever it was seemed to be more wonderful than anything that had ever happened to her in her entire life. She had had many adventures, many inner and outer experiences, but whatever was in that room was better than champagne, better than sex, better than anything she had experienced. It was perfect bliss to be in The Mother's room, and she did not want to go back down to the street, she wanted to go back into The Mother's room.

Mari came down to the step above her. She seemed to understand exactly why Roslyn had stopped there on the steps. She looked at Roslyn with a wonderful twinkle in her eye and assured her, "Don't worry, you can come back on Bliss's birthday."

By the time they had gotten to the bottom of the green staircase Roslyn knew she had already forgotten how much more marvelous it felt to be simply near Her, and was content to think of staying in Mother's World at least until Bliss's birthday in December.

Chapter V

Bernie, Ma Talyarcan, Gitananda

V

The earth's uplook to a remote unknown
Is a preface only of the epic climb
Of the human soul from its flat earthly state
To the discovery of a greater self,
And the far gleam of an eternal Light.
This world is a beginning and a base
Where Life and Mind erect their structure dreams;
An unborn Power must build reality.

Sri Aurobindo, Savitri

The Purusha, the silent witness, can dictate a harmony for nature to execute, not by interfering in our functioning. Purusha inclines us to a conscious regard that transmutes at once, or after much difficulty, into the idea and dynamic impulse.

First must be the freedom of the impersonal witness. Afterwards there can be the surrender to the control of The Divine Mother

See the ego as nothing better than a device and the interaction, an illusion. Step back, observe, unmoved by the grief and desire of the lower being. Wait for the intervention of a higher will and the intuition of a greater, more luminous knowledge.

Old habits must die, lose their frequency and be released. The supreme harmony can not come except by the cessation of the egoistic will and choice and act and the quiescence of limited intelligence. The individual ego must cease to strive. The mind must fall silent. The desire will learn not to initiate. Personality must join its source and from above all thought and initiation will come.

Action must be initiated by the working of an impersonal transcendent force. A cosmic mind, life, substance, must act on a pure self empowered with bliss. This is a state of freedom that can come in the yoga of works through a renunciation of ego and desire and personal initiation and the surrender of the being to the cosmic self or the universal shakti.

(from Jim Bean's Journal extracts from Sri Aurobindo's Synthesis of Yoga.*)*

Roslyn put some stuff together for her trip to Rameshwaram, but she did not have any money to stay in Rameshwaram. She had been able to borrow only enough for the third class train ticket. She hoped since Panditji had invited her, and was a great and powerful yogi, he would worry about the details, like money. She did not know how long she would be in Rameshwaram. She thought when Panditji found she had no money he might send her right back to Pondicherry.

She was not worried. She had her room in Pondicherry, and was expecting money at The Ashram Post Office. Leaving the guesthouse for the train she spent several of her precious rupees for a rickshaw to take her to dinner at Castelini with John Kelly on the way to the station.

Kelly was in the middle of moving out of Castelini to a guesthouse on the beach, where he would be able to stand in the garden at an easel and paint the ocean. He was still wearing mauve pajamas and drinking beer. The dinner that night was exceptional. The Countess de B. had had her cook prepare a special meal for them and sent it over, warm, in a tiffin. There was lobster in a wonderful sauce, and French green beans, and chocolate mousse. Gabriel brought some Coca-Cola with ice and Kelly told Roslyn, "You haven't seen anything yet."

She replied, "It seems my life is very different to other people's. I have had some really unbelievable and wonderful experiences, like meeting Mother today, but I have had some terrible hard times, much worse than what I see happening to others."

Kelly replied, "It is the yoga. Your soul is being prepared like steel, first fire then ice."

She answered, "How can that be yoga? Mother said equanimity is an indication of spiritual progress. I am either rejoicing or suicidal."

"How do you feel today?" Kelly asked.

"Ecstatic because of meeting Mother and frightened because I am going to Rameshwaram without any money."

"Don't be frightened. You have always had what you need, why should that change?" he asked.

"Maybe I shouldn't go. My room and food are already paid for here," she said.

"No, no, go. It is an act of faith. You can always come back."

They ate quickly and she went to the train station. The train was already there. She bought her ticket and boarded.

The first leg of the journey was quiet and easy even though it took the train an hour to get to the large junction fifteen miles west of Pondicherry. Then she had to get off the train in the big station, tired, carrying Bliss and her bag, and find the train to Rameshwaram.

She had to climb the dirty stairway to the footbridge so she could cross over the tracks and platforms to the platform where the Rameshwaram train was waiting. Even in the middle of the night it was not cold. It was hot and dusty and there were many very exotic looking people.

She finally found the train and boarded. It was crowded, but she found an empty luggage rack, curled up with Bliss, and went to sleep. During the night she needed to get up to go to the bathroom. She left Bliss and her bag in the luggage rack for a couple of minutes. Then she crawled back onto the rack, next to Bliss. With her head on her bag, she went back to sleep.

When she woke up the fingers of dawn were already streaking the morning sky. She got down from the luggage rack. Many of the people who had been on the train had gotten off at the many stops during the night. There was a place on the seat below. The train pulled into a little station. There was a boy at the window selling tea and cookies. She took some tea and cookies from him and went into her bag for the money to pay him. The money was gone! She was very upset. All her money, although it was only a few rupees, was gone. Someone must have taken it from her bag when she went to the bathroom in the night.

A man from the second class carriage that was next to the women's car noticed her distress. He asked her if he could help.

She explained that she had just wanted a cup of tea and some biscuits. When she went into her bag to pay for them, she found that all her money had been stolen.

He bought the tea and cookies for her. She was very grateful.

She had not a paise, not even the smallest coin. She was on a train with Baby Bliss in southern India. She was trying not to worry. Panditji had invited her. If he was really a great yogi he would look after her.

The train chugged along slowly through the hot bright South Indian morning and stopped at the next tiny station, a few palm trees, a cement platform, a small brick building, a sign, and a few huts on the sand under the palm trees.

The man, who had bought her the tea and cookies, came to her window, waving his arms trying to get her attention.

He handed her a wad of rupees, and explained, "I took up a collection in the second class car where I am traveling, because I did not want you, a foreign lady, to think badly of the Indian people. It is not much." He gave her a good thick wad of rupee notes.

She had not told him that she had only had twenty rupees, and she probably should not have accepted the money, but she figured it was Panditji's way of solving that problem, and accepted it.

"My pleasure," he said.

The whistle tooted and he got back into the other car. She counted the money, over 300 rupees, a fortune!

Then the train was on the bridge and they were in Rameshwaram.

Her bag was full of rupees and Bliss was laughing on her hip. It was a golden soft sunny morning. They got off the train.

She took a rickshaw directly to Panditji's house.

There was no one on the varandah, and no one in the central courtyard. Panditji was sitting in his meditation room chanting mantras. The glow of the ghee lamps and the smoke from the incense billowed around him creating a strange other-worldly atmosphere. Roslyn sat down with Bliss, resting her back and her bag against a big pillar and watching and listening in the silent morning. Panditji was playing with water, flowers and fire, chanting mantras with more syllables in a moment than seemed possible. He seemed very calm and strong. The photos around the doorway of his puja room of The Mother, Sri Aurobindo and his guru, seemed to be resonant with benedictory force. She sat there feeling blessed, in the presence of Masters. Bliss sat, as quiet as a doll next to her, her hand resting lightly on Roslyn's lap as though in meditation.

Roslyn had done the thirty-four day practice, and felt much more stable than she had when she met Panditji. She did not know why he accepted her, or why she accepted him, but there seemed to be an understanding between them, a rapport, which had nothing to do with language, culture or appearance. He was a friend, guru, guide, in a very gentle form. He was jovial and lovable, consistently engrossed by The Divine. He was a devoted shakta, devotee of The Lord who believes the goddess, shakti, to be the immanent active energy of the transcendent and remote Shiva.

Panditji was ringing a bell and chanting a mantra that sounded like Omaha Cream Cheese. He mumbled some more mantras. The atmosphere changed after he rang the bell. He got up and came out of his meditation room with his little cup and spoon.

Roslyn had been careful to make no sound, he could not have seen them without eyes in the back of his head, but he knew they were there. She took some of the water in her palm and drank it.

He brought them two bananas. His daughter came and brought them coffee and took Bliss.

Panditji asked about The Mother, and Roslyn remembered that She had given a flower for him the day before. She went into her shoulder bag, from which her money had been stolen on the train. Her passport was still there, and all the cigarettes, matches, comb, candy, and other junk she always carried in that small cloth shoulder bag, and under it all she found the fluffy green marvelously fragrant flower. It was still fluffy and sweet smelling. It should have been a crushed nothing. She was amazed that flower had survived the journey from Mother's room to Panditji in Rameshwaram.

Panditji was very pleased to receive a flower from The Mother. He took it immediately into his meditation room and sprinkled some water on it and offered it to The Goddess, The Mother, Shakti, the active powerful component of the Lord, Shiva, who abides in deep contemplation.

The Mother is the female active aspect of god, destructive and beneficent, Durga, the ten armed goddess riding a lion in battle against evil. When there is neither light nor heat nor sound, even then, within, is Her great warmth, the soul, the timeless one in everyone.

Panditji told Roslyn a story about Durga. There was a devoted Hindu prince on his way to the Durga temple with his entourage for Durga puja. India was ruled, at that time, by the Moguls. A Mogul Muslim captain intercepted the Hindus on their way to the temple, and insisted they forfeit their religion or their lives. They persuaded him to accompany them to the temple. When they got to the temple, the Muslim captain slit the throat of the Hindu prince's horse and told him and his entourage that if the goddess they had come to worship did not restore the life of the horse he would kill them all, and take their horses and the offerings they had brought to the temple to his Lord. The Hindu prince was distraught, and went into the temple with the captain, drew his sword, and cut off his own head, rather than become a Muslim or let the Muslims murder him. The goddess was pleased with his devotion, so she restored his life and the life of his horse. The Mogul captain stopped harassing Hindus from that day.

Roslyn stayed in Rameshwaram for a few days at Panditji's guesthouse, a beautiful old, very comfortable house near the temple. He had two other disciples staying there, a man from Kerala and his teenage son. It was a traditional South Indian house, with big old wood pillars supporting the roof over the entrance, and built around courtyards, like in ancient Rome. There was a servant to look after them. The other disciples never exchanged a word with Roslyn, and hardly said a word when they were with Panditji.

It was peaceful, but slightly austere. There was no one she could talk to in Rameshwaram except Bliss and Panditji. She took Bliss to the beach. She took Bliss to the temple. She took Bliss to Panditji's. They ate sweets, drank coffee, watched the elephant and the procession around the temple. They heard the mantras chanted over the loudspeakers. It was nice, but very boring, except when she could be with Panditji; and then she would feel her being fill with light, and take on a consciousness that would straighten her spine and flood her from within and without with tranquillity and joy. It was quite inexplicable, that she would go to Panditji's house and sit on the terrace while he was sitting in his meditation room chanting mantras, and some magic would pour through her. She felt love, and joy, and peace, but she wanted to go back to Pondicherry where she was having a lot of fun. Ananta had invited her to the island for the last night of Durga puja, the "Victory." She asked Panditji if he would give her a mantra and he said he would see her in Pondicherry in December.

Roslyn took the long slow dusty train ride back to Pondicherry with the last of the rupees the good Samaritan had given her. They left Rameshwaram at noon and arrived back in Pondicherry at dawn the next morning.

The sun was just coming up as they got to the station. Pondicherry was glowing in beautiful dawn colors. Roslyn had written to her father Bernie, "Pondicherry by the sea, this is where I want to be."

She got a rickshaw from the train station to Shelter Guesthouse. Everything was exactly as she'd left it in her room, and her servant Marie came to look after Bliss. The dhobi came for the dirty clothes. Roslyn went off to the Post Office and to see her friends.

At the Post Office there was a letter from her father, with money. He had written that he was coming to see her in Pondicherry for Bliss's birthday in December.

She cashed the check. In the bazaar she bought some cloth that she took to the street of tailors. The street of tailors was a little alleyway across the street from the bazaar where there was a row of Tamil men, tailors, sitting at their sewing machines all along one side of the alley. She left the cloth with one of the tailors, who promised to have her new clothes ready for her by evening. Then she went and bought a bicycle and ordered a basket for Bliss to be attached to the handle bar.

She stopped by Lorelei's, but Lorelei was grouchy and busy, and it was nearly lunchtime, so Roslyn went back to get Bliss and pay the maid at the guesthouse.

There was an Italian woman in the room next door who had moved in a few days before she left for Rameshwaram. She was an older person, but very chic and amusing. She was vociferous of her disapproval that Roslyn did not wear any shoes, that Roslyn left the baby with the servant in the mornings, that Roslyn was not married, etc. She grabbed Roslyn walking past her room.

"So you are back. I heard the baby crying."

Just then the door to Roslyn's room opened and Bliss emerged, all clean, with a bow in her hair, and a clean dress, in the arms of the nice Tamil woman who was looking after her. Bliss looked just fine with Marie, but she immediately made a fuss when she saw Roslyn, demanding to be held.

"Are you going to lunch?" her neighbor asked.

"Yes."

"Where are you going?"

"I don't know, maybe the Continental," she replied. She always enjoyed The Continental Hotel on the beach with its dining room looking out over the sea. The food was non-vegetarian, good, and inexpensive.

"Why don't you try the new Ashram restaurant on the beach, 'Tous qu'il faut?'"

"There is only vegetarian food in Rameshwaram. I am looking forward to a non-vegetarian meal."

"It is non-veg. It is run by Mother's granddaughter, and she has very commendable steaks."

Roslyn laughed. "We must be in the only Ashram in India that has a steak house."

She had been very impressed by Mother's granddaughter when they met on the balcony outside Mother's room. She was very elegant. Things in Mother's world were somehow better, cleaner, nicer, than things in the real world, so Roslyn was glad to hear that there was a non-veg restaurant associated with The Ashram.

It was a little blue/gray/white building on the beach road, near The Continental. There was no sign on the door, but the door was open and there was a room full of white tables and stools, and people eating.

It was amazing. There were very few Indians, nearly all Europeans. Roslyn had not seen another white face or any non-veg food for days. She went into the next room, where The Mother's granddaughter was serving food from a long table covered with a clean cloth, a buffet, all you could eat for a few rupees, including filet mignon, fish, pommes frites, salad, vegetables, rice, dal, chappatis, bread, yogurt and fruit. Exactly the restaurant Roslyn had been looking for all her life, except there was only tea, coffee and lemon juice, no Coca-Cola.

Roslyn piled the food on her plate, and balanced it in one hand and Bliss on her hip. She sat at one of the white tables in the front room.

Bliss sat on the table and shoved her hands into the food on Roslyn's plate. She put food on her face, her shirt, the table, the floor, and even a little in her mouth, while Roslyn ate, ignoring Bliss, looking out the window across the empty street, onto the beach, the sparkling clear sea, and the bright blue sky.

Bliss was pounding rice into the table top with her fists.

Roslyn's neighbor came and asked why she had not left the baby at the guesthouse with the servant, instead of bringing her to the restaurant where she was disturbing everyone.

She was not disturbing Roslyn. Roslyn could not believe that anyone might be disturbed by a baby smashing rice into the white table top, so she ignored the remark and told her Italian neighbor, "The food is very good."

"That baby should wear diapers," she replied.

Roslyn gave Bliss a piece of fish to play with.

Her neighbor walked away and did not talk to her anymore.

At lunch she saw Ananta's friend Joe, who was also going to the puja on the island that night. He suggested they share a taxi with a lady from New York, an old friend of Ananta's, who was visiting in town for a few days. He told Roslyn they would pick her up at 6 p.m.

She spent a quiet afternoon with Bliss getting ready for the gala puja on the island.

She wore her beautiful red Chinese silk brocade dress from Nepal. She spent hours painting her face like a Suerat painting with blended dots of color around her eyes and cheekbones. Bliss wore her black cotton shirt with the gold dragon. They were looking terribly exotic, when the taxi pulled up with Joe and Ananta's old friend, Miss America Pie, who was wearing loafers with stockings and an impeccable Peck & Peck skirt and blouse. Joe was his usual Mr.Clean image, in his starched shirt and shorts.

Joe asked Miss America Pie if it was true that she rode her horse in Central Park every day, and she replied, "Not when I am in India." After that there was no more conversation in the taxi.

They got to the island, and Countess B. was there with Ananta looking entirely bewitching. They were both drunk. Ananta greeted his guests perfunctorily, and then disappeared into the bedroom with the Countess, closing the door. The three guests who had had nothing to say to one another in the taxi still had nothing to say to one another. Joe pounded on Ananta's bedroom door, "Ananta, do you have some brandy in there?".

"I think we should go if he is going to behave like that," he said to Roslyn and the lady from New York.

They went out into the garden. The sun was setting. Lights went on suddenly all over the island, the great light on the pillar of Zeus, strings of Christmas tree lights on the temple, and lights in the garden lighting the statues of Athena and Varuna and the lotus ponds. Ananta and the Countess finally joined them. Together they walked down the swept path to the temple where there were three chairs. Ananta sat in the middle chair, with the Countess de B. on his right. Miss America Pie sat in the other chair on his left. There were mats on the ground for Roslyn, Bliss and Joe.

Roslyn was very disappointed that Ananta was no longer paying any attention to her. The priests began chanting, and the musicians playing the strange South Indian music. She seemed to lose contact with time and space and enter a strange new dimension.

The Tamil orchestra played the chenai, tabla and harmonium, while the priests chanted and played with flowers and other offerings in the temple. Roslyn felt a huge luminous presence on the little quiet island. Two priests dressed in white longis and white threads over their left shoulders sat chanting mantras inside the temple, which was glowing with the light of many shining ghee lamps.

Roslyn overheard Ananta explaining that the priests had been trained by Panditji in Rameshwaram to perform the rituals in his temple. This was the great victory celebration of The Divine Mother as Durga, over the monster Maisha, the buffalo of ignorance. The purpose of the ritual was not simply to celebrate Her victory, but also to invoke Her presence.

The tropical evening was full of the sweet fragrance of flowers, exotic music, glimmering lights, glowing lamps, chanting of mantras, and a great stillness. As the ceremony continued the priests decorated the statues in the temple with flowers, and performed rituals with water, flowers and various implements. The musicians played strange exotic music, and it was like being in Panditji's house, because suddenly everything was different, and Roslyn felt marvelous. It was as though she was no longer confined to her body; the irritants and discomforts of her personality vanished, and she was part of something wide and vast that flowed through infinity into time.

The priests came out of the temple and built a small fire in a little pit, all the while chanting mantras. The feeling of a deep serenity and joy held her enthralled. Bliss sat quietly. The priests were throwing ghee, flowers, handfuls of rice, and so on, into the fire, and chanting rhythmic mantras. The music held everyone spellbound. Then the priests went back inside the temple, said some more mantras, and rang a bell. They came out and gave Ananta and each guest and servant some red kumkum powder, some white vibhuti, some sacred water, flowers, and finally a little leaf with some food on it. Everyone stood up. Two of Ananta's servants took the large brass deity out of the temple and placed it on a piece of silk in a small gilded palanquin. They lifted it and carried it on their shoulders. They were followed by the priests, who were still chanting mantras, carrying burning incense and a brass tray with stuff on it. The palaquin was followed by the musicians, Ananta, the ladies, Joe, Bliss and Roslyn.

The procession went around the island propitiating the various deities, and even the deity of the river, which surrounded the island, and then back to the temple.

Ananta had invited everyone for dinner, but suggested they propitiate his pet boa by feeding it the baby. Roslyn did not think it funny, and was really feeling put out with Ananta.

There was a table with a linen tablecloth, napkins, silver and china and crystal, and an excellent four-course dinner with wine and brandy. Ananta excused himself after coffee, having ignored Roslyn and Joe all evening, and went into the bedroom. The Countess de B. followed him, and closed the door! The others were left. Miss America Pie was very displeased to have come all the way from Central Park to visit her friend, only to be left sitting with a glass of brandy while he disappeared into the bedroom with a French Countess. "I guess we may leave now" she said, setting down her empty glass. They left. The taxi had waited for them on the opposite shore. Joe thought the women were very funny over-reacting to Ananta.

Pondicherry was certainly the place to be that fall for a single woman with a baby. At that particular moment in time it was a very unique community with a very far-out attitude towards a single mother. The Mother welcomed Roslyn, and everyone accepted her and Bliss as part of Mother's dream of a New World sailing in across the waves on the horizon of time. An entirely new evolutionary species of wonderful beings, with a new consciousness that did not include ownership or the conventional nuclear family, was expected. Each person in the community thought of him or herself as a single person, a person whose primary relationship was with The Divine. In all other relationships everyone is equal, a child of The Mother. Each person was free to relate to anyone else, and everything in the world is part of Her great manifestation.

The project, Auroville, in 1969 was called by The Mother, "A cradle for the superman." The entire community of The Sri Aurobindo Ashram seemed to be very enthusiastic about Mother's project, and excited about the babies coming to Auroville. There were some who thought it was too liberal on Mother's part to open the doors wide to Her children from all over the world who were traveling to Pondicherry to meet Her. There were those who claimed that as Sri Aurobindo had opened the path to the Supramental world in The Ashram, in Auroville Mother had opened "The sex center."

She was beckoning a future, wide and unknowable. She had opened the door for a new world to manifest in time and take humanity through the evolving planetary crisis to the future.

Mother had spoken of her inner vision of Auroville, "That same thing which, in the history of the universe, had made the earth the symbolic representation of the universe so as to be able to concentrate the work on one point, the same phenomenon is taking place now: India represents all terrestrial human difficulties, and it is in India that there will be the cure. And it is for this that I have been made to start Auroville."

The Sri Aurobindo Ashram was a spiritual, largely celibate, and very traditional ashram. Suddenly Mother started a town without rules. Babies arrived, and were welcomed by The Mother as part of the community and citizenry of the new town. Roslyn arrived there with Bliss, the nicest person she had ever known in her life, in her arms, and they were greeted as though they were not only expected, but very welcome.

It was as though all of Mother's World had been organized to greet them, and inspire them with the ideal of Auroville. Here was a new family, which involved the whole village that is a microcosm of the world, as the villagers are from all over the world. There was a great deal of to-ing and fro-ing from one country to another and back to Pondicherry, making the quiet little backwater the hub of an international scene. The beautiful tropical town has always offered a lovely site for travelers. Roslyn had heard that the great Alexander was in Pondicherry. The town is ancient, and it is said that the Sri Aurobindo Ashram is located on exactly the same site as the ashram of the great Vedic Rishi Agastya and his great shakti, Lopamudra. Pondicherry was perhaps Veda Puri in ancient times. The town, la ville, is rumored to have been designed by Louis XIV of France, The "Roi de Soleil." It is built around a park, the streets like rays of sunlight from the park, looking over the beach a block away. There is a grand promenade along the sea which is a wonderful place to walk in the morning. Sri Aurobindo when seeking refuge from the British went to Pondicherry. People devoted to him from all over India and the world followed him there. He has been revered by philosophers and psychologists for generations. Readers of Sri Aurobindo's great works have visited The Ashram in Pondicherry. Many stayed for years or visited regularly.

The people from all over the world who had come for a visit and chosen to stay, or came back regularly, were all devoted to Mother and Sri Aurobindo.

The organization of the Sri Aurobindo Ashram was extraordinary. It housed, fed, cared for and educated thousands of people. There were industries, libraries, Nursing Homes, dental clinics, handicraft workshops, a perfurmerie, businesses, playgrounds, a swimming pool, a beach, tennis courts, a printing press, guesthouses, a dining room, a restaurant, a gas station, and movies on Saturday night at the playground. It all moved together very smoothly.

Everyone involved was deeply committed to The Mother, and treated everyone else with respect. Mother was absolutely in charge and responsible for every detail.

Roslyn made new friends every day. Everyone was amiable. There were so many interesting people, from everywhere. She finally started to eat in the Ashram Dining Room at least twice a day because it was just around the corner from the guesthouse. The food was very healthy, and she met likable people there. She usually had lunch on the beach at "Tous qu'il faut", where the food was invariably marvelous.

She visited Lorelei nearly every day. They would sit, stitching and gossiping, and the children would play in buckets of water or with balls of yarn like kittens. Roslyn had many new clothes made in the bazaar for herself and Bliss.

Lorelei and Roslyn took the children to "Equals One," an experimental center for children where they were experimenting with new educational approaches that could work for children beginning on a path of evolutionary yoga, as at Auroville.

There was a big red-headed Canadian psychologist there who had been German Swami's disciple and Mari's inspiration for the hero of her book, Austin.

Austin had been either a patient or a student at the Jung Institute in Zurich. He had a room full of small sandboxes and toys he called the World Game. They would take the children there because neither Bliss nor Lorelei's children had toys. The children would play with the toys in the sandboxes, and Lorelei and Roslyn would talk to Austin or the other people around there. Everyone was full of enthusiasm about the wonderful new creation that was beginning. The "Age of Aquarius", which people were singing about in San Francisco, Mother was greeting with a new town, a material site for the new creation.

Young people, old people, black people, white people, people from all over the world, came together to play in Austin's sandboxes. "Equals One" was run by a French woman dentist, who had left her home, husband and practice in Paris, because she thought she was really an artist and liked to live in Pondicherry. She adopted a Tamil girl who was very beautiful and very friendly with Roslyn. The Tamil girl wanted to try LSD. Roslyn didn't have any.

Lorelei had to be home in the evening in case her husband, who did not talk to her, happened to be home. Roslyn was free to go out and meet other travelers at Equals One, or listen to music at the Ashram Library, meditate, or go to a movie at the Ashram playground.

There was rain, and sometimes even a lot of rain. The streets were like rivers during the monsoon. Meanwhile the caravan of pioneers from Paris was coming to Auroville, overland. The community was waiting for these pioneers with excitement. Something wonderful was expected from Auroville.

The caravan was going to live in Aspiration, an experimental temporary model community which had been built as an experimental model that would be the model for Auromodele, which in turn would be the model for the town, Auroville. Aspiration had been built on the edge of a great plateau of eroded wasteland overlooking the sea. Thatched huts with bathrooms and electricity had been built, perhaps a score of huts, beautifully designed to accommodate a single person. Two huts shared a bathroom and a small corridor in which there was space for a hotplate and a small food cupboard. There was a community kitchen looking out over the parched plain to the Bay of Bengal. This had been designed by the architect for the town, Andre, and built and paid for by the Sri Aurobindo Society.

Every hut was freshly painted. There was not a crack in the cement. There were fresh new vessels for food in the kitchen. The community in

Pondicherry waited for the caravan to arrive, and Auroville to begin. Although the opening ceremony for Auroville had happened on February 28th, 1968, there had been very little development in Auroville by the end of 1969. There were a few scattered huts built by some crazy foreigners, who felt called to live in the wilderness, a few huts near the Madras road at Hope, a farm, and the maternity clinic at Promesse.

The maternity clinic was interesting. It was not simply a place to give birth. It was a series of apartments. when women in the community became pregnant they could go to this quiet, peaceful, comfortable place, and spend their pregnancy in contemplation of the Divine, listening to music, living quietly, healthily and harmoniously so the child would acquire a consciousness and aura of inner peace from before birth. The practical problem became apparent when the pregnant mothers had their small babies and did not want to move out of the comfortable apartments. The complex of huts at Aspiration had been built. Twenty-five hundred acres of land had been bought by the Sri Aurobindo Society. A caravan of vehicles full of people from Paris, who had joined with the aspiration to live in Auroville and had pooled their resources to travel together and start Auroville, were on their way.

One evening Roslyn stopped by Austin's and met a beautiful couple there. He was impossibly handsome, open, friendly, charming, and she was more beautiful than any movie star. They had a five year old child with them. They were not only gorgeous to look at but intelligent and amusing, and they lived in Auroville. They were building the first permanent house in Auroville. They were the parents of the first child born in Auroville, the one who had drowned as an infant.

If these were the type of people who were going to be in Auroville, then Roslyn wanted to be there too.

Her friend, the Tamil girl at Equals One, disappeared when the caravan finally arrived. She had gone to live in Aspiration with the pioneers who had come with the caravan. Roslyn would see them charging into Pondicherry in their old white Citroen vans that they had driven from Paris. A couple of Australians arrived at the guesthouse. They went to visit the community in Aspiration and as there were still empty huts - were given two huts and invited to move in. Roslyn wanted to live in Auroville very much.

The people from Aspiration were a very beautiful and distinct group on the streets of Pondicherry. There was an incredibly tall and handsome black North African who Mother named Krishna when they all went to see Her when they first arrived, and a beautiful Frenchwoman who had

had a baby a few weeks after they arrived. The rest of the people were all Europeans, and wore shorts and tee-shirts and had an atmosphere of exuberant energy. There were always several of them together when Roslyn would see them, and they never spoke to her.

Her Tamil friend from Equal's One had fallen in love with a tall French man and was going to move into his hut. She offered Roslyn her hut.

For Roslyn, Auroville was more real than Pondicherry, or any other place she had ever been. It did not matter that it was really a few huts on a piece of wasteland pockmarked with impoverished villages. For her it was a place where there were other people sharing the same inner vision that had guided her to India. This inner life and its demands had guided her, and she was very grateful that she had found a place which aspired to be what her soul was seeking.

Her friend said, "Take my hut, I am staying with my boyfriend in his hut."

Roslyn and Bliss went on the van to Aspiration with her in the afternoon, to stay in her hut.

The colony was very French, and most of the people ignored Roslyn entirely, although there were a few smiles. Someone came up to her and told her that she could not stay in Auroville without The Mother's permission. She had not brought anything with her to Aspiration except Bliss, so she had to go back into Pondicherry the next day anyhow. She decided to leave a letter for Mother with Mari asking for permission to live in Auroville.

That night she was sitting with Bliss on the hard red soil outside the hut after dinner. The evening was very still and there was a full moon. The stars were very bright, and sitting there, looking at the stars, she had a wonderful inner experience that seemed to her to confirm the vision that had led her away from Arizona, from Bliss's father and America, to come to India.

The next day when she went into Pondicherry she went to see Austin at Equals One and told him about her vision. He told her that she should write about it to The Mother; it could have been a hallucination rather than a vision.

So she wrote a letter, several pages long, telling Mother about the vision in Arizona, the vision in Aspiration, and asking Her permission to live in Auroville, then left it with Mari.

She went back to Aspiration. The community was not very friendly. The Australians who had moved in a few days earlier seemed like part of the community, but no-one talked to Roslyn, no-one sat with her at meals, the woman with the baby was too busy with her new baby and other children to greet her as another mother. Everyone was very busy. She felt a little bit like she and Bliss were intruding on the Aurovilians, but why were they "Aurovilians" and she only an ordinary mortal?

It was an uncomfortable feeling, and she felt like a stranger. She knew she was supposed to be in Auroville, but the people in Aspiration seemed to feel that she did not belong there. One of the men came over to where she was sitting at dinner. "Tomorrow everybody working on the road. You come working on the road."

"I have to go into Pondicherry," she replied.

"Tomorrow everybody Aspiration working road."

"I cannot work on the road, I have to go to Pondicherry."

He got up and walked away.

She felt as if she had blown it, but she did not want to work on the road, and hoped for a message from Mother in Pondicherry.

She got up the next morning and went to the dining room for breakfast. One of the Frenchmen came up to her, "You coming to work with us on the road?"

"No, I am going to Pondicherry."

"Everybody in Aspiration today is working on the road," he said.

"I am not working on the road, I am going to Pondi," she replied.

He walked away. She watched everyone carrying shovels and pans for moving dirt going to work on the road as she waited for the Land-Rover to come and take her and Bliss to town.

Finally it arrived in a cloud of dust. The Auroville plateau was hard red dirt. There was no green to be seen. It looked dry, brittle, finished. She got in the vehicle and rode into town. It was the only 4-wheeler on the road. The driver held his palm on the horn and frightened children, chickens, cows, goats, cyclists and rickshaws out of his way. He drove down the middle of the road, constantly slapping his palm on the horn, and it was only a few minutes before they reached the town.

Roslyn's servant, Marie, was waiting for her in her room. Roslyn gave her Bliss and went off to see her friends and eat.

Before she went back to Aspiration that evening on the van, Roslyn saw Mari and received Mother's answer. Mari explained to her that usually when the Mother received a letter She would listen only to a few words or a single sentence and be able to give Her reply, but She asked Mari to read this entire letter, several pages long, and then replied, "Bon."

What did that mean? The French word "bon" means "good" in

English, but what was She replying to? Roslyn was asking permission to live in Auroville at Aspiration; did "bon" mean yes? She had written Mother about the vision she had had in Arizona and the vision she had had in Aspiration, did "bon" mean something in relation to those visions? It didn't matter. Roslyn was okay with it, and went back to Aspiration.

At dinner the Italian guy who had told her the night before that everyone in Aspiration was going to work on the road in the morning, came over and asked her if she would come and work on the road the next morning. She had to go into Pondi again. She was waiting for a check. She needed to go to the Post Office to check the mail.

He walked away, back to the table where all his French friends were sitting. Bliss and Roslyn were sitting alone at the edge of the dining room, because there was no place for them at the large table with the others. The people in Aspiration were not at all like the people in The Ashram, or the people she had met at Equals One, they were very unfriendly. Roslyn would smile at them and they would look at her as if she was not there. She hoped it would get better. It was a very pleasant place to sit on a warm clear tropical evening. She could see the moonlight shimmering on the ocean.

Several of the people from the big table, including the Italian guy, were walking back towards her.

The Italian guy asked her, "What you think is Auroville?"

"Freedom," she replied.

"What that mean? You think Auroville a free hotel, you come and you sleep and you eat and you go to Pondicherry all day and out to lunch?"

"Auroville is Mother's World."

"Yes, and you cannot live in Auroville without The Mother's permission, so please you go tomorrow."

"No, I have permission from The Mother."

"How you have permission from Mother?"

"I sent Her a letter."

"With whom you send Her a letter?"

"I sent it with Mari."

"No, only Poorna can take letters to Mother about Aspiration."

"I will take a letter to Mother tomorrow to Poorna, asking for permission to stay in Aspiration."

"Can you give some money to the community while you are staying here?"

"Yes, of course," she knew that the people in the caravan had pooled their resources in Paris, and, that the money was supposed to maintain the community for a year in Auroville, but after a few weeks the money was finished and the community was now running on a budget given by the Sri Aurobindo Society.

"How much you give?"

"I don't know. I don't have any money at present. I am waiting for money."

"Why you coming here?"

"I want to live in Auroville."

"Okay, you go live Auroville, you no stay here."

"This is the only place I can live in Auroville, you have running water, electricity, transport to Pondi, a community kitchen. I am alone with a baby. The rest of Auroville is only empty land."

"Yes, I know, you go."

"No."

"Yes."

"I will take a letter to Mother tomorrow."

"Okay." And they walked away.

She sat there alone with Bliss. Her Tamil friend had been absorbed into the French group, and it did not seem to be the chic thing to do to talk to Roslyn, so she also ignored her. There was an old white haired Frenchman living with a very young woman, who introduced himself, but he also did not seem like part of the group around the French table in the cafeteria in Aspiration.

There was an entirely humorless Frenchman with glasses whose wife had donated a large part of the money to build Aspiration, who was a self assigned "in charge."

He went over to Roslyn and told her, "I hope you understand Auroville is not for everybody. It will not grow in the right way unless we do what The Mother wants. You cannot stay here. You do not have The Mother's permission."

"I don't have your permission, I have The Mother's," she replied.

"No. This is not the right place for you."

He walked away, and she sat there looking at the moon rising and its reflection on the ocean, feeling that she was where she was supposed to be. Even if Aspiration was not where she was supposed to be, she felt certain that maybe the purpose of her life was to come to Auroville and live the experience that would happen in a place consecrated to the ideals of the Auroville Charter.

"Auroville belongs to nobody in particular. Auroville belongs to humanity
as a whole, but to live in Auroville one must be a willing servitor of the Divine Consciousness.

"Auroville will be the place of an unending education, of constant progress, and
a youth that never ages.

"Auroville wants to be the bridge between the past and the future. Taking
advantage of all discoveries from without and within, Auroville will boldly spring towards
future realizations.

"Auroville will be a site of material and spiritual researches for a living embodiment of an actual Human Unity."

Roslyn believed that she had been dragged across the world by destiny to the experimental utopia because nothing else made sense, and there was nothing else she wanted to do and nowhere else she wanted to be. She wanted to be near The Mother. She wanted to be part of the Auroville game.

Pondicherry was very delightful, but she did not want to live in Pondicherry. She felt she needed to be part of the new community, Auroville, but she had to write another letter to Mother asking again for permission to stay in Aspiration.

She took the letter and Bliss to Pondicherry in the morning.

Late that afternoon she was resting in her room before going back to Auroville. The guesthouse manager knocked on her door.

She opened the door.

"Mari called on the phone and asked me to ask you to come to her house now. She has a message for you from The Mother."

Roslyn was surprised. She thought it would be a day or two before she got a reply, and as she had sent the letter through Poorna she expected the reply through Poorna.

She grabbed Bliss and went to Mari's on the way to the van.

She rang the bell, and the servant admitted her and offered her a chair in the garden. She sat there, and after a few moments Mari came out.

"Hello Roslyn. How is Bliss?"

"We are fine. What is the message?"

"Mother asked me to tell you that you have to leave Aspiration and move back into Pondicherry."

Roslyn felt as if she had been struck from behind with a sledgehammer.

"I don't understand," she stammered.

"You still have your room in town, don't you?"

"Yes."

"You have an appointment with The Mother in two weeks for Bliss's birthday."

"I have to go or I will miss the van."

Mari hugged her, and said, "Don't feel bad. It is not yet time for you to move to Auroville."

Devastated with disappointment she got back on the van, spent another lonely evening in Aspiration, assuring everyone she was leaving forever in the morning, and brought her few things back to town the next morning.

She really did not feel too bad. In Pondicherry she was nearer to The Mother, and Mother was much more interesting than Auroville. In Pondicherry she had friends.

She went back to her room in the morning. In the evening Poorna's servant came to her room with a tray that had a magnificent lobster mayonnaise and a chocolate mousse on it, and a note from Poorna saying she hoped Roslyn was not too disappointed to be back in Pondicherry. It was such a great gesture, Roslyn had to reply that she was not disappointed. She was delighted to be back in Pondicherry.

For the next couple of weeks the days blended into a happy haze. Roslyn would get up early, walk to the beach and swim at sunrise, have breakfast in the Ashram Dining Room, and spend mornings visiting friends, usually Lorelei, where she would stitch, and Bliss would play with the children. Then lunch, a nap, tea, and more friends. She met some other people from Auroville, Americans who lived in huts near the center. They were friendlier, and she liked them better than the French at Aspiration, but she did not think anymore about moving to Auroville. She was in Pondi, and she was happy.

Bliss's first Birthday

vi

O Sun-Word, thou shalt raise the earth-soul to Light
And bring down God into the lives of men:
Earth shall be my work-chamber and my house,
My garden of life, to plant a seed divine.
When all they work in human time is done,
The mind of earth shall be a home of light,
The life of earth a tree growing towards heaven,
The body of earth, a tabernacle of God
Awakened from the mortal's ignorance,
Men shall be lit with the Eternal's ray,
And the glow of the sun -lift in their thought,
And feel in their hearts the sweetness of my love,
And in their acts my Power's miraculous drive.
My will shall be the meaning of their days;
Living for me, by me, in me they shall live.

Sri Aurobindo, Savitri

116

The surrender of the being to the cosmic self or universal shakti can come in the yoga of knowledge by the cessation of thought, the silence of the mind, the opening of the whole being to the cosmic dynamic and the supreme reality, or in the yoga of devotion by the surrender of the heart to the hands of the all-blissful, the adored Master of our existence.

A divine descent requires no less than an ascent to the Divine; there is a prospect of bringing down a future perfection and a present deliverance. As knowledge widens, it becomes increasingly evident that it was for this that the Master of works cast down the soul within each as a spark of the Eternal light into the darkness. It can grow here into a center of the light that is forever.

There is a light where the transcendent and universal and individual Divine are blissfully joined. For this realization an ascent out of the mind is imperative. There must be with the ascent a dynamic descent of the self-existent truth that exists always, uplifted on its own, above mind, eternally present in the manifestation of life and matter.

The individual consciousness will recover its true sense and action; for it is a form of a soul sent out from the supreme and, in spite of all appearances, a nucleus or nebula in which the Shakti Force is at work for the victorious embodiment of the timeless and formless Divine in Time and Matter. This will reveal itself slowly to our vision and experience as the will of the Master of works and their own ultimate significance, which alone gives to world-creation and to our action in the world a bright meaning.

(from Jim Bean's Journal extracts from Sri Aurobindo's Synthesis of Yoga.)

"Pondicherry by the sea, this is where I want to be," Roslyn had written to her father, Bernie, after meeting Mother in October. He replied he was coming for a visit.

Bernie and Roslyn had finally become friends a few years earlier when he visited her in Mexico and she fed him LSD. They spent a memorable day running around in his rented Volkswagen bug with her Indian friend Antonio, from the jungles of Nayarit, playing with the ocean on the beach in Matachan and drinking tender coconut water. They laughed a lot, and Bernie started a beard that he wore until he died.

They had really connected on some level, after being part of a family wherein there was not much affection or communication. That day they laughed so much together that the relationship changed. Bernie's role changed from the responsible unapproachable parent, to the friend.

Bernie was an American Jewish dentist. He was a person concerned with and committed to the community. He lived most of his life in the small town in Pennsylvania where he was born and where Roslyn was born. He was always active in local organizations, that worked for the benefit of the town at large, or to help people to help themselves. He had dabbled in real estate and construction, but his basic income was from dentistry.

He was always trying to push Roslyn to shape-up, if he paid any attention to her at all. When they tripped together in Mexico he had enough self honesty to laugh a lot.

He had come to see Roslyn in Berlin after Bliss was born. People in that family simply did not go around having babies out of wedlock, but he was willing to forgive-and-forget and take Bliss back to the USA and find someone to adopt her.

Roslyn told him to "Fuck off!"

They flew to Crete, because she convinced him that she was going to India with Bliss, and Crete was East of Berlin and warmer in winter. From Crete he flew back to Pennsylvania. He left Roslyn and Bliss in Crete with about $20 and a promise of $100 a month - mailed to wherever Roslyn told him to mail it - for a year.

The year was ending, and Bliss and Roslyn were in Pondicherry. Roslyn was happy and comfortable. She was thinner than she had ever been in her life. She had a bicycle with a basket for Bliss in the front, and they were both well and happy riding around town from the beach to The Ashram, to friends, to Equals One, to the Dining Room, to Tous Qu'il Faut, and to another eatery called Gompatram's. It was a daily round of simple wonder. In the evening sometimes Roslyn would give herself a treat, and go to the bazaar and have a Coca-Cola with ice. She was happy and active from morning until night, and every day she would find a new fragment of The Mother's World and learn something new.

For anyone who had ever imagined that they might like to live as part of a community rather than as an individual or nuclear family, The Mother's World, the Sri Aurobindo Ashram in Pondicherry, was an astonishing organization of like-hearted people. One of the premises of the yoga is that all relationships begin anew every day. The only thing to rely on is The Divine.

The yoga of The Mother and Sri Aurobindo, Integral Yoga, encompasses every part of life. Roslyn had met the nicest and most interesting people she had ever met living in Pondicherry that fall. By the time her father arrived she had friends from Italy, France, Holland, Brooklyn, Boston, Canada, Sweden, Germany, fascinating people, beautiful children, and felt part of a community with the goal to build the new town of Auroville. She wanted to be in Auroville.

There were little quotations of The Mother posted and changed regularly in the library, Dining Room and Ashram playground. Roslyn always found these quotations inspiring. "Auroville will be a place for all who aspire to live the Truth of tomorrow." "Auroville will be a place where people can live away from all national rivalries, social conventions, self-contradictory moralities and contending religions." "All those of goodwill who find that the world is not as it ought to be are welcome." Roslyn, reading these aphorisms, felt she was being reminded of what she knew she really wanted and what would make her happy. She wanted to live in Auroville with Bliss.

Bernie arrived at the Madras airport after days of sitting on airplanes from Philadelphia to New York to London, Frankfurt and Kuwait, then finally Bombay, where he had gotten a hotel room for a few hours before getting on another plane to Madras. He arrived in Madras to get in a taxi with Roslyn and Bliss for the four hour ride from the airport to Pondicherry.

It took Roslyn about a year to get from New York to Pondicherry. He had done it in two days. The car was a standard Indian taxi, with a driver who drove on the wrong side of the road, because everyone drives on the wrong side of the road in India. Bernie was not feeling good when he got off the plane.

He was not in the taxi for five minutes, then it started.

Roslyn said, "We are going to meet Mother tomorrow."

"Who is this Mother?" he asked.

"The Divine Mother."

"I am taking Bliss back to America with me. Children die in India. You can do anything you want with your life, but she deserves a chance."

She let him go on for about five minutes. He was just like he had been when he arrived in Mexico. She knew it was going to be okay, but she had to stop him from going on in that vein because it was not interesting, and it was leading to a big argument between them. She interrupted him and said, "Look Bernie, tomorrow I am taking you to meet The Mother, and if you think you can do more for Bliss than She can, then you can take Bliss."

So it was settled; no argument, he was going to take Bliss back to the USA and find some nice people to adopt her, and Roslyn was going to keep Bliss in Pondicherry and take her to Auroville.

"There used to be a guy in Philadelphia who called himself Father Divine," Bernie said.

"I don't think it is the same as The Divine Mother," Roslyn replied.

"He was a con."

"Let's not talk about Mother until after you meet Her," she suggested.

"Did you bring me any money?" she asked.

He unbuckled his belt. She became worried, frightened he might hit her with it in the taxi because she was already giving him a hard time, but he grinned at her as he pulled it through the loops of his pants — which didn't threaten to fall down without it. Bernie had a very big waist, and his exceptional black leather belt had a zipper which ran the full length of the inside of the belt. He handed the belt to Roslyn. She opened the zipper. There were neatly rolled wads of hundred dollar bills around the entire circumference. He took it back before she opened the zipper all the way, but it was clear that he had enough money for a very fun couple of weeks in Pondicherry.

"You told me to bring cash," he said coyly.

She did not want to fight with him. She wanted him to give her some money to repay some of the hospitality she had been receiving from her wonderful friends. She had planned a party for Bliss's birthday, and invited all her friends from Pondi, even some of the friendlier people from Aspiration. She did not have the money to pay for the cakes she had ordered from Poorna.

The road was terrible, because it was just after the monsoon and there were parts that were washed out. They had to drive across muddy detours. The car was hot and uncomfortable, but there were palm trees and a new horizon, and as soon as they stopped laying trips on each other it was fun being together. Bliss was his first and only grandchild then, and she was very charming, with blonde curls, quiet and cuddly. She seemed to recognize him, although she had not seen him since she was three weeks old. He was in India, which was not where he had ever imagined he might be. Rudyard Kipling was as close to India as he had hoped to ever get, and there he was in a hot car on a dusty road with a little black driver that was going like hell down the wrong side of the road, barely missing bullock carts, cows, people on bicycles.

Halfway between Madras and Pondicherry, after Roslyn admonished him for his back seat driving, Bernie got out and went to sit in the front seat with the driver, taking Bliss.   For the rest of the ride Roslyn leaned over the back seat talking to him, while he made friends with the driver and stopped and admired flower garlands and ancient villages and skinny little children.

Roslyn had arranged for Bernie to stay at The Grand Hotel on Rue Suffren in Pondicherry. John Kelly and Ananta's friend, the Countess de B., were staying there rather than in an Ashram guesthouse, because they enjoyed the brandy. The countess was looking for an apartment. She had decided to stay in Pondicherry. Roslyn, Bernie and Bliss arrived at the hotel. Kelly and the Countess were sitting on the upstairs terrace near Bernie's room. They invited Roslyn, Bernie and Bliss to dine with them on the terrace.

Bernie took one look at the Countess and thought he was in love. She was, as usual, beautifully dressed and made up, with her honey blonde curls delicately framing her very lovely face. She said, "Excuse me, I don't speak English."

He replied, "Excuse me, I don't speak French."

She smiled at him, "I speak a little English, no?"

He was devastated by her charming accent.

Kelly introduced himself, and offered Bernie a drink. They were soon all sitting and chatting on the terrace like old friends.

Bernie gave Roslyn a trunk full of clothes and toys for Bliss that her mother had sent, and she took it back to the Shelter Guesthouse where she and Bliss were still staying, to change for dinner. She had made new clothes for herself and Bliss in gold satin and purple satin, but she had beautiful silk to wear over the satin, and Bliss had a pile of adorable new dresses from grandma.

It was a great evening. M. Magry had found a set of candelabras somewhere. The moon was full, and there was a light breeze from the sea. There was white wine at the beginning of the meal and red wine with the meat. Stories of the French Resistance and American Liberation in W.W.II, were included with the wine, and champagne with dessert. More stories with dessert, coffee and brandy, about The Mother and Sri Aurobindo.

Bernie had flown to India to rescue his starving granddaughter and was met by this great colonial sartorial splendor, the comforting companionship of another American, John Kelly, and the enchanting companionship of Countess de B., who was not much less glamorous than Garbo, and maybe more interesting, but he was not interested in The Divine Mother.

Roslyn left Bernie and Kelly in rattan chaise lounges smoking Bernie's Cuban cigars in the moonlight and swapping lies. The Countess had gone to her room. Bliss and Roslyn left promising to return for breakfast.

Bliss's first birthday dawned bright and clear. Bernie was pounding on the door to Roslyn's room before she was even out of bed.

He was in a great mood, excited about being in India and Pondicherry. He had come in a bicycle rickshaw that he had hired for the day. He wanted to see what they did in the morning, so Roslyn got on her bicycle and he followed her in his rickshaw, pedaled by a thin little black man who was less than half his size. They went to The Ashram beach for a swim. Bernie was horrified to see Roslyn in the ocean with the baby loosely tucked into her arms. Roslyn told him the terrible story about how one day she was in the ocean with Bliss and a wave came and knocked the baby out of her arms, and for a moment in the vast sea she'd lost her, and was terrified that she might have lost her forever, but when she reached for her there she was. The sea had given Bliss back to Roslyn.

Bernie thought Roslyn was interesting, but too loose to be a responsible parent. He reassured Bliss that she would be okay because he would take her to the USA and find her a good home. Bliss liked Bernie and was very nice to him. She treated him as though she knew he was her grandfather, but Bliss and Roslyn were inseparable. Bliss did not like it much if she could not reach out and touch Roslyn, and she refused to tolerate it if she could not see or hear Roslyn. They had been on the road together, step by step across half the world, and Bliss was very clear that Roslyn was her person. She did not like it if Roslyn was not right there. Roslyn liked Bliss, although she would go off at times without the baby — and Bliss often screamed until Roslyn came back. Bliss had no fear of other people, and would happily go to anyone as long as Roslyn was there, but she did not like to be left with other people, and usually gave the servant, Marie, a hard time when Roslyn would leave them together.

Bliss was one year old, and had survived and thrived. Although Bernie was relieved to find that she was a very happy and healthy child, he still thought she would be better off in the USA.

After a refreshing sea bath and an argument because Bliss deserved a more responsible parent, they went to the hotel for breakfast. Puffy golden omelets done to a turn and fresh French bread. They ate, and met Kelly, who was taking them out to where his servant Gabrielle lived. They all got into the ancient car Kelly had gotten and drove out to this little village at the edge of town. Tiny huts roofed with palm leaves were packed tightly together. Whole families lived in each hut. Gabriel, his wife and all their children (seven or eight) welcomed them warmly on the dusty street outside their hut. The hut was so small that it seemed difficult to imagine where there would be room for everyone, even standing up. Gabriel's neighbors joined them on the street, and gave them flowers. Bliss was sitting on the arm of one of the women, and Roslyn picked up one of the other children. Bliss shouted at her from the other side of the circle of people, "Mama!!"

It was her first word. Kelly thought she was mute. Bernie thought there was something wrong with her hearing, because she seemed very quiet when he'd gone to see her when she was born in Berlin. She never cried. She was so quiet he suspected she was deaf, so he clapped his hands loudly over her as she was lying on the bed, looking peacefully up at him. She did not stir, not a start, not a quiver. She did not respond at all to the loud noise he had made. He was certain there was something wrong with her. Roslyn did not feel there was anything wrong with her. She did not talk, but there were occasions when she screamed. She was very capable of communicating, even without talking. She really did not like Roslyn picking up other babies. So, she had something to say, and she said it.

Bernie gave some money to Gabriel, and they got back in the car and went to The Ashram to get bouquets of flowers to offer to The Mother in the afternoon.

Back at the hotel it was lunchtime, and another huge meal. Bliss was drinking beer with John Kelly, who was going to meet them in the afternoon - after they had been to Mother - at a friend's apartment above Tous Qu'il Faut on the beach, for Bliss's birthday party. Bernie had brought a bottle of Jim Beam for the occasion.

Roslyn rushed to the guesthouse after lunch to dress to go to The

Mother, then cycled to The Ashram to meet Bernie and Mari.

Mari was waiting for them at the gate, and had a little gift for Bliss. Bernie arrived a moment later.

Mari led them upstairs to a beautiful little balcony off Sri Aurobindo's rooms, at the bottom of the staircase to The Mother's room, and asked them to wait. She told them she would call them when The Mother was ready to see them, and disappeared up the stairs.

Bernie pulled one of his huge cigars from Havana out of his pocket and proceeded to clip the end and light it.

Roslyn was so embarrassed. "You can't do that here."

"Why not? We are the only people here." They could see down into The Ashram courtyard at other people, but no one was looking up towards them..

"It is forbidden to smoke in The Ashram," Roslyn said.

He took another long puff on the long brown pungent cylinder, smiled at her, and said "Relax."

She had put Bliss on the mosaic marble floor with the flowers. She was sitting there in the sun surrounded with flowers, like a cherub Buddha.

Bernie took another puff on his cigar, and another great cloud of pungent smoke went into The Ashram atmosphere. Roslyn was trying to quiet her mind, and compose herself to be receptive to The Mother.

Mari came back. "Mother is ready to see you now. She said the cigar smoke reminds Her of Sri Aurobindo."

Bernie put out his cigar. Roslyn scooped up Bliss and the flowers.

Mari said, shyly to Bernie, "People kneel in front of Mother, to make it easy for her to look at them."

Bernie replied. "I do not kneel in front of anyone."

Mari did not say anything more and led them up the stairs and into Mother's room.

Just as She had been when Roslyn was there in October, Mother was sitting in Her chair in the center of the medium sized room, only the room was full of baskets of treats that Mother was preparing for her disciples and guests for Christmas. Roslyn ignored Bernie, went and knelt in front of Her, and set Bliss down on the carpet.

Mother said to one of Her attendants, "Please bring a chair."

Bernie said, "I don't need a chair," and knelt in front of Her.

No one said anything for a long moment. Then Mother turned to Roslyn and asked her, "Where are you staying?"

Again, Roslyn was speechless.

Mari answered for her, "Shelter Guesthouse."

Mother turned to Bernie and gave him a small green plastic basket full of little gifts, then She gave Roslyn a small green plastic basket also full of gifts. She gave Bliss a little hand made stuffed animal plus some sweets and flowers. She gave Bernie and Roslyn roses. She gave Bliss a birthday card, and told Roslyn, "Bring Bliss to me again, next year, on her birthday."

They all shared a moment of silence. Mother smiled at them, then Mari led them out of the room.

Roslyn did not know why, but being in The Presence of The Mother was one truly marvelous experience. People seemed to actually change in the seconds or minutes they spent in that Presence.

When they got to The Ashram gate Bernie stuffed all the things in his basket into the corner of the seat of his rickshaw, put the little green plastic basket upside down on his head, and started skipping down the street to the beach. Bernie weighed around 300 pounds, and was wearing Bermuda shorts, high socks, nice comfortable shoes, a clean white cotton sports shirt, gray hair, receding hairline, small goatee, and was not at all the kind of person you would expect to see skipping down the street with a green plastic basket on his head in South India in the middle of the afternoon.

"What are you doing?" Roslyn asked him.

His little man with the rickshaw he had hired for the day was following him. She easily kept up with him on her bicycle.

"I am only doing what everyone else is doing here," he replied, "Turning inside out.   I think I haven't skipped since I was a kid. It's fun!" but then he got back into the waiting richkshaw.

Bernie left after New Year, 1970.

Bliss and Roslyn were in Pondicherry, and Bernie had agreed to continue to send Roslyn $100 a month.

She was in better shape than she had ever been in her life, and weighed less than she had weighed at sixteen. She looked well, she felt well, she was happy.

Each day dawned bright and clear. She would get on her bicycle with Bliss and go to The Ashram, offer a flower and a stick of incense at Sri Aurobindo's tomb, and sit under "The Happiness Tree," for a little while.

The rest of the day would be spent swimming, eating, visiting friends.

By Mother's birthday, February 21st, she was feeling a bit bored with her wholesome life, and felt she was ready to meet an interesting man.

All the devotees gathered around Sri Aurobindo's Samadhi at ten in the morning for meditation. It was Mother's birthday, and there seemed to be a special glow or hum in the atmosphere.

By ten in the morning The Ashram was full of people. Even at six in the morning there were hundreds of people, and the flower arrangement on Sri Aurobindo's Samadhi was exquisite. There was a special silk canopy over the tomb. Roslyn was sitting daydreaming in the soft, sweet early morning. Many people were wearing white. All the women in The Ashram had been given new saris by The Mother, white voile saris with Mother's symbol printed along the border. There were many of these, and a few splendid silk saris. Aurovilians were also there, looking very tanned, in shorts, a completely different vibration to the people living in Pondicherry. There were many visitors, quietly dressed. The Aurovilians were a vivid color, perhaps slightly barbarous in the quiet gentle group gathered around Sri Aurobindo's tomb. The other foreign visitors to The Ashram had opted to nearly blend in with the respectful, devout community of The Ashram, wearing white or modest pastel colors, but the Aurovilians seemed to be another resonance. Even though there was profound silence in the courtyard as they sat alone or in groups among the silent devotees, the Aurovilians seemed somehow to be more noisy. Roslyn sat alone in a beautiful silk sari, with ardent devotees around her. She was sitting silently in Mother's garden under Mother's windows, behind which She sat in silence radiating blessings to the throng of devotees filling every nook and cranny of The Ashram. The place was redolent with harmony, love, peace and prayer, full of gratitude that She had brought everyone together, Her children in Her garden, from every part of humanity, representatives. All this struck Roslyn as she sat on a step in the staircase near the foot of The Samadhi, dressed in her gorgeous silk sari made in The Ashram.

She felt alone among all the people. She did not belong to The Ashram or Auroville. She was there invited by The Mother, welcomed by The Mother, and content to sit in Her courtyard on Her birthday among Her devotees, but instead of asking for the Supramental transformation or something useful or important, she was thinking, "Mother, I would like to meet a really interesting man."

That afternoon Roslyn ran into Ananta and Kelly at Darshan, and they invited her to have dinner with them at The Liberty Hotel.

The Liberty Hotel in Pondicherry is the set for all those bad bars in all the old movies, with scenes usually starring William Holden, down and out, in the last port along the last sandy beach. There's usually a whirling ceiling fan, which doesn't move fast enough to bother the flies, and Holden's is typically the only white face in the room.

The Liberty Hotel is on a dusty road behind the railroad. Occasionally one could run into a Greek sailor there, and Ananta loved Greeks. Kelly liked it because it served good hard whiskey.

There she was sitting at the table next to the door, with her good friends, and in walked an incredibly handsome man. He was over six feet tall, with the most handsome face, blue eyes, and long carefully combed brown hair, worn like George Washington, in a small bun on his neck. His was a princely demeanor, and he walked like a wary animal.

He looked at Roslyn. She looked at him. Collision!!

Roslyn was the only woman in the room except Bliss, who was 14 months old and sitting demurely in a chair. Ananta was also instantly smitten. The tall handsome stranger walked over and introduced himself, Edward Loring. He asked if he could join them and buy a round of drinks. Ananta said something in Greek, and Edward replied in Greek. Kelly kind-of looked at the ceiling and just said, "Oh my God!"

Loring was not only handsome and elegant, but gracious, spoke Greek, and bought everyone drinks. As usual, Roslyn was drinking Coca-Cola.

Kelly explained to Edward that they were meeting on an auspicious day: after all, it was The Mother's birthday. Edward had never heard of Mother, but he spoke Greek, and Ananta assured him that the great Greek demi-god Alexander had also visited Pondicherry. There was a very exuberant atmosphere. The bar closed at eleven, and finally the barkeeper turned out the lights. Edward bought ten bottles of beer and invited everyone to join him in his room. Kelly bid everyone goodnight and got in a rickshaw to go home to bed. Ananta and Roslyn were feeling rowdy. They went upstairs with Edward, into a room with a large bed with a blonde woman in it.

They all sat on the bed because there was nowhere else to sit. The blonde woman paid no attention to them. She did not seem to be asleep, just not sociable. Edward assured them they were welcome.

Roslyn was sitting there with Bliss. Ananta and Edward were drinking beer, when suddenly Ananta threw himself into Edward's arms. Edward said, "Pardon me, but I am a lesbian," and made a lunge for Roslyn. Then they were lying on this bed smooching between a sleeping blonde woman and Bliss. Bliss started screaming.

Roslyn had noticed Ananta creeping out with all the unopened beer bottles. It wasn't comfortable to be making out and listening to Bliss screaming, so she untangled herself from Edward and said she had to go home.

Being in a super gallant mode at that moment, he would not hear of it unless he escorted her home. She agreed.

She was living in a little cell with a narrow single bed for herself and Bliss, but she let Edward put them in a rickshaw while he accompanied them on her bicycle.

It was very romantic sitting in a rickshaw moving soundlessly down the quiet moonlit streets, with a beautiful handsome stranger riding alongside to protect her from any dark forces that might waylay her in the night.

They got to the guesthouse and found the street door locked. Roslyn had to bang on it and shout until she woke the watchman, who then came down and unlocked the door. Edward seemed unwilling to say goodnight there, so she invited him into the room. They put Bliss on the bed and laid the mat on the floor. He told her great stories of romance and heroism. They got up in the morning and went to find a place to stay. He and the blonde lady were only friends traveling together. They didn't want to travel together anymore. He wanted to stay with Roslyn in Pondicherry.

She told him about Auroville. He thought it sounded interesting.

February 28th is Auroville's birthday. For that year, 1970, Mother gave Auroville a word for the day, "Change."

Austin from Equal's One was moving to his hut on Quiet Beach in Auroville. He had invited many of his friends to join him on February 27th in the afternoon, to go with him in a long boat, a traditional large balsa wood fishing boat which had neither a sail nor an engine, just a crew of several Tamil fishermen with oars. Tamil fishermen had been using boats like that since time immemorial.

Edward was still with Roslyn and Bliss. They had spent the week in the hotel on the park, eating huge meals and making love. Bliss was not happy sharing Roslyn.

Edward had confessed to Roslyn, as all lovers do, that he had been married twice and had no children, but had many lady loves. He had only been really in love once before, and that was when he was young and studying at a European University. He had fallen in love with a very beautiful, very young woman named Lorelei, and she suddenly disappeared from his life one day.

In the late afternoon on the 27th of February they met Austin and a bunch of other people on the beach, and got into the boat, which put out to sea. Riding in the prow Roslyn felt like Cleopatra on her barge, with Bliss on her lap, her lover at her side, friends all around, and a crew of small black men singing a song nearly as old as the sea as they rowed.

They watched the white houses of the town disappear, and saw little villages interspersed with large coconut groves, and long white beaches. The boat floated over the surf into the shore.

There was a large compound, a big piece of sand surrounded by a hastily constructed fence made from casurina poles and coconut palm leaves. There were some small huts like in German Swami's ashram, with mud walls and coconut palm roofs. In one of these huts dinner had been prepared for them by Austin's Tamil servants. They consisted of a nice looking young man with a mustache and open smile named Kennan, Austin's butler or batman, and his very pregnant wife Elamma, who cooked, plus her mother Ellamalu, who just sat near the fire.

There was a very strange equality in Mother's world. There were ten or fifteen guests who came in on the boat and six or eight fishermen. Bamboo mats were set in a large square on the sand and Austin invited everyone to sit. Ellama, Kennan and Ellamalu served a memorable high tea on banana leaves, with stainless steel cups for tea and aluminum cups for water. Everyone was friendly, happy, jovial. There were people from Italy, Canada and France, Tamil fishermen, and Austin. Austin was a great red headed Irish Canadian dressed always in a plain white cotton longi with a white cloth over his shoulder, constantly regaling everyone with lyrical stories of his adventures and his delight and gratitude as a child and devotee of The Mother. Austin loved women in general, and The Mother in particular.

He was fun to be with. It was a crackling and very sandy tea. After tea they went down to the beach for the sunset, and Edward swam so far out into the Bay of Bengal that people on the shore were concerned; for his safety. Everyone went back into the compound and slept on mats on the sand using longis for bedsheets.

At dawn some people from Pondicherry came out to join them for meditation on the beach, as the sun was rising over the ocean at the beginning of the new day, Auroville's birthday. The Mother had given Auroville a word for the day, "Change."

Roslyn's friend Lorelei had come with the group from Pondicherry. She and Edward took one look at one another and ZAP! There she was! The beautiful, wonderful, adorable Lorelei, the woman, who had just disappeared one day from his life, the woman he had never been able to forget, and in that instant Roslyn was forgotten.

But she was with Bliss in Auroville. The adventure had begun.

Nothing belongs to anybody in particular in Auroville. No one belongs to anyone in particular. Auroville belongs to no one in particular, but to humanity as a whole, and is an experiment.

Roslyn's great quest, her great adventure, her big trip, had led her to Auroville through vast spaces without and within.

By the time Bliss and Roslyn went to live in Auroville on February 28th, 1970, Roslyn was convinced that she had been called to come with Bliss to participate in the great experiment which The Mother was building there to the north of Pondicherry.

It was to be a place of transcendental truth. Ego would not be sovereign; people would be kind, and aspire for peace, human unity, the Supramental transformation, etc. But what people would these be? People like Roslyn? She was just not a great person, in some ways. She was one of the all-time spoiled brats of American civilization.

When her father, Bernie, came to see her when Bliss was born, he accused her of having broken all the ten commandments.

She could not plead guilty or not guilty. She only knew and felt a sound within which resonated as her path. She was committed to following that.

Her sweet, kind, loving grandmother once looked at her with gentle affection and said, "You are a lost soul!

Despite all of that, she felt confident that she had been called by The Divine Mother to participate in Her great experiment — to build a town which would celebrate the "truth of human unity," a town which would belong to no-one in particular, but to humanity as a whole, and would be a precursor of the Supramental transformation of the planet. It would be the perfect town. A gorgeous model had been designed by the famous French architect. Architects from the United States and Europe had come to live on the site and help the great vision of a truly new city, not just another city, but a truly new city, built in a new way, on new precepts, by people dedicated to the future.

She did not care what her father and grandmother thought about her. She did not know what she wanted, but it was not what they were trying to give her. She might not have been a perfect person, and probably the others who came to work together as a representative humanity were equally imperfect, but all shared some identification with the goals of Auroville.

Mother had said at one point, something like, "You can not have Auroville, and ego." They were all full of ego and ignorance. There, even on "the sunlit path," they were able to create huge pockets of darkness.

And then there was the challenge of Auroville itself. Shayma, who had brought a bit of the earth of Sweden to the opening ceremony on February 28th, 1968, to mix in the urn at the center of Auroville with bits of earth from everywhere else in the world, plus the earth of Auroville, told Roslyn that there was a quality of great heroism in the opening ceremony. The representatives of all the nations made their offering at the urn, mixing the earth of their native lands with the earth of all the other nations in a gesture symbolising the unity of Mother Earth. The urn was sealed with a piece of marble into which the Mother's signature had been engraved, like a great mantra. The representatives of the children of the mothers of the world sat in a circle around the urn with other guests and devotees of The Mother, listening together to the tape The Mother had prepared for that event. She read the Auroville Charter in English and French. Shayma said, "It was like a declaration of war on the dark forces. Nothing like that had ever happened before in the world. It was almost frightening, The Divine had claimed a bit of earth for the Supramental transformation and something new and marvelous had been declared."

Sri Aurobindo had said, "Everything is Divine, even the devil is Divine."

The yoga of Sri Aurobindo and The Mother is a process of transformation. The process of transformation is an integral part of the substance of every yogi, leader, teacher. From some plane there is an empowerment of a being to be in the physical dimension, but somehow seemingly transcending normal limitations.

The whole project of Auroville was bathed in charisma. "The cradle of the superman" promised to transcend everything which had been done before. There would be no need to make all the same mistakes everyone else had already made. Mother had said of Sri Aurobindo, "He has done everything for us." Roslyn took that to mean that going to Auroville would be like going to the Supramental world, and everything would always be wonderful, golden and blissful there. The City of God, utopian communities, spiritual communities, have always been attractive to some weird people.

A friend had told Roslyn that Mother had been working with the community around Her in Pondicherry for countless lifetimes.

It was a very eccentric, but cohesive community. The ingredients were as disparate as possible. People were from all over the globe, from all walks of life, from every imaginable spiritual background, all bound by the personal belief in one's own individual experience, which resounded so profoundly with their personal inner truth that they dropped their real lives in the real world and came to live in Mother's World.

The Ashram had 2,000 residents in 1968, and an excellent school. There were industries, businesses, galleries, playgrounds, farms, a theater, but it was not like a kibbutz. There didn't seem to be any rules, just the expectation of simple human decency.

Mother ruled absolutely, a benevolent dictator, and she said, "If you do not like it, leave." Those who stayed loved it. Many people loved The Ashram and Mother and Sri Aurobindo, but did not come to live in Pondicherry, they just visited regularly. There is great joy and power in a large group of people around an enlightened master.

Then The Mother, with the help of the Sri Aurobindo Society, started Auroville, as a town which would be a great experiment in human unity and community. Auroville would also demonstrate The Yoga in day to day life.

The first three people who went to stay near the Banyan Tree and site of the amphitheater at the center of Auroville in 1968 - Arindam, Gene and Jane - were constantly fighting, and there were letters to Mother day after day. Finally She responded: "Goodwill towards all, goodwill from all is the basis of peace and harmony." She then named the center area of Auroville "Peace!"

On February 28th, 1970, Mother had given Auroville that word for the day, "Change."

Roslyn woke up that morning on a bamboo mat on the beach in Austin's compound at Quiet Beach in Auroville, between Bliss and Edward. They had gone with the others down to the beach at sunrise for meditation. On the beach they met Lorelei, Edward's long lost true love.

Everyone sat on the sand above the high tide mark and watched the sun rise over the Bay of Bengal. Was it only because they were watching, or because it was a special day, the birthday of the City of Dawn, that it seemed the sunrise was a light show of unbelievable splendor?

By the time the sky was the clear light blue of a typical South Indian morning, they were all ready for the long trek from the beach to the center of Auroville, along a path Austin had chosen through desolate land and ravines. They walked through the thorns and up the steep ravine first to Aspiration, where they had breakfast. Most of the people already living in Auroville joined them there for the walk to Auroson's Home, the first real house built in Auroville. Lorelei played her silver flute and Edward walked next to her, while Roslyn lagged far behind carrying Bliss, who at fourteen months did not know anything about walking.

At Auroson's Home they listened to some inspirational poetry by Rod, and then continued down the long hot dusty road. Roslyn had been traveling for 22 months, since the moment of the vision calling her to India, of Mother calling her to Auroville, and there she was walking alone, carrying Bliss down the hot dusty trail, far behind the group of Aurovilians and friends of Auroville walking together. She knew Edward had left her the moment he saw Lorelei. They were in the middle of the crowd in front of her. She had never felt more hot, tired and alone than she did that morning, walking to the Banyan Tree at the center of Auroville.

Near the center there were cars and a bus parked. Many people from the Ashram and the Sri Aurobindo Society had come to meditate at the Banyan and listen to the music The Mother had chosen for that event.

The meditation was over. A short guy came over to Roslyn and Bliss. He was wearing glasses, white shorts and a white shirt, but his feet were the red color of the Auroville earth. Everyone had gotten up after the meditation and were piling into the cars and bus, or into the trailer at the back of a tractor, ready to leave.

He was shaking his head, and said, "Look at everyone getting back in their vehicles to go back to Pondicherry, this is only the beginning of the meditation. This is Auroville. This is Auroville's birthday."

"Is it possible to stay here?" Roslyn asked.

"Certainly. There is an empty hut over there" he said, pointing to a cluster of three huts not far from the Banyan on the dusty plain.

"If we stay how can we get back to Pondi?" she asked.

"No problem. There is a Land-Rover that makes two trips every day into Pondi, and there is always the village bus."

"Let's stay," Edward said. Lorelei was going back on the bus.

"What will we do for food?" Roslyn asked.

"You can have lunch with me," the short man with glasses offered.

They accepted with alacrity. He introduced himself as Constance.

It seemed that everyone else had packed themselves into the vehicles that slowly pulled out down the dusty road. Suddenly there was just Edward, Bliss, Roslyn and Constance on the hot dry plateau that was the center of Auroville, and a small wizened Tamil woman who came out from her little hut near the Banyan Tree.

Constance took them over to one of the huts on the other side of the Banyan Tree. It had a concrete slab floor and palm leaf and bamboo walls and roof. "I can probably find you a couple of bamboo mats if you stay here tonight," he offered.

"That will be fine," Edward said.

"Where is the water?" Roslyn asked.

Constance replied, "I live next to the only working well in the center area. My house is called The Pump House."

"Are you the only one who lives here?"

"No. There are two other Americans - one an old friend of mine, the other a Japanese American - and a Canadian woman."

"What do they do for water?"

"Well, there is a bullock cart that carries a water tank which fills up at the pump and delivers water to everybody. There is going to be a new well near the Banyan soon."

"Could I live here?" Roslyn asked.

"Why don't you come and have lunch and we 'll talk about it."

He led them down a shallow rocky ravine and up an embankment onto a rocky, dusty road with deep ruts. All around the land looked hot, dry, parched. They came to a water tank and tap at the side of the road. "We keep this tank full for village people," Constance explained.

The tank was next to a gate in a fence around a field where some young trees had recently been planted. They entered the gate and saw the big round hut with a thatch roof that dominated the field. The hut had just been built using casurina poles in a circle, and tying the tops of the newly harvested green poles together in the middle of the roof to form the basic structure. Palm leaves, bamboo and thatch covered the structure. There was a cement floor and short brick wall between the casurina posts, and a space of about a foot and a half between the walls and the roof. The whole structure seemed to be held together by a large casurina center-post to which the treetops had been tied, and around which the roof structure had been built. It was imaginative and attractive, but did eventually collapse.

Outside in the garden were a couple of other huts. One housed the diesel pump that was used on the well, and the other was a small kitchen.

Constance bade them make themselves comfortable and disappeared into the kitchen.

The minute Constance left them alone Edward turned on Roslyn.

"You are not my woman and that is not my baby."

"What do you want to do?" she asked, feeling embarrassed and crushed.

"I like this Auroville project. It is interesting. I think it might be fun to stay here for a while. Maybe we can make a place here. I don't mind if you live with me, but I will not make love to you and I am in no way responsible for you and your brat."

Money was not really a problem for her at that moment. She had just received a large bonus from Bernie and her regular check for March.

She was sitting there, cut to the quick, when Constance arrived bearing a tray with tea and fried bread.

Edward asked Constance if there was any place near the pump where they could build a hut. Constance replied, "Just beyond the fence is a small village field, and beyond that a field which belongs to Auroville, which you could probably use. You would need Mother's permission and the chief architect's permission. Maybe the villager would let you put a water pipe across his field, so you could get water from the pump, but in any case the bullock cart could give you water."

Roslyn had no idea what she was letting herself in for. She was enjoying the fried bread and tea with raw palm sugar called jaggery. She decided that the first thing she would buy would be a gas stove, so even if they did not have any water they could eat. If they had a stove and some water, food could be brought out from Pondicherry. Constance told them that everyone living in Auroville got a half loaf of bread from the Ashram every day. No problem. Excellent whole wheat bread, a bullock cart to bring them water, a bamboo mat, checks from Bernie, and Roslyn felt she had all she needed to live in Auroville, which was where she wanted to be.

Edward and Constance were going to walk over to the field that Constance had proposed as a place where they might build. They invited her to join them, but she declined. She could see the piece of land they were talking about, a huge field, surrounded by a ring of ancient Palmyra trees.

Before they left she asked Constance to turn on the pump, so she could wash the dishes and take a bath. The water poured out of a pipe about waist high in front of the house into an irrigation ditch.

Constance and Edward came back. Edward said it was a fantastic piece of land, there wasn't even any soil, only rocks.

Constance warned them that because that field was in the area of the future town, they could only receive permission to build a temporary structure there. Roslyn had enough money to build a hut, not a house. She did not want to build her house. She wanted to live in Auroville. After more tea and fried bread they went back to the hut near the center with two borrowed bamboo mats to sleep on.

When they got there they noticed the door to the nearby hut was open. Standing in the doorway was Constance's friend, Rod, dressed all in white, with a long sparse beard and long hair looking a little bit like photos of young Sri Aurobindo, but talking with a soft Texas drawl. He seemed delighted with Bliss. He told them he was making a school near the other Banyan tree near the center of Auroville.

"But there aren't any children," Roslyn replied.

He laughed at her. "There are many children. There are thousands of Tamil children in the Auroville area. There are 23 Tamil villages in the area."

"Do you speak Tamil?" she asked.

"I am trying to learn," he replied.

They spent a very uncomfortable night in the hut, and Roslyn added mattresses, pillows, mosquito net, bedsheets and kerosene lamps as well as a stove and food to her shopping list for the next day.

The Land-Rover was not going into town until 11 o'clock, so they decided to walk to the village and get the village bus. They went to meet Constance, and he led them down the ravine road in front of his gate, across a big parched area with thorn fences, past scrawny dark brown children dressed in rags following emaciated cows and goats.

They heard the blast of a horn.

"Hurry up," Constance said, and burst into a run. Edward followed him. Roslyn could not keep up. She was carrying Bliss. She tried to run. They were in the village. She could hear the bus drive by and another blast of the horn. Edward and Constance had just missed it. They were standing under a big tree at the side of the road surrounded by the most pathetic group of children imaginable, when Roslyn caught up to them panting. The children were begging for 10 paise. Constance asked them why they wanted 10 paise. They replied that they wanted to buy a bit of tapioca. They were covered with running sores, their eyes were inflamed, and the boys wore only a scrap of rag tied to a string around their waist, the little girls tattered dirty skirts that nearly dragged on the ground. Roslyn was horrified. Bliss was clean, plump and astonishingly healthy by comparison: how could she live with her in a world where the local children were so filthy and ragged, with oozing eyes and sores?

"We can wait here for an hour, or we can walk to Coot Road on the Madras road, which is not far and catch a bus there," Constance suggested.

"Let's go." Edward said.

They set off on foot down the long hot dusty road. It was in fact a very beautiful road. At one point it was like a grand dusty avenue with huge coconut palms on either side. There were rice paddies on one side of the narrow dusty road, which was not wide enough for two cars, and a beautiful lotus pond on the other side. They passed a very ancient temple.

Roslyn finally caught up with Edward and Constance at a little tea stall where the dusty track met the Madras road. A few minutes later a bus stopped and they went on to Pondicherry.

Chapter VII

Forecomer's Dance Drama

vii

A vast Unknown is around us and with;
All things are wrapped in the dynamic One:
A subtle link of union joins all life.
Thus all creation is a single chain.

Sri Aurobindo, Savitri

In reality, no man works, but nature works through him for the self expression of a Power within that continues from the infinite. Not desire, not attachment, must drive him, but a Will that stirs in a divine peace, a knowledge that moves from the transcendent light, a glad impulse that is a Force from the supreme Ananda.

To love God in the world and to act so that the Divine may more and more manifest Himself. So the world will go forward by whatever way of its obscure pilgrimage and move nearer to the divine ideal.

All our concentration is merely an image of the divine tapas by which the self dwells gathered in itself, by which it manifests in itself, by which it maintains and possesses its manifestation, by which it draws back from all manifestation into its supreme oneness.

Being dwelling in consciousness of Bliss, this is the divine tapas.

This concentration goes on by the Idea, using thought, form and name as keys that yield up to the concentrating mind the truth that lies concealed behind all thought and name and form, for it is through the idea that the mental being replies to that which is experienced.

The self is eternal and all things are becoming.

I am that, the pure, the eternal, the self-blissful.

To find, know and possess the divine existence, consciousness or nature, and live in it is our true aim. The Divine is the one perfection to which we must aspire.

(from Jim Bean's Journal extracts from Sri Aurobindo's Synthesis of Yoga.)

Auroville might be just another variation of the hero in the contemporary planetary saga. The tale of the hero, from every climate and every culture, remains the same, an endless variety of details in many mirrors.

The hero has to strive to emerge from the mass, the transliterated external circumstances that represent the miasma of the past, the subconscious that he and everyone inherits.

Something extraordinary happens to the hero that prompts his awakening. He fights his ego and wins his soul.

The amazing aspect of Auroville's heroism is that Auroville does not represent the traditional hero, the individual. A group of people, caught in a process of manifesting a great vision, are forced individually and collectively to behave heroically.

Everyone who comes to live in Auroville must forsake the ordinary path his or her life might have taken among family and friends. Although everything that is happening everywhere never happened before, the permutation between what is happening in Auroville and elsewhere is obviously going to be more intense. It is a unique situation in the late twentieth century, the most dynamic and dangerous time in recorded history. Auroville is a place where people from all backgrounds, cultures, religions, walks of life, have come together for an experiment in human unity that would find the way through the soup of planetary disaster to a future humanity.

Auroville was a dream, a vision of the future imposed on the bleak South Indian landscape. People from Europe, the United States, India, answered Mother's call for people who were looking for something different in their lives, people who wanted to live a life dedicated to future humanity, and all that implied.

All this was marvelous and exciting, but, where and how were these exotic creatures going to live? They were just people, with two arms, two legs, a head, a torso, male, female, young, old, rich poor, skilled, unskilled, all obsessed with the mad thought that they wanted to live in the twenty square mile area which had been designated on the architect's map as Auroville.

The area was full of termites and mosquitoes, poor villages, with 100% illiteracy among the 20,000 villagers in the area, and no electricity. The land according to local legend had once been a forest, but there were no forests, the forests had been cut and the land badly eroded. Roslyn's friend, Edward found evidence of an ancient burial ground near the center of Auroville, that he said proved that in recent years all the topsoil had been washed away by monsoon floods because of the deforestation of the area. Roslyn remembered that during the monsoon rains the ocean near Pondi became the red color of the Auroville earth!

There was hardly a tree to be seen in whole area. The land was parched and hard, and herds of emaciated cows and goats, rambling in searching of any bit of green they could consume, had consumed nearly everything but the rocks. The plan for the town in the office in Pondicherry looked a bit like an intergalactic space station. Anyone with even a little bit of sense would have run away, but Roslyn did not have any sense, and she thought that the time was coming for something different from what her mother had achieved and offered her.

Stability, security, comfort, did not mean much to Roslyn, because she had always had them. She wanted something else, but she did not know what. Auroville sounded different from anything she had ever heard of, and completely in keeping with her ideals. A miniworld, a giant sandbox, where - protected by The Divine Mother - she and Bliss could play.

Roslyn was into joy, and blissing out, sharing and caring, just living. She had listened to Bobby Dylan and liked to think she was just a rolling stone.

But she was not a stone: she was a young woman with a little baby and she needed a place to live where her child could grow. She did not need to own anything, but she wanted a home.

The City of The Future was a noble vision that conformed to Roslyn's personal ideals. The City Earth Needs. In Pondicherry there were fancy and famous people talking about the most gorgeous town with the most wonderful gardens that ever were. Auroville was a majestic but very naked red clay plateau.

When Roslyn first went to Auroville she was told that the local zamindars* paid the villagers one rupee a day to work in their fields. Auroville paid three rupees a day and gave lunch, so all the villagers wanted to work in Auroville.

Roslyn had sent a letter to Mother through the chief architect asking permission to build a temporary house for herself, Edward and Bliss on the empty Auroville field near the Pump House. Mother replied, "Love and Blessings."

Roslyn took Bliss and walked to the big empty field surrounded by huge ancient Palmyra trees. She walked around the field and sat for a while under one of the Palmyra trees. She tried to understand what it would be like to live on that field in rural India, and decided to put a small hut there and find out. She would at least be living in Auroville. A young Tamil man approached her.

"My family was having this land before," he said.

"I am building a house here," she replied.

"I can help you," he said. "I am Ramchendran."

Roslyn introduced herself and Bliss.

"Where is father?" he asked.

"America," she replied.

"When you want starting building?"

"Tomorrow."

"I don`t know tomorrow starting. First I buying materials, everything, then starting."

Just then Edward arrived.

He extended his hand to the Tamil man, "I am Edward Loring."

Ramchendran took his hand briefly, and introduced himself.

"I am Ramchendran. My family was having this land before."

"I am building my house here," Edward said. "You can help me."

"I thought I was building my house here," Roslyn said.

"You his husband?" Ramchendran asked.

"We are friends. I will build a house here for her and then a house for myself.

"How big house you want?"

Edward gave Roslyn a stick and told her to draw the house she wanted in the dirt.

She had not really thought about it, but she drew a U shape, which she divided into two rooms with a side entrance and a front entrance. Edward asked her where she wanted to build. She said the corner of the field where they were standing was fine.

Edward went over to the Pump House and borrowed a measuring tape. Five minutes later he and Ramchendran were putting sticks in the ground where they would dig holes for the posts that would support the roof.

Roslyn asked Ramchendran to arrange a bullock cart. Edward made an appointment to meet him at Ganeshan Bamboo in Pondi the next day, and after tomorrow work would begin.

Roslyn and Edward were hardly talking to each other, but they were both involved in building the hut. Constance invited them to move in with him, and they were happy to leave the little hut at The Center.

They slept on mats on the floor, like spokes of a wheel around the center post, Bliss next to Roslyn, the two guys on the other side of the room. They had bought barrels for water, and Constance had arranged that the bullock cart would bring them a load of water every two days.

The roof went up very fast, and did not cost too much, but then it seemed the floor took a long time and cost a lot. They needed broken bricks, lime, cement, sand and small stones for the foundation. Roslyn was running out of money. Two more people had come to live with them at the Pump House, a young German couple Roslyn had met in Pondicherry, Geof and Gabi.

Edward was living with Jane, and never spoke to Roslyn.

The house was just a roof and a floor. There was no money left for walls, but the workers who had done the roof offered to make walls out of mud painted with whitewash, and so it went on, very slowly, with more expenses every day. A Dutch woman and her daughter who had met the German couple in Pondi came and stayed with them at the Pump House. There were seven or eight bodies sleeping on mats around the center pole every night, sharing food and sharing their lives. Roslyn seemed to be the only one with any money, so she was buying most of the food, but she had chosen to live in a community in Auroville, and did not regard money that came to her as exclusively hers; everything was now Mother's. Bliss and the German girl adopted one another, and this made Roslyn freer than she had been since Bliss was born.

She would leave Bliss in Auroville and go to Pondicherry, visit friends and shop. One day she went to see Mari.

Mari said that Mother had given her the name and blessings packet for Roslyn's house. She handed it to Roslyn, and Roslyn gave a loud whoop of laughter. Mari put her finger to her lips telling her to ssssh.

Mother had named Roslyn's house, "Silence."

Roslyn sent Mother a letter asking for permission to see her and receive her blessings before she moved into her new house. Mother gave her an appointment for Easter morning.

Easter is in April. It is indisputably hot by then in South India.

Roslyn felt that a darshan with The Mother certainly merited a new dress, and since she did not have much money she bought a secondhand purple silk sari in the bazaar. She went to the ribbon stall and continued to spend more money than she would have spent if she had bought a silk sari. She bought ribbons: satin ribbons in beautiful solid colors and plaid ribbons. Then she designed and made a dress that was very simple, but did not at all conform to the dress code standard of that time or place. It is strictly and horribly taboo for a woman to have uncovered shoulders in India. The dress was held up with ribbons, and had ribbon ruffles around the top and bottom. Ribbons tied in bows, or in double or triple bows with streamers of every length, were stitched haphazardly over the front and back of the torn purple silk.

She walked into The Ashram carrying Bliss on Easter morning, dressed in her crazy new dress that was already falling apart because the silk was so old.

She was feeling very sorry for herself, because Edward was being so hostile to her. She did not know what she was doing; she was just doing the best that she could in the circumstances, and she felt ridiculous in her new dress that had started to fall apart the moment she put it on. She did not even know why she was going through the trouble of going into Pondi to see The Mother, but she still had her room at Shelter Guesthouse.

It was the first time she had a morning appointment with The Mother. She had received a card that gave her a 9:30 a.m. appointment. She had a bouquet of flowers for Mother. As she went into The Ashram, from the gate to the staircase she felt people staring at her. Her dress aroused a very unfavorable reaction. She did not know about the taboo on naked shoulders. She tried to ignore the bad vibes and went on up the stairs. She went straight up to the balcony outside The Mother's room, and was amazed to see many people sitting there quietly, all apparently waiting to see The Mother.

There were pale blue awnings protecting the terrace from the direct onslaught of the sun.

For a moment Roslyn was overwhelmed to find there were so many people, but she adjusted to it and found an empty place next to the balcony rail where she sat with Bliss. There must have been at least a hundred people on the balcony, and at 9:30 a.m. it was already hot. It looked like a long wait. She may have recognized some of the faces, but they did not recognize her.

Most people were wearing white. There were many big gold symbols on thick gold chains. Everyone was very quiet. There was an atmosphere of meditation. Even Bliss was extraordinarily quiet, for a while. They sat and sat and sat. More people came, and the terrace became more and more crowded. Occasionally Mother's attendant would come and call someone into the room. Nothing was happening except that the terrace became ever more crowded. Roslyn felt increasingly lonely, and wondered if she could hold on. It got hotter and hotter, and Bliss started to fuss.

Hours passed. Roslyn would have left if she had anywhere more interesting to go, but she was having lunch at the Grand Hotel d'Europe, and it would not be served until one, so she had nothing to do and no place to go until then. She sat there, and watched the sky and what was happening in The Ashram courtyard, thinking about a quiet mind and a silent mind and silence.

The attendant came out and said, "Birthday people."

Many of the people stood up and formed a queue. The queue moved slowly but steadily, and then there were only a few people left sitting on the terrace, who one by one got up and joined the line. Finally she was the only one left, so Roslyn joined the end of the queue. She felt like crying. She was so depressed.

Then she was in The Mother's room, Bliss on one hip, a bedraggled bouquet in the other hand, moving towards Mother. The person in front of her moved away, and she went down on her knees in front of The Mother, who looked up at her and laughed ...and laughed ...and laughed, until Roslyn and Bliss were laughing with her also, like three happy fools. Mother gestured to Her attendant to give a little stuffed toy to Bliss, while she gave flowers and blessings' packets and her hand to Roslyn. Roslyn was overcome with love and joy. She got up and walked out feeling happy and confident that God, She, is alive and well in Pondicherry.

Roslyn felt beautiful as she came down the stairs from Mother's room. She went to The Hotel with Bliss and sat alone in the dining room at a table with a white starched cloth and napkin, set for one, and ate her way through a full four-course meal, Bliss sitting on her lap eating little tidbits out of her hand. She even let M. Magry persuade her to have a half bottle of wine with lunch.

The next morning it was time to go back out to Auroville. It was hot. Roslyn was still cheerful from Mother's Darshan and the good lunch of the day before. That is, she was still cheerful riding out in the Land-Rover, until she ran into Edward and Jane where the Land-Rover stopped at The Center. They were going into town. Roslyn had a hard time getting out of the Land-Rover with her shoulder bag, Bliss and two large wicker baskets of food for the community. Finally the driver of the Land-Rover got out and offered to help her, because the other passengers had emerged without offering any help. They had come out to work for the morning in The Nursery of the Matrimandir Gardens. One of the ladies had a big straw hat, a long Southern drawl and a name like Scarlet Finkleberger.

People were already talking about The Matrimandir, the Mother's Tomb, but Roslyn could not imagine why people wanted to build a tomb for Mother. Mother was doing the Supramental transformation and was not going to die.   Mother loved flowers and gardens.

It was commendable that ladies with widebrimmed straw hats would venture out into the day to work at The Nursery, that was running on two bullock carts of water a day, meanwhile dreaming of the great garden that would surround Matrimandir..

The City of the Future looked a long way away It was a long walk from where the Land-Rover stopped to the Pump House, and there were no rickshaws. Roslyn had given her bicycle to Lorelei, because Lorelei could not afford rickshaws and did not have a cycle and needed one. Bliss was not into walking, but seemed to enjoy riding Indian-style on Mama's hip.

Edward and Jane did not look at or speak to Roslyn as they got into the Land-Rover. Roslyn left the baskets of groceries with the watchman, hoping that one of the other people living at The Pump House or their tamby* would fetch them. She had more than enough to carry with Bliss and her shoulder bag. She considered leaving Bliss with the watchman, but she would have howled, so Roslyn set out from The Center to the Pump House. Although the Pump House is only a few furlongs from The Center, it was so hot that Roslyn could hardly breathe by the time she got there.

She dumped Bliss in the German girl's arms, and collapsed.

"Didn't you bring us any food?" the German guy asked.

"Yes, but I left it at The Center."

"Yes, just as I thought. I will go and get it; who will come with me?" Geof asked.

The Dutch lady's daughter offered to go with him. There was a new face under an unkempt beard, dressed in tattered cloths wrapped or flung over parts of the body, speaking with a broad Australian accent.

"Hi, I'm Owen. Geof and Gabi brought me here on Saturday night, and I have decided to stay."

"But you can't just decide to stay here, you have to ask The Mother's permission," Roslyn said.

"How do I do that?"

"You send her a letter. Sometimes She asks for a photo."

He shrugged his shoulders, "Whatever; but anyhow I'm here now. I am working over there on the new house site. I hear we're all going to be thrown out of here."

"What?"

The Dutch lady interjected, "Constance has had to ask us to move on, because he had been asked to vacate. Some guy who lived here before was having an affair with an American lady in Pondicherry. He seduced her seventeen-year-old daughter, and claims they were married by The Mother. He wants to bring his bride home to his place in Auroville. This had all happened in the last couple of days."

"That place isn't ready!"

"We have to move out of here today. Constance already left. He decided to move back to Pondi for a while."

"We'd better build a kitchen over there. With so many people in the hut we have to have a separate hut for our food trips."

Roslyn was relieved that Bernie had sent her some extra money. She had written to him that she was building in Auroville.

They made a great feast and moved into the new house, 'Silence', that night. She and Bliss slept on the sand pile in front of the house. It was a little chaotic, but somehow it was alright until the next day, when Roslyn received a summons to the Auroville Office in Pondicherry. Mr. Vasudeva, who was acting chief, said there had been complaints that there were people living at Silence without Mother's permission. Roslyn found out that Edward and Jane had been complaining, and it seemed Edward wanted Mother to throw everyone out of Silence and take the place himself. Mother sent a reply, "Nothing belongs to anybody in particular in Auroville, everything is to be used for the welfare of all."

Roslyn felt this reply supported the community at Silence, and thought that would be the end of the matter, but Jane and Edward wrote again to The Mother. This time Mother's reply was to suggest to Roslyn that she move 'Silence' across town to a field where there was a big well, but no other Auroville development. Roslyn did not want to move, and the matter was dropped finally when Jane left for Canada to raise money for Auroville and Edward went to Europe.

They finally all got permission from The Mother to be at Silence, and Silence was accepted as another sub-community in the growing community of Auroville.

The summer was uneventful, except that it was very hot. Owen left, after going to The Ashram Playground roaring drunk for a Saturday night movie, and getting Aurovilians banned from The Ashram cinema forever. Margie moved in. Roslyn built a kitchen, and a patio connecting the kitchen to the house. The Dutch lady built another hut and then moved to Pondicherry. Margie built a small hut at the far end of the field. Mother named it "Surrender."

The honeymoon couple moved out of the Pump House after a couple of weeks, and a pregnant Chinese/Malaysian woman and her French husband moved in.   They already had a daughter, Aura, who was a few months younger than Bliss.

They were all friendly, working with Lorelei in Pondicherry, and had started using the name "Aurocreation" for the product of their creative community.

Friends of Roslyn's from California came for a visit with their little girl, who was Bliss's age.   She was 6'2", he was 6'5" and their daughter was twice as big as Bliss and four times as big as Aura.   They ate more than everyone else all put together, and they had no money.   Somehow everyone adjusted.   The German, Geof, suddenly came up with some money, and life remained a moveable feast.

All those meals for all those people was a full time job for several of them, because the shopping had all to be done in Pondicherry, except for bread and eggs that came from The Ashram in the Land-Rover and milk from the village.   They had a little motherless boy from the village who did everything for them.   They would leave the dirty dishes in buckets in the kitchen at night, and he would bring the milk in the morning and wash the dishes.

They used kerosene lanterns for light.   There were always visitors. Roslyn met an amazing man from Madagascar in the Park in Pondicherry, wearing the red robes of a Tibetan lama and playing a flute.   She brought him home for dinner, and he stayed in Auroville for ten years and painted exceptional paintings.

There would be official Auroville meetings occasionally.   At one meeting the people who lived in Pondicherry, and thought they were "in charge" of Auroville, met with the people who were living in Auroville to tell them that the program for Auroville from August 1970 to August 1972 was to build Auromodele, the model community for the future town, and Matrimandir.   Questions about the Tamil villagers living in Auroville, especially the old Tamil lady whose hut was next to The Banyan on the proposed site of Matrimandir, made them so angry that they stopped the meeting and went in their cars back to Pondi.   The old lady's hut burned down a few days later.   Everyone suspected the Pondicherry office was responsible, but it refused to take any responsibility to provide a new hut for the old lady, so some of the people in Auroville built her a new hut near the village.

There were also many social gatherings among people living in the various settlements. The people from Silence would go to visit Forecomers and there would be a party.   The people from Forecomers would visit

Silence and it would become another party. The French had a different life in Aspiration, with toilets, running water, and electricity. They were too busy from the beginning reproducing the lives they had left to try anything new. The experiments on the edge were usually failures, but were often hilarious. At Forecomers, for example, someone built a bamboo globe on the edge of the canyon, and thought to live in it, but it fell into the canyon with the first big wind. Luckily noone was in it when it rolled over the edge and down the sleep slope.

Another couple moved into Jane's house, a guy from Bombay and a luscious blonde from Canada. They would show up at Silence at least twice a day for food. It was the only community kitchen in the area, and Mother had said, "In Auroville people will eat in community kitchens." People from other communities and Pondicherry visited Silence. The blonde girl from Canada fell in love with a Frenchman from Aspiration with long blonde hair, and the guy from Bombay went back to Bombay to reappear a couple of months later with another blonde. Fortunately by that time his other girlfriend and had left with her new boyfriend. Edward came back alone for a few days and spent an evening with Roslyn singing mantras, and gave her a copy of Sri Aurobindo`s great epic poem, "Savitri."

They had survived the summer and the summer monsoon. There were hints of green on the great red Auroville plateau. There were even a few flowers around the house at Silence. It was October, and Roslyn's birthday. She had an appointment in the morning to see Mother. She gathered most of the flowers from the garden at Silence - and a few from the Nursery - to present Mother with a bouquet of flowers from Auroville.

She was glad she had not brought Bliss. There were a lot of people on the balcony. She had to sit there for a long time, but it was very pleasant. It was very quiet, and the atmosphere created by the aspiration of the other people sitting there waiting for a blessing from The Mother was very soothing. The morning was pleasant, and Roslyn had managed to find some clean clothes in her cupboard. She hadn't even been able to get a new dress together for her birthday. She was so busy living, building, feeding people.

Gradually, one by one, the attendant called all the people. At first it was very slow, then it started to move a bit faster, then the attendant signaled to her. She got up and walked across the little hall into The Mother's room. Mother was sitting in her chair, very still. Roslyn went in front of Her and knelt, and offered Her the bouquet, flowers she had picked in a garden in Auroville. Mother accepted the flowers, and meditated on them for a moment, accepting the spirit of the offering as well as the offering. Then She gave Roslyn a bouquet of the same flowers, but much stronger and more vibrant from her Ashram gardens.

Roslyn wanted to thank Mother for the wonderful days she was having, but she could not speak. She could only look at Mother, who was looking at her with gentle affection. Then Mother smiled and gave Roslyn a rose and a card, and Roslyn got up to go.

She floated down the stairs and on through the bazaar, picking up a cake she had ordered. She stopped for a quick meal at The Continental Hotel on the beach. She left her parcels in her rickshaw and went into The Continental. It was on the beach road in Pondicherry, and had big rooms, a bar, comfortable rattan furniture, and an excellent view of the beach. The food was okay.

Roslyn was not surprised to find Kelly there. It was one of his hangouts. He was staying just down the road at a guesthouse on the beach.

They greeted each other affectionately, although they had not seen each other for months. It's my birthday," Roslyn announced.

"Wonderful, my dear, allow me to buy you lunch."

What a pleasant surprise. After months of feeding everyone, buying and preparing baskets of food, someone to buy her lunch. Happy Birthday!

"So tell me, how are things in Auroville," Kelly said after ordering food and a Coca-Cola for Roslyn.

"Wonderful. I am so happy." she replied.

"How is Bliss?"

"Nicer and nicer. You must come out and see us. I have built something and there is a community of maybe fifteen or twenty people emerging there. We are really having a good time."

"But what are you doing?"

"Living."

"Do you have water yet?"

"We have been waiting for a rig to bore a well for months."

"How do all of you people live together without water?"

"Well, a bullock cart with a water tank on it comes by every morning at around ten. There is more water in the tank than our two water barrels can hold. We put all the buckets and pots and pans where the hose from the tank reaches into the kitchen. We all take our clothes off and pour buckets or pots or pans of water over each other until the tank is empty. We relate, get clean, and clean the kitchen and the pots and pans at the same time. It's lots of fun."

"And you think that is the Supramental Manifestation?" he asked.

"Maybe. It certainly doesn't hurt anyone, although it may shock the bullock cart driver."

"Are any of you people doing anything?"

"Maybe we will do some handicraft workshops and a boutique in Pondi with Lorelei."

"That sounds good. Tell me, what do you hear from your father?"

"He is coming with my mother in December. My sister is coming next month."

"I look forward to seeing him again," Kelly said.

They ate quickly, because Roslyn was in a hurry to get back to Auroville and Bliss. She thanked Kelly for the lunch and treated herself to a taxi back to the dusty field where she lived with her friends.

Geof greeted the taxi with a spoon in his hand. Roslyn laughed at him and suggested he help unpack everything from the car to the kitchen before he started to eat.

Everyone was very jolly. Friends from other parts of Auroville visited in the evening. Someone brought a tape recorder so there was even music and dancing under the stars.

The days were filled with happy routine.

Roslyn went with Joe to spend a few days in Rameshwaram. When she got back Bliss just curled up on her lap and would not leave her arms for an hour or two, but then she was running around with the other children again and trailing after Gabi.

Roslyn's American friend was pregnant, and eating more than ever. They were waiting for money to invest in carpets and things before they left. Roslyn was wondering how her sister would react to living in a hut with eight other people.

Roslyn walked past The Ashram gate one day in Pondicherry, and ran into Mari, who was just coming out of The Ashram. Mari was glowing. She had just come down from Mother's room. She was in a daze, but she stopped Roslyn and said, "Look, Mother just gave me a flower for you."

It was a sprig covered with little white flowers.

Roslyn accepted it.

Mari looked at her, and said very quietly, "This is a water flower."

Roslyn hated to think how badly they needed water. They had been waiting six months for a bore rig that had been hung up for months boring unsuccessfully through rock at Forecomers, only to find more rock than water.

She got home, and there it was, already set up on the field, the boring rig. The men would be coming in the morning. They were going to start digging her well, but she had to pay them seventy five rupees a day. Her sister was bringing money from Bernie for the well. Meanwhile, she had to keep the work going on and pay for it day by day.

She had about exhausted her credit, but her sister was arriving in Madras. She was about to go to meet her sister's plane when she got a telegram. "Robbed in Delhi. Arriving Madras Monday at 11 a.m."

Roslyn tried not to panic. She was already worrying about the money she was borrowing to keep the work on the well going, and she had a long way to go. The first day the crew was very excited because they struck water at four feet. The foreman suggested they might have hit an underground lake, but they couldn't stop there. They had to go on through layers of clay and sandstone, and finally granite, until there were several aquifers to draw from.

Every day she had to come up with the money for the crew and the rent of the rig. The next step was steel pipes, and it had to be done immediately because the casing had to be put in while the bore well rig and crew were there, or they would go off and it might take months to get them back to put in the casing.

She went with Bliss in a taxi to the Madras airport.

Roslyn's sister Dorrie arrived traveling from Delhi with a blonde Frenchwoman, who reminded Roslyn of Simone Signoret in "Ship of Fools." She was old enough to be interesting, yet had a rare glamour with knock-out, white blonde hair, every hair in place in a chignon. Breathtaking. Simple, haute couture safari clothes and beautiful warm flashing blue eyes only confirmed the first impression of a real lady. Dorrie introduced her sister to the French lady, "Yvonne LeMieux."

"May I come in your car to Pondicherry?" the French lady asked.

Roslyn was happy to have such a fascinating companion for the long ride with her uptight older sister, who was already treating Bliss like a baby, speaking goo-goo. Roslyn got the luggage in the car while Dorrie held Bliss.

Finally they were all in the car and heading to Pondicherry. Roslyn turned to Dorrie: "What happened in Delhi?"

"I was robbed."

"How did it happen?"

"I locked the door and went to sleep, and when I got up in the morning my bag was gone. Someone in the hotel must have done it."

"What was in your bag?"

"Everything. Money, passport, tickets, traveler's checks."

"What did you do?" the French lady asked with genuine concern.

"I called the US Embassy and American Express, and my father, and got everything back except the money Bernie gave me for you,." she said to Roslyn.

"But I need money. I'm digging a well."

"Don't worry, Bernie sent some to the bank in Pondicherry."

"I hope it arrives; it can take years to get money sent through the bank in India."

"Cheer up. I am your sister, and I have not seen you for a long time. Tell me, where are we going in this car?"

"I am taking you to where we live in Auroville."

"That is interesting," the French lady said. "I am very interested in Auroville."

"We will drive through Auroville before the taxi takes you into Pondicherry."

"Very good. I like to see Auroville. How is it going there?"

"I am very happy there." Roslyn could honestly say.

"May I tell you a funny story?" the French lady asked.

Roslyn and Dorrie were happy not to have to confront each other, and Roslyn did not want to think about her money conundrum that she would have to solve or go into the debtor's prison in India.

The French lady told them, "I have been coming to Pondicherry regularly since my husband died. My grief was formidable when he passed away, and the only solace I found was in a place I found somewhere in my dreams which was very quiet, a tomb perhaps, covered in flowers, but there was a sense of joy there which shattered my grief's incarceration of my soul. I felt again alive, as I was sleeping and dreaming, but I seemed to become dead again when I woke up. I had this dream night after night, and gradually the days became better.

"I had never been to Pondicherry, but the day my husband's obituary was in the paper there was also the obituary of a Frenchman who had died in Pondicherry with the Indian name Pavitra. I thought that strange, and as I am traveling often to India I decided to visit Pondicherry. I am French, and I know that there is a French Consul there, because Pondicherry was a French colony until recently, but I had never any reason to go to Pondicherry. I remembered, after my wedding, I was sitting next to my husband's friend from Bombay at dinner, and I asked him, "Where do I go if I need help?"

He replied to me, "Go to The Mother."

"Who is The Mother?" I had asked.

"An old French lady in Pondicherry," he replied.

"Numb with grief and the prospect of years of widowhood and loneliness; feeling unable to go on. I had no place to go. Twenty years after my husband's friend told me that I should go to The Mother if I ever needed help, I got on a plane and traveled to Pondicherry."

"I went to the Grand Hotel d'Europe, and took a room. It was very pleasant. After a good dinner I went to bed, to sleep. I woke at four o'clock in the morning because someone was calling me. I could even hear it, when I was awake. The voice was urging me to come. I did not know who or where. It would not allow me to stop and dress, so I just threw on a robe and slippers and was out the door down the stairs into the street. I had never in my life done anything like that, in a strange town, in my negligee, alone in the middle of the night, but I could not stop I had to answer the call. I walked through the empty street, glowing with bright moonlight in the hour before dawn, afraid I`d gone completely mad, but unable to stop myself. On through the comfortably lit park. Instead of feeling frightened or endangered, alone before daybreak on a strange street, not knowing where I was going, I felt unafraid, and it was beautiful. I just kept going until I came to an open gate under a light and went in. It was just as it was in my dream.

"Strange story, no?"

Roslyn replied, "That's a very nice story. Did you get to see The Mother?"

"Yes, her granddaughter, Poorna, introduced me to Mother."

"We are going to see Mother tomorrow," Roslyn said to Dorrie.

The French lady, Yvonne LeMieux, said, "I spend so much time traveling that I often bring messages from one person to another. I have a very important message for Mother from France."

She sounded as if she was talking about Louis XIV himself.

She was very entertaining, this alluring lady. She had been recently in Mexico at the wedding of the President's daughter, and was going from Pondicherry to Bombay to visit her friend there who was so famous that even Roslyn recognized the name.

The driver stopped and everyone got out for tea at a little village stall. Yvonne refused to sample any of the exotic treats, but Roslyn urged savories and sweets and tea on Dorrie. They ate with Bliss.

Yvonne commented on what a nice child Bliss seemed to be, and Bliss picked up a bit of an iddly rice cake and threw it at her, but it landed on the table. Bliss occasionally acted like a baby when she was not getting enough attention, but she usually acted like a person, in fact almost invariably, from the moment she was conceived.

Bliss did not talk a lot. She seemed to agree with Roslyn that the non-conformist lives they were leading were fine. She was happy, loving, and related to many people rather than a nuclear family.

They got back into the taxi, and Roslyn told them about Auroville. Dorrie told them about her new lover whom she was planning to meet the next week in Bermuda, so she had to cut her trip to India short.

They turned left off the Madras road at the little Ganesh temple that marks the entrance to the Auroville area. Dorrie could not imagine why Roslyn was so enthusiastic. It was The Emperor's New Clothes. To Roslyn a city more beautiful than the Emerald City of Oz was an ever-present mirage on the horizon. To Dorrie it looked like only heat and dust.

The taxi stopped at the little cluster of huts next to two 50-gallon drums that were used as water barrels. Lounging around under the big roof was a disparate, disheveled group.

Yvonne bid them, "Good luck," and rode off in the taxi to Pondi.

Dorrie wished she could have gone with her. Roslyn begged her to stay for at least one night.

Dorrie agreed finally, but only after Roslyn established that if she really hated it she could move into Pondicherry the next morning.

One of the rooms of the hut had been set aside for Dorrie's use. The other five people had piled into the other room, covering the floor with their sleeping bags. There was a bed with a mattress, pillow, sheets and a mosquito net for Dorrie. She had never used a mosquito net, but she had been to the movies and she knew she was not going to like it.

She had a pile of gifts and foodstuffs from Bernie for Roslyn and Bliss. She had brought a dress for Roslyn made of a new synthetic fabric, a jungle print. Roslyn was happy to have something to wear to see The Mother.

As Dorrie was unpacking her bags a mongoose ran through the room, and then she saw a huge cockroach. She told Roslyn, "I will move into Pondicherry tomorrow."

Roslyn and Bliss had a wonderful dinner of salami and chocolate pudding.

In the morning the tamby helped them carry Dorrie's luggage to the Center, and they went to Pondi in the Land-Rover to meet Mother and find a guesthouse for Dorrie

By the time they got to Pondicherry it was too late to see the man in charge for a room in one of The Ashram guesthouses; he had already gone to lunch. They parked the luggage at The Auroville Office and went out to lunch.

After lunch they had an appointment to meet The Mother with Mari.

Dorrie was pretty uptight. She had been living and working in Manhattan for ten years, and that was not what she wanted to be doing for the rest of her life. But she did not know anything else. She certainly did not want to live like Roslyn, in a hut without a telephone or television.

Roslyn was very happy living in her hut. She enjoyed the community; she was happy that she did not have another parent in the relationship with Bliss. She loved living in Auroville, where, no matter what appeared to be happening, every possibility was there. Roslyn was very grateful to The Mother for having created the concept and reality of Auroville.

Roslyn and Dorrie went into The Mother's room with Mari and knelt in front of Mother.

Mother looked at Dorrie, smiled at her, and gave her a flower. Then she looked at Roslyn.

Roslyn's mind was full of all the details of her life, Bliss, money, her friends, the community. She wanted to thank Mother for giving her such a unique, free and wonderful life experience. Then abruptly and unbidden, "Silence," the name of her house, came to her mind. She remembered reading something Mother had said during the Darshan she gave the people from Aspiration, that their minds were too noisy. Roslyn stopped thinking. She stopped trying to be polite and say the right thing to Mother. She just sat in front of Mother, still, silent, and instantaneously she was filled with an energy she had never experienced before. It seemed somehow to be exactly the opposite of the energy she knew as herself.

It was very wonderful and vibrant, as though every cell of her body was suddenly turned on, but it happened in a flash, and when her mind perceived something else happening, it stopped. Then Mother smiled at her and gave her a flower.

Roslyn and Dorrie got up and went downstairs. In the courtyard Roslyn stopped at Madhav Pandit's office. She greeted him and explained she had just taken her sister to meet Mother, and her sister needed a room in a guesthouse for a week.

He was very friendly, and made out a card for "Good Guesthouse."

Dorrie was singularly nonplused at meeting Mother. "She seems terribly fond of you, but I don't know why you are so fascinated by her," she said.

Roslyn put Dorrie in a rickshaw with her luggage and agreed to come in for lunch the next day at the guesthouse. She dashed off to catch the Land-Rover back to Auroville, and left her sister to fend for herself in town.

The next day she went back to Pondicherry in the morning to meet her sister for lunch.

Good Guesthouse was next door to the Hotel d'Europe. It had a very different atmosphere. On the street there was a blue/gray/white wall with a freshly painted pale blue gate. Boughs of bougainvillea hung over the wall. The gate opened into a garden with guest rooms on either side, and then a large verandah, which had been made up like a sitting room looking out onto the garden. Large photos of Mother and Sri Aurobindo dominated the space.

Dorrie was waiting there. She looked much prettier than she had when she arrived in Madras.

"You look as if you're not finding Pondicherry all that hard to take," Roslyn said.

"I am enjoying it. There are some interesting people staying here in the guesthouse, and the food is superb,"

"I am happy to hear that. I feel like I am starving. When is lunch?"

Dorrie walked over to the desk and asked the manager who was buried behind a newspaper, "Excuse me, when is lunch."

He was a very mild man, dressed in spotless starched white shirt and shorts. He had a pleasant smile. "At 12:30, in about ten minutes." He introduced himself to Roslyn, "I am Mr. Doyle."

"I am Roslyn. I live in Auroville."

"Oh yes, how nice. Your sister was telling me. I must go look after things in the kitchen," he said, and disappeared through the curtains into the dining room, where Roslyn could see tables set ready for lunch. She was feeling ravenous.

"What did you do here yesterday?" Roslyn asked Dorrie.

"There is this guy staying here who went to Harvard. He went out and bought some beer that he brought back in his green book bag. There is a pretty young French Canadian girl also staying here. We all got drunk together. It was fine; but not what I would have expected in an Ashram in India.

There was a flash of white, and the most handsome human being in the world was bent over Roslyn's outstretched hand, that had somehow met his hand in space. She looked into eyes that seemed to tell the story of every spring forever. He was saying, "You must be the terrible sister who lives in a hut in Auroville."

"And who are you?" she gasped.

"James Anthony Drummond Bean IV," he replied. "May I escort you in to lunch?"

Roslyn thought for a moment she was Vivian Leigh on the set of "Gone With The Wind." She had strolled away from the battlefield of dust and fried bread in her fresh frock into a dining room with clean tablecloths and napkins, matching silver, and a servant in clean crisp white clothes ready to serve course after course of exquisitely prepared food. Her sister cooed unintelligible babble to a man infinitely more attractive than any movie star.   His brown hair was not long enough to be hippie or unkempt, but long enough to soften his very long and thin face. Roslyn kept getting lost in those dreamy hazel eyes, and could hardly listen to, much less, take part in, the light repartee, just like any junk novel heroine.

They all glittered through the soup course, fish course, entree and dessert, and then chose tea rather than coffee. Jim invited Roslyn out to ice cream after lunch on her way to the Land-Rover.

Lunch might have been paper for all she noticed of the food as she swallowed it. He became her Ice Cream Jim.

She went in to lunch every day with her sister, and sometimes she took Bliss with her. Jim always joined them, and took her out for ice cream after that huge meal.

Roslyn booked her parents, Bernie and Anna, into Good Guesthouse for their proposed Christmas visit. Jim told her he would be joining his parents in England for Christmas.

Roslyn asked him, "Where are you going? Have you met Mother? Where is there to go?"

He laughed at her and bought her another ice cream.

Dorrie left and was married two weeks later. Every time Roslyn went into Pondi she seemed to run into Jim. He would always buy her an ice cream. One day when she ran into him, she had just run out of money, and she needed to finish the shopping for the community, so she borrowed a hundred rupees from him.

A few days later she picked up her parents at the airport, and took them to the guesthouse, promising to come the next day for lunch.

When she arrived in the morning, her mother was already pissed-off. Jim Bean had asked for the 100 rupees he had lent Roslyn. Then another guy from Auroville had come in and spent the morning talking

Bernie into giving money for a dairy in Auroville.

Jim Bean walked through the lobby with a statuesque blonde.

"There is your friend, Jim Bean," Anna said sarcastically.

"Yes, I know. Who is the blonde?"

"She is a Swiss writer."

Bernie came in puffing on a cigar and making a big fuss over Bliss. Anna was a little less uptight with Bernie than she had been with Roslyn, but she did not like India.

They ate together, but Roslyn was finding it very hard to talk to them, especially because the only thing she seemed to have to say was, "I need money."

A small funny looking man followed by a woman with a basket on her head and a little boy appeared. "I show you magic," the little man said.

"How many rupees?" Roslyn asked.

"What you like you give."

Suddenly there was a beautiful rose in his hand that he gave to Anna.

She said, "Thank you very much," but as he was handing it to her it became a silk scarf that unfurled for meters and meters, until there was a pile of silk on the floor.

Then he asked Bernie for a rupee.

Bernie handed him a rupee. He folded it carefully and then unfolded it, and it became a hundred rupees note. This he ripped in half and put it together, and it became a twenty dollar bill.

The woman had set down the basket.

The magician was telling stories in a language that was not identifiable, but nonetheless understandable and amusing and fascinating.

He took a small clay pot from the basket, and filled it with water from a tap in the garden. He poured the water onto one of the potted palms and kept pouring and pouring and pouring. It was like the pitcher of Bachhus.

Then he brought a pot with a small mango tree, less than a foot tall, out of the basket. He refilled the water pot and started pouring water on the little tree. The tree started growing, and within five minutes had grown inches and acquired more leaves.

"Wow!" Roslyn exclaimed. "We really need this guy in Auroville."

"Yes, what you saying?" the magician responded.

The next day was Bliss's birthday. Mother had not been seeing people for a few days, so there would only be the party in the late afternoon at Silence.

Anna and Bernie were planning on going to the party by taxi.

"Tomorrow you coming here going taxi Auroville?" Roslyn said in her best Tamilais.

"Yes," and he seemed to pull a pile of multicolored satin ribbons from the air.

The guest house manager came into the lounge. "I am very sorry, but this is an Ashram Guesthouse. We do not want magicians here."

"Why not?" Roslyn's mother asked.

"Please, I am sorry, but this fellow has to leave."

The Magician packed up his things and put the basket on his wife's head, and Roslyn went out with them and arranged for them to go to Auroville the next day. She gave them 100 rupees, and hoped they would show up the next day.

Roslyn's American friends had left finally for California. They had been there three months, and spent their last weeks after their money arrived buying things to sell in the USA. Roslyn had finally asked them to contribute something to the community, and they promised to do something before they left. Roslyn returned one day from Pondi to find them gone, two baskets of groceries on the table with a note. "Thanks a lot, see you around." So there was only Geof, Gabi and Margie now living at Silence. Margie had her hut, Surrender. Geof and Gabi were moving into the hut built by the Dutch woman, and for the first time since she had built it only Roslyn and Bliss lived in her hut, although they all still shared the kitchen. If her parents had arrived when there were eight people sharing one hut they would have freaked out, but as it was, it looked okay.

Everybody from Auroville and many people from the nearby village had been invited to Bliss's party. Gabi, Roslyn and Margie had been baking cakes and cookies for days. The palm roof on the patio between the hut and the kitchen was being redone because the original structure had been built too fast and the angle was not steep enough with the result that it was disintegrating after only one monsoon. They had already done the new structure, but not the palm leaves, so Ramchendran spent the day blowing up balloons and tying them on the new structure, so the roof was only sky and balloons.

Then they hung up some fairy Japanese lanterns Roslyn had found in Pondicherry, and Ramchendran said he would light the candles in them when it was getting dark.

There were flowers, food and drink, a small Tamil band with chenai, harmonium and tabla, and many people by the time the taxi arrived in the late afternoon.

Roslyn was surprised to see Jim Bean alight from the car with the magicians and her parents.

The magician immediately included the Aurovilians in his act, and everyone was immediately involved, enthralled, as he went on to do the tricks he had done the day before, and many many more. There was much laughter and joy, and Roslyn sat quietly on the ground with Bliss on her lap and watched what was happening. It was fun, a real party. The magician had everyone laughing - flowers, seashells, small animals, all kinds of things were appearing and disappearing, and he seemed to include everybody there as part of the magic.

One friend from Forecomers brought fireworks and was shooting off rockets in front of the hut. Ramchendran went to light the lanterns, and Bernie freaked out. "You're crazy. You are going to burn the house down."

One of the great frustrations of Roslyn's childhood had been that fireworks were forbidden. She loved fireworks. She and Bernie started shouting at each other, and Bernie and Anna took the magician, his wife and son and left. Angry.

Roslyn found in the kitchen a huge wide mouthed thermos full of ice cream. There were people everywhere eating and drinking. A tape recorder was playing pop music and people were dancing. Roslyn left Bliss sitting on one of the round cement tables in the patio and circulated a bit among her friends. When she came back to Bliss someone had given Bliss a stuffed toy elephant, and people had put bangles on her little chubby wrists, flashy necklaces around her neck and ribbons in her hair; she seemed to be enjoying herself.

Shortly after dark the party began to break up, but there were several old and new friends who stayed the night.

Roslyn's parents showed up in the morning in a taxi. They were angry at her, but they wanted to spend the day with Bliss. Her mother told her to bathe Bliss and dress her so they could take her to town for the day. Roslyn dunked Bliss in a full water barrel.

"Is that how you bathe her?"

"Why not?"

Roslyn was actually afraid Bernie and Anna were going to try to kidnap Bliss. They were very angry at her, but they thought Bliss was nice.

She did not want to give them Bliss for the day, but she also did not want to fight with them, so she gave them Bliss; but she was very relieved when they brought her back in the late afternoon.

An uneasy truce held among them. They saw each other nearly every day. Her parents also saw a lot of John Kelly, Mari, the Countess de B. and other people in Pondicherry, so for all their disapproval of Roslyn it was clear that her parents were fascinated by Mother's World.

Roslyn invited them to come with Kelly for lunch on Christmas Day. She spent the morning baking a cake. Her guests arrived, and everyone was very jolly as they enjoyed the fried potatoes with salt and drinking water from the new water filter for lunch. Roslyn was hoping the cake would save it. She tried to cut it: the knife bent before entering the cake. The cake was harder than the brick on the floor. Roslyn was so embarrassed. Then Gabi admitted having bought rice flour instead of wheat flour.

After that sumptuous feast and a walk around the arid plateau, where it was hot even in December, her parents only went on and on that she did not have to live like that. If she wanted to live like that she could live like that, but Bliss deserved something better, on and on.

Finally they got in their taxi and went back to Pondicherry.

A monumental feast had been prepared that evening at the Pump House. Roslyn was surprised to see Jim Bean arrive in the late afternoon with his Swiss lady friend.

Roslyn was wearing her red Chinese silk brocade dress, which she had only worn twice before. It was the most beautiful dress she had ever owned. Jim and his friend came into the gathering with a bunch of other people, and after greeting a few friends, came over and said "Hello, Roslyn."

He asked her something, and they started to talk, standing there, as the sun set. The moon came up. Supper was served, and neither of them moved, as though they had stopped for a moment in space to say "Hello," and time and the world stopped. They stood there without moving towards one another, nor away from one another. They had not seen anyone nor heard anything. Abruptly the Swiss lady was standing there saying, "It's 9:30 and they lock the doors at the guesthouse at 10:00. Shall we leave?"

"But you haven't had anything to eat," Roslyn said, looking at the table, finding nothing but empty plates there.

They'd missed dinner!

"That's all right," said Jim, smiling with his arm around the Swiss lady, as they walked off to the taxi.

Roslyn had a hard time making anything of all that, but her sense of self preservation took over, and she went to see if there were any crumbs left over from the feast.

On January 1st Mother proclaimed 1971 "A Sweet Year!"

Bernie and Anna went back to Philadelphia from Madras. They had paid for the well, the pump, the electrical installation, a cow for the Auroville dairy, a given a donation to The Ashram. Anna commented at the airport, "I think we could have stayed in the most expensive hotel in New York and gone out to lunch and dinner every day and the theater every night, and spent less money than we have spent in two weeks with Roslyn in South India."

As much as they'd done, as much as they'd given, it wasn't enough. There was still a Pump House to build, pipes and paint to buy, and Roslyn didn't feel very settled. She was happy. There would soon be running water and electricity. She just felt that shopping and cooking for the people at Silence was not going to be her job for much longer.

Jim Bean had gone away for a few days with the Swiss lady for New Year. Roslyn really decided to make a point of forgetting about that very weird, albeit, very handsome, intelligent, rich, and mesmerizing man.

There were a few quiet days at Silence. Roslyn was talking a lot with her neighbors at The Pump House about starting a community for artists and artisans which would also involve Equal's One and education for the children. They were talking about something new, different, fun, exciting, ideal, and were not sure quite what it was they hoped to achieve that no one else had ever done before.

Roslyn occasionally ran into Jim Bean in Pondicherry. She hardly had time to stop and have ice cream with him.

Most of the people in Auroville were working together on a dance drama that was being staged at the edge of the canyon at Forecomers.

A poem had been written by Rod called: "The artist before dawn and the dream of victory.

> *Why does the wild wind wander on this planet*
> *while the hunter runs among the stars?*
> *and why does the flute caught wind*
> *call softly to the moon*
> *when clarity wears the gown of night?"*

Then there were pages of poetry conjuring the images Rod reckoned would come into play with the manifestation of the new town. There were dancing bureaucrats and magicians, young men and women, friends, dreamers, people from different countries and backgrounds, coming together sharing the dream of the artist, until at the end of the poem:

> *"O the city rises round the rim*
> *as night's armor clatters to the ground*
> *and in the utter silence*
> * men of light noisily launch their ships*
> *to the sun—*
> *O the kingdom rises round the rim."*

The best pop music of that time, like The Beatles' "Here Comes the Sun," orchestrated the dances and play. The play ended with the players inviting the audience to dance around a Maypole with long colored streamers, and everyone was happy imagining that the age of Aquarius, friendship, and universal realization had already begun in The City of Dawn on the Coromandel Coast.

There were two performances. Roslyn wore her red brocade dress again, but it was a little tight.

Jim Bean was there for the last rehearsal and both performances.

Roslyn asked him, "When are you moving to Auroville?'

"I am leaving for Hobe Sound in three weeks," he replied.

"Where's that?"

"Florida."

"Why?"

"My parents have invited me for Easter."

"I thought they lived in London?"

"They have several homes."

"That's nice."

"If you give me that big thermos I brought to Bliss's birthday party I will fill it up with ice cream when I come back out."

"When are you coming back out?"

"I heard that work is starting on the Matrimandir after The Mother's birthday."

"I thought you said you were going to Florida."

"I don't need to be there until Easter."

"If you like Auroville so much, why are you leaving?"

"It is going to be very hot here in a few weeks."

"That's the dumbest thing I ever heard." Roslyn walked away.

Both performances were a great success, and both the players and audience were amazed at how much fun - and yet inspirational - the evenings were. An immense cut out larger-than-life photo of Mother was standing above the center of the proscenium of the makeshift bamboo and palm arch above the stage. By then, at the end of each evening everyone was dancing with joy, as beautiful Auroville was right there - everybody happy, everybody smiling, here comes the sun, in the city of dawn.

Roslyn's friend who hadn't showed up in Istanbul now showed up with her German boyfriend, and they moved in to Silence, then to Forecomers. An American couple with a Mercedes van and a little boy two months younger than Bliss parked one day near the kitchen at Silence. He came over and asked, "Is it okay if we park here?"

Roslyn had seen him once or twice in Katmandu. It was okay.

A German guy who made musical instruments out of a coconut shell and a stick and string appeared one day, and stayed. A completely crazy American lady with a thirteen year old daughter showed up, and disappeared leaving her daughter behind. The van stayed next to the kitchen. He was often around in the evening, and the little boy was around some of the time, but most of the day Bliss seemed to be hanging-out in the van and Roslyn never even saw the mother of the little boy.

They'd been there a few days. He came over to the gang gathered around the breakfast table drinking tea, and said, "Goodbye, thank you for everything."

He gave them all a friendly smile and wave, and then the lady, who was really very beautiful, came out from behind the van, gave a little wave, and also said a shy "Goodbye."

All the people sitting in the patio smiled and waved, and the van pulled out.

It was a very cool scene. People came and went. There were always people around. There was a food scene happening in the patio from dawn to dark. If no-one was drinking or eating, people were talking or there were children playing. The little Tamil tamby went around behind everyone cleaning up. The electrical lines had been installed, the Pump House had been built, the pump installed, a shower had been built, and it had all been inspected. They were just waiting for the Tamil Nadu Electrical Board to turn the current on; meanwhile, they were still living on two barrels of water a day.

An hour after the Mercedes van had left it was back. The couple got out of the van with their little boy, and walked into the patio.

"Hello," she said shyly.

"Hello," Gabi said. "Did you forget something?"

"We got to the Madras Road, and couldn't figure out where we were going, because this feels exactly like the place we've been looking for, so we came back. We would like to stay, and build a house."

Roslyn had other friends building a palace of bamboo and palm leaves, in a nearby grove of Neem trees. His family were big water supply merchants from Bombay, so he was going to help put together the water scene in Auroville.

It was nearly Mother's birthday, and work was to begin on The Matrimandir. Ram, from Bombay, had a pump to install for the well near The Banyan to get the water running for the inauguration ceremony for the Matrimandir.

The night before Mother's birthday it was clear they would have to work the whole night, and then maybe if everything worked right they might have water for the ceremony scheduled for dawn. Roslyn went to help keep him awake while he encouraged the mechanics and electricians as they worked through the night. Slowly, carefully, they inserted the new pump at the end of a length of pipe into the well, and then joining it to another, and then another length of pipe, without dropping it and losing it forever in the well. Finally, just before dawn, Ram pressed a button, water flowed, and they were all deliriously happy.

Ram went home to sleep, and Roslyn went to the place prepared for the ceremony. She sat on one of the few mats, and drifted between wakefulness and sleep. The stars faded and the sky became lighter. Quietly others came from Auroville on foot or by bicycle, drifting into the area and sitting quietly nearby.

The sweet early morning bird calls and quiet hum of a South Indian morning were interrupted by the noise of a bus, the Land-Rover and several cars coming from Pondicherry, that seemed to all emerge in the morning light, shattering the magic stillness.

One of the people who had arrived in the motor vehicles told Roslyn to move because she had plunked herself down on one of the mats reserved for the VIP's. She felt like a VIP, having spent the night with Ram getting the well working. She remembered the attitude of some people in Pondicherry towards the Aurovilians: the rough and tumble Aurovilians were just the workers; who had come to build Auroville, like a house. The workers would come, build the house, and then leave, after which the owners could come and enjoy the place.

She felt angry and betrayed at being asked to move over for someone more important, so instead of moving into the appropriate section for the proletariat, she walked back to Silence and missed the ceremony.

A few days later it was Auroville's birthday, February 28th. Everyone in Auroville was going to the Banyan tree to meditate at dawn.

Roslyn walked up to the Banyan tree, leaving Bliss asleep in the hut. By the time she got to the tree the sky was already perceptibly lighter and the first colors of morning were brillaintly coloring the sky in the East. She could see the shadow forms of other Aurovilians. The morning was very quiet. It was a special quiet, without the croak of a frog or whine of a mosquito; the stillness was nearly luminous, with a sound of its own.

Roslyn had been looking into spiritual mysteries for years, but no one had ever been able to tell her how to meditate, or had given her a mantra. The only thing that she was able to clearly infer from what she had read and experienced was to be quiet.

She was sitting there, deliberately trying to stop thoughts from flowing into her mind, watching the early morning sky as the stars faded. There was a dazzling array of every color from pale gold to deep purple splashed across the sky, flowing with kaleidoscopic grace, seeming to fill the sky and the new day with color. Then all the colors ran towards the horizon, and melted into the salmon pink nimbus around the sun peeping over the edge of the earth.

She was not thinking anymore. She was there; and she heard The Mother telling her, "Your work is finished at Silence." She saw big white cement buildings descending onto the field.

Roslyn was in shock as she walked away from The Tree. She could not greet or talk to anyone. She had just spent a whole year trying to make a place habitable. Everything was ready and paid for, but the water was not yet running, and she did not want to leave. She had spent a small fortune, and her parents would never forgive her. She didn't know what to do. She went to Pondi to talk to Austin, who told her to write to Mother and look around Auroville for another place to live.

"But why?"

"Well, if it was a true vision you will not be at Silence much longer."

She had to agree, but she did not want to move. She wrote to Mother, and got a blessings' packet for a reply. Roslyn was not sure if the letter had really gotten to Mother, because Mother was only receiving correspondence from Aurovilians through Vasudeva, and he had an attitude towards Roslyn that made her feel that he held her in little regard.

She decided to go to Rameshwaram and visit Panditji.

She met Jim Bean on the street and mentioned she was going to Rameshwaram.

"I would like to go with you. I met Panditji last month when I was traveling in the South, and he gave me a 34 day practice that will be finished in a few days. Let's consult the I Ching."

The I Ching said, "Three days before starting."

They agreed to meet in three days and go to Rameshwaram.

Roslyn got to town three days later - without Bliss - with her gear for the trip, and went to meet Jim.

He had consulted the I Ching again, and was told, "It does not further to cross the great water," so he was not going with her.

She went alone, and stayed for a few days. She asked Panditji what she should do.

He replied, "Look after Bliss. Bliss is very nice."

She asked him for some practice.

He told her, "Don't worry."

Finally she went back to Auroville. It was hot, and there was not much happening. She was still spending long evenings talking with her neighbors, and designing a new community built of interconnecting bamboo and palm structures which would house workshops, studios, classrooms and play rooms, a kitchen, a dining room, sleeping areas and social areas, like a giant hive.

They had no money at all. None of them had any money. Roslyn knew that if she moved Bernie would be angry about all the money he had spent at Silence, and might not give her money to build again, but she decided to move nevertheless to a large piece of empty beach land owned by Auroville near the village of Chinnacalapet.

She had written a letter to Mother about her vision on February 28th and received a blessings' packet.

She now wrote to The Mother for permission to move to the beach.

Vasudeva said, "Speak to the chief architect."

The architect said, "No. It is better if you build something in Auromodele."

"I do not want to move to Auromodele. I want to move to the beach. Please ask The Mother's permission for me," she begged.

He asked Mother. She gave permission and a blessing packet.

Roslyn went to see Jim Bean and told him she was starting a new community on the beach in Auroville, and asked if he would contribute some money to help the work.

He gave her 100 rupees.

Roslyn moved on the first of May, without even having seen the land she had chosen from the map in the Auroville office. Dhyan and Guiom and their small son moved into Silence.

Panditji

viii

The knowledge in our hidden parts we keep;
Awake to a vague mystery's appeal,
We meet a deep unseen Reality
Far truer than the world's face of present Truth:
We are chased by a Self we cannot now recall
And moved by a Spirit we must still become.

Sri Aurobindo, Savitri

Even when we get rid of the 'I' of body, mind, heart, desire, self, there remains a substratum ego, pure fundamental ego power that supports itself, the consciousness of the mental purusha. Man mistakes this indefinable self for the infinite, or a shadow of the Purusha, but it must disappear. By its disappearance it will reveal the spirit's unclouded substance.

The Lord is subject to nothing. The individual soul-form is subject to its own highest self, and the greater and more absolute that subjection the greater becomes its source of absolute grace and freedom.

The difficulty for the mental being is to bridge the chasm between the lower and higher consciousness. The mind can rise by a great, prolonged, concentrated, and all forgetting effort out of itself into Samadhi, or it can try to call down the divine into itself so that its mentality shall be changed into an image of the divine.

This is done by the mind's power of reflecting that which it knows and contemplates its consciousness. The mind is really a reflection and a medium. Ordinarily the mind reflects the status of mental nature. If it becomes clear, passive, pure, by the renunciation of activities, and of characteristic ideas and outlooks of the mental nature, then; as in a clear mirror or the sky on a clear day, without ripples, unruffled by winds, the divine is reflected.

One has to concentrate on and realize the one Brahman in all things as conscious force of being as well as pure awareness of conscious being.

The Self is All, not only in the unique essence of things, but in the manifold form of things, not only containing all in a transcendent consciousness, but as a step towards true union with existence.

(from Jim Bean's Journal extracts from Sri Aurobindo's Synthesis of Yoga.)

Until February 21st, 1971, as far as Jose was concerned, Auroville could go screw itself. He heard some conversation in Pondicherry about the inauguration of The Matrimandir. There would be buses leaving from The Ashram at 5 a.m. on Mother's birthday. He wasn't going on no bus to Auroville at 5 a.m. on Mother's Birthday.

On Mother's Birthday he woke up at 4 a.m. He tried to go back to sleep. He woke up his wife and told her he was going on the bus to the meditation in Auroville. A seductive force was pulling him out the door, into the bus, to Auroville.

He had been living with Ethel in The Ashram since 1965, and nothing like that had ever happened to him before. Nobody bothered him and he didn't bother nobody. He was from Harlem, and his wife was from New Jersey.

He had left his mother's house when he was fourteen, and was as bent a hipster as could be found on the streets of New York in the fifties. He was "Who" the Beats were all writing about.

In his sickness he was bent. Did his business as he went. Furtive, feral, roamed the street, lipped hip knowledge, incomplete. When he'd hear a cop's whistle he'd eat humble pie and proclaim, "God's my witness, I don't know nuttin."

In reform school, back on the street, rolling whores and drunks, making marks, then scoring. He was so cool he thought he'd left no spoor. But back up the river he went for another term and back out into the world of lies which was his to cheat. He robbed the rich, sometimes the poor. He never stole from an honest person, because he'd never met one. Solid fences made good neighbors.

Nightly he stalked the gawking crowds, past gilded bars and grills, weaving lightly through theater throngs, as he snatched the unsuspecting purse. His face a stone, as the victim screamed. His heart was alight with speed. His adolescence was an embodiment of greed. He plundered the canyons of the west-side city streets where pushers spoon-fed junkies, pimps pushed prostitutes. His gun, inspired awe.

The victims waited for his crime; half-dead, lost in his underworld of dread. He'd raped life like a king, strong-arming everything that inflamed his greed, until the day a heist 'went wrong.'

Then he heard the losers' blues, because he had graduated from reform school and was on his way to jail. His hands were cuffed, and screaming sirens sang. The game had ended with a crash. He stopped as death ran near, enraged. The cops had fists, and his hands were cuffed together.

In court everyone agreed the thing to do would be to lock him up and throw away the key. Fifteen years hard labor they all agreed.

A living death was his new life. He slaved while time passed, guarded well. He wanted revenge, but his common sense cautioned guile, enforced restraint. He got out on parole after five years of good behavior, but they promised his cell would be waiting for him when he got back. At last he was free.

Lone as a wolf, lean at the door, he decided he had to find another way that would not take him back to the prison cell. He registered at a university and was paid to go to class. He read conceited folly's dusty tomes, and learned to speak in subdued tones. In school he sought his soul and found his wife, a gal with enough money that he no longer had to steal.

He knew that was not his scene for long, so he decided they should make the most of it while it was happening, and see the world.

They had met The Mother on their trip around the world in 1962. They had been traveling on a long honeymoon by freighter from one port to the next. The boat they had gotten on in Madras to take them across the Indian Ocean to Africa stopped a few hours after leaving Madras in Pondi, and they were told the boat would be taking on cargo for two days.

They got off and found a bang-up bar looking at the grand promenade and the ocean. They were enjoying the breeze and the cold beer. A drunk from Boston with peroxide blonde hair offered to buy them a round of drinks. He joined them at their table, and they fell into some somewhat long exchanges of words. The queer fellow told them he had been living in Pondicherry for nine years.

"Why?" Jose asked.

"Because The Divine Mother is here."

They did not believe him. The drunk Bostonian invited them to meet him in the bar in the morning, and he would take them to The Mother.

It had been a fascinating evening. Jose didn't much like the guy from Boston, but the beer was cold, the food was good and cheap, and they didn't know any other place in town, so they were in the bar in the morning.

The drunk American with peroxide hair and an exotic Indian name burst into the bar just as Jose was finishing his coffee. The Boston Brahmin had made it clear to Jose that his Puerto Rican mother, years in the penitentiary and CCNY had not made him an American. Jose did not want to even bother with the guy. Ethel was curious about "The Divine Mother," and since she seemed to be bored by nearly everything but sex and food, why not? They could always laugh about it later.

"You must come at once."

"Hey man, come back in half an hour, or we'll catch you later." Jose said. He had just lit a cigarette. He didn't feel like jumping.

"You have an appointment in five minutes with The Mother."

The Bostonian said something to the waiter in the local lingo and the waiter said, "You asking bill sir?"

Jose paid the bill, and with Ethel, followed Ananta as he walked briskly across town through the park. Ananta stopped in the park and picked some flowers, and gave them to Jose and Ethel to present to The Mother.

They went in a gate, through a courtyard, up a stairway, and felt as if they were going to meet some VIP. They were standing on a balcony in the sun under an awning with about twenty people. It was very quiet.

"Hey man!" Jose said, turning to the Boston Brahmin.

Ananta said, "Please be quiet, we may have to wait for a few minutes."

Jose and Ethel looked at each other and giggled. They stood looking over the rail at the scene in the courtyard below, and out onto the street. All the buildings were the same blue/gray/white color and the fresh sea breeze was pleasant.

A little old white haired man with a wispy white beard in a spotless crisp white dhoti, wearing a white string, looking about as close as possible to St. Peter at the Pearly Gates, came onto the terrace and beckoned to them.

They followed Ananta into Her room.

She was sitting there on Her Chair.

Jose had no words to describe what happened to him in the next few moments.

Coming down the stairs after meeting Mother he said to his wife, "When the boat gets back to New York I am getting on a plane and coming back here to be with Her."

As they walked through the courtyard they stopped at the tomb. Jose felt something pulling on him, as though the ground around the tomb was magnetized to his feet. As he followed Ethel walking towards the gate he said silently to Mother, "I'll be back."

They had been living happily in The Ashram for six years. They were comfortable. They knew where they were going to sleep. They knew they were going to eat. For entertainment there would be a movie at the playground on Saturday night. A harmonious peace, and feeling of simple well being that he had never imagined possible had entered his life.

He didn't want to go to Auroville. He didn't want nothing to change. Things were good as they were, but the force that dragged him out of bed demanded he go on the bus to the ceremony in Auroville.

The laying of the cornerstone was simply a child offering flowers and incense to a picture of The Divine Mother. Then most of the people left. A few stayed to start digging the foundation of Matrimandir.

Jose stayed. They broke the hard earth with a crow bar, and put the dirt in pans and dumped the pans into a wheelbarrow. Somebody had to take the wheelbarrow to the side of the site and dump the dirt. Jose decided he would be the somebody on the wheelbarrow.

All day he worked with the Aurovilians. When the tour bus came out in the afternoon he caught a ride back to Pondi, not noticing he was covered with the red dust of Auroville. Ethel told him he looked very dashing and dangerous with his dirty feet.

He wrote to Mother; he wanted to work on The Matrimandir. She sent him a blessings packet. His wife agreed that he could spend a few days - or even a few nights - a week in Auroville. He did not want to have to stop work in the afternoon and go back to town. He wanted to work until it was finished, until it was built, a room for Her in Auroville.

The first night he was out there he was going to sleep under the Banyan. Nearby, huts, bathrooms, a kitchen, were being constructed for Matrimandir workers. One of the guys, another New Yorker who sang Bob Dylan songs all day long as he worked with the crow bar gouging the earth, told him he could come to Silence. There was a reasonable new hut that had been built for chickens where he might be as comfortable as under the Banyan, and there would be something to eat. It was like being back in hard labor pushing the wheelbarrow all day, but different.

Jose sighed. There were some exciting looking chicks at Silence, although he heard that Margie was moving to Forecomers. There was a sign in The Ashram in Mother's handwriting in a huge scrawl, "No Gossip!" The community was so small and so tight that everyone knew everything about everybody else, and more.

Jose liked living quietly in The Ashram. He wanted to be the invisible man, not a topic of gossip. There were too many broads in Auroville, and they were all wearing short shorts and sleeveless Banyans when they came to work on Matrimandir. Maybe they thought with all the dust nobody noticed, but he noticed, and it felt so good to be seeing something that looked so good. He and his wife were "Doing yoga." They didn't fuck except to make babies. She had two babies. He hated yoga. He loved women. The American woman with the Indian husband and the roving blue eyes, were they looking for him? She had a little baby. His wife had two little babies. Enough babies.

People in Pondi were saying shit like, "Mother finally made a mistake, Auroville."

"Mother opened the sex center, Auroville."

It wasn't like The Ashram where all the chicks were swathed in white cotton like babies or dead bodies. Living with Ethel in The Ashram he thought he had transcended all that shit of being excited about a piece of ass, but he felt about a hundred years younger. Some part of him simply responded to women. It made him happy to be working on The Matrimandir and looking at beautiful women all day long. He suddenly remembered that he had a cock and he wondered if he had forgotten or only hoped he had forgotten. Anyhow, it was back, and he sat in the dark corner of the patio where the chicks and everybody were gathered around the two cement tables. He felt more at home in his chicken house than in the apartment where he and Ethel had lived for six years. He hadn't come to Auroville for chicks. He had come to work on Matrimandir.   He loved it from the morning to night, pushing the wheelbarrow and looking at all the gorgeous chicks in their shorts, bending, stretching.

He tried to think about something else. He found he was hardly thinking at all. The body moved, worked. He had never been happier. Eating, sleeping, nothing was important, the only thing he wanted - because he was so happy - was to do something for Her.

He visited Ethel in Pondicherry. She told him that someone had told Mother, "Some of the people in Auroville think they are Supramental beings."

Mother replied, "They are inframental. They are behaving like cats and dogs."

Jose was jolted back into another reality, but after a few days again felt the urge to go to Matrimandir, so he went back for a few more days. He hardly noticed that Roslyn had moved out and Dhyan had moved in.

Dhyan was so happy that Mother had given her permission to move to Silence. She had been so unhappy and lonely living in the orchard at Hope.

She had arrived with Guiom in Pondicherry the previous spring. She was not yet eighteen, and already married and pregnant. She had met

Guiom in the village near the convent, at a patisserie. He was very handsome and looked like a wolf with his long red hair and red beard. She knew she was very beautiful, but her mother wanted her to become a nun. She was living in the convent studying, preparing to be a nun, and she met this handsome wolf at the patisserie in the village. He bought her and her friend cakes, and was so very different from anyone she had ever seen or known. He was Guiom de Juin and he had just come back from the Baleares and was on his way to India.

Dhyan's father had been a house painter who had fallen, broken his neck and died when she was eleven, and her life was completely shattered. Her mother sent her to the convent where she spent hours a day on her knees praying and scrubbing the floor. She had heard about the Baleares and India in her geography classes. She would get into much trouble at the convent if they found out that she had spoken to a strange man and allowed him to buy her a cake.

The other girls didn't mention it because they also liked talking to strange handsome young men and eating cakes. There were never any cakes in the convent. They were rarely allowed to go to the village, but whenever she did manage to get out, he seemed to always be there, waiting for her. He asked her to marry him and go to India with him.

They arranged to elope to France where they would be married on their way to India. She told her Mother Superior and nuns that she wanted to visit her mother, so she got permission to leave the convent. Guiom met her at the train and they were off to France. She wrote her mother that she was married.

She was starting a new life of love and adventure. The world suddenly seemed to explode. Instead of being on her knees praying and scrubbing floors she was in a bistro in Paris. She could not believe how wonderful life could be with Guiom and others drinking coffee and laughing at a conversation full of sexual nuance that she could enjoy. She wondered if she could thank God that she had escaped the nuns.

She received a letter from her mother telling her to go back to the convent, the nuns would forgive her. Her mother was saying a mass every day for Dhyan's soul. It made her shudder. She decided not to write to her mother for a long time, maybe when they were in India. Guiom was working as a taxi driver to make money for the trip.

She felt very shy among Guiom's older, exotic, bohemian friends. She would sit and listen to strange people, strange languages, strange ideas. These strangers might almost have come from another planet, they were so different from the people she had known. Even though these people were new and strange to her, she felt more intimate with them than the people she had known all her life. She had studied languages in the convent, and could understand French fluently, also some English, as well as Dutch.

She was very happy with Guiom. He was very gentle and careful with her and did everything for her. He found them a place to live in Montmartre and shopped for them, fed her, bought her a beautiful white Mexican wedding dress from Oxaca with pale blue embroidery. When he was working she was at the cafe drinking coffee and wine with their friends. Sometimes they smoked kief. She was not feeling shy anymore. She was feeling sexy, beautiful, loved, slightly drunk, and she was beginning to feel a little sick.

She was pregnant! Guiom was astonished, but did not want to stay in Paris, so amid tears and embraces they took The Oriental Express to Istanbul. It was a long train ride, but they were cozy in the little compartment. Then there was another long train ride across Turkey and days of buses across Iran and Afghanistan. In Afghanistan it seemed there were only men. She did not see any women on the streets or in the shops. She was really feeling sick. She had stopped smoking and drinking. She was puking and pregnant, following blindly the prince charming, who; had snatched her from the convent. Together they were crossing Asia like Alexander the Great. Each day facing her fear of the unknown from morning to night, she longed for the comfort and safety of the familiar.

She had been traveling for weeks, across Europe and Asia. Sitting next to the window in the bus from Kabul to Lahore, she knew she was seeing some of the most beautiful terrain in the world. She sat, contented to be next to Guiom, always there. protecting her, far from the gray world of the convent, showing her to the sunlight and majesty of the world. The pass through the Himalayas, the Hindu Kush, was awesome. The day was clear and bright. Every color in every hue imaginable sparkled off hillsides, and mountain lakes. There was a magnificent play of light and shadow between the mountains and the valleys. She felt she was really traveling through the foothills of the gods.

In Pakistan they stopped briefly in train stations packed with people, people sleeping on the platforms, beggars everywhere. She could not imagine where they were going. Women with children in their arms, hanging on their skirts, pregnant, she wondered whether there would be more for her and her child than sleeping on a concrete platform in a train station. They took another bus to the border and were finally in

India. Train stations, tea-shops, buses up into the mountains, and then back down to the plains. They stayed in cheap lodges and ate with local people avoiding expensive hotels and restaurants, but their money was running out. Guiom was getting anxious. He wanted to find a place for them to stay, where she could have the baby. Train stations, cheap hotels, hostels, houses, filled with travelers and lice. They went from one place to the next. Someone mentioned Pondicherry in South India. They went there after Madras.

They took a room at a cheap lodge on the main street and went to the Indian Coffee House for something to eat.

There were no empty tables. At one of the tables there was only a fat Western woman who looked like a hippie with a young child. Guiom asked if they could sit with her. She said, yes.

The fat woman said to Dhyan, "You are very beautiful."

Dhyan was wearing her Mexican wedding dress.

The waiter came and they ordered coffee.

"Are you traveling?" Dhyan asked.

"No, I live here."

"Where?"

"In Auroville."

They drank coffee.

The fat woman picked up her child and her shopping bags.

Guiom and Dhyan went to the Sri Aurobindo Ashram and were directed across the street to the Auroville Office.

Dhyan in her Mexican wedding dress and Guiom with his red beard and white longi looked more like Mary and Joseph than most Christmas cards.

They saw the exhibition declaring that a new town was being built. The sign at the door said, "Greetings to all people of good will."

They looked at the display and read the Charter, and felt that if Auroville belonged to no one in particular, but humanity as a whole, and welcomed all people of good will, it would also welcome them.

They approached the desk.

"Yes, may I help you?" the lady in a white sari with a long white braid over her shoulder asked them.

"We would like to live in Auroville," Guiom said.

"We prefer applicants to apply from their country and come only after they have been accepted by The Mother."

"We have traveled overland from Europe. We do not want to go back to Europe to write a letter to asked permission to come to Auroville,"

Guiom replied.

"I will give you an application and if you bring it back to me, with photos, I will give it to The Mother."

They went and had photos taken, and the next day went back with the photos and the applications. The lady took the papers and asked to see their passports. She told them to come back on Monday morning.

There were cockroaches in the room at the lodge. To escape the dreariness they went for a walk and found the beautiful promenade along the beach. At the end of the promenade was an Ashram Guesthouse. Guiom suggested they move there, and out of the dreary lodge by the bazaar. They got a room overlooking the sea that was clean and cool. Dhyan felt better at once, being in a clean place.

They walked along the grand promenade three times a day to the park and The Ashram Dining Room. The food was very inexpensive and good.

It was too hot in the middle of the day, so Guiom bought a tiffin in the bazaar and brought Dhyan her lunch so she did not have to walk in the heat of the day across town.

They went swimming in the sea behind the guesthouse and felt more relaxed and happy than they had ever been. They were hoping to be allowed to stay in Auroville.

Monday morning they went back to the Auroville Office. The lady in the white sari said they could live in Auroville. There was an empty apartment in Promesse, the community that had been built for expectant mothers. They would have to move somewhere else in Auroville after the baby was born. There was an agricultural community, Hope, near Promesse, where some new huts were being built. If they gave 15,000 rupees they could have a hut there when the baby was born.

"But that is all the money we have," said Guiom.

"Don't worry. The Mother has accepted you in Auroville. The Sri Aurobindo Society provides Prosperity for Aurovilians."

"But we do not know anything about Auroville except what we see here." The exhibition hall was full of machetes of the exploding galaxy that would be the city. Futuristic buildings connected by moving sidewalks, a large golden ball with rosewood petals around it, interlocking buildings of weird shapes, plans for a new city, but it was not clear how much of the new city had been built.

"Perhaps you would like to see Auroville before you decide. There is a tour for visitors which leaves here in the afternoon at 3:30 and comes back by six. If you come here this afternoon at about 3:25 you can go on the tour and see Promesse, Hope, the center, Aspiration. It will cost you ten rupees each for the tour, and then you can come tomorrow and tell me what you have decided."

"That sounds all right," Guiom said.

Dhyan felt hostile and confused that the woman had asked for all their money. On the wall in big letters she had read, "There will be no exchange of money in Auroville."

Guiom's family was not sending him money. They did not seem pleased that he had eloped with a young Belgian girl. They were Dutch. Dhyan's mother was not going to send her any money. If they gave the money for their hut they would be entirely dependent on Auroville, but they would have a house of their own for the baby forever, although, "Nothing belongs to anybody in particular in Auroville."

It was too confusing. It felt like a miracle that a place had been offered them to live in while they were waiting for the baby, and a house of their own, but they would be stuck in India without any money. Would they never go back to Europe?

They had to decide to use the money they had to go back to Europe, or stay in India. They did not want to go back to Europe. She was happy to have found a place that offered a nest where she could give birth. They agreed that they were very fortunate to have found a place in the world where they could have their child.

The first place the bus stopped on the tour was Promesse. There, The Mother had built a community of dwellings; simple nice apartments, with bathrooms and kitchens, fans, a delivery room and a dining hall, to be used for the mothers-to-be in the City of the Future. A place providing them with a pleasant, carefree atmosphere for their pregnancies, and for the first days of the lives of the new beings that were coming to The City of the Future.

The tour guide showed Dhyan and Guiom the apartment that would be theirs if they chose to remain in Auroville. It was brand new. No one had ever lived in it, and it was all freshly painted. Everything was provided, even teacups and bedcovers.

Then the tour went to Hope, where their hut would be built. It was an agricultural community with a few huts in the middle of vast acres of orchard and farm-land. There were trees covered with fruits and nuts. They would not starve there.

The bus took them to the center, where they did not see any Aurovilians or buildings. There was only a Banyan tree, and a little old Tamil woman sitting outside her hut, not far from the tree.

Then they went to Aspiration, which looked wonderful. There were beautiful neat white thatched huts on the red plateau overlooking the sea, and many European people wearing shorts and Banyans, ignoring the visitors. Dhyan thought it looked much more attractive than Hope. Guiom liked the solitude of Hope, and wanted to work on the land. He did not want to live with a bunch of unfriendly French people.

They went back to the Auroville Office the next morning, and gave the lady in the white sari their money and asked when they could move to the apartment in Promesse.

She told them they could move out that afternoon on the bus, or on the Land-Rover the next morning. They were eager to move out of the guesthouse that was costing twenty rupees a day.

"What will we do about food?" they asked her.

"There is a community kitchen where you can take your meals. I believe that everyone takes turns cooking, although there is a servant to keep the kitchen clean. There is a servant who will clean your apartment and a dhobi who will wash your clothes."

"But what will we do about other things we need, like clothes, toothpaste, soap, and things for the baby?"

"You make a list every month, and bring it here at the end of the month. At the beginning of the month Prosperity is distributed. Please give me a list of what you need and we will try to get whatever is on your list for you."

"We would like to move out on the bus this afternoon."

"Very good," the lady in the white sari said.

"Do we meet The Mother?" Dhyan asked.

"Bring me a letter to Mother, and maybe she will see you."

"I want to meet Mother," Dhyan said.

"Maybe you would like to give me a letter for Mother before you get on the bus this afternoon."

"Yes. I would really like to see Her."

"It may not be possible. Usually She does not see people."

"I will write asking Her permission to see Her."

"Yes."

"Thank you."

The lady in the white sari gave them a receipt and they left, had lunch in the Dining Room, and then went back to the guesthouse to pack and check out.

They went to Promesse on the bus in the afternoon with all their belongings in their well-traveled bags. Waiting for them at the bus was an Italian couple. He was very tall with silver hair and she was very short, Lucio and Mariana.

They explained that the office had called to say they were coming, and they were greeting them on behalf of the community. A little girl came and stood shyly next to them. They introduced her as their daughter. Mariana was expecting another child in December. Dhyan's baby was expected in October.

One room in the compound had been set aside as a delivery room. It was very very clean, and the walls, furniture everything in the room was white. There were fresh flowers in a vase. The compound was full of flowering trees, shrubs and flowerbeds. It was apparent that a big effort had been made to create a pleasant atmosphere.

The Italian couple admitted that they were both architects. They gave Dhyan and Guiom tea in the community kitchen. Everyone in the community took food there and they all took turns cooking. Guiom and Dhyan would have to cook twice a week. They carried the bags to the apartment. There was a Gujarati midwife who came out on Wednesday mornings to see expectant mothers, and who attended the deliveries.

The agricultural community, Hope, where their hut was being built, was just across the highway. They could walk over there and watch the work, but apart from cooking twice a week they had nothing to do. The other people were from another age, another world; they reminded Dhyan of her mother.

She had not written to her mother since France. She decided to wait until the baby was born. There was nothing to do. There were some books by Mother and Sri Aurobindo in the community kitchen. They took them to their room and read them. They saw the fat hippie woman on the Land-Rover a few times. She seemed to be surrounded by hippie friends. They seemed happy and not as serious as the people at Hope and Promesse. Everyone was always polite, but there seemed to be a curtain between her and the others.

Dhyan received a note telling her she that and Guiom had an appointment with Mother. She went to Pondicherry with Guiom in the Land-Rover. They spent the morning on the hot balcony waiting to be called. Dhyan was feeling very sick and pregnant, when they were finally called into The Mother's room.   Dhyan nearly collapsed at The Mother's feet as the blast of the air conditioner nearly knocked her over after standing on the terrace in the sun for more than an hour under the cotton awning. She hated waiting. She was slightly angry that though she was pregnant she had had to wait while others went before her. She would not have waited except that she had been deeply moved by a little book of prayers and meditations she had found and been reading. Traveling across Europe with Guiom she half expected to give birth to the baby in a stable. She was amazed they had found an environment where she was protected and nurtured in her pregnancy. It seemed that along with the child within her she had been offered a new life. Her child was just another part of the new world that was being born, and the new world, the Supramental world, seemed to have begun with the fragile beautiful lady in muted silk, looking like Elizabeth I of England with pink hair, sitting on Her chair in her room. Dhyan saw nothing in the room but a carpet and a chair and a wonderful presence that emanated from Her. Dhyan felt perfectly happy curled up at The Mother's feet, but eventually she felt a gentle hand on her shoulder. She looked up and was dazzled by the tender gaze of the old woman. Dhyan felt her illusions of self pity and discomfort dissolve. She did not feel sick and pregnant: she was young and strong and had been drawn to The Mother to be part of the great adventure of consciousness and joy, Auroville.

She was so proud and full of joy, tears were streaming down her face and she was clutching the card and flowers Mother had given her. She felt confident she and her child had been chosen to fulfill a wonderful role in the unique drama that was unfolding, part of The New Creation in the planetary evolutionary cycle.

They had lunch in the Dining Room and waited in the park until it was time to get the bus back to Promesse. They were exuberantly content with the chance of a life that promised transformation from within and without.

It was a very special place to be having a child. The children of the new town were the future, and the most important citizens of a community solely dedicated to the future. Promesse had been one of the first priorities of The Mother for the new town, a place clean, comfortable, safe, with an excellent atmosphere, removed from the normal cares of day to day life for the mothers of the new beings who were coming into new bodies.

It was a place where many languages were spoken, and all very gently.

Nearly all the people in Promesse were involved as expectant parents in the miracle of birth. There was an American couple working in the Matrimandir gardens, though she was not pregnant, and there was an old French couple who looked after the cows at Hope and were waiting for their house to be ready, but everyone else was waiting for the stork.

It was as though these were the first babies to be born, the children of Auroville, the new beings who were coming to help humanity find its way to the new creation that would be the future. It was the time and place to be having a baby, and she could not accept that she had just stumbled into it on her blind peregrination. She felt that she had been chosen, called, with the new being within her as part of the Mother's design for the future.

The days were beautiful. She and Guiom were happy together and in love. They would walk over to see what was happening on the hut being built for them. They would stop at the little temple across the road and delight in the blue plaster statues of the god with a head of an elephant. There was not much traffic on the highway, and there was only foot traffic on the dirt road into Auroville, a few Aurovilians on bicycles, the Land-Rover in the morning, and the bus in the afternoon. There was a pool in the orchard and many birds gathered in the trees nearby. At night she would hear the jackals howling. There were four guys living at Hope who always had dirty bare feet and ate lunch in the community kitchen in Promesse.

She hardly ever looked at anyone, she was very absorbed in the minutiae of her life. The Gujarati midwife came out from Pondicherry every week and took her blood pressure and told her to be careful not to eat too much salt.

Some days it seemed a long time from one meal to the next, with not much to do in between. She read somewhere that Mother had said, "One should eat to live, not live to eat," but meals were the high point of the day. Only the men talked at the table. She could not really understand everything that was said because the conversation was in English, German or Italian. The guys from the farm came in, sat down, ate their food, and left. They often did not say a word. Guiom was absorbed in some books by Sri Aurobindo. He would sometimes read aloud to her. She did not understand anything, but it was pleasant and peaceful after crossing the world through crowded cities and train stations beset with unruly mobs.

Dhyan and Guiom soon became friendly with their neighbors in Promesse, Ram and Susan. They were in the next apartment. He was a rich Indian from Bombay and she was American. They were expecting a baby in January. They were building a house in a grove Neem trees near all the happy hippies at Silence. She was busy stitching clothes and a quilt for her baby. Dhyan could hardly keep her few clothes mended. Guiom had adopted the local dress of a longi over the bottom half of his body and a towel over his shoulder. It had been suggested that he help work on the farm. He was gone most of the day. Even though he was working they were not given any money. They had no money at all. Susan would take Dhyan to town and out to lunch or shopping, because Ram would go visiting friends or on a drinking spree and she would not see him for days. They had plenty of money from his rich family in Bombay. It would get him angry that she spent it, but she was angry that he would disappear for days. When they were in their apartment there were loud arguments that everyone in the compound could hear. She would lock him out of the apartment and he would be banging on the door yelling at her. Sometimes she ignored him. Sometimes she yelled back. Everyone ignored them. Guiom sometimes went off with Ram to Pondicherry and came home drunk. Dhyan didn't talk to him for two days after one excursion, so he didn't do it again.

Ram was wonderful when he was sober; just a loud drunk. There were no rules in Auroville. Whatever happened was "Mother's Grace," and it was okay. The Italian couple tried to counsel Ram and Sue . They were told to mind their business. Even when Ram and Sue were screaming at each other everyone else walked around with a rather silent blank expression, which Dhyan hoped was an expression of inner peace or yogic calm.

In the dining room the conversation began to include the guys from Hope, who were all unhappy - like Guiom - that they were working all the time on the farm for the Sri Aurobindo Society and getting no money, only food, shelter and toothpaste.

Dhyan was still very optimistic. She and Guiom had a close and warm friendship with Ram and Sue. There was a great psychic thrill at having entered The Mother's world, and to be having a baby, a new child for the new town.

The pains started in the middle of the night. They had not made any arrangement for that eventuality, so there was no one to call. Dhyan writhed on the bed while Guiom stood helplessly nearby until morning. He went to breakfast and said, "Dhyan is in labor. What should I do?"

The Italian woman immediately offered her help to move Dhyan into the delivery room. Her husband said he would call the Gujarati midwife and tell her to come on the Land-Rover.

The pains were terrible. Each contraction left her exhausted, and afraid, unable to protect herself from the torture of the next contraction.

Mariana was holding her hand and telling her to take deep breaths.

Someone lit some incense under a photo of The Mother. Dhyan wondered if Mother would or could help her. Her breath caught as another contraction wracked her body, and she was thrown back into the vast cave of pain.

Finally the midwife came. She examined Dhyan and noticed the baby was in position for a breech birth.

The labor went on for more than two days, and finally a beautiful child was born. The Mother named him Auro.

Exhausted, humiliated by pain, in awe of the strange child lying on her stomach, Dhyan finally slept. She was tired and depressed after the birth, though she adored her little golden son who had a crown of golden down.

He was a preposterous baby, because he looked like an old man and seemed to understand everything, especially her. She did not feel Guiom, her mother or anyone else except her father had ever understood her, but this little baby seemed to know and understand her completely. They were asked to move out of their apartment immediately after the birth because another pregnant woman needed the space. Guiom exhausted himself getting the hut ready for her as she was recuperating. She was slightly appalled by the whole process of giving birth, feeding the baby, and wanted to sleep, but had to be there for her little son. She did not want to be awake to feed and care for him, but every moment she was with him was something very special. To her he was like God in a little baby.

They moved to the new hut. It was very satisfactory and clean, smelled of fresh paint, and was surrounded by young cashew nut trees. There was a bathroom, running water, electricity, a small kitchen alcove and three rooms under the fresh and golden thatched roof. Guiom was supposed to bring her meals from Promesse, but he fell ill two days after they moved into their hut. For a day he tried to continue, at least fetching the food, even if he could not work on the farm; but then he had to ask one of the other guys if he would bring the food for them, and collapsed with a raging fever. He was delirious and barely coherent for days, and no one intervened. Dhyan was barely recovered from the delivery and had barely enough strength to go to the bathroom, and she had a tiny baby and a delirious man to look after.

The neighborly Belgian guy from the farm saw that Guiom was very ill, and after a few days called the midwife. She diagnosed typhoid. They could not put him in a Nursing Home, it might be contagious:

Dhyan had to look after him.

She was only eighteen years old, but she did what she could, and did not fall ill, but she hated Guiom. She never wanted to touch him again after cleaning him while he was sick. She had moved into one of the other rooms in their hut with the baby, and as he got better she remained there with the baby. Giom continued to dote on her, but she could not stand the sight of him. She was living with him, yet she could not even stand to talk to him. There was no-one to talk to except the baby that grew more beautiful and radiant day by day. He was Lord Krishna in a Wagnerian hero's baby body. He was a joy to be with.

Guiom was better, but not well enough to go back to work on the farm. He just moped around behind her all day long. She tried not to notice, to take walks alone with the baby. She never looked at or spoke to anyone. If she did not have the baby she would have just run away from Guiom as she had run away from the nuns. He was dogging her every step.

She began to notice other people. She would meet them in the Land-Rover or the dining room at Promesse. They smiled at her and the baby, and she felt a community of friends around her. She was cut off from them in her hut in Hope. She felt she could not breathe when she was with Guiom; he wanted to be with her constantly. If she even smiled at any of the other men Guiom would be raging with black looks for at least a day. He was wrapped around her like a snake. She refused to sleep with him or even in the same room with him. She stayed with the baby.

She saw one beautiful man who wore crisp thin white clothes and looked like an angel with laughing eyes, and was nearly as thin as his bicycle. He and the cycle looked weightless as he rode slowly, effortlessly, in a motionless motion past Hope on the road into Auroville.

One day in the Land-Rover she met an American with long tangled black curls like an unclipped poodle. He nonchalantly put his arm around her. She had wedged herself into the last place on the seat, and Guiom had to go sit in front with the driver.

She was blushing furiously and had to turn away when the man whispered in her ear, "You are the prettiest girl in Auroville."

She could not move away from him because she was wedged between him and the door.

Guiom was giving her dark furious looks, when the fat hippie's little girl climbed off her mother and over the guy with tangled curls to get closer to Auro. The little girl and the baby seemed to be fascinated with each other, clasping fingers and laughing, and then the other child in the Land-Rover, a little boy about the same age as the little girl, also climbed over the other people. The guy sitting next to her had to move his arm fast or the child would have landed on her lap on top of the baby. The affection and friendship that happened spontaneously and instantaneously among the three children enchanted the watching grown-ups. The two older children wanted to go with the baby when the car stopped in Pondi, but their parents pulled them off in other directions.

Guiom heard Roslyn was moving to the beach to start a new community. He asked her if they might write to Mother for permission to move into her hut at Silence. She had no objection. She had given the hut to Mother. Mother gave Dhyan and Guiom permission to move to Silence.

Dhyan was happy to move near to where her friend Sue was building, and where there were other children for Auro. She told Guiom, "In Auroville nothing belongs to anyone in particular. I am not your wife."

He did not care what she said. He loved her - madly, passionately, and forever. He felt like killing himself the way she was ignoring him and flirting with all the other men. He did not want to beat her up, but how else could he get her to submit to him?

He could see that she acted as though she hated him after his illness. It was not his fault that he had fallen ill. He did everything he could think of to please her, but nothing that he did pleased her. He hoped that moving to Silence with all the strangers around she would turn to him.

The Sri Aurobindo Society was building a workers camp and community kitchen near Matrimandir, but until it was ready the only place for people to stay near Matrimandir was Silence. It was full of guys with curly hair and guitars, beautiful women, and a surly Puerto Rican who lived in the chicken house. It was a mish-mash of humanity, but Dhyan thought she wanted to be there, not at Hope. They were leaving their comfortable hut, but that was what she wanted.

He had hoped they would have the whole hut for themselves, but there were too many people. They only got the back room. Dhyan told Guiom. "If you touch me I will scream. I don't want you to touch me ever again, not even my hand or my toe."

He could not understand why or how she could feel like that. He loved her. He would do anything he could to make her happy.

"The only thing you can do to make me happy is leave me alone," she said.

He felt close to tears.

In the morning he got into the Land Rover and decided to go to Pondicherry and swim to California.

Ram got into the car. "Are you happy in your new house."

Guiom admitted, "I have never been more unhappy. Dhyan doesn't even want to look at me. I think I will try to swim to California."

"Why don't you come with me. I am going to see Panditji."

Guiom went with Ram. When they got to Panditji's house in Pondicherry Panditji said to Guiom. "Good. You have come. I have been waiting for you."

A bullock cart had arrived at Silence just after dawn and Roslyn put her mattress, her clothes cupboard, a stove, a food cupboard, and two chairs on it. She told the driver to meet her on the beach near Chinnacalapet. She even left the blessings packet that had been given by Mother for Silence framed as part of a collage hanging in the house at Silence.

She went with Bliss to town in the Land Rover. Roslyn was walking from where the Land-Rover stopped to where she could get a taxi to take her to the beach, where bamboo workers were waiting for her to build a hut so she would have a place to sleep that night, when she ran into John Kelly.

He thought that what she was doing was so crazy that he insisted on joining her in the taxi out to the beach. He had had a vision of Auroville, a beautiful promenade along the long white beach. So although it was crazy it was perhaps exactly what had to be done, to start Auroville along the beach.

They rode down the Old Madras Road past villages, coconut plantations and tropical beaches, until Roslyn saw a flash on her right. She told the driver to stop. He stopped in front of a shack next to the road. There were about fifty men from local villages sitting there in various states of inebriation, the local grog shop. The grog shop was next to the large plot of Auroville land Roslyn was moving to.

Kelly was delighted. A grog shop and acres of undeveloped beach with little tiny fir trees sounded to him like a redefinition of paradise, specially after the second liter of toddy*. Roslyn had arranged for the bamboo workers to also bring a hand pump and a long pipe, and she was busy putting two little huts together, one for a kitchen, one for sleeping, and watching the little Tamil men force the pipe through the sand. They fastened the handpump, then - voila! - running water at last.

The bullock cart arrived with her things from Silence. She sent it into

Pondicherry to pick up more materials for the hut and a bamboo bed strung with rope.

There was a parade of Tamil men from the villages on either side of that strip of beach. The place where she was putting her hut was a little hill, and the whole strip of beach had small trees on it, so sparse and so small that she could see almost from one village to the other, except for the slight curve of the coastline.

The beach was used by the local fishermen. The headmen from both villages came to meet her. Kelly chatted and drank with everyone and arranged for one of the sons of the headman to work for Roslyn. A handsome white haired lady, the wife of the headman, brought rice and fish curry and took Baby Bliss to the village.

The old Tamil lady brought Bliss back several hours later with a ribbon in her hair, bangles on her wrists, a black dot between her eyebrows and on her cheek, and some fried fish. The hut was up and the hand pump working. The day was finished. Kelly was going back to Pondicherry, and Roslyn was alone with Bliss on the strange beach. It was too hot to sleep inside a hut, so she put the bamboo bed outside, and let the pounding surf and the wind in the trees lull her to sleep.

The next day was even harder to face. It was so hot that from nine in the morning to late afternoon she could not stir from the hut, because the sand was so hot it burned her feet and she still did not have any chappals.

She was putting a cement floor in the hut. She did not know how to begin to go about shopping and cooking. The Headman's wife kept bringing meals. Roslyn had hoped some of the people from Silence would move to the beach with her, but no one did, although they visited. Nearly everyone in Auroville was busy at Matrimandir. A camp was being built near the center for Matrimandir workers.

After a few days on the beach Roslyn finally went to Pondicherry by rickshaw. It was a long slow ride into town and a long slow ride back to the beach.

At the end of her second week on the beach several of her friends from Auroville came by bicycle to visit her to insist that she come to a meeting because everyone had been told to move out of Silence within fifteen days. The chief architect had decided to use that field to build Bharat Nivas, the Pavilion of India in Auroville. Money had been given by the Government of India to begin the building. There had been a national architectural competition to design the building and The Mother had chosen the winner. That field had been chosen because the grant did not include anything for the installation of water and electricity. Water and electricity were there. The Tamil Nadu Electricity Board had finally flicked the switch and turned the power on a few days after Roslyn moved out.

She visited Silence on her way to the meeting. It looked great. She could not imagine how or why she had ever left. The collage with the blessings' packet for the house was gone. She asked about it. "Some Dutch people who were traveling in a van stayed for a few days, and asked for it. We did not think you would mind if we gave it to them."

They all went to the meeting that had been called at the new dining room in the new workers' camp near Matrimandir. It was a bamboo and palm leaf temporary construction that had been designed by the chief architect in Pondicherry or Paris. He was there along with some others from the Pondicherry office in their white clothes.

With all sincerity the people who had come out in the cars from Pondicherry were trying to explain to the group of people gathered in front of them that although Auroville belongs to no one in particular, the twenty people living at Silence had two weeks to relocate themselves. If they were working on Matrimandir they could move into the workers' camp, or they could go and live at Forecomers, or go back to San Francisco. Nearly everyone was working at Matrimandir, but they found it overwhelming that the people from Pondi could come and turn them out of their huts, and they had no option but to move.

Auroville belongs to nobody in particular, but who was nobody in particular?

Silence

There is a power that knows beyond
Our knowings; we are greater than our thoughts.
And, sometimes, earth, unveils that vision here.
To live, to love, are signs of infinite things,
Love is a glory from eternity's spheres.

Sri Aurobindo, Savitri

All existence is to the Yogin soul forms, and not merely idea forms of the Self, of himself, one with him, contained in his universal existence. All the soul-life, mental, vital bodily existence of all that exists will be to him one indivisible movement and activity of the being who is the same forever.

We have to possess consciously the active Brahman without losing possession of the Silent self. We have to preserve the inner silence, tranquillity, passivity, as a foundation, but in the place of an aloof indifference to the works of the active Brahman we have to arrive at an equal delight in them.

To prevent a relapse into the old obscurity of spell-bound ploys, or into the old mental movement of identification when ego attempts again to ally with the activity of the world, the sadhak, has to hold fast to the truth of Satchidananda, and extend his realization of the infinite One into the movement of the infinite multiplicity.

We are not mind or life or body, but the informing and sustaining soul, silent, peaceful, eternal. This soul we find everywhere sustaining and informing and possessing all lives and minds and bodies, and cease to regard it as a separate and individual being of our own.

We have to realize this silent self as the lord of all the action of universal nature, the same self-existent displaying the creative force of its eternal consciousness.

We realize it as itself, going abroad in its power and knowledge, not only the source of works, but the creator and doer of works, one in all existence. For the many souls of the universal manifestation are only faces of the one Divine, the many minds, lives, bodies, are only His masks and disguises.

(from Jim Bean's Journal extracts from Sri Aurobindo's Synthesis of Yoga.*)*

Roslyn went back to the beach. Some of the people from Silence came and joined her. Bernie sent more money, and they used it to build a beautiful large beehive type structure out of bamboo and coconut leaves. The building had several wings off a large central courtyard that discretely housed a toilet and a shower and was the community kitchen and dining area. There was a workshop, a dance studio and space for three families.

New faces appeared and became old friends as they filled up the new buildings before the spaces were even ready, as new members of the community. They were all working together with Lila in Pondicherry and hoped to create an organization for Auroville artisans and artists called Aurocreation. Roslyn went to visit Bernie for Christmas, and when she returned at the end of January there was a young French couple she had never seen before staying in her hut. The community told her, "Nothing belongs to anyone in particular in Auroville, and it is not your hut!"

She wrote to Mother and asked what she should do. Mother replied, "Find your psychic being. Try and I will help you."

She used the money she had brought from Bernie to build a new hut near the Kottakarai village, where some of her friends from Silence hoped to move. However, she never moved into the hut, she just gave it to friends who had no place to go and wanted to be part of the new community in Kottakarai. She moved into a hut built by John Kelly near the Bharat Nivas.

Kelly was living nearby in another hut on the Bharat Nivas field, supervising the construction. Jim Bean was living in the Matrimandir Camp and came by each evening after dinner for coffee and conversation. Bernie came to visit in April and offered to buy her a house on the beach road in Pondicherry. She said she did not want a house in Pondi.

After Bernie left she moved to an empty hut in Hope where she became friendly with an Italian man who talked her into building a hut next to the one he was building on a small piece of land near Erinchavadi village. They built two beautiful multi-level huts, with real bathrooms and septic tanks. She talked him into giving Auroville the hut he had built for a shop so that it could be used as a Free Store, because there was to be no exchange of money in Auroville. When her hut was ready she only stayed there for two days, because every time he passed her he smacked her on the ass. She gave her hut to a German girl who had moved in with her, and was all over the place, making her thoroughly uncomfortable. She moved to Ram's house. They were leaving Auroville because his wife had been having an affair with Jose.

Roslyn stayed there for six months, then Ram came back. She gave him back the house and moved into the house of a German friend on the beach. She felt like part of a community by then. Working together, playing together and sharing had created for her an illusion of a strong bond. All the products of Auroville, from the farms to the handicraft workshops, were being sold and exported by Aurocreation. Creating goods that could be marketed to generate an income for the community and doing environmental work like planting trees and building dams had become the two focal points of the community. Because there were so many small children, education was also an important activity.

Jose was living in the camp. He had built a house for his wife and children, but she had thrown him out, so he had moved and was working on Matrimandir.

Dhyan had moved into a house in Kottakarai and had another baby.

Bernie fell ill and wanted Roslyn to bring Bliss to the USA. Roslyn's on-again-off-again thing with Jim Bean had really hotted up. He was taking her off on lost weekends that would become lost weeks. Bliss, having been left behind with nobody in particular, was furious! Jim promised Roslyn he would follow her to the USA. She had a return ticket, good for four months. It was a hard farewell at the Madras airport. Roslyn told Bliss they might not come back to India. Bliss said, "We have to come back to India, Mama."

Roslyn asked, "Why?"

Bliss replied, "Because of my children."

"What children?"

"My Tamil children."

Roslyn landed in the USA with Bliss in October 1973. She went to her parents' apartment in Pennsylvania and was told Bernie had retired. Anna was now handling the money, and there was no money for her and Bliss. They could go back to India, they could stay in the USA, but Anna felt that Bernie had supported them long enough. Bliss was not too old. She could still possibly be placed in a good home if Roslyn could not look after her.

Bernie gave Roslyn an old white station wagon, and her grandmother had sent her $500 for her birthday, so she got in the car and drove away with Bliss.

She headed straight for San Francisco. It took her several weeks. She would call Bernie regularly. When she called from New Mexico he told her that The Mother had passed away.

Roslyn was stunned. Mother was doing the Supramental

Transformation. She was not supposed to die! Roslyn, and perhaps others, had imagined that the transformation would slowly change the Mother's body into a new body, a new species, Supramental beings who never need to eat, die, shit or fornicate.

It was not to be. Perhaps Mother's physical body was too small for Her, and when she left it She entered a new body that was everywhere in the whole world at the same time. Nonetheless, Roslyn was desolate. Jim Bean wrote saying he wanted to spend his life growing gardens around the Matrimandir, which was to be - at least symbolically - The Mother's Tomb.

Roslyn did not know whether to use her plane ticket and go back to India to be with Jim Bean, or to continue on to San Francisco. She had received blessings from The Mother before she left Pondicherry to begin a community in California, Auroville West. Mother had said the second city of Auroville would be in Northern California. Roslyn decided to go on to California. By the time she got there she was in contact with an old friend, an artist, who was leaving for Colombia, abandoning his wife and his studio on a cliff in a town called Bidonville, 25 miles north of San Francisco, overlooking the Pacific. He offered her the studio. The studio was owned by the neighbors. They lived in San Francisco, and used their house only occasionally on weekends. They were happy to have someone living on the property.   They did not charge any rent. They did not feel it was an adequate liveable space. They were so concerned about her comfort that they ran an electrical line from their house to the studio so she had electricity.   She had no idea how miraculous it was to get a rent free space with an amazing beautiful view of the ocean in the USA, and in one of the nicest communities!

There was no bathroom in the studio. A nearby neighbor on the other side of the studio, Frankie, offered Roslyn and Bliss free access to his bathroom, which had a door that opened onto the back of the house, so they could even use it without going through the house.

Frankie and his wife were French. They had grown up in neighboring castles in the South of France. As her parents had no son, and she was the eldest daughter, Suzanne had inherited the title and was a Countess. She did not like to speak about this. She had been taught about the French Revolution in school, as a child, and was terrified that one day she and her parents would be murdered because they were aristocrats. They had a marvelous old palace with winding stairs, towers, and numerous rooms that helped to compensate for the dangers of having titles.

Frankie, on the other hand, was born before his parents were married. His mother, Francoise, was the only daughter of a Baron! She had eschewed the life of the aristocracy and had fallen in love with Paris in the thirties. She had visited the salon of Gertrude Stein, knew F.Scott Fitzgerald, Anais Ninn, Picasso, and numerous bohemians. She was gorgeous, and not at all interested in making a suitable marriage or making her papa happy.

She was bursting with generations of comfort and tradition and wanted something else. She became part of a very bad crowd - Jean Cocteau, Henry Miller, and her lover, a young American with a heroin habit. She was finally rescued by a handsome American who had been a dentist; but, fled middle class respectability. He had come to France in search of adventure, and bought a boat in which he sailed around the Mediterranean.

She left Paris with him, to Nice, where they got on the boat. She was nauseous all the time. By the time they got to Istanbul she was certain she was pregnant. He protested undying love and wanted to marry her immediately. There and then, she saw the value of all she had rejected. She did not want to be married in Turkey. She wanted to be married in France. She did not want to get back on the boat and spend months, sailing back to France.

She sent a telegram to Papa, and he replied, "All is forgiven, come home. Love Papa. 10,000 Francs enclosed." She booked a suite on the Orient Express to Paris and bade a fond farewell to Frankie's papa, who promised to set sail immediately for France.

He promised to come to her father's castle and ask him for permission to marry her. He even agreed to marry in the Catholic Church; anything she wanted. He loved her and wanted her happiness. Would she reconsider and travel back to France with him on the boat? No! She would not.

They wept in each other's arms, and he had to jump from the moving train. They waved, and then she relaxed in her luxurious compartment, and ate and slept all the way to Paris. Papa met her in Paris and took her home. Her mother had died when she was born. Her father had never remarried. They had fifty servants in the house and hundreds on the estate. He did not know what to make of her returning alone, unwed and pregnant, but he was happy that she had come home, and that he would have a grandchild.

She loved her American Mr. Smith. Papa was so overjoyed to have her back he indulged all her whims and fantasies, but seemed disappointed when Mr. Smith finally arrived. Frankie was already some weeks old by that time. Francoise was overjoyed to see him. They were so obviously in love that her father had to agree to a wedding, but insisted that Mr. Smith sign a premarital agreement that he would never lay claim to the estate.

They were married and given a suite of rooms in the castle. If life were a book, one could close it here and say that and everyone lived happily ever after, however, life is a little bit longer than that.

Mr. Smith sold his boat because Francoise refused to ever set foot on it again.

They were certainly very comfortable in the castle. Much to Frankie's chagrin, another baby arrived, but he was very well loved and looked after, and was a special favorite of his grandfather. Although he was given most of his meals in the nursery by his nurse, on Sunday he was allowed to join the family and grandfather in the dining room for lunch. There was a footman behind every chair.

Life was wonderful. There were dogs and horses, gardens, and people constantly paying attention to him. A teacher came from the village to teach him. After a time, each Sunday when he would go to lunch with his parents and grandfather he could see that his father and grandfather disagreed about Hitler.

Grandfather felt it did not matter to France what was happening in Germany, and Mr. Smith saw Hitler as a threat to Europe. The argument became more fierce each week. When Frankie was seven years old Francoise, Mr. Smith and their children were banished from the castle to the fifteenth century priest's house several furlongs from the castle. The teacher no longer came from the village and Frankie had to go to the village school. Mr. Smith went off to fight Hitler. After some months there were no more letters from him. For Frankie it was the end of childhood and the beginning of anxiety. He had lost his father. Was he dead? Had he abandoned them and gone back to the USA? It was years before they were told he had been killed serving the allies in the OSS. During that time Frankie passed into puberty and met the girl next door; or the princess in the other castle in their valley.

Grandpa invited Frankie for tea one afternoon and asked him if he would like to be the next Baron of Monte d'Or.

Frankie was only thirteen, but for him his father was a hero and his grandpa a villain, so he replied, "My father was Mr. Smith, and I shall be Mr. Smith. I do not want to be The Baron!"

His grandfather was furious and gave the title, castle, and everything to his sister's daughter, Mathilde. Francoise and her children had only the 15th century priest's house and a little bit of land. It was a very hard time for them. Nonetheless Frankie remained Suzanne's dearest friend. She thought it was wonderful that he had stood up to his grandfather.

They both went away to school, she to Switzerland, he to some relative of his father in Ireland. They met during holidays. When she was 18 her parents arranged a marriage for her with a Belgian Marquis. She and Frankie were lovers!

Her parents were shocked! They refused to see him. They referred to him as, "Francoise's bastard!" Suzanne was distraught. Her parents promised to disown her if she continued to see Frankie. Frankie had nothing to offer her. He went to Paris, claimed his American citizenship, and joined the army. Suzanne was sensible and married the Marquis.

Frankie fell in love with the USA. He served in the army, then traveled around from coast to coast for a few years. Finally he decided it was time to visit his mother.

When he got to Paris he decided to call Suzanne at her apartment, although he did not expect to find her there. She was there. She was overjoyed to hear his voice. She had a baby daughter and had left her husband. They had filed for an annulment with the Vatican. Frankie was pleasantly surprised to hear this. He called his mother to say he would spend some time in Paris on the way home.

He moved into Suzanne's apartment and looked for work. Her parents did not know that Frankie was there, and were being very generous hoping that she would soon come to her senses and go back to her husband.   They tried to be understanding, that marriage and motherhood had come as a shock to their very gentle daughter. When her parents came to Paris she would meet them at their apartment, or in a restaurant..

Love was invented in Paris, and Frankie and Suzanne had a marvelous season of love in Paris. His mother sent him some money. He worked occasionally. Her parents and her spouse gave her money. They had a lovely apartment in the 16th arrondisment. Nanette would go off to nursery school in the morning and Suzanne and Frankie would drink coffee and chatter endlessly about everything until it was time to fetch her in the afternoon. Nanny would give the child supper, but Suzanne had to give her a story and a goodnight kiss. Then there were the evenings. Suzanne and Frankie would either go out, or friends would drop by. Little white lies to mummy and daddy during shopping trips to the Champs-Elysees was Suzanne's worst problem, until she realized that she was pregnant. She had been terrified of becoming pregnant again, and was a devout Catholic, so they almost never made love. She had not wanted to become pregnant. But she was pregnant.

He was overjoyed. Her parents were at home, in their castle. She had to tell them. Frankie agreed they had to be told. He would go with her. They would explain that they would be married. She begged him to let her speak to them alone at first. He had to wait at the bottom of the path through the orchard to be asked in. They had never invited him into their palace, although Suzanne's mother and his mother had been girlhood friends, and even gone to school together; but Suzanne's mother had married a banker.

Suzanne gathered all her courage and went to see her parents in the afternoon when she knew they would be sitting in the conservatory among the plants having tea.

"Suzanne, how good to see you. Where is Nanette?"

"I left her in Paris with the Nanny. She will be all right overnight."

"How did you come?"

"Frankie brought me."

"Frankie? Surely you are not going to start that again."

"Yes, Daddy, I am. We are going to be married."

"Impossible. You are married to George."

"No, Daddy. You know very well that I have applied for an annulment of that marriage. I am going to marry Frankie, and we would like your blessing."

"You must be mad!"

"Maybe, but Frankie and I are going to be married by the Justice of the Peace in the village and I would like you to be there."

"Never."

"Impossible."

"Why?"

"I am pregnant." she said, bursting into tears.

"There, there, my dear girl, that is no reason to marry him. I am certain your husband will be very happy with another child."

"Daddy, I am not going back to George. I am going to marry Frankie."

"Never."

"Impossible."

"We will disown you."

"It does not matter."

"She is mad. We shall have to lock her in her room and call the doctor."

At that, clutching her handkerchief, Suzanne fled. She ran down the stairs, out the door, through the arbor into Frankie's arms, as he stood there hoping to be invited in.

A few moments later the butler came out and said to Frankie, "Excuse me sir, but the Count has said that you are not welcome here." They got back into his dilapidated Deux Chevaux and went to his mother's house.

His mother was very pleased to see her elder son after several years, and beside herself with joy at the news that he and Suzanne were being married and were already expecting a baby.

They married in the town hall and went back to Paris. The apartment was hers, but she was informed that the rest of the estate would be given to her younger sister, although the title was hers.

There was no more money from her husband, and no more money from her parents. There was no more Nanny for Nanette. They had a roof over their head, but Frankie had to work, or ask his mother - who had very little - for money. The only jobs he could find were menial ones, as waiter or dishwasher. He was a graduate in hotel management, but the only jobs he was offered were dining room attendant or room clerk, that paid barely enough to feed them.

The baby came, and it was babies. Two blonde haired blue eyed boys, like Romulus and Remus. Suzanne's mother broke down and visited, bringing two complete layettes and a Nanny. She refused to even look at Frankie when she visited, even though he served her tea. Suzanne tried to smooth things over, but her mother said, "Please, do not ask me to speak to him!"

Frankie was furious; his feelings were hurt. He was broke, but they had their two gorgeous children, and he was sick of Paris.

He persuaded Suzanne that they should rent the Paris apartment and go to the USA. There they would be able to live like kings on the rent, and he would be able to collect benefits from the GI bill because he had served in the army during the Korean conflict.

It was obvious to her that they had to do something, so she agreed. Frankie's mother sold a ring from her mother's dowry and gave them the money to pay for their passage to New York. Frankie had some friends in New York who were interested in starting an import-export house. He got a part time job as a waiter where he got good tips, and finally invested all their money in a scheme that was to make them rich on the latest fashion - underpants with the days of the week embroidered on the right hip. Ten thousand pairs of underpants from Hong Kong, and on each pair the day of the week was misspelled!

He was not only broke, but in debt. He had to make a move. He was also slightly frightened that Suzanne would call her father who would send her a ticket to get on a boat and go back to Europe with the children. He persuaded her that they had not gone far enough into America. "If you haven't seen California you haven't seen America."

"But what will you do there?" she asked. He laughed at her and piled her and her children into the old Studebaker he had just bought with the rent from Paris, and took them on the long ride from New York to San Francisco.

He remembered Bidonville from an earlier trip to California as a beautiful small town on the ocean. After six days of driving with two restless four year old boys, and a little tearful, insecure, seven year old girl, they pulled into the parking lot of the only motel in town, above the bar.

They got out of the car feeling that they had arrived. They walked around downtown observing the quiet desultory pace of the charming small town, and when they saw the beach the children were enchanted and immediately caught up in the play of other children. The surfers in wet suits and beautiful women sunbathing in the fog struck them as hilarious. One guy with long stringy hair, dressed in black, barefooted, was playing a saxophone to the ocean. "Wouldn't you love to live here?" Frankie asked Suzanne, and she looking at the strange motley of eccentrics and exotics on the beach and had to say, "Yes!"

There was a small restaurant in the town run by an old drunk who offered Frankie a job as the cook when he went and asked her for a job the first evening they were in town. He accepted it although the salary was less than the minimum wage. He liked the old drunk and was happy to help her out. The restaurant had not been open for months, but it was summer and there were tourists in town. The old drunk promised to ameliorate the meager salary, by giving him permission to feed his family out of the kitchen. She also promised him a bonus at the end of the season. They were terribly crowded and uncomfortable in the motel room, two adults, three children, and all their possessions.

They visited the real estate office and saw a picture of a red house on a cliff overlooking the ocean. The real estate agent took them to see it. It was a dream. The house was ordinary and insignificant, but the view was superb. It was love at first sight. They had to have it. Frankie was eligible for a GI loan and the restaurant owner agreed to say he had been working there for a year at a very high salary. They got through the paper work very fast because the owner was eager to sell. Frankie and Suzanne were handsome and elegant, and with the children made a beautiful family, a real estate broker's dream. Because Frankie had arranged the mortgage through his GI benefits there was no downpayment. The monthly mortgage payment was exactly the amount they were receiving from the Paris apartment.

Frankie worked at the restaurant for two weeks, but then when the owner refused to pay him even the meager salary he had promised, he quit.

They were broke, but had made many friends, and most of them were on welfare. Frankie took Suzanne and the children to the Civic Center to apply for welfare. Frankie thought it was a lark. Suzanne was embarrassed.

The social worker tried to give him a hard time, insisting that he at least look for a job and furnish proof that he had looked for work. After months of receiving forms duly filled out and signed by the garage owner, the grocery store owner, and the bar owner in Bidonville that Frankie had looked for work but there was no work to be had; his social worker insisted he do some social service and arranged for him to paint the fence around the local bird sanctuary. He had been working on that for several years when Roslyn arrived, broke, with Bliss, on his doorstep. He was happy to take her to the Civic Center and help her apply for welfare. She was given a check immediately as a single mother, and they were ecstatic.

Suzanne had found a very poorly paid job as assistant librarian in the local library, and the amount of her paycheck each month was deducted from the welfare check, which made Frankie furious. Suzanne also would take old bluejeans from the free box and very carefully, with about forty hours of arduous hand stitching, transform them into very fashionable skirts that she would sell for ten dollars at the local secondhand clothing store. She managed to do one or two of these each month, using the money to pay for the gas in her ancient Studebaker. It usually ran, even if it took two gallons of gas to get up the hill in front of the house.

Frankie had become great chums with a very wealthy lady who called herself She. He had built a sauna in her house, and created a beautiful Japanese garden for her. She had given him a small old school bus that he completely renovated and painted mauve with the legend 'Hacienda de Valdez' and a big glowing sun on the side.   It was a comfortable house on wheels for six people overnight, and even more people could be accommodated on a day trip. Frankie was often asked by She to take her hang gliding. She was about sixty years old, and had snow white hair, but was not ready to be an old woman.

Frankie had finished the work on the sauna and garden for She. She had a young man from Texas staying with her and seemed to be trying to take a distance from Frankie.

He was at loose ends. Suzanne was struggling to make ends meet. Nanette had gone to stay with her grandparents, and was going to boarding school in Belgium. The boys were typical seven year-old rowdies, furious with their parents because they did not have a TV, new cycles and all the other things their classmates had.

The family was hanging on by the skin of their teeth at the edge of a cliff that was slowly crumbling in front of their eyes into the ocean. They would wake each morning grateful the house had not slid down the cliff into the ocean, wondering if or when it would. One of the houses nearby had had to be evacuated because the ground under it had fallen into the ocean, their foundations had caved in, and the owners were trying to make an insurance claim. Roslyn and Bliss crashed into this world like visitors from another planet.

It was friendship at first sight between her and Frankie, kindred souls. They were both in love with the adventure of living, and condemned by everyone else as totally impractical. They had both traveled widely and loved a good yarn. Frankie was a philosopher extraordinary and Roslyn was a great story-teller. They loved to come together every afternoon at the round table in the red house, in front of the picture windows overlooking the cliff, and drink tea. Suzanne stitched on her interminable skirts, and they would rap.

Roslyn had only been there a few weeks when Frankie left for Mexico with one of the boys. He had been planning to leave when Roslyn arrived, and put off his departure for a few weeks, but as the weather continued cold and wet, he took off in search of some sunshine with the welfare money for the month.

People were saying it was the worst winter they could remember. It rained all the time, when it was not raining it was foggy. There was not a glimpse of sun for months. There was no heat in the studio and Roslyn's silk clothes from India did little to keep her warm. She could hardly bear to get out of her sleeping bag, except to go to Suzanne's house. There they would sit next to the fire with warm cups of tea and soothe one another with stories of the past and dreams for the future.

Suzanne had only the fireplace in the corner of the living room for heat. They had very little firewood, so each day the fires were smaller and smaller, until they were practically homeopathic. Suzanne would wait until Roslyn arrived to light a few twigs. It was a siege of cold and damp. Eventually they ran out of wood. Roslyn suggested they visit Frankie's friend, She, in her little oak forest on the edge of town where She had cords of firewood stacked neatly along her fence. She frequently had given Frankie permission to help himself from the woodpile.

They drove over there in the old car. She was not there. She had once asked Suzanne if she had conceived the twins by artificial insemination: the relationship between them was so cool, it could perhaps be described as chilly. She had invited Roslyn once for a sauna. She gave her a clean towel and disappeared. They had not spoken fifty words to one another. She seemed to be only interested in men. Suzanne and Roslyn were happy that they did not have to ask her for firewood, and filled the car with as much wood as it would hold, then rushed home for a cup of tea and a big fire. Curled up next to the fire they could watch the storm raging over the ocean. Suzanne was constantly worried that the cliff would collapse. Perhaps one night while they were asleep the house would tumble down onto the beach, into the crashing surf. It made it more interesting. It was a bit like being shipwrecked.

Between them they had two children and were living on welfare and foodstamps that never quite stretched from one distribution day to the next. They shared what they had, but they did not have much except their wits, which they would parry with one another until they were usually both convulsed with laughter. They turned everything they did not have into a joke, and thoroughly enjoyed what they did have, which was one another's company. Suzanne's little boy would come in, "Mom, is there anything to eat?"

"Not right now," she would replay with a twinkle in her eye. "Time to do your homework."

"Can I do it in here? It's too cold in the room."

"Only if you are very quiet."

"Can I have some tea?"

"Well, as it is very weak tea, I suppose you may have a cup, but no sugar. Sugar is bad for your teeth."

Roslyn would explode with laughter. They would re-use old tea leaves until the tea was indeed very weak. She was amazed at how little milk and sugar Suzanne used, and tried to emulate her.

Bliss had found a family of five children who lived in the house across the muddy lane. Bliss was five years old and those children were two, four, five, six and seven. Their father was always drinking beer, the television never was turned off, and the mother did not seem to object - if she even noticed - that she suddenly had a sixth child around. Bliss would go there from school and stay for dinner. Then she would go looking for Roslyn at Suzanne's and try to cadge another dinner. Roslyn would take her back to the studio, light some candles, and read her a story. The studio had been a garage, built in the early years of the century, with a storeroom downstairs. The whole structure was built of wood and stone, and the redwood walls were beautiful in the glow of the candles. Roslyn's friend had replaced a large section of the shingled roof with a Plexiglas skylight. The rain fell on the Plexiglas like sticks on a drum. There was no insulation. The artist had also cut a window in one wall. Roslyn in her sleeping bag, Bliss in her sleeping bag, cuddled close together for warmth as they slept.

Suzanne was always working. In the morning she would go to work in the library. In the afternoon she would stitch endlessly on the skirts she sold for so little money. Roslyn made a doll for Bliss, but was too busy enjoying the culture shock of being in Northern California to do anything.

Roslyn was very inspired by Suzanne's nobility. She never lost her temper. She never said a harsh word, although she could be terribly ironic. She never complained. She seemed to relish the hardships. Suzanne's account was overdrawn and overdue at the grocery store because Frankie had used up all their credit provisioning the bus for the trip, but Suzanne was not angry. She seemed to flourish on weak tea and dry toast, and the weaker the tea and the drier the toast the more pointed the humor, but there was always something nice to eat for the children. She was amazing.

Finally it had gotten to the point that they had only a quarter between them until the next checks. Suzanne decided to go ask She for a $20 loan.

Roslyn waited for Suzanne at the house. Suzanne came in with a bag of groceries and flaming eyes.

"I see you got the $20." Roslyn said happily.

Suzanne turned on her and said, with fury, "Yes, and She made me sign an IOU!"Roslyn found that terribly funny and finally Suzanne saw the humor in it; they both had a pleasant evening laughing by the fire. By the next day, however, they were feeling bleak. It was cold. It was raining. Roslyn had to wade through mud up to her knees to get to

Suzanne's house. The checks were still two days away. The provisions Suzanne had bought the day before were finished. Suzanne actually said to Roslyn, "I wish you'd stop laughing. It isn't funny."

Jut then a brand new Land-Rover pulled into the drive. Old friends of Frankie had come for a visit from Southern California, and had thoughtfully brought boxes of provisions and a case of champagne. Suzanne introduced them to Roslyn and they laughed and laughed around the fire as the storm crashed around them, munching caviar on toast and drinking champagne. Roslyn said to Suzanne when she left to go home that evening, "It is — very droll!" Suzanne cracked up, and Roslyn and Bliss went out into the storm to the studio replete with good food and friendship.

Spring came. Frankie finally returned from Mexico.

Suzanne would go to work at the library every morning after the children left for school, and Roslyn would join Frankie for breakfast and coffee. After coffee they would go downtown to the Post Office, then, often, get some provisions from the grocery store and go off for a picnic in the bus.

By the time they got back to the house Suzanne had cleaned up the mess they had left in the morning, and it was time for tea. They would sit together in front of the big perpendicular picture windows watching the sun set over the ocean beyond the cliff, and never ran out of things to say. Roslyn told them about her grand romance with Jim Bean, and Frankie said to her, "A bird in the hand is worth two in the bush."

Roslyn replied, "I'll wait for the bird in the bush. He is a fantastic bird."

They agreed to call the house The Peacock Court, headquarters for the Bindoville project in Bidonville.

Frankie's girlfriend She called him soon after he returned, and he was again pressed into service chauffeuring her around, escorting her to the opera, etc. One day She invited Roslyn for tea. They had nothing at all to say to one another. Finally She got up and went to her piano and played some pieces by Debussy, beautifully. Even so, Roslyn did not feel there was any base of communication.

Frankie was very happy with his three ladies, and the ladies were all happy with him. Roslyn and Bliss had made many other friends in Bidonville.

One week in the Bidonville News there was a virulent article against proposed development near the beach. It ended with the sentence, "The land belonged to God before it was owned by men." It was signed by Billy Skylar. Roslyn had already heard about the legendary Billy Skylar and Skylar's Ranch, an 'open land' community in nearby Sonoma County that had been closed by the county. Nearly a hundred families of happy hippies had settled there in rough shelters they had built for themselves, independent of any building codes. The ranch had quickly become a legend, a hangout for musicians, and a center for equinox and solstice festivals and other universal occasions. Hundreds of people would come out from San Francisco for these celebrations. The annual Maypole was a vision of lovely young ladies with long multicolored ribbons swirling around one another in a multi-hued rainbow of harmony and beauty. There were frequent gatherings in the evening around campfires listening to and playing folk music, often including some of the most famous names in pop music.

Skylar's neighbor was a farmer named John Kelly. He must have been the shadow side of Roslyn's great friend John Kelly. Farmer Kelly did not like all the cars driving though his land. He had sold Skylar a thousand acres of his three thousand acre ranch, but the only way to get to Skylar's was through the Kelly land. Skylar and Kelly did not get on well with one another. Kelly accused Skylar and his friends of stealing his sheep. He had thousands of sheep. Skylar thought he was hassling him because he wanted to force him to buy his other two thousand acres, but Skylar did not want to buy it, and did not have enough money. Kelly went to the county with complaint after complaint until finally the county sent in bulldozers to knock down all the illegal buildings on the land, including the house Billy Skylar had just built for himself and his family. Not up to code, no building permits.

Whatever happened to life liberty and the pursuit of property? Skylar got a bill for a hundred thousand dollars from the county, for the destruction of his house and the homes of his friends.   Skylar had to hire a lawyer, so he would not have to sell the land back to Farmer Kelly to pay the county for having bulldozed his house.

Kelly got an injunction that no one could use the road through his land to Skylar's land except Billy Skylar. There was no other way into the land, except by foot through the rugged hills. No one could live on the land. It was just land. Rocky, hilly land, running streams, verdant forests, no road access, no buildings. To walk into the land took a whole day. Billy, while fighting to try to keep the land and the dream he had lived there, and the dream he held for the future, moved to Bidonville. He bought a big house where he and his wife, his ex-wife and daughter, and his ex-wife's boyfriend and a few others were living.

In the days following Billy Skylar's letter in the Bidonville News everyone Roslyn met seemed to have a story for her about Billy Skylar, and Skylar's Ranch. She was dying to meet this living legend.

It was a Saturday morning and pouring rain. Frankie was busy with She, so Roslyn got into her old gas-guzzling station wagon and went downtown to check the mail, hoping for a letter from Jim Bean.

The Post Office box was empty. She still had some food stamps, so she bought some food at the grocery store for herself and Bliss and turned around to go home. At the bottom of the hill, where the road from the commercial to the residential section of town started, were two guys, who looked as if they were trying to hold one another up while trying to hitchhike. They really looked drunk, and it was only midday. Roslyn nearly passed them, but one of them was really and truly handsome. She stopped.

The handsome blonde guy opened the back door and poured his friend onto the back seat, slamming the door after him. He opened the front door of the car, and then asked, in an incredibly sexy voice, "Do you mind if I sit up here with you, Ma'am?"

Roslyn thought, 'I must be an idiot, but this looks like another fantastic bird!' She gestured to the empty seat beside her, and said, "Be my guest."

He gave a slight bow, uttered a softly drawled "Thank you ma'am," and got into the car. He was soaking wet, very drunk, and gorgeous. Long blond ringlets fell over the collar of his rough woolen shirt. The truly eccentric people in Bidonville did not wear conventional plastic rainwear. His friend said, "Hell, it's raining too much, let's go back to the bar."

"There is mulled wine waiting for us at home. Let's go."

"Okay," his friend agreed, slumping over the back of the front seat. He asked Roslyn, "You gong up to Elm?"

She nodded.

"Thank you Ma'am for the lift. My friend here was feeling a little porely."

She laughed at him, and he rolled his big blue eyes at her.

Bidonville has one street down town, at the edge of the little peninsula, where there is the Post Office, liquor store, laundromat, grocery store, bar, restaurant and beach. Then there is a paved road that leads up to the residential section of the town, that is on a mesa, surrounded by cliffs and beach. Only a thin neck of land connects this peninsula to mainland USA. The main road on the mesa is paved. Most of the houses are off the main road on little muddy lanes.

"Tell me when to stop," Roslyn said.

The rain was pouring so hard that she could hardly see the road up to the mesa along the cliff where there were frequent landslides. The handsome drunk was making comments about the weather. "It looks as if tomorrow is going to be a nice day."

She was beginning to feel a little uncomfortable with him. They got to the top of the hill.

"Well, ma'am, you can set us down right here, if you like."

"We will drown in this rain!" his friend shouted from the back seat.

"Like hell we will."

She looked at them. They were both scruffy, and the guy in the back looked fairly old. "Where do you want to go?"

"Well it is just down here a piece," the old guy answered.

"How bad is the road?" she asked. The road to her studio was terrible, she had had to find a way around and about, rather than approach the studio from the main road, because in the rain the road became a waterfall, and there were deep invisible ruts and holes. She could not risk it in her low slung station wagon.

"The road is okay," the blonde reassured her, and pointed to a mud road on the left. It looked okay. There was only a little water. It was fairly level, a few puddles, but she could see nothing terrible until she had gone too far. There was no place to turn around, and suddenly the road looked like a river in full spate.

"Don't worry, just drive slowly. It's not as bad as it looks," he said.

She was furious with herself for having stopped and picked them up. She felt trapped, which was how she usually felt after an impetuous and generous deed, by which usually she seemed to cause herself unnecessary hardship. She wished she had insisted they get out on the main road. The car would probably die in the middle of the rushing water and then how would she get home? She had no money for garage bills.

It did not die in the rushing water, but she was afraid it would do so after she dropped them off and was on her way home alone.

"Don't worry," he said, as though reading her thoughts.

They were still going forward slowly in the blinding rain when suddenly he shouted, "Whoa!"

She stopped the car. They were in front of a big redwood house with about six vehicles in the drive.

"Come on in for a glass of wine," he said.

"No, no, I have to go home."

"Yes, you can go home after you have drunk a glass of wine with us," he said looking at his friend.

His friend also insisted that she join them for a glass of wine.

"But I don't drink wine," she said.

"That's okay. We'll find something else for you, but you have to come in. You were so nice. You brought us all the way home in the rain. Please ma'am, please come in for a few minutes."

"No, I don't think so, I really have to go home. I have a little girl."

"Well hell, so do I have a little girl."

She smiled at him.

"Come meet my little girl," he said.

"No, I don't think so."

"Hell Billy, you must be losing your charm," his friend in the back seat said.

"Please, I want you to come in my house," the handsome man insisted, not taking no for an answer.

She did not know what to do.

He got out of the car, came around and opened her door, bowed, and said "Billy Skylar at your service, ma'am."

She was flabbergasted. The one person she wanted to meet in Bidonville. "Are you really Billy Skylar?"

She looked at his friend when she asked this question.

The friend laughed at her and replied, "Yes, you have nothing to worry about. He is Billy Skylar."

She got out of the car and followed this man whom she had been dying to meet into his house. The house was full of people. An exquisite woman with long blonde hair in a flowered print dress greeted Billy and his friend, scolding them for being late, wet and drunk: Billy's wife.

He ordered her to give a glass of mulled wine to the exceptional lady who had save them from certain death by drowning in the deluge.

The blonde woman looked at her askance. Roslyn introduced herself.

Billy Skylar looked at her, "I've heard about you. You lived in Auroville."

"Yes."

His friend, Lou, said, "I met Mother in 1965."

"Come, come, sit," Billy said, dragging her across the room to a chair by the fire, from which he evicted a scruffy little girl with big eyes by picking her up and setting her down gently on a big cushion on a beautiful handmade hooked rug.

Roslyn had a glass of warm spiced wine in her hand. There seemed to be many people in the room, but it was very peaceful and harmonious. It seemed that they all lived there.

She asked Lou, "How did you come to meet The Mother?"

"A few years ago I felt it was time for me to go to India. I had heard that if you have a guru he will find you at the right time. I decided that if I had a guru it would make it easier for him to find me if I went to India.

"I visited all the holy places, the temples, the Ashrams, the mountains, the seashore, and met many gurus and holy people, but somehow it didn't change anything for me. I finally realized that my spiritual path is not in India, but here in California, and there is no guru but the guru here," he said, pointing to his heart.

"I was ready to leave India, but I had to wait for several days in Madras for my flight to San Francisco. I had of course heard of the great sage of Pondicherry, Sri Aurobindo, and knew that he had passed away years ago, but as I had nothing more exciting to do I decided to visit his ashram.

"Even now, particularly on a day like today, the memory of that place is like Xanadu."

"I had been traveling in India, Ceylon and Nepal for nearly a year when I arrived in Pondicherry. What a beautiful place! I had seen wonderful places, but they were always surrounded by the chaos of poverty and disease that is everywhere on earth, but especially evident in India. The Taj Mahal Hotel in Bombay was the most beautiful and luxurious hotel I had ever seen, and I am a professional musician, so I have seen many hotels, but the beggars ruined it for me.

"I do not know what Pondicherry is like now, but then, it was unbelievably clean, quiet and beautiful. I was given a room in an Ashram guesthouse on the beach. There was a beautiful promenade along the ocean, no cars, only cycles and cycle rickshaws. Many people wore white. When I got up early the next morning I walked along the promenade, absorbed in the early morning peace. There were a number of people walking and jogging, but no one disturbed my peaceful solitude, walking slowly looking at the gentle waves lightly touching the shore, and the sunrise. There the sun rises on the ocean. Here it sets on the ocean. There, there was a little man who had an urn of excellent hot coffee on the back of his bicycle. I stopped and stood there drinking my coffee, watching the people in white walking briskly, and a few jogging smartly, and thought that if there was another place in the world for me, besides California, this could be it.

"I had heard a rumor that the town had been designed by Louis XIV, the Roi de Soleil, which was why it was set out with broad avenues radiating out from the central, very charming park, like rays from the sun. Along these avenues were high walls over which I could see flowering trees and shrubs. It did not look like any place I had seen anywhere before. There was such a peace, such tranquillity. I was there in the middle of the winter. The weather was lovely, cool and fresh in the evening, bright and warm during the day.

"It was the last thing I expected, to find such a charming place in India!

"I walked from my guesthouse to The Ashram, and just for the hell of it asked for a darshan with The Mother.

"She made me wait for a week. I had to go back to Madras and change my plane reservation. There wasn't a travel agent in Pondicherry and the phones were hopeless, but I hired a car for a day from The Ashram and went to Madras and canceled my reservation and booked a new flight for three days after my appointment to meet Mother.

"While I was hanging around Pondicherry, it seemed everyone I spoke to, everyone I met, was all excited about Mother's plan to build a town for the realization of Sri Aurobindo's yoga.

"I thought it sounded like a great idea, and when I went to see Her I asked Her if I could use my ranch in California for the same purpose.

"I had bought fifty acres in Sonoma, years ago, and had never done anything with it. I wanted to do something for The Divine.

"Mother promised to help me."

Roslyn could not believe it. "You mean you started a community here in California with Mother's blessings?" she asked incredulously.

"Yes. It was called Morningstar Ranch. Aurobindo means Morningstar, so we chose that name and used the native American eight pointed star as our logo.

"I felt I had to give the land to The Divine, so I tried to transfer the title to 'God.'

"I wrote to Mother. Billy do you have the copy of those letters I gave you?"

Billy went over to a desk and pulled a file folder out of a drawer and gave it to Roslyn.

There it was. She could not believe her eyes. Copies of Lou's letters to Mother and Her replies.

Lou had written to Mother; he wanted to deed his land to God. She wrote back telling him she thought that was a very purposeful thing to do.

Then he wrote and told her that he had invited many people to come and live on the land. She wrote back saying that was very interesting, and asked him to send her photos of the people.

Lou sent her a black and white photo, a copy of which was in the file. Fifty hippies, bearded, bedraggled, ragged, rugged, flashy, uniformly unkempt, with Lou and a woman kneeling toute nude in the center.

The next letter in the file was from one of Mother's secretaries saying she was too shocked by the photo to show it to Mother.

The next letter in the file was a letter from the same secretary apologizing for her letter of the day before.

Then there was the final letter of The Mother. It completely blew Roslyn's mind. These letters had been written in 1966. In 1970 a friend in the USA had sent Roslyn some LSD by mail. Many people in Auroville had expressed an interest in taking LSD. Roslyn had no desire to be an acid guru in Auroville, so she had offered the acid to Mother. She had sent it in a letter to Mother, through Mari, and explained, that if Mother gave Her blessings for her to use it and distribute it in Auroville, she would.

Mari brought her a reply from Mother saying, "Mother said she had never been offered the substance before, and so She wanted to convey her thanks to Roslyn because it would give her the opportunity to work on the substance. But, for the moment, She did not think Roslyn needed to take any LSD; but," Mari said, laughing, "Mother said She promises you a trip!"

What a trip! Years later to discover that although Mother had never been given the physical substance LSD until 1970, she had written a definitive essay about the psychedelic experience in 1966. Roslyn was blown away. Of course what Mother had written about LSD was the most insightful writing about LSD Roslyn had ever read, and she had taken plenty of LSD. She would never forget the final sentence of that letter, "But if the psychic being could use this substance the result would be miraculous!"

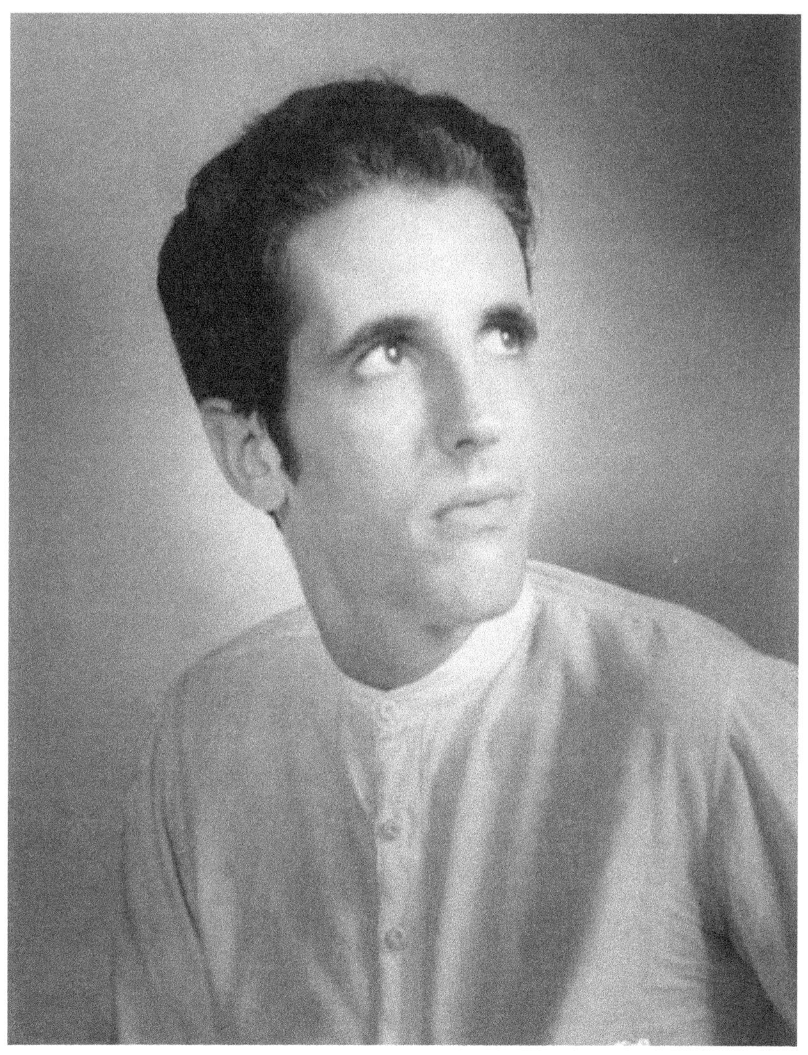

Jim Bean

X

There is a consciousness mind cannot touch,
Its speech cannot utter, nor its thought reveal.
It has no home on earth, no center in man,
Yet is the source of all things thought and done.
The fount of the creation and its works.
It is the originer of all truth here.
The sun-orb of mind's fragmentary rays,
Infinity's heaven that spills the rain of God.
The Immense that calls to man to expand the spirit,
The wide Aim that justifies his narrow attempts,
A channel for the little he tastes of bliss.

Sri Aurobindo, Savitri

To realize and unite oneself with the active Brahman is to exchange perfectly or imperfectly as the union is partial or complete, the individual for the cosmic consciousness.

One arrives at that, becomes that, whether by breaking the walls of the ego, by identifying oneself with all existence in the One, or else from above by realizing the pure self or absolute Existence in its outgoing, immanent, all embracing, all constituting self knowledge and self creative power.

It is as the immanent silent self in all that the foundation of this cosmic consciousness can most easily be laid by the mental being. The Witness is pure and omnipresent who regards all the activities of the universe as the Conscious Soul of the Cosmos, Satchidananda, for whom Nature displays the eternal procession of her works.

Sat: He is beyond the conception of space, time and causality that he creates phenomenally as the conditions of manifestation. There is no cause for this existence, no object, no increase, no decrease, no change. It is not subject to time, causality, space. He alone is. Nothing else exists. He must necessarily exist by Himself, in Himself, to Himself. He is absolute existence.

Chit: We are not conscious of external objects, only of certain perceptions and impressions as this is all being can grasp of external things. Consciousness is the fundamental thing from which all existence proceeds. All things are but the distortion of the absolute consciousness. All sentience is ultimately self-sentience, sat/chit, sentience in the condition of existence. Transcendental existence is one and simple without parts. Consciousness therefore does not proceed by the same laws as our individual consciousness. Consciousness does not proceed by differentiating subject from object, knower from known, but simply is by its pure right of unqualified existence.

Ananda: Where there is no limitation there is no pain. The Bliss of Brahman is therefore absolute in its nature.

If we can by the mind and heart get at the truth of the spirit, receive the powerful descent of the divine into this lower humanity and change our nature into a reflection of the divine nature, we can break down the walls of ego.

The complete realization of unity is therefore the essence of the integral knowledge and of the integral yoga.

(from Jim Bean's Journal extracts from Sri Aurobindo's Synthesis of Yoga.)

Roslyn went back to the studio, to tea with Frankie and Suzanne, who agreed that meeting Skylar and finding the letters from Mother was a clear sign that she had been sent to Bidonville to help start Bindoville. It was very exciting to feel that Mother was not only a part of Roslyn's past in India, but also of the present and future in California.

A few days later Roslyn was cleaning up some of the dead leaves around the studio when a bald man with a long red pony tail came by. He asked, "Are you Roslyn from Auroville?"

"Yes."

He extended his hand to her. "I am Saschwa, founder of The Church of the Gentle Brothers and Sisters."

She took his hand, and looked at him and saw he was extending an offer of friendship as well as his hand.

She invited him into the studio, where they sat on cushions on the floor because there were no chairs or beds.

He told her that he had sought her out because he had heard that she was a devotee of Mother and had even met The Mother in Pondicherry. He asked her to concentrate with him on Mother.

Roslyn sat there and tried to quiet her mind. She had learned in Pondicherry that a silent mind was the first step towards meditation. She looked at Saschwa, and could not believe what she was seeing. His face, which was slightly puffy and ordinary, seemed to dissolve. Face, hair, everything changed, as though it was made from water. Roslyn gasped. For a moment it was Mother sitting there in front of her.

Saschwa said, "Yes, I am a medium and a healer."

Her mind rebelled at the thought of what she had seen and what he had said, but he was so genial. There was nothing menacing about the entire experience, except that it went beyond the bonds of anything she had ever experienced.

"I love you," he said. "I feel you are the sister of my soul."

She said, "This is all a bit much for me. Come let's visit my friends and have some tea." She took him over to The Peacock Court.

Frankie and Suzanne found him very interesting. They all agreed to go to lunch at the large house he and his disciples had rented downtown behind the Post Office.

They were impressed by the old big white house, possibly the largest house in town. There was a huge drive and several cars were parked along the edge of the drive, all fairly ancient. They entered through the front door into a large room with no furniture. They were very caught up looking at one another, laughing through their eyes, very skeptical.

The Church of the Gentle Brothers and Sisters? Saschwa had told them that their logo was two hands. They were healers, and healed by simply laying on hands and invoking the force. They were also palmists. He had promised to read their palms. He said he was a channel for a power that could heal.

The room Suzanne, Frankie and Roslyn had entered was dominated by a large portrait of Helen Blavatsky.

Saschwa greeted them and introduced everyone to everyone. All his followers had names like, Moonglow, India, Soma, Krishna. New Age names that they had received with their initiation into the church. There was a cute little roly-poly, swarthy, slightly bald, bearded guy named Scotty who bragged that he had been friendly with Saschwa for more than fifteen years, longer than anyone else in the group. He had painted the portrait of Blavatsky.

The others were all much younger than Saschwa and Scot. They were a group. Although they were different ages, sexes, backgrounds, they were somehow all the same. They seemed to each be making an effort to be more spiritual, more esoteric, less externalized. Saschwa was the guru. Everyone seemed to hang on his every word, and he delighted in it.

Lunch was fried tofu and brown rice with vegetables. Suzanne remarked that she thought the food was lovely. Frankie mumbled he thought the food might be good for rabbits, and hardly ate anything. The group did not drink black tea, which was the primary fuel of The Peacock Court, but only green tea. Frankie liked Saschwa, but hated watching all the reformed hippies drinking green tea and waiting for their guru to say something. Everyone was very sweet. There was only honey for the green tea, no sugar. The basic sacrament of life, at least for Frankie, was black tea with sugar. If green tea with honey indicated spirituality or yoga or The New Consciousness, he did not want anything to do with it. He was feeling very uncomfortable, although Suzanne and Roslyn seemed quite happy with the group. Saschwa, of course noticed Frankie becoming increasingly uncomfortable, and asked the group to excuse him and his guests so he could take them to his house to meet the girls. He did not live in the large house with the rest of the group.

He and his companion, Moonglow, had a separate house on the Mesa. He promised Frankie a real cup of tea, and they followed his car in the bus. The other disciples were not happy not to have been included in the invitation, but Saschwa had made it clear to them that they were welcome in his private space only by invitation, and they were clearly not included in the invitation. The disciples were nearly obsequious in their relationship to him, but he really was something of a phenomenon.

His personal domain was a beautiful house overlooking the ocean. He lived there with Moonglow and two little Chihuahua dogs. They were very small and went wild with yips of delight when he walked in the door. The first thing he did when he walked in the house was to pick both of them up and greet them with love.

He welcomed Frankie, Suzanne and Roslyn and told them they would all remain lifetime friends for they had already been friends for many lifetimes.

His house was full of extraordinary pieces of exotic art. A pair of Chinese ancestors painted on silk hung near the fireplace. There were beautiful bowls, vases filled with lovely dried flowers, and comfortable expensive furniture. There was a kitchen stocked with beautiful gleaming pots and pans hanging over the stove, and there was lovely china stacked in elegant cupboards with carefully wrought glass doors in wooden frames.

Saschwa said to Frankie, "I noticed you did not have much of an appetite at lunch, would you like some smoked salmon on toast with your tea."

"What is that all about? Your disciples are vegetarian and drink only green tea and live without any furniture in that huge house, and you live like this?"

"Karma, my dear, karma. It is my karma and dharma to live like this. My lovely little dogs need certain amenities. They are very delicate."

They certainly looked delicate. They were hardly as big as his hands. They were so thin. They had so little fur. They looked more like mice than dogs.

Saschwa was preparing tea, toasting bread, doing this and that, and all the time holding his dear little dogs, or setting them down just next to his hands when he needed both hands.

He finally set them down on a deeply upholstered chair when he went to pour the boiling water into the kettle. His gentleness with them was amazing, and of course they adored him. When he set them down, they whined. He told them to be good girls, and they were quiet and curled up against one another and watched him.

When everything was ready he carefully picked them up and sat down with them on his lap.

At last there were cups of good black tea, with sugar and milk, and little plates of tea sandwiches and cakes. While they drank tea Saschwa told them a little about himself.

He was from New York, where he had studied business. He had worked for a firm of stockbrokers, but at the same time had always had deep, intense and strange inner experiences. He finally decided that he was not supposed to be living and working in New York, just as most of the people around him decided he was a little stranger than most people.

He went to Mexico.

There he discovered he could heal people by touching them. At first it had frightened him, but then he began to enjoy it. His old friend, Scotty, also was unhappy in New York. Within a couple of months he joined Saschwa in the little village where he had been living in Mexico. They would go up to the border every six months and then go right back to the village, always loading up with vitamin and mineral supplements for the villagers, because Saschwa felt that many of the people were simply suffering from malnutrition.

They made friends with other gringos who were also living in Mexico, and moved into a small ranch at the edge of the village where people from the whole area would come with their sick friends and family members. They called him 'brujo' which means something like witch, shaman, healer. The people would often bring him small gifts, a chicken, a half dozen eggs, a bag of grain. There were even people who asked him to take their children, and look after them. He had not been willing then to take the responsibility of children, but he had a dream of building an orphanage for orphans who are maimed, crippled, or terminally ill, a house of love. Some of the people in the group had been traveling in Mexico, and heard about him from other travelers. They came to meet him, and simply stayed with him until they were all asked to leave by the federales. Saschwa had become too well known. Someone blind could suddenly see, and every day people were coming from all over the area to be healed. He returned to California with a little band of followers.

The rest of the group included people who had joined them while they were living in San Francisco. When he arrived in San Francisco they were only a group of five, including him and Scott. They rented a large flat to live in and a small hall where they would give readings and healings on Sunday afternoons. For some reason the results were not as spectacular as they had been in Mexico, but people were attracted to him, and kept coming back week after week. He gave courses on palmistry and psychic healing, and most of the people who had joined the group had come from these classes. He had registered the group as a Church for tax purposes.

He did not really like living in the city. They had driven out to Bidonville usually once or twice a week for months, and had fallen in love with the little town. One of the people in the group had just inherited some money, so they were able to afford to move out of the city. They had all agreed to moved to Bidonville.

They had no income, except from the donations they received from their congregation for the Sunday afternoon palm readings and healings.

There was a copy of Sri Aurobindo's "Savitri" on the coffee table.

Roslyn felt that between herself, Saschwa, Frankie and Suzanne a bond of spirit had been forged, a friendship that would weather the storms of time and life.

They were all enchanted with one another, but saw that somehow this had come from The Mother and Sri Aurobindo, like the contact with Skylar. Saschwa spent several afternoons with them in the next weeks. Sometimes he would come alone, sometimes with Moonglow. Roslyn went into The City with them one Sunday afternoon and found it somewhat sad to see the poor and ill or disturbed people coming and giving their contribution to receive a healing, a palm reading, a bit of hope.

Then Skylar came one afternoon for tea and asked if Frankie would like to make a trip up to the land on the bus with Suzanne, Roslyn, himself and a friend. Frankie loved to travel anytime, anywhere, in the bus.

The bus was a self contained world on wheels. There was a tiny kitchen, with a sink, an ice box, which needed only a block of ice and would keep things fresh for days, a drawer for crockery and utensils, and a sliding shelf for a kettle and pots and pans. There were two broad comfortable benches that faced one another across a table where six could sit comfortably and drink tea. The table could be moved at night and set between the benches to become a large double bed. There was a very comfortable armchair-type seat in the front of the little kitchen, as well as, of course, a seat for the driver. There were curtains between the front part of the bus and the back, which could be tied back to open to the front, or closed for privacy.   In the back there were two sets of bunk beds.

Frankie had developed the fine art of the minimal in the bus.   To travel with him was to travel, with wonderful meals and endless pots of tea, adventuring into strange places, off beaten tracks into unknown wildernesses, all very comfortably.   There was always a stream or a traveler's rest, or a State Park to provide fresh water, and everything else one needed was contained in The Hacienda.

They intended to set out in the morning. Roslyn had arranged for Bliss to stay with the neighbors. They had to take the boys with them on the trip. Skylar had arrived with his friend, Danny, who had golden red hair, a short furry beard and merry eyes, and another little boy. They went downtown to buy some supplies, then decided to have lunch at the Court because it had gotten to that time by the time they had gotten back from downtown. It was November 17th, 1974, exactly a year after the Mother had left her body in Pondicherry.

Finally by early afternoon they were ready to start.   It is in fact less than an hour from Bidonville to the land, but Skylar showed Frankie a dirt road that led off into the hills and took them to some hot springs. The pools were there at the end of the barely discernible dirt track. Hot water in deep pools flowing up from the earth. They all took off their clothes and soaked, then dressed and had tea in the bus. By then it was late afternoon. Frankie turned the bus around and took them back to the main road and on into Sonoma County.

Skylar explained that since the land was closed they would go to a neighboring ranch, Star Mountain. There he had friends who were expecting them for the evening, and in the morning they would go look at the land.

Star Mountain was at the end of another dirt road off the main road. All the people there seemed happy to see Skylar and meet his friends. It seemed that there were about ten or fifteen people living there, including several women with small children. There was a large community building, cum kitchen, cum dining room near where they parked at the end of the road near some old pickups and a couple of cars. There was also a van. The residents lived in little homemade huts in the forest. Each one, different from the other, lovingly constructed and maintained. There was a vegetable garden and flowers carefully planted and cultivated near the community building, around the huts in the forest. Skylar reminisced that whenever someone wanted to put up a new house on the land the whole community would come together to help. One could see that happy thought led him inevitably to remembering that all those houses had been destroyed by bulldozers, and he was being charged to pay for the bulldozers.

Roslyn found a quiet place under the trees looking out onto the silent hills and tried to remember Mother.

Dinner was very jovial. There was wine and beer and good food that Frankie heartily approved of. Suzanne found it rustic and charming. Someone played the guitar and sang. Others joined in and sang along. It was very cozy; a community.

In the morning Skylar decided that instead of taking the bus to the land they should all go in his old red fire engine that he had parked in the barn at Star Mountain.

It was a forty-five year old fire truck, bright red. It had a big bell that someone banged with a stick because it was built before fire engines had sirens. They had to push it to get it out of the barn. They poured some gasoline in the gas tank.

Bill got in the cab and tried to start it. The people from Star Mountain started laughing. This had obviously happened before. Billy got out of the cab and opened the hood. He asked for some tools and someone ran and fetched them. He twisted and fiddled for a few minutes. Then he opened the radiator. He put his had in and started pulling out handfuls of straw and mice. Everyone was roaring with laughter.

He asked for water. Someone brought a bucket of water. He poured it into the radiator, got back in the cab, and amazingly enough after a few gasps it started. Everyone piled in. They got half way down the hill to the main road and it stopped. Billy fussed and fiddled, whacked the engine with a stick, pulled a few more handfuls of straw and mice out of the radiator. Before he started again, Frankie got out and said he would walk back up the hill and follow them with the bus.

Billy looked as though his feelings were hurt, but he said, "Okay, if that's what you want."

Frankie walked off, and the fire engine started off slowly again with Frankie's friend, Danny, hitting the bell with the stick Billy had used to hit the engine. They got nearly to the main road and the thing again stopped. After a couple of minutes everyone got out and watched and laughed as Billy tried to start it again. Finally he asked everyone to push. Even then it would not start. Just then Frankie arrived in the bus.

Billy threw up his hands, admitting defeat. They pushed the old fire truck over to the side of the road, and cheerfully climbed into the bus.

Billy gave directions and they drove down Coleman Valley Road to Farmer Kelly's gate, locked with a combination lock. There was a big sign. No Trespassing!!! Billy got out of the bus and opened the gate. They drove through the land, past the barn and farmhouse. Billy had Frankie stop the bus at the top of a hill that led down to the valley that was Skylar's Ranch. Billy said that as far as he knew, no-one had been over the road in over a year, and at the best of times it was not good, so after the rains and all it could be impassable. It was better to park at the top and walk down.   Everyone was willing to walk down to the valley. The road looked like a dry riverbed rather than a road. There were broad and deep crevasses that ran unevenly from side to side. It was even difficult   walking.   The bus might not have made it, although Frankie insisted he could have done it without mishap. It was a long walk.   There were beautiful old trees everywhere, weeping willows, oaks, intermingled with pines and other indigenous species. Finally they came to a running stream where they all sat for a few minutes.

"This is it. This is Skylar Ranch," Billy said sardonically.

It looked as if no one had ever lived there.

"Can you imagine, three years ago there were three hundred people living here?"

The County had taken Lou to court and said he could not deed his land to God. They were going to close Morningstar. I was already friendly with Lou, and enjoyed going over to Morningstar in the evenings. There was always good music. Lou asked me if I would let the people from Morningstar come here when the County closed Morningstar and bulldozed their homes. I said, 'Sure!'

"In four years here the community grew from fifty to three hundred people. My daughter was born here. Then one morning the bulldozers came and it was all gone."

The hilarity was suddenly gone and everyone was quiet. They walked back to the bus, drove to Star Mountain, said goodbye and went back to Bidonville.

Six months later Roslyn bumped into Billy downtown at the ice cream parlor.

"Just the girl I was looking for," he greeted her. He was with his friend, Danny. "We were going to come over to Frankie's to see if you want to come to a Mayday party on the land."

"How can you have a Mayday party on the land?"

"Danny just bought Farmer Kelly's ranch."

She was astonished. She could not imagine anyone being rich enough to buy all that land. She looked at him, "Did you really buy that land?"

He was a young guy with a wife and three kids. They had come out to the Peacock Court several times for tea. They had all gone in the bus to the hot springs once. They were very charming, but Roslyn never imagined they might be seriously wealthy. They had invited her and Frankie to their house in Belvedere each time they met. They were wasting so much good time having good times that they had never gone over there.

Danny laughed at her. "Yes, we bought the land, although we are going to have to sell the Belvedere house. You better come visit us before we move."

"This is exciting!" she exclaimed.

"We think so," Billy agreed.

"Will you come for Mayday?" Danny asked.

"Will you fix the road?" Roslyn asked.

Billy laughed, and promised, "Just for you we will fix the road, okay?"

"Okay, okay, we will come, but you have to come with me now to tell Frankie. I know he will be pleased."

"Sure, we could use a cup of tea."

Frankie and Roslyn went to the meeting at Skylar's on May 1st, 1975.

It was a glorious day. The sun was shining and the sky was bright and clear. When they got to the dreaded gate on Coleman Valley Road it was open. They decided to risk the road down the hill since Skylar had promised to fix it. It was not too bad, but they were surprised at how many cars, trucks, buses, and people there were at the bottom.

They might have buried the last hippie in the Haight Ashbury in 1969, but hippiedom looked alive and well on that hillside in 1975. The women wore flowers in their hair and ribbons and bright dresses, or flowing robes. Most of the guys wore beards and bluejeans. There were many many children.

There was music and a Maypole. One of the children became lost. Everyone went out to search for him. He was found. There were many reunions of old friends. Saschwa and Moonglow came and stayed for a little while. By evening most of the people had left. Billy asked Roslyn and Frankie to stay. There were about forty other people who stayed.

There were two campfires. The people sat in circles around the fire. There were some guitars, a flute and drums. The music was the music of the people, and the bad-old good-old days. Roslyn was sitting between Billy Skylar and Zen Jack, an old hippie.

The evening became night and they all sat there without moving, listening, hearing, going deep within with the sound of the unity there in that small community under the stars near the fires with their music. The current of the magic of the land seemed to grow, and the music became more and more beautiful.

Roslyn was dreaming of Jim Bean and Auroville and India. She felt as if a telephone wire stretched between the land in Sonoma and that dream and The Mother's Dream in South India. Suddenly the circle was silent. She could hear the om being chanted in a temple in India just as the group around the fire began to om.

It was only a moment. Then the guitars began again to play the songs of the people, and slowly the fires died down and everyone stretched out where they had been sitting. Some people had sleeping bags, others didn't. Frankie brought mats from the bus and blankets for himself, Roslyn and Skylar.

There was a strange aura of peace in that place that night.

They all woke up early in the morning, cold and stiff, complaining of the damp.

Summer came. Suzanne took the boys and the dog to France to visit her parents and Frankie's mother. It was August. Jim Bean was finally coming to visit Roslyn, nearly two years after he had kissed her good-bye at the Madras airport, squeezing an amulet into her hand at the last moment, whispering in her ear, "I love you truly."

Frankie received the rent check from the apartment in Paris. Instead of spending it on the mortgage payment, Frankie and Roslyn agreed that probably Jim Bean would offer some money to The Court, Bindoville, an Auroville community in the USA. They spent the mortgage money on a movie camera.

Jim Bean had finally set his date of arrival for the day before Sri Aurobindo's birthday.

That summer the town had initiated a New Age college. Residents were asked to offer courses in any area of knowledge or discipline in which they had some expertise. Roslyn had offered a course in "The Adventure of Consciousness and Joy, Sri Aurobindo's Yoga."

A group of people who were interested in Sri Aurobindo's integral yoga had met every Friday evening for eight weeks at The Peacock Court and read and discussed the book, Adventure of Consciousness. The last class was scheduled for August 15th.

Jim Bean arrived at 1a.m. the day before. Roslyn met him with Frankie and Bliss in the bus. They drove from the airport to a hot spring where they soaked. They drove up to Skylar's where Frankie parked the bus under a beautiful old weeping willow tree. They spent a delightful day with Billy and his wife who were rebuilding their house. There were four walls, but no roof. They cooked on a campfire. There were a few others who had already moved back to the land, who joined them in the evening at the fire. They slept in the bus, and left in the early morning to be back in Bidonville before noon. They stopped at the nursery on the way for flowers to dress up the house for Sri Aurobindo's birthday, and for a willow tree to plant on the cliff to stop the erosion.

Jim Bean was charming and delightful. Everyone had a marvelous time.

Champagne sadhana. Sacraments were consumed. Suddenly during the evening, all the people from the class, and many of Frankie and Roslyn's friends, including She, were sitting and listening to a tape of music Jim Bean had brought from India. Roslyn realized, Jim Bean was not there. She looked around. He definitely was not there. She wondered if he was gone forever, or for another two years, or what?

Suddenly he reappeared, at her side. "Where were you?"

"I took Bliss up to the studio. She was tired. I read her a chapter from Narnia, and waited until she fell asleep before I came back."

He was a very exceptional man.

Roslyn and Frankie went to visit Mount Shasta with Bliss and Jim Bean in the bus. The Gentle brothers and sisters were going to meet them up there. They left Bliss with Frankie, in the bus and Roslyn and Jim Bean walked through Panther Meadow to the source of the Sacramento River through fields of wild flowers along the beautiful clear stream that flowed gently down the mountain.

They found a big tree overshadowing some large rocks near the stream where they stopped for several hours to read a canto of Savitri. When they finally reached the source of the river there was another person there. Zen Jack, who had been sitting next to Roslyn at the fire at Skylar's. He was living in a cave on the mountain for the summer.

When they got back to the bus that evening, Saschwa was there with a gaunt, rather wild eyed looking blonde man who Roslyn and Jim Bean recognized as someone who had visited Auroville briefly. He had been fasting on the mountain for forty days, when, he had been discovered by the Gentle brothers and sisters that morning. They were concerned for his health. They tried to persuade him to eat. He refused to eat anything. He said he was fasting until he received some sign from The Divine Mother, so Saschwa had brought him to the bus. When he saw Roslyn and Jim Bean, who he recognized from Auroville, he felt that was the sign he had been waiting for, and accepted some pollen and green tea with honey to break his fast.

They spent several days on the mountain. It was heaven. The weather was wonderful. It rained one night, but they were cozy, warm and comfortable in the bus. Driving back to Bidonville, Frankie could not help taking a side road off into a forest and they got totally lost. They drove on and on over dirt roads without a clue as to where they were, for hours, without seeing another vehicle. They were in danger of running out of gas. They stopped, and made a camp for the night on a stream by the road.

The next morning some forest rangers came and asked them what they were doing. Frankie explained that they were lost, and the rangers gave him directions to the highway that was only a few miles away. Roslyn loved being lost in the forest with Frankie, Bliss and Jim Bean, and had hoped they were lost forever.

They had a pile of dirty laundry when they got back to The Peacock Court.

The next morning Roslyn left Bliss with the neighbors and set off with Jim Bean and Frankie to the laundromat and self service dry cleaners that were about twenty miles away, across Mount Tamalpias.

While the clothes were going through the machines they sat at a chic little cafe next door and had lunch. It was only early afternoon, and the clothes were all clean. Frankie suggested they visit Danny in Belvedere. Roslyn and Jim Bean had a long history of lost weekends between them and were ready for anything.

They went to Belvedere and found Danny's house, the last house on the point.

They drove through the gates into the estate. A large swimming pool dominated the front of the house. Danny seemed delighted that they had come. He and his wife, children and the friends that lived with them were all preparing to move to the land. They had sold the house, and would be moving out in a few days. The house was large.

Roslyn asked, innocently, "How many rooms does this house have?"

Danny corrected her, "Not how many rooms, how many wings?"

He led them down a corridor with paintings on one wall and windows on the other overlooking the bay, an island and San Francisco, through a grand salon into a little glass enclosed five sided nook with a cane table and big cane chairs with large round backs. There they had some tea, and were finally persuaded to stay for dinner, then overnight, and accompany Danny up to the land the next day for his first night in Farmer Kelly's land. Only his five year old son would go with him. His friends, wife and daughters preferred to enjoy the enormous mansion as long as possible, but Danny was eager to move up to the land. Roslyn, Frankie and Jim Bean refused to stay in one of the guestrooms, preferring the bus. They were happy to receive a grand-tour tour of the house and grounds.

Jim Bean's parents had a house on Fisher's Island, a house in Georgetown, a house on Hobe Sound, an apartment in the Dakotas in New York City and an apartment in London, but he was staggered by the incredible luxury in this house.

It was as large as a small hotel. Some of the rooms were enormous. The ceilings were twenty feet high in the main rooms, and everywhere there were picture windows looking out over breathtaking views. The master bathroom was larger and had more space in it than most houses. From inside the house it could be entered from one side from a hall, and on the other side through the master bedroom. Both doors opened into a large graciously furnished room with many mirrors, alabaster sinks, and glass shelves filled with exotic beauty paraphernalia. There were several louvered doors leading to a shower, bathtubs, toilets. Off one of the toilets and the shower there were doors into the sauna, which also had a door that opened onto a deck just above the swimming pool, where there was an enormous jacuzzi. Danny took the tarp off the hot tub in case they wanted to use it, and turned on the jacuzzi and sauna.

They had a light supper with the family, then spent the next several hours enjoying the thrill of staying in the sauna until they were nearly unable to breathe, then jumping in the icy pool, or luxuriating in the swirling waters of the hot tub.

They felt renewed, purified. Jim Bean tried to explain to Frankie and Roslyn that the reason it had taken him so long to leave Auroville was because he had built an open well-cum-swimming pool on the unfinished well where Auro, Dhyan's son, had drowned the year before. He loved California, but the community in Auroville had become dependent on him. There had already been trouble with the Sri Aurobindo Society. Aurocreation had broken up, and everyone was minding his own business. He had been contributing his entire income to help to maintain the community. He felt he was needed in Auroville. Was Roslyn ready to go back to India?

"To be with you?" she asked.

"To serve The Divine," he replied.

"I have no money," she said.

"What are you worried about?" he replied. "Sri Aurobindo said, 'The victory is assured.'"

"I don't know."

"We don't have to decide anything tonight. Maybe after my sister's wedding I will come back here and we can go back to Auroville together. Maybe we can spend six months a year here and six months a year there," he suggested.

Frankie suggested to Jim that he buy the large empty plot of land next to The Peacock Court.

Jim promised to think about it and discuss it with his bankers in New York.

They followed the path along the far side of the house out to a point. There was a pier where a small yacht was anchored. It was a perfect view of Golden Gate bridge. From the pier they could see a small island where there were no houses, San Francisco and the Golden Gate bridge..

Jim Bean said, "I wonder how much money he got for this place? Probably enough to build the Matrimandir."

Roslyn said, "He bought two thousand acres of land, liberating Skylar's land, giving Skylar access, and wants to use the land for a community."

"Are you really as committed to this place as you were to Auroville?" Jim asked Roslyn.

"I don't know."

Frankie told them they should not waste such a beautiful night worrying about the future, but should enjoy the night, and they did.

A few days later Jim Bean left for New York, for his sister's wedding. Before he left he did the I Ching. The hexagram he threw was, 'The Well.' He read it to Roslyn. "They can move the town, but they cannot move the well." He interpreted it to mean that he had to go back to Auroville.

Suzanne arrived the night before Jim Bean left. There was a ball commemorating the end of the first term in the new college the town had begun over the summer. Jim Bean wore his pink silk Nehru jacket, and Roslyn wore an old black velvet Afghani dress. They had a marvelous time. They got back to the studio after midnight. Bliss was there alone, asleep. She had lit some candles, so the place was lit with a warm soft glow when they opened the door. At some point during the night Bliss crawled into bed with them. Roslyn was perfectly content, squashed between Jim Bean and Bliss.

The next night Jim Bean flew back to New York.

Frankie and Roslyn had climbed a stairway to the stars, but, when Jim left at the beginning of September he did not offer any money, having spent all the money he had with him keeping the show rolling while they were creating a memorable movie, at least in their heads, if not on celluloid. No one had really asked him for any money, and the August mortgage payment was not made at the end of the month the September mortgage payment was due. Frankie sent the September payment, and the mortgage company sent a polite note to say they would not accept the September payment without the August payment, on which there was a later fee of $23.

Frankie hadn't told Suzanne that he had not made the August payment, nor that the September payment had been returned. He did not want to spend the money that had been returned as the September payment, but there were expenses from using the movie camera, and school was starting. Suzanne was upset because they could not afford new shoes for the boys, so Frankie bought the boys new shoes.

By October they were three months behind in the mortgage payments. Roslyn was hoping Jim Bean would return to California for the winter after his sister's wedding, but he called to tell her he had decided to go back to Auroville rather than return to California, and offered to buy her a ticket to Madras. She did not feel that was an acceptable offer. She felt like throwing herself off the cliff, but she went to stay with an old boyfriend in Los Angeles for the winter and learned how to put beads on leather.

Frankie drove down to Los Angeles a couple of times during the winter to visit Roslyn at her friend's, and they always had a wonderful time, but the mortgage had not been paid since August.

Finally in February Frankie called Roslyn and said he was going to fly to Auroville to ask Jim Bean to lend him the money to pay his mortgage.

Roslyn wished him 'Good luck,' but could not imagine that would be very successful.

Several weeks later Frankie was back from India, and had not even bothered to ask Jim for the money because it was clear all of Jim's resources were committed to maintaining Auroville; but Frankie had fallen for Auroville and was eager to go there with Suzanne.

"But what can we do about the mortgage?" Roslyn asked.

"You have to come and stay in the house so I can go to Europe and persuade my mother to help me."

"Fine. I am bored to death with the scene here, but what will I do when you come back?"

"I don't know. We'll see. Something will work out. I will drive down to LA on the weekend and pick up you and Bliss."

So Roslyn went back to Bidonville. She was still receiving occasional letters from Jim Bean saying that he might be coming soon, but she and Bliss were alone in the house. She rented the living room to the local band to help pay the rent, electricity, etc.; let a mother with six kids, who had been evicted, live in the bus; and another homeless person was in the trailer.

The Court without Frankie was like riding a bicycle with a flat tire.

One day the full length mirror in the hall for no apparent reason fell and crashed.

A week later Roslyn spoke to a friend in New York and was told that Dhyan had fallen from the Matrimandir and was in a coma. Jim Bean was busy looking after her.

A few weeks later Frankie returned from France and threw everyone out of the house and paid the mortgage with money his mother gave him. His girlfriend, She, bought Roslyn and Bliss tickets to fly back to Auroville, as a gift on Sri Aurobindo's birthday, after Roslyn sewed beads all over her leather coat for free.

The Kottakerei Community 1973

O mortal, bear this great world's law of pain,
In thy hard passage through a suffering world
Lean for thy soul's support on Heaven's strength,
Turn towards high Truth, aspire to love and peace.

A little bliss is lent thee from above.
A touch divine upon they human days:
Make of thy daily way a pilgrimage,
Through small joys and griefs you mov'st towards God.

Sri Aurobindo, Savitri

All unity is an intensive, pure and infinite realization, all difference an abundantly, rich and boundless realization of the same divine eternal being.

How shall we be deluded? How can there be sorrow when everywhere is the oneness?

Every finite is an infinite and has to know and sense its intrinsic infiniteness as well as its surface finite appearance.

Purusha/Prakriti in their union and duality arise from the being of Satchidananda.

The principle of Yoga is to turn "Godward" all the powers of the human consciousness so that through that activity of the being there may be contact, relation, union.

To the Yogin, action is chiefly important not for its sake, but as a means to the growth of the soul.

In the tantric method Shakti is all-important. In Integral Yoga, spirit, soul, becomes the path to Shakti.

Our synthesis takes person as spirit in mind much more than a spirit in body. It assumes he has the capacity to begin at that level, to spiritualise his being by the power of the soul in mind, opening itself directly to a higher spiritual force and being to be perfected by that force bringing it into action.

The principle is a self-surrender, a giving up of the human being into the being, consciousness, power, delight, of the Divine. The liberated individual being, united with the Divine in self and spirit, becomes in his natural being a self-perfecting instrument for the perfect outflowering of the Divine in humanity.

The object of the integral perfection is to grow into the truth and power of the spirit. By the direct action of that power to become a fit channel of its self-expression, a life lived in the Divine, the divine life of the Spirit in humanity.

The change is evident where there is the aspiration for a spiritual realization of the Divine, and the Divine perfection. When there is unity in all the being and a spiritual perfection in nature, it is complete.

(from Jim Bean's Journal extracts from Sri Aurobindo's Synthesis of Yoga.)

The wheels of fate were turning. The Mother's children, their bright and dazed eyes on the stars, their feet began to slip on treacherous paths. An invisible cloud of disharmony began to gather in the atmosphere. Non recognized the approach of terrible confusion.

Jose had been busy working on the Matrimandir and living in the Workers' Camp. The Camp had been built for Matrimandir workers, by the Sri Aurobindo Society; the administration office of Auroville. Jose had also built a house for Ethel and their two little girls.

Instead of killing Ethel when he noticed that she was having it on with a big Dutch guy, he split. He left the house and did not go back, for years. It was okay having a room in the camp, when you could go back to your wife and comfortable house, but to just live in the camp and eat in the dining room was not his scene. It was too much like prison. Everyone was uptight about sex. The food was so bland it was like science fiction rations, but even duller.

He would get up every morning in his room that was like a cell, only there were no bars on the window and the roof was made of palm leaves and was full of squirrels. He hated the squirrels. They would shit on him. He would wake up every morning, and would get mad if he stepped in some squirrel shit on the way to the john. He was usually the first one up. The whole place was quiet. Within fifteen minutes he would be at the Matrimandir site. No matter how early he got there, or how late he stayed, from dawn to dark there were always a few people at work there, sometimes many people. Everyone in Auroville seemed to come at one time or another to work on the Matrimandir. He watched them with disdain. They would come, work for an hour or two, complain they were tired, then they would stop for a tea, and come back again a few weeks later. He worked from dawn till dark every day. He would start pushing a wheelbarrow loaded with dirt when he got there in the morning. Dump it on the pile. Then take it back to where they were loading wheelbarrows with the dirt they were taking out of the hole for the foundation, and take another loaded wheelbarrow. Dump it. He stopped, a few times during the day for brief meals, then right back to his wheelbarrow. Dump it.

At night he crashed. Exhausted. After a couple of years of pushing those loaded wheelbarrows he was in great shape, like a weight lifter.

He was beginning to go nuts inside his head. Then one of the French broads noticed him. She had come with a group of people from Aspiration, wearing short shorts and a halter-top, for a concreting. She took a long look at his muscles while he took a good look at her legs and shoulders. Even though she did not speak much English, Jose was sure this was a gift for him from Mother for all the loads of dirt he had been pushing around and dumping.

He could not take her to his room. Sex was forbidden in the Camp. She invited him to visit her in her hut in Aspiration.

He borrowed a bicycle and followed the van that had taken her back to Aspiration. She was a little surprised to see him taking her up on her invitation immediately. He knew what would happen, and it did. She was sure she was in love.

She lived with her little girl in a one room hut. He lived in his room in the Worker's Camp. They were in love. They wanted to be together. They wanted to sleep together. They wanted to wake up in the same bed. They had no money. He had not needed any money until he met her. He had given all his money to Ethel when he left.

There was a big empty three room hut near hers in Aspiration. They decided to move into that hut. It was a hut that someone had given to the Chairman of the Sri Aurobindo Society, who had been raising funds for Auroville and administering Auroville since its conception.

The Chairman of the Sri Aurobindo Society never used his hut. Once every few months he would come out in his car with a visitor and show them how simply he lived in Auroville, but he did not live in Auroville. He was never there. Was Auroville going to be like everywhere else in the world, full of empty houses owned by the rich, and no homes for the people?

Within a few hours of Jose moving into the Chairman's hut, the police were called and arrived in Auroville with a warrant ordering them to arrest everyone in the hut. There were seven men in the hut and they became the seven samurai in the ensuing battle.

The seven samurai were taken to jail and eventually bailed out by the community.

A disciple of The Mother, Victor, wrote to the community of Auroville, "No, it is not a quarrel between two camps: it is an evolutionary choice between the earth's past and its future. And ultimately it is the choice of the entire Earth, as one day we had to choose between Hitler (still another "brother") and the Resistance, or between pithecanthropus and Homo Sapiens. And now it is another species. It is another little vibration to catch and to live."

He enclosed a letter Sri Aurobindo had written on the 13th September, 1936: "No doubt hatred and cursing are not the proper attitude, it is true that to look upon all things and all people with a calm and clear vision, to be uninvolved and impartial in one's own judgment, is a quite proper yogic attitude. A condition of perfect samata can be established in which one sees all as equal, friends and enemies included, and is not disturbed by what individuals do or what happens. The question is whether this is all that is demanded from us. If so, then the general attitude will be one of a Neutral indifference to everything. But the Gita that strongly insists on a perfect and absolute samata goes on to say, 'Fight, destroy the adversary, conquer.' If there is no kind of general action wanted, no loyalty to Truth as against falsehood except for one's personal sadhana, no will for Truth to conquer, then the same samata of indifference will suffice. But here there is a work to be done, a Truth to be established against which immense forces are arrayed, invisible forces that can use visible things and persons and actions for their instruments. If one is among the disciples, the seeker of this truth, one has to take sides for the Truth, one has to stand against the Forces that attack it and seek to stifle it. Arjuna wanted not to stand for either side, to refuse any action of hostility even to the assailants. Sri Krishna who insisted so much on samata, strongly rebuked his attitude and insisted on his fighting the adversary, "Have samata," he said, "and seeing clearly the Truth, fight." Therefore to take sides with the Truth and to refuse to concede anything with the Falsehood that attacks, to be unflinchingly loyal and against the hostiles and the attackers is not inconsistent with equality. It is personal and egoistic feeling that has to be thrown away; hatred and vital ill-will have to be rejected. But loyalty and refusal to compromise with the assailants and the hostile, or to dally with their ideas and demands and say 'After all we can compromise with what they ask from us,' or to accept them as companions and our people — these things have a great importance. If the attack were a physical menace to The Mother and the work and the Ashram, one would see this at once. But because the attack is of a subtler kind, can a passive attitude be right? It is a spiritual battle inward and outward — by Neutrality and compromise or even passivity one may allow the enemy forces to pass and crush down the Truth and its children. If you look at this point you will see that if the inner spiritual equality is right, the active loyalty and firm taking of sides is also right, and the two cannot be incompatible...."

The Auroville jihad had begun.

The Sri Aurobindo Society was on a power trip. The Aurovilians had to defend the ideals of Auroville. By throwing the Aurovilians in jail the Chairman of the Sri Aurobindo Society had claimed ownership rights. The Aurovilians had to fight to free Auroville from this falsehood.

There was some discussion that it was perhaps only a problem of misunderstanding between those in the office and those in the field, but others agreed that this was Auroville's opportunity to shake off the management of the Sri Aurobindo Society. A few Aurovilians registered "The Auroville Society" and were taken to court by the Sri Aurobindo Society.

The Chairman of The Sri Aurobindo Society tried to promote himself to President, which had been Mother's role in the Society. He was accused of being an asura by Victor.

The Sri Aurobindo Society had been raising money all over the world 'for Auroville.' In September 1973, even before Mother had left her body, the Society, that had; since the beginning, helped to maintain the residents of Auroville; stopped giving even the minimal amount they had been offering to those who had no personal resources and were working on a recognized project like the Matrimandir. It was rumored The Sri Aurobindo Society was buying land and buildings all over India in the name of the Sri Aurobindo Society from money they were raising for Auroville.

When the Society suddenly stopped giving the soap, toothpaste, and Rs.150 per Aurovilian per month, the Aurovilians banded together and started a distribution service called 'Pour Tous'. Up to that time there was a lot of goodwill and sharing within the community. It was immediately clear that the only way the community could survive would be for the people with personal resources to share with those with nothing, so that everyone would have something, even those who had been dependent on 'Prosperity' and were suddenly stranded without hope of another paise.

Still, the Sri Aurobindo Society claimed the right to take and manage the money from the products of Auroville. Aurocreation was a service handling all the products of Auroville and Auroville related production units. They wanted to give all their profits to Pour Tous. The Sri Aurobindo Society claimed to own the profits and the right to spend that money as they saw fit. Someone raised some money in the USA to plant trees, and when the check came the Sri Aurobindo Society took half.

If Auroville was going to survive it seemed it needed somehow to establish its own legal identity. Meanwhile a couple of the production units disagreed with Aurocreation's policy to give everything to Pour Tous and wanted to decide for themselves how much they gave, and established separate business trusts.

The Sri Aurobindo Society borrowed a huge sum of money from the

State Bank of India using the deeds for the 2500 acres of land they had bought for Auroville as collateral.

The community went crazy. Peace and harmony disappeared and became confusion. No one knew whom to trust. The businesses that had not only broken away from the Sri Aurobindo Society, but also from Aurocreation, were still contributing something to Pour Tous. Aurocreation became a small Boutique that only handled the products of people who had tiny cottage industries, and then had to change its name because the Sri Aurobindo Society claimed that Aurocreation belonged to the Sri Aurobindo Society. The people who were exporting had established separate identities. The farms had established separate identities.

Everyone seemed to be fighting with everyone else about who was in charge of what.

Victor sent the community a letter beginning with an aphorism of Sri Aurobindo:

" 'Governments, societies, kings, police, judges, institutions, churches, laws, customs, armies are temporary necessities imposed on us for a few groups of centuries, because God has concealed His face from us. When it appears again in its truth and beauty, then in that light they will vanish.'

"In the meantime, let the Aurovilians follow their highest consciousness, and the results will be in exact proportion to their sincerity and their freedom from ego."

It seemed that the Sri Aurobindo Society was trying to step into Mother's place as the Administrator of Auroville. They were, however, imposing a different quality of administration and appeared to insist on rights of ownership privilege. They had not bothered to establish the trust and affection everyone had for The Mother. They simply presumed the privilege of being 'in charge.'

Mother had said, "Auroville will be a spiritual anarchy."

It was clear. One solution, revolution!!!

Someone wrote to Nolini, Mother's spiritual heir in the Sri Aurobindo Ashram. He replied with a quotation from Mother, and a comment, '"He who is for some and against others is outside the truth.' In the current struggle in Auroville, both sides are equally ignorant."

The Mother had said, "No politics in Auroville."

This was not political. It was a revolution for the preservation and maintenance of dharma, a battle against adharma. Auroville belonged to humanity as a whole. The Sri Aurobindo Society was claiming to own Auroville by its actions. Funds that the Chairman of the Sri Aurobindo Society had raised for Auroville had been used to buy a palace in Bangalore.

The residents of Auroville agreed that it was their responsibility to protect Auroville from the mismanagement of the Sri Aurobindo Society. Mother had said, "Decisions should be made and enforced by people living in Auroville."

The Chairman of the Sri Aurobindo Society did not live in Auroville. Even when he had been given a hut in Aspiration he had not come to live there. He had no right to make decisions for Auroville. It was wrong for him to raise money in the name of Auroville, unless he agreed to put that money at the disposal of the community. It was a real revolution; Power to the People.

After the Chairman of the Sri Aurobindo Society used police to reclaim his hut in Aspiration and had seven men charged, the seven invited all their friends to come and sit with them in that hut. Sixty people went and sat in the hut. The Chairman came out to speak to the community. He told them he was willing to forgive them. They told him to take his personal possessions out of the hut so it could be occupied by Aurovilians. He was not living there. It was unfair that he should occupy a three-room hut where he never stayed, while there were people in Auroville with no place to stay.

He said he needed the hut to show to people interested in Auroville, potential donors who were interested to see that he was living in a humble hut, or that if they were to come to Auroville they might have to live in such a hut.

The community told him they did not want him to raise money for Auroville unless he would give it without any strings to the community.

He told them it was impossible. He had responsibilities to the donors, had to maintain accounts, etc. Someone said, "You're a crook."

The vibe was definitely not cozy. Several members of the community said to the Chairman that he had no right to occupy a large family hut. He had not spent a single night there. Nothing belonged to anyone in particular in Auroville. That hut belonged to humanity as a whole, and was to be used for the welfare of all. The community had decided to give the hut to Jose.

The Chairman shrugged his shoulders in defeat, gathered his few personal possessions from the hut, and left. He did not drop the charges against the seven samurai, and did not drop the charges against the Auroville Society. Auroville had begun its day in court, which over the

next ten years went through the entire Indian legal system up to and including the Supreme Court.   The days of "Goodwill towards all, goodwill from all, is the basis of peace and harmony." were over. The order, goodwill towards all goodwill from all is the basis of peace and harmony; established by Mother when the first settlers began fighting with one another, was finished.

Jose moved into the hut with his French girlfriend.

It was a victory!

Victor wrote to Auroville, "As you know,, some people in Aspiration have tried to work out something for reorganizing this collective body, dealing with external relations — good or bad. I am not here to judge their merits or the soundness of the thing — but they have tried, and called all others to join in the attempt.   I received a letter about this from my friends in Auroville.

"So," the letter continued, sarcastically, "after an Auroville Management by The Divine Mother, Auroville had an Auroville Management by the Sri Aurobindo Society, and then proposed an Auroville Management by the Auroville Society , and now it has chosen an Auroville Management by the French.

"If this is all that this means, there is nothing left but to have an Auroville Management by nobody, or recall the Sri Aurobindo Society.

"There is a force that wants to destroy Auroville, is destroying Auroville.

"It plays on the mental level of doubt, distrust and jealousy, pushing everyone against one another.

"If this move is only towards French Management, why not next year German Management? American Management? Dutch Management?

"Everything is rotten and corrupt in advance with this kind of thinking.

"Will Auroville become a collective of Swedish radishes, Italian Matrimandirs, and Swiss cows?

"Auroville was put there by Mother as a place consecrated to the Supramental transformation. The people who are living in Auroville have a responsibility to humanity to realize Sri Aurobindo's evolutionary yoga!

"If the step being taken now by the community is just replacing the administration of the Sri Aurobindo Society with the administration by the Pour Tous Group, it is a waste of breath.

"Of course those spiritual leaders who have put Aurovilians in jail are just human beings, brothers, of those who went to jail. Everything is the same. Everyone is equal. We are all brothers, all children of The

Mother.

"Everything does not mean nothing!

"Auroville is not nowhere. It is here, put here by The Divine Mother. Why?

"Only there is a force of confusion which would equate dharma with adharma. Beware.

"I am also Mother's child, although I am greeted with contempt by many in Her Ashram and among the Sri Aurobindo Society.

"Auroville, arise. Stand on your own two feet. Be led by Her Divine vision, and not by petty bureaucrats, and white haired power brokers.

"Love, Victor."

Dhyan had gone with her children to visit friends who were building a hut near her hut in Kottakarai. The little girl, who was only two years old, kept trying to climb into her lap. The little boy, Auro, wandered off. She and her friends had tea and chatted about their lives there in the community. Water was a problem for everyone. Her friends were proud that they had begun to dig an open well near their hut. It was a big hole with about half of a meter of water at the bottom.

After tea Dhyan stood up, picking up her daughter, and started to call her son. He did not come. She called and called. She wondered if he had wandered off and gone home or somewhere else. Her friends invited her to look at their well that they had been digging themselves. They looked into the hole. She shrieked, and set her tiny daughter down on the mud as she rushed down into the hole to retrieve the body of her son.

They tried artificial respiration. Then; they heard the horn, of the village bus, and, ran to catch it, to take the child to the hospital to see if he could be revived. They buried Auro the next day outside Dhyan's hut. Dhyan and her little girl were in shock.

The people who had dug the hole left Auroville.

Jim Bean was living in a tiny hut called a capsule, a small hexagonal platform suspended about a meter above the earth with a coconut palm roof. The diameter of the hexagon was barely two meters. His capsule was in a forest of young casurina trees near the field where Auro had drowned. He was horrified. He had been very fond of the little boy, who often visited him in the afternoon. He decided to turn the well into a memorial for the child, and a water source and swimming pool for the community.

He and the father of Dhyan's daughter worked for six months all day every day with masons and coolies, assuaging their grief, by transforming that site of horror into something beautiful for the community.

Dhyan managed to recover fairly rapidly from her grief, thanks to living in a community. It was a large extended family, and everyone in the community was family. All for one, and one for all. Her grief belonged to them all. Her neighbors' children became her daughter's siblings to try to make up for the sibling she had lost.

Jim Bean was trying to sponsor the internal development of the community by starting a bakery to provide bread for the whole of Auroville. He also helped finance a leather workshop, a wood workshop and a pottery. His entire income was at the disposal of the community. He paid for the food for the entire Kottakarai community each month. They were not at all happy that he decided to go to visit his parents and Roslyn when he finished the well in the spring.

Everyone was happy to see him when he returned late the following winner. He had called Roslyn before he left the USA, and offered to buy her a plane ticket. He told her a friend of his sister would be traveling to India with him, and that he planned to be back in the USA for the bicentennial celebration in the summer. Roslyn did not feel inclined to accept a ticket from him then.

When Mother had been planning Auroville, she had originally placed the Matrimandir about a hundred meters from where it currently stands, right on top of the large banyan tree that is considered the center of Auroville. Before the construction began the spirit of tree came to Her in a vision and asked not bot be cut down, because it wanted to participate in the adventure of Auroville. In Mother's vision she saw the tree, not just as a tree but as an ancient spirit that had come to offer itself to the New Creation, and through it the whole world of Nature symbolically offering iself to the supramental transformation. Mother accepted this aspiration and moved the Matrimandir, welcoming a collaboration between past and future.

Panditji, also wanted to offer something to Matrimandir. He made a yantra in gold, the Mahasaraswati yantra of Tantrik tradition, and asked that it be placed in the foundation of Matrimandir. He had conducted an intense puja for half a year to consecrate and energize the yantra, he called it "harmony in human relations. Harmony in Human relations is one of the spheres of influence of Mahasraswati. At first no one seems to mind that the yantra be put in the foundation of the Matrimandir. But then a doubt crept in. Some questionn was raised about tis appropriateness, after all, Mother had not mentioned it in any of her conversations on Matrimandir. Panditji sugggested that they put it near

Matrimandir rather than in the structure. This was discussed, a debate smoldered, then was forgotten. The end result was the yantra was never installed.

Disharmony in human relationship has since reigned.

By the time Jim got back to Auroville the battle with the Sri Aurobindo Society was in full swing. Jim was amazed to hear that his name was on a list submitted to the Government of India, by the Sri Aurobindo Society, naming people in Auroville who should not get visa extensions.

The Sri Aurobindo Society said, "No-one should live in Auroville for more than five years. After five years the people should leave to make place for others."

The twenty-five hundred acres that had been purchased by the Sri Aurobindo Society was about forty per cent of the area designated for Auroville, "The City of the Future." And those acres had been mortgaged to the hilt. Even so, the land that belonged to Auroville was only sparsely settled. There was plenty of room for more people.

Dhyan was working at Matrimandir, learning to play the flute and getting into a relationship with a man who had just separated from his wife and two daughters.

Jim worked at the bakery and Matrimandir, and gave all his money to the community.

The situation was very tense, and he did not feel he could leave when spring became summer and the temperatures went up to 110 degrees Fahrenheit. Auroville felt as if it was going to explode. Jim did not feel he should leave although he had heard from Roslyn that she had moved back to Bidonoville and was waiting for him. There was not enough money. People were hungry. There was a legal battle to fight. He felt needed by the community.

Dhyan's friend had a dream of her falling from Matrimandir, which; at that time, was only four towers and a platform thirty meters above the foundation then. She laughed at him.

She had infected sores on her feet and legs and was tired of cleaning and bandaging them properly. They did not seem to heal no matter how many times a day she soaked them in hot water, or what disinfectants, creams or ointments she used. She finally ripped an old yellow longi, on which was written in red "Om namah Shivaya," into strips and wrapped them around her wounds and rode her old white bicycle to Matrimandir, leaving her daughter with her neighbor, who had a little girl about the same age. She had been doing this every morning for months.

Several people had suggested she stopped working for a few days to give her wounds a chance to heal. She believed no harm could befall her while she was working for the Divine.

She did not want to stop working. She loved climbing the perilous ladder and loved hanging suspended in space, thirty meters above the ground on a delicate grid of steel.

She had gotten nearly to the top of the ladder; and was hoisting herself with her hands onto the platform, when she fell. Through the scaffolding, breaking her fall and her bones on the iron bars every eight feet from the top of the ladder to the floor of the foundation, at the bottom of the great hole that had been dug for the construction, where she landed on her face. She broke her jaw, her neck, her back, her arm.

She did not regain consciousness for weeks.

Somehow her shattered body was lifted from the hole and taken to a nearby hospital. There wasn't an ambulance. Someone went by bicycle and fetched a van. The team of people who had been working with her moved her as carefully as they could, feeling it was urgent to get her to the hospital. She was broken and bleeding.

It was a horror in the emergency room. Finally there was a doctor who accepted to put her into intensive care. Jim Bean had heard about what had happened, and arrived. The people who had brought her were in shock. The staff of the hospital were overwhelmed.. It was fortunate that Jim Bean had arrived to state that no expense should be spared: transfusions, whatever was necessary. Everything possible must be done. Money was no object.

He arranged a roster of Aurovilian attendants, so there was not only a private nurse with Dhyan at all times, but two Aurovilians, also. She was to be surrounded in an aura of love and caring.

Victor sent a letter to Auroville. "It is necessary that in Auroville you must understand that that accident was not an accident. I am not a specialist of Kali, but Mother taught me to be able to see through what is happening. If you think I do not know what is happening in Auroville you are wrong. I can see exactly what is happening there. I am not blind.

"As regards that accident, each one must find its cause in himself, and his individual shortcomings. It is the real cause, the general condition of the community, not any single individual or group. All are equally responsible. If anyone feels that it has nothing to do with him, then he does not understand that whatever befalls a single member of the community is the karma of the entire community.

"Auroville must fight the falsehood of internal division. Those who say, 'We are building Matrimandir,' that falsehood enters Matrimandir.

"This accident occurred because there is a discord in the harmony of forces which construct the very base of reality. For such an accident to happen, the discord must be terrible, so it is not Kali who speaks, but Mother.

"In one of my conversations with The Mother she told me, 'Auroville is a Tower of Babel in reverse.'

"Thousands of years ago humanity came together to build the Tower of Babel, and became divided. Now humanity comes together again to become united. The Matrimandir is the symbol of this unity. How can such an accident happen at Matrimandir, unless Mother needs to make us aware that we are perpetuating the division rather than supporting unity.

"All those little I's that are screaming, me, me, me, and regard themselves as separate from this accident, or the expulsion of two Aurovilians and the harassment of others by police and imprisonment, have not understood that there is only one I in Auroville, Mother.

"The Matrimandir is Her new body. It is in Matter that this union of consciousness must manifest. It is in Matter that the yoga of The Mother has to be lived. It is through Matter, the matter of the transformed body, that the true Matrimandir is being built.

"The Matrimandir will be the reflection of what the community of Auroville will become whilst building it.

"People are transformed, and a new species will take birth. The Matrimandir will have meaning only if the Babel of Auroville is demolished.

"I must add that this attack on Auroville comes, not from without, but from within.

"Love, Victor."

The beginning of Matrimandir

xii

The spirit's strength shall make thee one with God,
Thy agony shall change to ecstasy.
Indifference deepen into infinity's calm,
And joy laugh nude on the peaks of the Absolute.

Sri Aurobindo, Savitri

The next stage of this yoga will be a persistent giving up of all the action of the nature into the hands of the greater power, a substituting its influence, possession and working, until the Divine to whom we aspire becomes the direct master of the yoga and affects the entire spiritual conversion of the being.

A yoga of integral perfection considers human beings as the Divine involved in mind, life and body. It aims therefore at a liberation and perfection of humanity's divine nature.

These three elements, union with the supreme Divine, unity with the universal self, and a Supramental life action from this transcendent origin; and, through this universality, but, still with the individual as the soul channel and natural instrument, constitute the essence of the integral divine perfection of the human being.

To discover the eternal Satchidananda, this essential self of our being within us, and live in it, is the stable basis to make its true nature evident and create a divine way of living in our instruments, supermind, mind, life and body, is the active principle of a spiritual perfection.

Prakriti has to reveal itself as shakti of the purusha.

There are three ways to intuit the difference between the mind and purusha: to observe the action of the mind with the witness purusha; or to see nature as an action reflected upon the consciousness and enlightened by the consciousness, but in itself other than consciousness; by feeling something larger and greater, the subliminal self; and, finally to be aware of the Supramental and spiritual being.

(from Jim Bean's Journal extracts from Sri Aurobindo's Synthesis of Yoga.)

Auroville looked beautiful in late August after the summer monsoon. Everything was very green. Seven years earlier when Roslyn had first gone to Auroville in August it had been a yellow and gray, hot dusty plain. During those seven years that parched plain had started to become a lush oasis.

The bus stopped near the center at the new community kitchen built by Vasudeva for the Matrimandir workers, called 'Unity Kitchen.'

Roslyn and Bliss left their bags at the kitchen and walked over to Matrimandir. From the road they could hear the unmistakable sound of the concrete mixer. Roslyn had never forgotten the concreting of the foundation of Matrimandir. It was a thirty-six hour uninterrupted pouring of fresh cement at the bottom of the great hole to form a single slab that would never crack. Everyone in Auroville was there. Many people from the Ashram came to help. Many people stayed from the beginning to the end. There was a continuous supply of peanut butter and jam sandwiches and lemon juice, tea and coffee in the little shed that served as a tea-room. Everyone was welcome to whatever they wanted. The work went on and on. It was an unbelievable atmosphere, as though everyone was drunk with delight, ecstatic to participate in the drudgery of pouring an enormous concrete foundation. It was positively festive. Roslyn remembered being amazed at the atmosphere and thinking, "Only Mother could turn a concreting into a party."

Many, many Aurovilians were working that morning at Matrimandir, and everyone seemed very happy. People dropped their pans of sand and came to embrace her and welcome her back. Bliss was jumping with joy. Roslyn was overwhelmed at being in Auroville, and excited by the changes she had noticed. She was amazed and happy to see how much Matrimandir had progressed. The bright South Indian light seemed to warm the cockles of her heart. She had come home. The people of Auroville, in their sleeveless Banyans and shorts, working together building Matrimandir, were her people. Someone told her she was expected to stay with Rhoda in Kottakarai.

She felt that she was on Sri Aurobindo's 'sunlit path' as she started walking with Bliss across the dusty plain towards Kottakarai.

She had left her bags at the kitchen, asked directions, and gotten a vague reply. The roads had been moved around a lot since she left. She walked with Bliss across the dusty plain in the general direction of Kottakarai.

She followed a footpath across a small ravine, through fields of grain, over small earth dams to a casurina forest. There was a small hut under construction. She knew it was Jim Bean's forest. More amazingly she recognized the pipe sticking out of the ground as the well where Mother had told her to move in 1970 when Edward and Jane were fighting with her. She was hopeful that the hut that was being built was being built for her, although it was very small.

She asked the workers where she was. One completely toothless, skinny, short, dark Tamil with long stringy hair and an enormous grin, brightly painted with kum-kum and vibhuti told her he was the watchman and this was his house. She asked directions to Rhoda's. He led her through the forest, along a narrow path that eventually became a road, past another hut, across a solid concrete dam. There was a beautiful wooden building with a tile roof in front of a large hut with a thatched roof. Constance, Rhoda's husband, greeted her from the porch of the pottery and sent a worker with a cycle to fetch her bags from the center.

Rhoda had prepared a room for Roslyn and Bliss in her house, moving with Constance and her two children into the other room, which was also where they cooked and ate. Rhoda and Constance had spent years building the Never Never Pottery. It was a beautiful place to make pottery, but the project had not yet made any pottery. They were experimenting with clay and finishing the kiln. Constance had come to Auroville in 1968 with the dream of building a pottery.

Rhoda was very shy, and beautiful. Her son was Bliss's best friend since the day they met, when they were both two years old. Between the house and the pottery the little boy suddenly appeared, hurling himself at Bliss. Bliss moved to the side and the little boy fell on his ass and was on the ground screaming. Rhoda came out, wringing her hands, "I don't know if you can stay here. Those two will be fighting and screaming all the time."

Just then Jim Bean came walking down the dusty road. He had spent the morning baking bread for the community of Auroville with Gary, the father of Dhyan's daughter. He had a loaf of fresh bread in his hand that he offered Roslyn. The children were at her side at once, saying "I want some. I want some." She broke off a piece for both of them, and a piece for herself. She put it in her mouth. It seemed the most delicious thing she had ever tasted. She laughed silently at herself for being so impossibly romantic, then looked at Jim.

He was looking at her, and suddenly they were back in that space where the rest of the world just disappeared. Jim apologized for not meeting the plane. Roslyn said that she understood. Somehow they had moved into Rhoda's house, and were curled up one against the other on a child's bed, shocked at the delight they each felt being with one another.

"There is an empty capsule near the well," he suggested.

"Will Bliss and I be able to live in a capsule? she asked.

"I do, and I love it," he replied.

"Yes, I am sure that would be better for everyone than if we stayed here, she agreed. Is it far from your capsule? Is it very small?" she asked.

"There is probably enough room in a capsule for you and Bliss to sleep. You will have to leave your things in the storeroom where I keep my things. My capsule is just across the next field."

"I guess I will have to build something to live in," she said. "I don't have much money."

"Don't worry. I will help you."

She was not worried. She asked about Dhyan.

Jim replied, "She knows you are coming and looks forward to seeing you."

"I brought her some miraculous golden seal healing cream made by a friend from Bidonville."

"Thank you," Jim said. "She is beginning to get terrible bedsores, and nothing we have tried seems to help. It is a miracle she is still alive. It is terrible for her. The first thing she said was, 'I wish I had died.' She cries a lot. She tries to be brave, but it is very hard for her. At the hospital they wanted to operate on her spine just after the accident, but they were afraid because they did not think she would be strong enough to survive the operation."

Roslyn could not begin to imagine what it would be like to suffer such grievous bodily injury. She was very glad that Dhyan had asked to see her the next day. They had always been friends. Auro used to come home with Bliss every day and spend the afternoon playing at their house, usually went home with the amah at the end of the afternoon. He was a very attractive child who seemed to be able to amuse himself endlessly with the simplest thing. Roslyn had been very fond of him. She wanted to be part of the team that would help Dhyan get back on her feet. It was unthinkable that she might not fully recover. It was impossible to remember Humpty Dumpty at that moment. Certainly all the love in Auroville had to be more effective than all the king's horses and all the king's men.

Until that time Dhyan had refused to see her daughter, Aura. That evening the little girl came to play with Bliss. She looked very sad.

The next day Roslyn went with Bliss to the hospital. Finally they found the room where Dhyan was staying. Dhyan looked beautiful. She was lying between immaculate white sheets. Her neck was in traction. Her arm was in a cast from her fingers to her shoulder. Her jaws were wired together. There were large freshly healed scars on her face. And there was an assortment of tubes attached to her body, here and there.

She looked like a priestess. She was radiant. An ancient wisdom blazed from her eyes that were more beautiful than sapphires. She was alive, and that seemed to be the important thing. Dhyan offered them cake that Gary had baked. Although she could not eat anything solid he sent her a cake every day from the bakery.

Despite the wires holding her jaws together, and her loss of teeth, she could speak, and be understood. She was charming. She was captivating. Her personality was more powerful than her injuries. She was determined to recover completely. Victor had told her it was her special work for The Mother. Roslyn thought it would be a very great work. Despite all the pain, sorrow, tragedy, Dhyan had borne, she mercilessly poked fun at herself, deriding her disabilities. Roslyn believed she had the courage to face the great challenge of restoring herself to health, and was willing to give anything she could to help her. She asked if she could join the team of attendants. Dhyan said, "No, but I will call you to visit me."

There was no sign of the depression Jim Bean had spoken about. Roslyn asked her why she had not called her daughter to see her.

Dhyan replied, "I am afraid it will frighten her to see me like this."

"You look great!" Roslyn told her. "She seems to be afraid that you disappeared and will not come back, like Auro. She needs to see you."

Dhyan asked Bliss if she would bring Aura to see her.

"Why do you include Bliss?" Roslyn asked.

"It will be easier for her if there is another child there. Especially if it is Bliss."

"Okay. Jim can bring them tomorrow?"

"Thank you," Dhyan said. Roslyn was holding her hand, and there was a great force of love and affection between them.

Roslyn went back to Kottakarai on the bus to the capsule, a small tetraoctahedron with a raised hexagonal platform under a palm roof. The capsule was next to the open well where Auro had drowned, that Jim had transformed into a beautiful swimming pool. She shared a mattress with Bliss. The capsule was not big enough for two mattresses.

Roslyn went to work at Unity kitchen. She heard people in Auroville gossiping that Victor was visiting Dhyan regularly, and had said she had been chosen to do the work of the Supramental transformation for the community. Everyone seemed impressed that the famous Victor, a recluse, was visiting Dhyan in the hospital.

Roslyn and Jim Bean were together every moment he was not with Dhyan. Roslyn started to build a hut in the forest near Jim's capsule. One afternoon she was alone in the storeroom, and Auro appeared, a shining, little ghost. He said to her, "Where is Jim?"

"He is building my house," she replied, nonplused at Auro's unexpected appearance.

The little shining vision that looked like Auro replied, "Why is he building you a house? I have already built you a house."

Suddenly there appeared a vision of the most beautiful house Roslyn had ever seen. It was nothing like the hut she was building. It was not as large as the house in Belvedere, but much, much more beautiful. It was a house like a song, a paean of harmony in space. White, with columns and shining white floors inside, and outside a garden!

Roslyn was stung by the vision of something unattainable, unimaginable. She said to the child, "I need a house here, in this material world, not there!"

He laughed and disappeared.

Just then Jim Bean walked into the storeroom holding his head.

Roslyn looked at him and asked, "What's wrong?"

He replied, "Your house just fell on my head."

The hut she had been building virtually had collapsed on top of him. The workers had dug him out immediately, and miraculously he had not been seriously hurt, but he had received a nasty blow to the head.

"I'm sorry about your hut. We'll have to start all over. Maybe we can build something on the other side of my capsule in the orchard. I will ask Gary to help us. He knows more about this kind of thing."

She took him into her arms. "I don't mind that the hut fell down. I am sorry that it fell on you."

Just then Aura came in looking for Jim Bean, and threw herself at him, howling, "My Jim Bean, my Jim Bean.!!"

He picked her up and gave her a hug.

They planted a tree of the variety Mother had called "The Beginning of the Supramental Manifestation" where the hut had collapsed, and built a large capsule in the mango tope, only a few feet from Jim's capsule.

The mango field had been named for what it aspired to be, not what it was.

Mother had called the mango tree, "Divine Knowledge."

The field had a living fence. There was no evident topsoil, and a big hole on one side where there had once been a well. There were a couple of small scrawny guava trees. There a worker was digging and composting holes, where evidently something would be planted.

Occasionally Jim Bean would spend a night with Dhyan in her hospital room, but usually he was in the forest. Nearly every morning before dawn he would come to Roslyn's capsule and call softly to her. She would jump up and crawl out of her cozy nest, and they would sit together in a corner of the well, in his capsule, under a tree, anywhere, and he would read sometimes in the soft glow of lanterns a canto of Savitri as the sun rose. Often their Dutch friend Ivar would join them.

One day Jim Bean said to Roslyn, "These are halcyon days given to us to give us strength through what is coming."

Other times he was bright and cheerful, still talking about six months a year in America and six months a year in Auroville, depending on Dhyan.

Roslyn visited Dhyan once or twice a week, and they both looked forward to these visits. Dhyan seemed to be moving from strength to strength. The cast came off her arm, the tubes came out, she learned to control her bladder and sphincter, the scars were disappearing thanks to a great cream someone had brought from Germany. Every time Roslyn went to see Dhyan she was more convinced that she would eventually get back on her feet.

One afternoon Roslyn was sitting with Dhyan. They were laughing together when Victor walked into the room.

He looked at Roslyn, "Excuse me, I would like to spend a few minutes with Dhyan."

"Of course." She went out and sat with one of the attendants on the porch.

Everyone seemed to think Victor was marvelous. She did not know why, but she was slightly frightened by his icy blue eyes.

When he left he said to her, "You can go back in."

She went in and continued her conversation with Dhyan. They parted with warmth and affection.

Jim Bean was coming 'On Duty' as she left. They said hello-goodbye, and she got the village bus back to Kottakarai, her capsule and Bliss.

Jim came the next morning. He seemed to be angry with her.

"What is wrong?" She asked.

"What did you do to Victor?"

"I have never done anything to Victor. He came in yesterday while I was visiting Dhyan. I left him alone with her, at his request. I have only seen him once before."

"When?"

"I was with Panditji on one of his afternoon walks. Did you ever walk with Panditji in the afternoon? "

Jim nodded. He had gone on afternoon walks with Panditji.

"Well, then, you know how it was. Whether here or in Rameshwaram, it was nearly inevitable during the course of an afternoon walk with Panditji that he would meet someone, usually someone quite extraordinary. I remember thinking that all the Vedic sages who suddenly seemed to appear during Panditji's afternoon walks were never visible to me when I was not with Panditji.

"We were walking around The Ashram in Pondi and suddenly, this short, skinny, gray haired Frenchman threw himself into Panditji's arms. Panditji hugged him briefly, something I had never seen him do with anyone else, and released him, smiling at him.

"I found it very strange. This man was doing everything to demonstrate intimacy and affection, but his eyes were like ice.

"We continued our walk. Panditji said to me, 'That is the great Victor.'"

"Victor was furious to find you with Dhyan yesterday. He told the attendant that you should not be allowed to see Dhyan because you are a Tantric Witch."

"He is crazy. When I see his eyes I think, 'Maybe next time he will take birth as a human being.'"

"Don't say things like that," Jim admonished her.

"Why not? Don't tell me you have become one of his devotees." She could not believe this was going down.

"Dhyan respects him."

"Shit. Why?"

"You may not visit Dhyan any more."

"That's unfair. I enjoy seeing her. She enjoys my visits. It keeps the relationship among the three of us cool. It is important that Dhyan and I see one another."

"It is not possible. Victor has forbidden her to see you. Forbidden the attendants to admit you. She listens to him. She thinks he will help her get well. Don't worry, it is only until she is better. Do you want to come with me today to see Dr. Sen?"

Dr. Sen was a famous surgeon in Pondicherry whom Jim wanted to consult about Dhyan's prognosis. They took the x-rays with them on the village bus into town and sat in the waiting-room waiting to hear some advice from this very respected doctor.

He had visited Dhyan just after her accident, and had seen the x-rays then and advised immediate surgery.

He explained to them that as it was already several months after the accident that it was no longer possible to do that surgery. There was nothing he could do. From the x-rays it looked to him as though the spinal cord had been cut at that point, and that it was unlikely she would ever walk again. He suggested that she receive some psychiatric attention to help her deal with the trauma.

Jim Bean said, "I cannot accept this. I will take her to the Stoke Mandeville specialist hospital in England. There she will receive the best treatment."

Dr. Sen said, "I have a friend who just retired from Stoke Mandeville living in Delhi. If you can take her to Madras perhaps he would be willing to come and meet her for a consultation."

"I was thinking about taking her to Madras. I think there may be better treatment available for her there than here in Pondi."

"Perhaps," Dr. Sen replied.

"Where should we go?" Jim Bean asked. Desperate for answers. Desperate for cures.

"You should probably consult with Dr. Ramakrishna, the chief neurosurgeon at the General Hospital in Madras."

"Thank you."

"Do you want to go to Madras with me?" Jim Bean asked Roslyn when they were back on the street.

"Love to," she said, grinning at him. He looked as if he had just been shot with an elephant gun and she could do nothing to help him. It all depended on Dhyan.

"Maybe we can take a van and get some fruit trees for the mango field at the same time," he replied, smiling shyly.

The next day Jim Bean received a note from Victor, "Each time a new truth has attempted to manifest itself on earth, it has been attacked at once and corrupted, spoiled by pseudo spiritual forces that represented a spirituality from the past, but was precisely that spirituality which the new truth wants to surpass. To give an example in history encumbered with unfortunate 'spiritual deviations,' Buddhism has been largely corrupted in much of the world by a whole tantric and magical Buddhism.

The falsity is not in the ancient spirituality that the new truth seeks to surpass, but in the eternal fact that the past clings to its powers, means and reign. As Mother used to say, in her simple words, 'The evil is to remain stuck there.' Sri Aurobindo with His ever-present humor said, "The spiritual truths of the past are perfectly all right where they are — in the past.' We could expect that this phenomenon would repeat itself today. In India, Tantrism represents a powerful discipline of the past, and it was unavoidable that Mother experienced the best as the worst of that system in Her attempt to transform all the means and all elements of the old earth. The Agenda has abundantly spoken of X, symbol of Tantrism. It so happens that we are witnessing the same phenomenon of 'deviation', and that today this same Tantrism seeks to embezzle the new truth by convincing as many adepts as possible not to repeat the Mother's Mantra, which is 'too advanced for most mortal men,' and to repeat in its place tantric mantras. This is an attempt to take the Mother's place. One must be very ignorant of the mechanism of the forces not to understand that, by repeating a mantra of the old gods, one puts oneself under the influence and in the orbit of all that. Mother had foreseen it and warned us about it in an entretien of October 16th, 1963. Unfortunately, we wanted to believe until now that Tantrism would convert itself. It is not so. Tantrism seeks to take the Mother's place and deviate those who are not sincere enough to want only One Thing; the new world. For those who are sincere enough we reveal the falsehood of the person called X. Victor."

Jim Bean was seemingly unmoved by this and arranged for a van to take him to Madras with Roslyn. Francis and one of the attendants called Boy asked if they could also use the van, as they had things to do in Madras. Boy was eager to help Jim locate the best possible treatment for Dhyan. Francis needed a new passport and some trees.

They left Auroville at about 5 a.m. and went directly to Vellore, where there is a hospital called The American Hospital with a rehabilitation center. It was a concrete block of rooms around a courtyard. The Administrator was slightly brusque explaining that the various therapies that were employed there were to help mostly accident victims recover and resume their lives. Many of the patients were sitting on wheelchairs or lying on beds in front of their rooms. Roslyn could see Jim, Boy and Francis rejecting this as a possible next step for Dhyan, even before the doctor finished speaking.

Back in the van, Boy quoted Sri Aurobindo: "The transformed body, not the crucified, is the body of the god."

There was a holy mystery around Dhyan. Hers was to be the transformed body. None of them were ready to allow that she might need the same therapy that would apply to lesser mortals chosen for less exalted work. She had survived to lead the community in the Supramental transformation. It was a sacred role. Tantra, medicine, all the old sacred cows were crucified on the path to the new being.

Boy reminded them that Victor had told Dhyan, "The doctors can do almost nothing. You must rely on Mother. Mother can do everything."

To Roslyn this did not sound like The Mother who had written in The Auroville Charter, "Taking advantage of all discoveries from without and from within, Auroville will boldly spring towards future realizations."

When she said what she was thinking, the three guys looked at her as though she was a Tantric Witch and ignored her. They were busy talking, and she was content to sit and listen. It was clear that her relationship with Jim Bean was in crisis, but she had no doubt it would survive the crisis.

Boy was going on and on about the great temple being sanctified with human blood.

What a terrible ancient barbarian concept, sanctifying the temple with blood. The only thing that could redeem the situation was transformation. Dhyan had to be completely healed. Roslyn thought it might be better if they slaughtered a goat to assuage the temple's thirst, and treat Dhyan like an injured human being; but she did not say it.

They went to the General Hospital in Madras and met the great neuro-surgeon. He looked at the x-rays and agreed to take on the case. He recommended they take a room for Dhyan in an exclusive Nursing Home. They went to the Nursing Home and made arrangements. The doctor in Madras agreed to invite the specialist from Stokes Mandeville for a consultation. They arranged to have her admitted within a week. It was a beautiful place. It was a very lovely, well maintained colonial style building, surrounded with a large immaculately manicured garden. The rooms were large, bright, and nicely furnished.

There was a couch for an attendant to sleep on in each room. The furniture was not strictly institutional. There were no metal cupboards, and there were comfortable chairs, wooden tables, attractive cushion covers and curtains. Whatever therapy was ordered by the doctor would be available to her there in the Nursing Home. They had an excellent physiotherapist. No mention was made of including a psychiatrist.

It was a long and not very pleasant morning, but they had

accomplished what they had primarily set out to do. They felt entitled to relax and enjoy the best lunch in town. They agreed to go to the Connemara for the buffet, but first they took Francis to the US Consulate so he could take care of his passport.

It was nearly mid afternoon by the time they sat down to lunch. Everyone was hungry, and so for a while there was not much conversation.

This was the first chance Roslyn had had to speak to Francis since she got back from the USA. She had heard gossip that he had been deported by the Society, and wondered if there was any truth to the story, so she asked him, "Were you really deported from India."

"No, I wasn't deported. Naren and I got Quit Notices from the Government of India and were given fifteen days to get out of the country. We decided to go to the USA, get new visas, and come back.

"I think the Chairman of the Society did not like us, and fed some poppycock to the Government of India that we were spies working for the American government. We decided not to try to fight it, just to go and come back, and try to raise some support for the Auroville community while we were there.

"The absurd thing is that the only organization in India that the Americans relate to is the Society for tax purposes. It was clear to us when we came back that Auroville has to establish its own identity. We spent three months is the USA trying to raise money for Auroville, mostly. We indeed raised some money to plant some trees, but then, as it was a tax-deductible donation, it went through the Society, and they kept half.

"We were really pissed about that.

"We decided it was time to come back. We went into the Indian Embassy in New York with our fingers crossed and asked for a visa. To keep it simple, we asked for tourist visas. No problem. We went back in the afternoon and our passports had been stamped with bright new visas.

"We managed to hold ourselves together while we were in the Embassy, but the moment we got out on the street we were whooping with joy and laughing at how easy it had been to fool the Society. We exchanged the return tickets we had purchased to help us get our visas for one way tickets, and were on our way the next day."

Jim, Roslyn and Boy were happily munching on their lunches as Francis went on with his story.

"We got to Bombay, Hi-Ho the dairy 'o! We marched confidently to Iimmigration, and wham. They looked at our passports, and said, 'Excuse me, will you come with me.' They took us with our passports into an office. The sign on the desk said, Chief of Immigration, but he was not there. There were two empty chairs in front of the desk. The guy said, 'Please take your seat.'

"I protested. There are people waiting for me. I don't have the time. If you like I can come back tomorrow, etc. The guy called in a few of his friends, and, still very politely, told us to sit down.

"We waited there, and waited there, and waited, until a fat cop came and sat behind the desk. He said he had arranged a flight for us back to the USA for that afternoon. Would we please give him $1,252 each.

"We don't want to go to the USA. You have our passports. We have valid tourist visas for the next three months in India." I said.

"But you are not tourists, you are foreign spies, and you will not be permitted to enter India.' The big man behind the desk said.

"Naren asked, 'Can I make a phone call?'

"No, no phone calls, nothing. Please you give the money for your tickets and you get on the plane to New York.'

"'We do not have that much money,' I said.

"Then we will call the American Consul and ask them to repatriate you. You may wait in the Transit Lounge.'

"They took us into the VIP transit lounge that was empty, and told us that if we left that room we would be under arrest and taken to prison.

"We asked them for something to eat and drink. Someone brought as a cup of tea and some sweets and savories.

"We sat there wondering what would happen. The afternoon turned to night, and finally someone from the US Consulate arrived. We told him we did not want to be repatriated. He agreed to tell the Immigration Officer that it would take a few days, and to call Auroville and inform the community that Francis and Naren were being held in the Bombay airport, and not allowed into India.

"He was a righteous guy, that guy from The Consulate. He came to see us a couple of times, brought us some chewing gum and Hershey bars, and was our only link with the world outside the transit lounge.

"The next time he came he told us that he had called Auroville and someone had flown to Delhi to try to get us released.

"We had a couple of novels with us that we finished in the first two days. The transit lounge overlooked the runway. There was a huge wall of tinted windows through which it was possible to watch the planes landing and taking off all day and all night. There was a loudspeaker that kept us informed about which planes were leaving or landing.

"We refused to pay for our food. We were being detained against our will. They had to feed us.

"They were not pleased with us. They wanted us to get on a plane and fly away. We wanted to come into India, to Auroville. Maybe I am paranoid, but I thought they were trying to drive us crazy by serving us mutton curry with raita and chappatis three times a day.   There was a water cooler in the lounge. There were fully equipped bathrooms. It was possible to sleep on the tufted, padded benches, despite the hum of the busy airport and the loudspeaker keeping us current with all the landings and takeoffs."

Francis was telling this tale with great relish as he was sitting at the opulent table in the five star hotel, wining and dining to his heart's content.

"The guy from the Consul came again and told us to be patient. Wheels were moving in Delhi, but it was taking time.

"We were trying not to go stir crazy. We started reading 'Savitri' aloud to one another, and agreed to leave the whole situation in the hands of Mother and Sri Aurobindo.

He looked at them intensely. "We were in the transit lounge for sixteen days, and nearly ready to accept the option of getting on a plane to the USA, when finally the door opened, and the Chief Inspector of Immigration came in and handed us our passports, saying, 'Welcome to India.' We nearly collapsed.

"He was accompanied by a man who said simply, 'Please come with me.'

"'Where to?' I had to ask. 'Don't worry, Sir, everything has been arranged.' He led us through the airport to a waiting limousine. I couldn't believe it. I felt like James Bond. The car took us to a gorgeous estate, and we were given a beautiful five-room, fully equipped guest cottage, complete with sauna and jacuzzi.

"The phone rang, 'Mr. Lala wonders if you would like to have dinner with him this evening."

"Lala, the biggest industrialist in India, the wealthiest and possibly most powerful person in India, was our host, supporting us and Auroville in the struggle against the Society.

"We felt we had just won a battle."

"What was Lala like?" Roslyn asked.

"He is great. Charming, and intelligent. One of his major interests for fifty years has been developing India's tourist industry. He told us that although he had heard about Auroville, he never felt involved until he heard that these young foreigners who had already spent years in

Auroville as honorary volunteer workers were being treated inhospitably. He felt honor-bound to rescue the image he had tried to create of India. He promised us he would help Auroville receive justice for our grievances against the Society."

They all ejoyed any number of desserts from the buffet. It was getting late. It had been a great lunch, but they had to complete their chores before they could return to Auroville. They went to the nursery and bought an enormous assortment of fruit trees that had already been grafted. Every nook and cranny of the van was filled with young, tropical fruit trees. The rack on the roof was full of fruit trees. Things were looking up for the orchard.

Francis was saying he thought that within a few weeks the Government in Delhi would give the power and responsibility of administering Auroville to the resident community. Boy felt they had taken an important step for Dhyan, and that under the eminent neurosurgeon, she would quickly recover.

They were all slightly euphoric after a long and interesting day.

They got safely back to Auroville, and stopped first at Francis's house. Someone was there waiting for the van to tell Jim Bean to go at once to the hospital. Dhyan had had emergency surgery.

The Banyan 1970

xiii

He is the godhead growing in human lives,
And in the body of earth-being's forms,
He is the soul of man climbing to God
In Nature's surge out of earth's ignorance.

O Savitri, thou art my spirit's Power,
The revealing voice of my immortal Word,
The face of Truth upon the roads of Time
Pointing to the souls of men the routes to God.

Sri Aurobindo, Savitri

Ego is the principle knot. Man is inseparable from the universal being, his body is a manifestation of universal force in matter, his life form is universal life, his mind is part of the universal mind, his soul and spirit are part of the universal soul and spirit. If he establishes this oneness and rises to be one with the Supramental soul and the universal spirit, he becomes the self-knower, self-ruler, and begins through this spiritual oneness to become a human master of his environment world of being.

To be an active master of the nature he must rise to some higher Supramental poise where there is possibly not only a passive, but; an active identity with the controlling spirit. To find the way of rising to this greater poise and be self-ruler is a condition of self-perfection. To draw the mental to the greater knowledge, the ideal knowledge soul, and that into the bliss self of the spirit, is the uttermost way of this perfection.

There are two forms of impurity at the root of the confusion; the defects from past evolution and a separate ignorance leaving a residue.

The basic mental consciousness is largely subconscious. The mind is unaware but it stores immense reserves of passive subconscious memory.

Physical habits are largely formed by these sub-mental memories and can be changed when a more powerful action of conscious mind and will is developed, and; by the reflective powers of the subjective inner being communicating to the subconscious will of the spirit for a new law of vital and physical action.

All the action of the mind or inner instrument arises out of the basic consciousness. When it is struck by the world's impacts from outside it throws up certain habitual activities, the mold of which has been determined by our evolution.

One of these forms of activity is the emotional mind. Our emotions are the waves of reaction and response that rise up from the basic consciousness by habit. These habits can be changed by the conscious will of the spirit. The true emotive soul, the real psyche in us, is not a desire soul, but the soul of pure love and delight. This can only emerge when the deformation created by the life of desire is removed.

(from Jim Bean's Journal extracts from Sri Aurobindo's Synthesis of Yoga.*)*

Roslyn went the next morning to a Pour Tous (all Auroville) meeting under the Banyan. It was hard for her to believe what she was hearing. A new court case had been filed by The Society against Auroville. The Society had told the Government of India that Auroville was an experiment set up by The Mother under their supervision and administration. No one should stay in Auroville for more than five years. No one should stay in Auroville without the permission of the Chairman of the Society. It was an experiment in non-ownership. People from all over the world were invited to participate on the land owned by the Sri Aurobindo Society, or on new lands that they could buy and donate to the Sri Aurobindo Society, develop, and leave. The Sri Aurobindo Society was prepared to administer the assets of Auroville according to this interpretation of the Auroville Charter.

The residents of Auroville decided not to apply any more through the Sri Aurobindo Society for visas, but directly to the Government of India, directly involving the Government of India in the conflict between the residents and The Society.

The atmosphere at the meeting was very bleak. Roslyn felt like crying. What had happened to beautiful Auroville? What had happened to those nice people in Pondicherry? How could the Sri Aurobindo Society claim to be nobody in particular? When she had arrived in Pondi, seven years earlier, Auroville welcomed all people of goodwill. How had all that hostility come to be? Were the residents of Auroville claiming to be nobody in particular?

Walking away from the meeting she bumped into her old friend, Sarah Ann, a minister's daughter from England, who had helped start the school in Aspiration in 1970. They looked at one another, each seeing the other's distress and confusion. Roslyn had not seen Sarah Ann since returning from California.

"Whatever happened to Auroville?" Roslyn asked.

"Let's sit at the amphitheater and have a talk," Sarah Ann suggested.

They left the others, noisily and angrily dispersing, and went and sat in the middle of the empty amphitheater trying to remember the dream.

"When did you get back?" Sarah Ann asked.

"A couple of months ago." Roslyn replied.

"Then I guess it comes as a bit of a shock."

"I don't understand it at all. I have heard the stories, about who did what to whom, but although I am horrified by what the Society is doing, I am even more horrified at the Aurovilian reaction. How can all this violence and self righteousness be Mother's Auroville?

"Who has understood Mother's Auroville? Do you remember that She talked about having a plan of the "ideal town," but that was during Sri Aurobindo's lifetime, with Sri Aurobindo living at the center. Afterwards, she was no longer interested. Then; the idea of Auroville. Huta wrote Mother her dreams: one or two sentences suddenly stirred an old, old memory of something that had tried to manifest — when she was very young and which she had forgotten. It came back with Huta's letter. All at once, she had her plan for Auroville. It is here, with The Pavilion of Truth at the Center," Sarah Ann said, pointing to the Matrimandir construction site.

"Have you memorized all Mother's writings?" Roslyn asked her.

"No, but I keep reading and rereading all the quotations about Auroville and Matrimandir, trying to understand what is happening within the context of what she said about Auroville and Matrimandir."

"Like that awful accident?"

"Yes, like that accident. How could that happen here? When Mother was explaining her concept for Auroville in 1965 she said something like, 'The center is a park which I have seen in a vision — perhaps the most beautiful thing in the world from the point of view of physical, material Nature — a park with water and trees, like all parks, and flowers, but not many flowers in the form of creepers, palms and ferns, all varieties of palms; water, if possible, running water, and possibly a small waterfall...'"

They looked at the dirt and dust around them, and again at the Matrimandir, laboriously coming up out of the earth like an ugly giant crawling out of a hole.

"She could not have been talking about this Auroville." Roslyn said.

"But it is precisely this Auroville." Sarah Ann insisted. "In this park she saw the Pavilion of Love. Divine Love. Then she changed it to 'The Pavilion of The Mother,' The Mother, the true Mother, the principle of The Mother, the 'creative principle,' Shakti, the principle of realization."

"It is a horror." Roslyn said.

"Oh, come, now." Sarah Ann insisted. "It is not as bad as all that. It simply is not finished. Did you know that the concreting of the first-level slab of Matrimandir began with a meditation on 11th November 1973. It was a huge work, needing clear weather. It went on for six days during the monsoon season. It was completed in the evening of the 17th of November. Not a drop of rain had fallen during those six days. The four pillars, representing the four aspects of The Divine Mother, were completed exactly at the moment of Mother's withdrawal from

Her physical envelope, at 7.25 p.m. on the seventeenth."

"Death and destruction. A temple of death and destruction. Maybe we shouldn't even finish it. Maybe we should just take it down and fill in the hole, and try to go back to friendly happy Auroville." Roslyn suggested.

"Unfortunately or fortunately we cannot do that. There is no way back. There is only the way through. Don't worry; be happy, do your work as best as you can, and let her do the rest," Sarah Ann said, solicitously.

"How can it ever be what She wanted? She said that things are no longer exclusive, not at all. She saw very well the possibility of using the most opposite tendencies at the same time! All together. This is what she wanted, to be able to create a place where all the opposites can unite. That is not what we are doing, fighting with The Society." Roslyn insisted.

"The situation today is what it is." Sarah Ann said. "You will have to find your path through the wild forest of confusion that seems to be growing in Auroville."

Roslyn smiled at her. "Thanks. It is helpful to have someone to talk to who does not see only 'us' against 'them'."

"The pleasure was all mine. I am happy you came back. Good luck."

Roslyn, impulsively gave Sarah Ann a brief hug, and they set out on foot in opposite directions.

Jim Bean did not come back to the forest for a couple of days.

When he came he looked awful. Gary came by in the evening, and Jim told him that he was ill and would not be able to go back to Dhyan for a couple of days.

Finally he confided to Roslyn that he had a painful earache. She got on her moped, and sped off to Pondi to buy him some eardrops, and rushed back to the forest. He just wanted her to sit quietly next to him in his capsule. He was apparently in great pain. There was nothing she could do. He asked her not to leave him. Finally, after a long silence, she hoped he had fallen asleep. He started speaking, very softly. She had to lean over to hear him, and then she thought, 'No, impossible."

He spoke the words in a whisper filled with horror, "She asked me to buy her poison. She wants to kill herself."

Roslyn could not imagine how Dhyan could have been so desperate to have asked that of Jim.

One of his old girlfriends had written him a few months after he arrived in Pondi that she would kill herself if he did not come back to her. He sent her a blessings packet from The Mother. A few months later she killed herself. When he heard, he was shocked, and grieved deeply for many months.

She sat with him all night, and in the morning, after a brief and troubled sleep, he got up and read a canto of "Savitri" to her from "The Book of Fate." They were both trying desperately to cling to Sri Aurobindo and survive the whirlpool in which they were caught.

For a few days they were very quiet.

The community was functioning on a purely idealistic financial system, where everyone was asked to give all their personal money to the community and it was redistributed so that everyone got a basket of food three times a week. Roslyn walked to the center nearly every day to prepare a meal for about 100 people at the center kitchen, Unity. Occasionally Bliss went with her. For the most part Bliss was with the other children in the community, and looked after by other parents. Life was very simple. Jim Bean used the Ashram laundry in Pondi to keep his clothes clean. Roslyn washed her clothes and Bliss's on a stone near the open well. She had one dress she wore nearly continually, a red cotton kaftan from Samarkand covered with embroidered flowers and birds, given to her by Francis's friend She.

Jim was busy preparing to move Dhyan to Madras. He was hopeful that the miracle everyone was constantly praying for would happen and the paralysis would disappear there. No ambulance was available, He had to build a bed in a van, in such a way, that an attendant could sit with her during the journey and try to minimize the shock of a four hour journey on a body that had been in a hospital bed for over two months. Jim made a trip by bus to Madras to arrange a suite in a hotel near the Nursing Home to accommodate the Aurovilian attendants, so there could always be two or three Aurovilians in Madras with her. A constant caring watch was to be maintained so she could never feel abandoned.

Victor had told the attendants they could reinforce Dhyan's will to get well, by doing whatever she asked and never challenging her will.

Roslyn was trying to be happy in her capsule. She went often to Matrimandir, and would sit in any of the pillars representing the four aspects of The Mother and concentrate on the mantra Mother had given her. For weeks she carried the little book by Sri Aurobindo and read and reread his beautiful descriptions of the four aspects of The Divine Mother in the pillars representing Mother in Her temple.

Finally all was ready, and Dhyan was moved from the hospital to the

Nursing Home in Madras. Jim confided to Roslyn that he thought it might be the first leg of her journey to England. They were still hopeful. He told her not to give up hope that they would be able to live in Auroville half the year, and in the USA the other half, if everything was well with Dhyan.

Jim took Dhyan to Madras and returned a few days later. Roslyn stayed quietly in Auroville. She attended more meetings. The tourist bus run by The Society was hijacked by a group of Aurovilians who felt that the bus belonged to Auroville, and should be used by the resident community, rather than by The Society to bring paying tourists to Auroville. The tourists had to walk back to Pondicherry. The police came and took the bus.

The school closed because many of the teachers came from Pondi on the bus, and the bus that took the children to school in the morning, and home at noon, as well as paying tourists in the afternoon, was in Police custody. Bliss and her friends had nothing to do but play together. Bliss was the oldest of the kids. Roslyn would often see her looking like a village kid with a baby on her hip, another child by the hand, and several other children trailing after her. She looked like a seven-year-old mother. It was not right. Roslyn felt she needed to do something for Bliss, but she did not know what, so she did nothing.

Jim Bean came back from Madras with a lovely willowy tall French woman in tow. Roslyn was shocked when she saw them strolling hand and hand into the forest. They looked like lovers! Jim introduced her to his friend, although she had known her for years. Roslyn had met Sari in Spain in 1968, and had been surprised to see her again in Auroville a couple of years later. Roslyn asked them what was happening with Dhyan.

Jim told her, "It is wonderful there for her. There is an excellent physiotherapist, and she is already sitting up without help from anyone. The famous neurosurgeon, after examining her and reexamining the x-rays, said that the paralysis is probably caused by a blood clot. It will dissolve. He could not say how long it will take."

"And the other specialist?" Roslyn asked.

"He will come in a couple of weeks; but by then Dhyan might be walking. She is getting better. She was very angry with us and sent us away."

"You are not going back?" Roslyn asked.

"I have to go back tomorrow, but Sari had been banished from the team." Jim said laughing, putting his arms around Sari.

Roslyn excused herself because she had to go to work in the kitchen.

Her emotions were like great waves crashing around inside her, but she was determined to remain blasé about whatever was happening between Jim and Sari.

Jim went back to Madras. The next time he came back to Auroville she saw him cycling near the center with Sari, before he came to the forest. He told her he was going to stay in the house he had just built for Dhyan. When Dhyan fell, her hut had been in bad shape. There were holes in the roof, holes in the floor, the walls were open, any thief could get in. There was no bathroom, no electricity. Jim had helped Gary re-do the whole thing so it was a cozy little cottage with a new roof, new floors, walls, windows, shutters, a bathroom and electricity. It was ready and waiting for her, but as she could not use it he decided to use it himself rather than his capsule for the moment.

That left Roslyn with Bliss alone in their capsule next to his empty capsule. Roslyn was too wounded to even think of making a scene. If he wanted to leave her she could only say, "Okay. Will you visit us?"

He looked at her, bemused. "Hey, don't take it so personally. I am just moving into a house for a while. I will be back."

At that point she did not even want him to come back, but she did not say anything. She turned away and went back to her capsule, and cried.

Bliss came and asked, "What's wrong mama?"

Roslyn could not explain; just read story after story to the child by the light of the kerosene lamp until late into the night.

For a couple of weeks Roslyn hardly saw Jim when he came from Madras, except with Sari. They looked beautiful together, both tall and slim. Occasionally Jim would come to the forest in the early morning and read a canto of "Savitri" to her.

For her the relationship had become an inner agony.

One morning Jim came to the forest. "Dhyan has asked to see you," he said. "Will you come with me tonight on the train to Madras?"

"Of course," she replied.

She went and asked her neighbor to look after Bliss for a day or two. Judy readily agreed. She had three little kids who loved Bliss.

Roslyn and Jim went together on the village bus into Pondicherry. She hardly said a word. He was being completely charming and thoughtful. There was time for dinner before the train, so they went to their favorite restaurant, The Continental. They had ordered and were sipping their lemon sodas, and Sari walked in. Roslyn just kept retreating behind the inner wall she was trying to build between herself and Jim to try to protect herself from the awesome pain that was threatening to break her into tiny shards.

"I decided to come with you." Sari said.

"You were not invited," Jim said, as gently as that can be said.

"Oh, it's okay, I won't see Dhyan.   I will just stay at the hotel."

"Not this trip. Would you like to have dinner with us."

She joined them at the table, and after dinner Jim asked Roslyn to excuse him for a minute while he walked her to her guesthouse. Roslyn felt like a bleeding corpse when they walked out of the restaurant together. She briefly considered just getting up and going back to her capsule, to Bliss, and forgetting the Madras trip, but Dhyan had called her. She had to go. Jim was gone only a few minutes, but for her it was a lifetime in hell.

For the first hour the train was crowded. They sat stiffly next to each other. After Villupuram most of the people got off. Jim went and stretched out on the opposite bench. Roslyn stretched out on her bench, her bag for a pillow, a longi for a cover.

They arrived in Madras just before dawn and took a taxi to the hotel. They were looking forward to getting into the delectable fluffy clean beds in the hotel and getting some sleep, but when they got to the suite, all the beds were full. Word had gotten out that Jim Bean was keeping a suite in Madras for nobody in particular, and the Aurovilian attendants of Dhyan felt free to bring their children and their friends with them to enjoy Jim's hospitality, on his tab. Roslyn could see him restraining his anger when he saw people who were not even looking after Dhyan using the bed he had hoped to fall into, but he had not set any limits. He apologized to the people who were there for waking them, and said they should go back to sleep. He did not want to sleep. He then turned to Roslyn and asked Roslyn if she wanted to sleep. "No, not at all," she replied, dying to lie down and go to sleep after shaking on the hard bench with hurt and fury all night on the train.

They went to the dining room that was just opening for breakfast. The hotel had an excellent restaurant that catered to tourists, rather than South Indians. Roslyn and Jim were both hungry and angry.

When Roslyn saw how angry and upset Jim was, she just forgot her own anger and wanted to break, through his self-restraint without hurting him or herself, then remembered what he had said to her when she was upset that he was leaving her in Bidonville. "What are you worried about, Sri Aurobindo said "The victory is assured.'"

She was not mocking him; she was trying to pull him out of a very bad inner space to a better space, because she saw he was overwhelmed by responsibilities, none of which he had chosen.

She was there for him at that moment, and had already forgotten how angry she had been at him all night. Jim took her hand. They were sitting face to face across a table from one another, but their heads were nearly touching. He started talking about things that he never talked about, because he was never in a situation where anyone wanted to listen to him. He was exhausted, mentally, emotionally, and financially. He said his parents were bewildered at the sums of money he was spending, and surmised it was because he was madly in love with Dhyan. But all the people using the suite, and the dining room bills, were costing thousands of rupees each day. He asked her if she would be willing to go with him to Mahabalipuram for a couple of days after she visited Dhyan.

Roslyn told him she was there for as long as he wanted to be with her.

They were back together, and happy as a couple of larks.

They took their bags with them, and left a message at the desk, after Jim paid all the bills, to the effect that he would be in Mahabalipuram for a couple of days. It was still early morning. There is a movie theater that opens in the early morning and runs continuously until midnight playing American movies. They went there, considering sleeping through the movie, but the movie was "Hello Dolly!" which made them both homesick for the USA.

They got to the hospital. The door to Dhyan's room was locked from inside.

They knocked. Dhyan said, "Come in." The door did not open. Jim went and called the nurse, who tried to open it with a key. But she couldn't, because it was locked from the inside and the key was in the lock. Dhyan was the only one in her room, and she could not move from the bed. Jim ran outside, climbed a tree, and climbed into the room through the open window. A second later he unlocked the door and admitted Roslyn.

The nurses on the floor asked how it was possible to lock the door from inside? No-one could figure it out. Jim told Dhyan that he had gotten money from the bank in Pondi to pay all the bills, and since the suite in the hotel was full he was going with Roslyn to Mahabalipuram for a couple of days. She thought that would be good for him. The consultant from Stoke Mandeville was expected the next day, she reminded him.   He assured her that one of the other attendants would be there with her when he came.

Dhyan sent him away and greeted Roslyn warmly. She was looking much better. She was sitting up straight, unassisted. Her hair had begun to grow back, and was like soft brown feathers around her face. She confided to Roslyn, "I want it to go away, just go away. I hate all the exercises. I want to wake up one morning and be able to walk, but my legs are getting thinner and thinner, even with all the massage and exercise."

Roslyn could remember her own acute emotional pain of the day before, and suddenly empathized with the deep traumatic agony Dhyan was experiencing.

"But you are getting better," she said to Dhyan.

Dhyan looked at her, and collapsed like a swan onto her pillows. "I don't know."

Just then Jim walked back in with Boy.

"Boy is here, and Armando and Miriam are at the hotel, so I guess I will push off," he said to Dhyan.

She smiled at him and Roslyn, raised her hand, as though giving her blessings, "Have a pleasant vacation."

Jim kissed her gently on the cheek, and her eyes sparkled at them conveying her deep affection for them both.

"I gather that Dhyan does not approve of Sari, and would prefer you to be with me rather than with her," Roslyn said as they walked down the hospital steps.

"Let's not talk about it. I have a vacation. Let's have a few days together," Jim said.

"I told Judy I would be back tonight or tomorrow," Roslyn protested weakly.

"Don't worry. Bliss is in Auroville. She will be okay."

"Are we going now to Mahabalipuram?" she asked.

"Krishnamurti is talking in Adyar this afternoon. Have you ever heard him?" he asked.

"No. Have you?"

"No. Shall we go have a look?"

"Sure, why not." They each carried a small shoulder bag that held the few essentials they would need for a couple of days.

They splurged and took a taxi to Adyar, and ate some puris and tea for lunch from a little tea stall.

Krishnamurti was going to talk under a beautiful tree in the garden near the large old lovely house where he was staying. Roslyn and Jim were very early. They laid their longis on the grass under a tree and went to sleep. They woke up a couple of hours later, and quite a crowd had gathered.

The great man was sitting on a chair talking. It had started to rain.

People were starting to move, because of the rain. Some were already leaving.

The great man was saying, "No, no, don't move, it is only a little rain."

The light drizzle continued while he was speaking. Now and again, someone would go to get up and he would say, "No, don't go, it is only a little rain." Roslyn and Jim were convulsed with laughter, and getting quite soaked.

Finally Krishnamurti concluded his talk and gave them all permission to leave, as he scurried into the house under an umbrella held by one of his friends. It seemed that the moment Krishnamurti went into the house the heavens opened, and the rain poured down in buckets She and Jim laughed and laughed as he mimicked the great man, "It is only a little rain."

After the deluge they made their way to the bus stand, where they found a bus for Mahabalipuram.

Roslyn did not like traveling on crowded Indian buses. She did not like being squeezed between many people, but she managed to get a seat next to the window, and with Jim next to her it was okay. They were still laughing and damp from, "It is only a little rain."

The bus was a rather ancient model, with large streaks of rust showing through its red and white paint, a crunched fender on the back, a crunched fender on the front, no doors, and was full of people. There was an aisle and parallel wide wooden benches that could comfortably accommodate four or five people. Every inch of space was packed with people. There were people on top of people. There were people hanging on the step. It was horrendous; but with Jim Bean between her and the rest of the world Roslyn was completely happy, and he seemed quite happy.

She could not close the window because there was no glass in it, but the heat between her and Jim and the hot wind soon dried their clothes.

The bus started, went a few blocks, and stopped. Some people got out. Others got on. A few more blocks, a few more people got down, and several more got on. Stop. Start. Ride a few blocks, and stop. Start. But finally they were through the town and on the open road.

Stop. The driver and conductor got down. Everyone else started getting down from the bus.

Jim got up and looked out the open window and saw the driver and conductor drinking tea.

"Would you like some tea?" he asked Roslyn.

She was hungry and wanted to piss, but she was afraid of losing her window seat if she got up, so she declined.

Jim went out. She got up and ran across the road, and squatted behind a tree. She ran back to the bus. Jim was standing there with a glass of tea in his hand for her. "Where were you?" he asked.

"Thank you for the tea," she replied.

They started laughing. The conductor was blowing his whistle. Roslyn grabbed her seat by the window while Jim returned the empty tea glasses. He had to climb over five people to get back in his narrow space, but he was very slim. It was funny, and they continued to laugh, pressed together like slices of bologna in a sandwich.

The bus continued to stop every few kilometers, and after a while there were perceptibly fewer people in the bus. They had already been on the bus for a couple of hours. There were no longer people standing in the aisles and hanging out the door. The bus stopped at the brightly-lit bus stand in Chinglepattu.

"What are we doing in Chinglepattu?" Roslyn asked.

"I guess this is the long way round to Mahabalipuram."

She looked at him, "I guess." They both found that very funny. It had started raining again.

Jim said, "It is only a little rain." They roared again with laughter.

The driver and conductor were laughing at them. They got out of the bus and bought some flowers from an old woman sitting under umbrella. Jim wrapped flowers around Roslyn's topknot, and she garlanded his wrist.

"Mahabalipuram?" Roslyn asked the driver.

He wagged his head.

The conductor blew his whistle.

"How long?" Roslyn asked.

The conductor wagged his head.

Jim and Roslyn laughed. There were not many people on the bus.

It trundled on slowly down the road, stopping at first every few furlongs, then every few kilometers, to let people off. Occasionally someone got on.

"We seem to have caught the local," Jim said.

They both burst into laughter remembering New York subways.

Finally the bus stopped in the middle of nowhere in front of a little shack lit by a tiny kerosene lamp. There was an old samovar. The driver and the conductor got out and invited Jim and Roslyn to join them for tea. The bus was nearly empty. They had been together on that bus for so long, the driver and conductor seemed like old friends.

Jim said to Roslyn, "What do you think we look like to these people?"

She was wearing her red embroidered kaftan. He was wearing a rumpled thin white cotton shirt and slacks, and blue velvet vest. "We probably look like a couple of butterflies on the run"

"Watch out," he said, winking at her, "There are the guys with the nets!" They ran around one another trying to avoid the nets they were pantomiming, laughing.

The driver and conductor were offering them tea. They stopped jumping and laughing and said, "Thank you."

The driver and conductor said, "Very good."

"Mahabalipuram?" Roslyn asked. They had been on the bus since early evening and it was nearly midnight. Normally it is possible to reach Mahabalipuram in one hour by road from Madras.

The driver and conductor wagged their heads.

They were nearly the only passengers on the bus. Roslyn was half asleep, leaning against Jim, when the bus finally stopped in Mahabalipuram. Near the bus stand there was a tall pink building with a big sign, "Hotel."

There was a body sleeping on a charpoy in front of the door.

Jim woke him, by putting a hand gently on his shoulder.

Eventually the man woke up, sticking his head out from under his longi. "Yes?"

"Have you a room for us?" Jim asked.

"Attached bath or common bath?" the man asked, sitting up, holding a big key in his hand.

"How much?" Jim asked.

"Attached bath, seven rupees. Common bath, five rupees."

Jim grinned at Roslyn, "I think we can go for an attached bath."

The man got up wrapping his longi around him, "Pay in advance."

Jim gave him twenty rupees. "For three days."

That seemed to make the man very happy. The twenty rupee note disappeared into his longi, and he opened the door to the building with his big key and took a smaller key off the wall. He turned on a dim light and led them upstairs into a small room, with a tiny bathroom. There was a little wire and ribbon butterfly attached to the latch on the bathroom door.

Jim said, "Look, we have come to the right place."

Roslyn said, "Excuse me, but I need some sleep," and crashed.

The next day after prolonged morning rituals they walked through the little village. Jim found a barber he remembered from a previous visit, and enjoyed a shave with hot water and a hot towel on his face, sitting on a stool on a sand floor. He told Roslyn that he had stopped in Mahabalipuram when he had first come to India on his way to Pondicherry, and fallen in love with the place.

The village was full of little shops where stonecutters plied their ancient craft.

The town had been a center of a great kingdom in ancient times. Next to the tiny village, which is right on the sea, there was a rocky hillside with lots of carvings, from the base to the crown. At the bottom there is a huge room carved into the hill supported with great stonecarved columns depicting ancient gods and goddesses. Outside there is a huge carving that is called Arjuna's penance. Arjuna, the survivor of the Battle of Kurukshetra, perhaps had something to do with the carving of that enormous stone, telling of the aftermath of the great battle. It is a glorious piece of sculpture. They walked past the sculpture up the hill. The stones on the path were worn by the tread of many many people over maybe a thousand years, worshipping at these shrines, viewing these sculptures. There was a marvelous sense of antiquity and continuity. At various places along the eccentric path there were small caves, each a temple dedicated to various aspects of deity, each filled with wonderful ancient sculptures, some incomplete. At the top there is a great unfinished Shiva temple, and an old light-house and a new lighthouse.

There are huge flat rocks to sit on in the sun. Jim loved the carvings and the ancient temples. He was happy to give homage to the old gods. From the top of the hill they could see the sea sparkling blue like Dhyan's eyes in the sun. They offered incense and prayers.

Roslyn had visited Mahabalipuram a few years earlier with her father and John Kelly, and there had been nothing there, except the ancient carvings and temples. It was a tiny Tamil village, with a small Government Tourist Bungalow near the Shore Temple that seemed to be slowly sinking into the ocean.   Since then, during the intervening five years, it had become a center of tourism. There was a string of hotels and housing developments along the beach to the north of the village that boggled her imagination, because there had been nothing but beach before. As they walked along the sand they passed hotel after hotel, and then some housing developments. They could see yet another hotel a few kilometers in front of them near an ancient temple, on a jutting promontory.

They found an unblemished deserted beach near a casurina forest that looked a little like the forest where they lived in Auroville. They spent much of the day frolicking in the ocean. Roslyn loved to body surf with Jim Bean. She was a completely unathletic person, but with Jim's expert coaching she would find her way occasionally to the top of a wave that would take her on a bed of moving water, living energy, right up to the beach. Heavenly. Exhilarating. After each ride they would plunge back in and laugh with one another. Sometimes she would just dive under the wave and watch Jim ride it in to the shore and come back to her. He was unbelievably graceful in the water. It didn't matter whether he was riding a wave into the shore or coming back out, he was always on top of the water — like a flying fish. She knew she was clumsy, and had once had a bad accident when she tried to body surf without him. She had been grabbed and churned by that rushing water, and felt like a piece of stone being churned to a grain of sand, overwhelmed as the great weight of the wave crashed down on her..

But that day, there were no accidents and they rode and played with the waves until they were exhausted. They walked back along the beach past the hotels into town, to their little room where they left their wet clothes and changed into dry clothes for the evening.

Jim had noticed a little restaurant near the Shore Temple that he wanted to try. Roslyn was famished. They felt very good. The restaurant was a simple hut with Roses growing in pots near the door, The Rose Garden. Roslyn recognized one of the people sitting in the restaurant, Serafina, a friend she had not seen for several years. Serafina was surprised and happy to see Roslyn. She had just gotten back to India. She was with her husband on their honeymoon. They all sat together at a little table, on rickety old wooden folding chairs, on the sand floor, and laughed a lot. Jim ordered a lobster that cost less than a bowl of cornflakes in the hotel in Madras.

They had a marvelous evening guzzling lemon sodas, and munching broiled lobster.

The next day was more of the same. Roslyn thought about Bliss, but did not say anything, hoping that she would be all right. She was seven years old, and could take care of herself. Jim thought about Dhyan, but felt he needed extra days on the beach more than she needed him.

After breakfast they walked down the beach again and spent hours playing in the surf, building sand castles, talking, being together. Roslyn felt completely at one with him, completely in harmony with him, as they started walking back to the village..

Suddenly Jim stopped short. Roslyn was in such a fog of love, she had not seen anything. She looked up. Standing in front of her was Sari.

"I decided to go to Madras anyhow, and there they told me you were in Mahabalipuram, so I came. I hope you don't mind," she said to Jim.

"Not at all," Jim replied. "Where are you staying?"

She pointed to the nice new expensive hotel with a swimming pool they were just passing.

"Would you like to come and see my room?" Sari asked Jim.

Roslyn felt like an asshole when he said, "Yes."

Jim asked Roslyn to wait for him, and left her on the beach as he went with Sari into the garden of the hotel. Roslyn could see them walk past the swimming pool and into the hotel. She felt herself sliding into an abyss. She sat on the beach alone, wishing she had taken a bus back to Auroville that morning. Regretting the happy day she had just spend with Jim. She was furious with Jim for waltzing off with Sari.

"A penny for your thoughts."

He was standing next to her, and she was so sunk in gloom that she did not even want to look at him.

"Come on," he said, sitting next to her. "It is not that bad."

She could not even look at him. She was afraid she would cry.

He got up and gave her his hand to pull her up. "Look how beautiful it is," he said, looking at the clouds outlined in pink and gold in the sunset.

She said, "I really need to get back to Bliss."

He said, "No. I need you here for at least one more day. Please."

So she stayed.

They met Serafina and her husband again at the Rose Garden for dinner. The fish steaks were grilled to perfection. The conversation traveled from Australia to Afghanistan to Istanbul to Hawaii. By the time they got back to the hotel Roslyn had persuaded herself to forget Sari.

The next morning after their ablutions and rituals they went to the Rose Garden for breakfast. Across the road from the little hut, that they agreed was the finest restaurant in the world, was a granite floor and four columns, perhaps the ruin of a small temple. Jim felt like sitting and talking. This was very rare, for he seldom spoke about himself, his family, or his life before he had met her, and she was fascinated. They sat on the stone floor in the corner farthest from the road, against a carved granite column and one another. Jim talked. It was as if he was trying to put who he was into words. Trying to find himself in his past, as though the search could lead him through his current dilemma.

Roslyn loved the sound of his voice, and was fascinated by the stories he told of the world where he grew up and came of age. She was amazed to learn that he had joined Scientology, and that he was a high level adept. He told her about healing techniques in Scientology that he would like to try with Dhyan. She could not remember the accident. According to his understanding of the techniques he had been taught, he thought that if she could remember she would be healed. He also demonstrated some other healing techniques, and talked about his passion for architecture, probably the result of his affection for his mentor in boarding school, an architect, who had become a priest.

He talked about his family's homes on Fisher's Island and Hobe Sound, his grandfather's house in London, and running around with The Velvet Underground when he had finished Harvard. He talked about Harvard, and about Hawaii. He wanted to take her to Hawaii to show her the volcano. He talked, and she listened. They went across the road to The Rose Garden for lunch and sat outside at a little table, as Jim continued to talk and Roslyn listened.

Jim talked about his parents who had left him and his sister with nannies and a governess when they were little. They had sent them off to boarding school when they were older, so he hardly saw them; but he adored them, both of them. His mother was older than his father. They had met in Rome where her father was the ambassador to the Court of St. James. The night they were to announce their engagement her father had sent his valet to the bank to get the family diamonds out of the vault for her to wear at the great ball that had been prepared for her. The valet never returned from the bank. The jewels were lost, heirloom diamonds that had been in the family for generations. Later they heard the valet had bought a villa in Tuscany and was making wine.

He spoke of the wonderful relationship his parents had, traveling together, doing things. He spoke of them with great love and respect, though he wished that he had had more time with them. Perhaps when Dhyan was better he would be able to spend time with them.

After lunch they walked back across the road to their little roofless ruin. Jim talked and Roslyn listened. She listened to him talk about being part of Bobby Kennedy's campaign team, and the shock when Kennedy was shot in front of him. How he had gotten into his grey Mercedes and driven up the coast until he had come to Bidonville, where he had stopped and sat in the bar until a woman picked him up and took him home. He stayed with her, although she had five children, and was helping her look after them all. One afternoon he came home and found her in bed with another man. He packed and left. He drove back down the coast to leave his car with a friend, then got on a plane to Hawaii. He had worked on the local elections there, and his candidate was defeated in a landslide victory for his opponent. He decided to travel to the East.

He spent some time in Japan, in Bali, in Singapore, and finally arrived in Madras.

He had gone to Pondi. He met Mother. He met Roslyn.

He called Roslyn's attention to the street passing the little granite floor where they were sitting. There were no walls, no roof, they were sitting in plain sight of god and everybody.

Sari was walking down the street looking as though she was looking for something, not seeing them.

"This is the fourth time she has walked past us." Jim said. "I told her the view was wonderful at the lighthouse at sunrise. I think she might have thought I would meet her there."

"Jim, that's mean," Roslyn said.

"Would you mind if I invite her to dinner with us to night?"

"Yes, but I guess I shouldn't."

While they waited for her to come back, searching for him, Jim continued to talk.

A hut in the forest

xiv

Always we bear in us a magic key
Concealed lie's hermetic envelope.
Only when we have climbed above ourselves
A line of the Transcendent meets our road,
And joins us to the timeless and the true;
It brings to us the inevitable word,
The godlike act, the thoughts that never die.

Sri Aurobindo, Savitri

The sense mind is the activity emerging from the basic consciousness that makes up the whole essentially of what we call sense. The inner sense mind has subtle sight, hearing, power of contact of its own that is not dependent on the physical organs.

Buddhi is a construction of conscious being that quite exceeds its beginning in the basic mental. It is the clear intelligence with its power of knowledge and will, originally thought power and will power of the spirit. It has the power of arranging or selecting reason and will. Beyond that it will be the instrument of the sadhak in the pursuit of pure truth and right knowledge, opening another reality where ego is a disembodied symbol, and no longer sovereign.

One purified instrument helps purify the rest. We enjoy God in the world, the Ananda in things, enlightened enjoyment by aesthetic and emotive mind and secondarily by the sensational nervous and physical being but subject to right reason, order.

When desire, vital craving, enters limited life's instinct for possession and satisfaction which derives from physical perturbation and through severance from the universal life force, become aware of the mind as a separate power, isolate it and distinguish too the psychical and physical life and cut the link to dependence. Be a transmitting channel for the Idea and Will, and let the breath become a means of effecting the mind's direct control of the physical life.

Desire is only a deformation of will in the dominant bodily life and physical mind of the will to delight. It is necessary to distinguish the inner will to delight and the outer lust and craving of mind and body.

Find the pure will, undeformed by desire, for the purified emotional mind will choose right reason and the psychic being can come to the front. The receptive sensational mind responds to contact with pure luminous delight and the active sensational mind is an impartial channel for the dictates of the pure intelligence and will, or the Supramental purusha.

(from Jim Bean's Journal extracts from Sri Aurobindo's Synthesis of Yoga.)

That evening after dinner at the Rose Garden, Jim excused himself to walk Sari back to her hotel down the beach.

Roslyn went to the room and locked the door.

A few minutes later there was a knock on the door.

"Who is it?"

"Me."

She unlocked the door.

"Were you expecting someone else?" Jim asked when she opened the door.

"No, but I wasn't sure you would be back."

"Don't be stupid," he said, and went to bed.

The next morning Roslyn got up and started packing her things.

Jim Bean opened his eyes slowly, watched her for a while without saying anything. She closed her bag, picked it up, and started for the door.

"Where are you going?" he asked.

"Back to Auroville, back to Bliss."

"What's wrong? I thought you would go back to Madras with me to see Dhyan and find out what the specialist said."

"My daughter has a birthday tomorrow," she said, opening the door and walking out.

There was a bus ready to leave for Chinglepattu where she would get a bus to Pondi. She had only a few rupees, but it was enough for a bus ticket.

Just as the bus was pulling out Jim Bean dashed up to the bus and handed her through the window a seashell with "God is Love" written on it.

She felt completely lost in her relationship with him, and was happy to be going back to Bliss who was always sweet, faithful and constant in her affection.

She got back to the forest in the early afternoon. She went looking for Bliss. Judy said, "I haven't seen her for a few hours, but when I do I will send her home."

Roslyn went back to her capsule, and then to Unity Kitchen to help prepare the dinner for the community of Matrimandir workers and people living in the center area.

When she finally got back to the capsule in the evening with supper for Bliss in a tiffin, Bliss was there. She had used Roslyn's special silver scissors to cut Roslyn's beautiful red kaftan into a pile of ribbons, and was in the process of cutting the ribbons into little bits.

Roslyn screamed at her.

Bliss broke into tears. She was so angry at Roslyn for going off and leaving her. "I am only a little girl and nobody cares for me," she said.

Roslyn felt guilty and embarrassed, and felt she was the worst mother in the world.

She took Bliss into her arms. She put her hand on Bliss's head. Bliss pulled away. Roslyn grabbed the child, and looked at her head in the light of the kerosene lamp. She gasped with horror when she saw that the child's head was covered with crusty sores teeming with lice. She was furious with herself, and even more furious with Jim Bean. Their adolescent romance was hurting Bliss.

She tried to pull herself together, not to express her horror, and just be kind to the child she had ignored for months. She had forgotten the most important thing, and had gotten absurdly involved in the drama of the Auroville story at that moment.

She read Bliss stories and made the child laugh and forget her discomfort. When Bliss was sleeping she went around the community to find some lice medicine. Judy didn't have any, but someone else did. She took it back to her capsule, woke Bliss, gently applied it, and wrapped the child's head in a piece of the red kaftan before she went back to sleep.

In the morning she took the child to the hand pump and washed her hair. It was the first time Roslyn had washed Bliss's hair since they had come back to India. She was consumed with guilt, that she had been so neglectful of her precious child.

She didn't know what to do. She was alone and penniless, dependent on the community. Running around with Jim Bean and cooking in the center kitchen left her no time to make little beaded bags, and there was no market for her little beaded bags locally, except at prices that barely covered the cost of the material. She had demonstrated that she made lovely things with her hands, but no one was helping her to start a workshop.

She felt she had nowhere to go and no one to turn to.

She had been so involved with herself that she did not even see that she was shamefully neglecting Bliss.

The next day was Bliss's birthday. Roslyn spent the day and most of the night cutting up one of her old silk dresses to make a vest for the child.

Jim Bean arrived in the morning with a shiny red bicycle for Bliss and announced he was moving back into his capsule in the forest. Bliss was delighted with the bicycle, and disappeared on it the next minute.

Roslyn and Jim were alone in the forest. He looked awful.

She made him some tea at the watchman's house. The stove was three bricks set in a U and small twigs from the forest. Nonetheless, the tea was very tasty. Cooked over the wood and pine needles at the watchman's hut it tasted surprisingly like Lapsang Souchong tea from the smoke. Jim had stopped at the bakery on his way to the forest and bought some cinnamon rolls. Roslyn was astonished to find butter, jam and peanut butter in the food safe at the watchman's hut, which had come in the Pour Tous basket that week. Sometimes there was only half a cabbage and two carrots for three people in the basket for three days.

The watchman and the old woman that lived with him helped her carry everything down to the little glade near Jim's capsule, where they had a hammock and some bamboo mats.

Jim greeted the watchman and the old woman affectionately, and asked them if they were well. They smiled hugely and said they were very well. The old woman was called Dosama. She had been an eccentric, a single woman living alone in the village. She had left her husband because he beat her, and went into business making and selling dosais in the village. She was successful enough to survive. She liked to drink the fermented wine from the coconut trees, and was usually tiddly even early in the morning. The watchman had invited her to share his hut although she was ostensibly much older than he. She moved from her hut in the village, because she had been offered work for the most affluent family in the Kottakarai community - cleaning, looking after the children, and cooking - and seemed very happy in her little hut with the watchman. Jim loved the little family in the forest. He was delighted that after years of living in the forest with no amenities he suddenly found he could come home and for high tea. He seemed very pleased.

Roslyn was happy to have made him happy, but he still looked pale and drawn and upset about something. After eating Roslyn took the dirty dishes back to the watchman's hut and then went back to Jim and asked him what was bothering him.

"I got back to Madras and found Dhyan hysterical. The specialist told her she would never walk again."

"How could he say that?"

"He examined her and the x-rays and concluded the spinal cord had been cut. If they had operated immediately after the accident, perhaps something could have been done, but they couldn't. She probably would not have survived an operation at that point. Anyway, he says it is hopeless. She begged me to give her poison."

"Is there no hope?" Roslyn asked.

"She wrote to Victor. He replied, 'The Mother can do everything. Have faith in Her. Call Her.'"

Roslyn looked at him in horror, "Demand a miracle?"

Jim got angry. "Don't be such a cynic. We've done everything we can. Dhyan has had it with doctors. She wants to come back to Auroville and concentrate on the Supramental transformation, and I will be there to help her as long as she needs me."

"Sounds like that could be for a long time," Roslyn said.

"Mother can do everything. You have to help, you have to believe Mother will heal her."

"Tinkerbell power, yes, why not. Of course I have faith in Dhyan, and in Mother, but the Auroville Charter says Auroville will take advantage of all discoveries from without and within."

Jim said, "I know, but what can we do? We have seen half the doctors in South India in the last six months, and even flown in a consultant from Stoke Mandeville. What can I do? She wants to come to Auroville. She believes Auroville will heal her."

"I just hope she is right," Roslyn said.

Jim read some Savitri to her.

Someone with a fine house in Certitude offered Jim his house for Dhyan and moved into a hut in Aspiration. Gary and Dhyan's daughter, Aura, were living in Dhyan's hut in Kottakarai. Aura had become inseparable from the tribe of children that hung out and played with Bliss all day, every day. The kids were remarkable. They seemed able to make a game of everything.

Jim arranged for the van to pick Dhyan up in Madras on Christmas Eve. Roslyn was deeply moved that Dhyan was coming back to Auroville for the first time since her accident in July for Christmas. She felt that was auspicious. After Bliss's birthday she took Bliss to Rameshwaram for a few days to ask Panditji to please help Dhyan.

He said, "She will be alright, but it will take time."

There was still a dim hope that the great neurosurgeon had been right, and it was only a blood clot which would dissolve and she would be able to walk again; that the great specialist was wrong!

Dhyan came from Madras. Roslyn went to take her some flowers on Christmas Day, but was turned away by the attendant. "If she wants to see you she will call you."

Roslyn was hurt and disappointed, but she respected the fact that Dhyan had a very difficult task ahead of her and had to choose how she would go about it. Roslyn was grateful that she could turn around and walk back to the forest.

Jim spent every minute he was not with Dhyan with Roslyn. Roslyn hardly ever saw Bliss. With her cycle Bliss wandered all over Auroville, stopping here, staying there, having lunch here, taking a bath there, having some lessons with some Aurovilians who were concerned that there was no school for the children.

On the mornings when Jim was not in the forest Roslyn would get up at four and go to the center kitchen, sometimes with Bliss, and cook breakfast for fifty people it to be ready and on the table by 6 a.m. When Jim was in the forest they would always begin the day with Savitri.

Roslyn invariably spent her mornings, and usually her afternoons, stitching on something. If it wasn't little beaded leather bags, it was vests for the children in the community, or tapestries, but she felt that if she could keep her hands busy, somehow she would find her way through the impossible situation she was in.

Occasionally Jim would take her to Pondi. Once he took her and Bliss to Kancheepuram where they stayed with an old yogi who did pujas and told fantastic stories.

He gave them some kum-kum and vibhuti for Dhyan and promised that he would help her. The women in his house painted the palms of Roslyn's hands and the soles of her feet with drawings in henna. It was fun.

Back in Auroville, nothing seemed to change. Roslyn used to go often to Matrimandir in the evening, climb to the first level, and concentrate on the mantra Mother had given her. For a few minutes she would feel better, then she would go back down to the world below.

Jim never gave her any money. He said that Dhyan had accused him of buying his friends and had told him not to give her any money. There was nothing she could say to that. She knew that he was giving all the money he had to the community anyway, paying everything for everyone, food, electricity, forests, everything. If Jim had take Dhyan out of India for further treatment, who would have paid the bills?

Meanwhile two little local boys of Bliss's age had moved into the watchman's hut. Roslyn had to maintain the whole scene out of her Pour Tous basket. She usually ate at Unity Kitchen or at a tea stall in the village where she could get ten puris for one rupee.

Everything might have turned out differently; if they all had been older and wiser; but, they were young and foolish; short of words to tell one another what was happening then and there; however much they could say to one another about the past which had no bearing at all on that situation.

Sari would flit through the forest occasionally. They had a bamboo mat with a tiger painted on it which Roslyn sat on most of the day, stitching, when she was alone, or talking with Jim when he was there. She was becoming very put out with the situation.

Jim was still part of a team of attendants, all entirely devoted to Dhyan. There was a room for an attendant in the house where she was staying — and she had a beautiful room that looked out onto a lovely garden. Jim would go to "work" looking right as rain, and come back a day or a day and a half later looking as if he had been shot at and hit.

One afternoon he came back after having been away for a couple of days. Roslyn was lying in the hammock. She had not been feeling well. He pulled a crumpled telegram out of his pocket that he had been carrying around for a couple of days. It was from her mother, "Dad passed away last night."

Jim offered her a glass of brandy. Roslyn went to look for Bliss. Bliss had loved her grandpa.

Roslyn vaguely hoped that Bernie might have left her some money, but she got a letter from her mother telling her that Bernie had given her all his money in 1973, and there was nothing in his will for Roslyn. She briefly considered going to the USA to sue her mother for a portion of her father's estate. She might be entitled to something legally, but then she decided she did not want the karma of taking her mother to court. How her mother spent her father's money was her karma. For Roslyn, having nothing there in the forest was like a birth of a new being, which was not the child and dependent of those parents in far away America, but the child of The Mother and Sri Aurobindo.

She was sitting in the forest one evening with Jim a few weeks later. He had come back from work, looking as though he had been beaten with a stick around the head and shoulders all day long, and would not say anything to her.

She freaked out and told him that he was not making things easy for her.

He walked away.

He came less frequently to the forest, but he still came. When he was there she would be kind to him, quiet, undemanding, serving, but he never spoke to her. He would sometimes read Savitri to her. His voice was like a caress.

Roslyn was very unhappy. She asked Gary if Dhyan had ordered Jim to stop talking to her.

Gary replied, "It might be better for Dhyan and Jim if you just left Auroville."

Roslyn wrote to all her friends and told them that if they sent her plane tickets for her and Bliss she would be happy to visit them.

None of them replied.

The Kottakarai community cut off her Pour Tous Basket.

Boy came to the forest and told Roslyn, "Jim doesn't need your love. If you love Jim, then you must understand what he feels towards Dhyan, who also loves him. You should go."

Roslyn would have been happy to go anywhere, but where to go? She wrote to her sister that she was alone and penniless and friendless.

A few weeks later she received a letter from the US Consulate in Madras to the effect that her sister had contacted them, saying that she was alone and penniless and friendless, and they would be happy to repatriate her.

She let that offer pass.

She sat on her mat.

Bliss's Eighth Birthday

XV

The great are strongest when they stand alone,
A God-given might of being is their force

Sri Aurobindo, Savitri

The purification of intelligence and will is a development of organizing the crude stuff of consciousness. The body becomes an instrument with a capacity to disengage and separate to a greater or less extent through action from the sense mentality, able to draw back and observe sense data and act on it from above by a free intelligence.

The higher mind must be purified of all that makes it subject to the sense mind and then purified of its own limits and the inferior mental intelligence and will be converted to the greater action of a spiritual will and knowledge.

The philosophical mind can overcome and contain first sense impressions, and an ethical mind and intelligent will sets itself over the impulsive reactive sensational mentality, but even a low of true delight and beauty are still incomplete in the yoga of self perfection.

Greater and greater detachment from lower suggestion and an increasing discovery of a self existent being, light, power, bliss, which surpasses and transforms the normal humanity to become what it can be.

The ethical mind becomes perfect in proportion as it detaches from desire, sense suggestion, impulse, customary dictated action and discovers a self of right, love, strength and purity in which it can live and make it the foundation of all actions.

The aesthetic mind is perfected in proportion as it detaches itself from all its crude pleasures and from outward conventional canons of the aesthetic reason and discovers a self-existent self and spirit of pure and infinite beauty and delight that gives its light and joy.

The mind of knowledge perfected away from impression and dogma and opinion discovers a light of self knowledge and intuition that illuminates all the workings of the sense and reason, all self experience and world experience.

The will is perfected when it gets away from and behind its impulses and its customary ruts of effectuation and discovers an inner power of the spirit that is the source of an intuitive a luminous action and original harmonious creation. A complete detachment from desire, impossible without an entire self-government, equality, calm, is the surest step towards the purification of the mind.

A calm, equal and detached mind can alone reflect the peace or bare the action of the liberated being.

(from Jim Bean's Journal, extracts from Sri Aurobindo's Synthesis of Yoga.)

Roslyn sat on her mat in her capsule and cried for months. Jim Bean would come by occasionally, sometimes stay for a day or two, never speak to her, eat with her, read Savitri to her, sit with her, spend sometimes forty-eight hours at a stretch with her, then disappear. She had no idea when he would reappear. He took her moped, got a flat tire, and just left it somewhere on the other side of town. When she asked him for money to repair the tire, he said to Gary, who was visiting them in the forest, "Tell her, you can stand on your own two feet." Gary did not have to repeat what Jim had said. Roslyn started screaming at him, "You stupid son of a bitch!" and throwing whatever came to hand. He and Gary ran out of the forest.

She was shocked and horrified that he could say such a mean thing to her, after not speaking at all to her for weeks. Then Jim did not come by for some time. Boy told her Jim had promised Dhyan not to speak to her until she walked.

Roslyn asked Gary if it was true. He refused to answer her. He fixed her moped and kept it.

Roslyn was still hoping that Dhyan would walk, but wondered if she would be afraid to lose her control over others. Roslyn felt Victor's advice was perhaps bad advice. Perhaps confrontation would do more to strengthen her will than acquiescence, but nobody asked her opinion. Victor had told the attendants that it would reinforce her will if they would do whatever she said. The world around her was to be only exactly what and how she wanted it to be, except for, of course, her disability, which she was determined to overcome, but then if she did overcome it she would perhaps lose control of everyone who was waiting on her. She had to have courage. She had to let go the superficial and find within herself the strength to stand on her own two feet. Everyone and everything around her was committed to this goal. Victor took Jim aside and told him to have nothing to do with the tantric witch, Roslyn. Jim, Boy and Dhyan's other attendants were committed to their work with her. What would they have done if she suddenly stood on her own two feet? She refused to use a wheelchair. She wanted to walk. Until she could walk they agreed to carry her. Everyone was praying, and hoping that one day the paralysis would disappear. Would she be willing to go back to living in her hut?

Roslyn was not very concerned about what would happen if Dhyan walked. It seemed that Dhyan was not about to walk. Despite all the massage, exercise and therapy her legs were looking like toothpicks the last time Roslyn saw her sitting on her bed in her room, surrounded by attendants, flowers, a larger than life photo of Mother, refusing to admit her.

Roslyn had to forget Dhyan and Jim. Her great love for Jim Bean had been so central to her life for years that it was difficult. Even after her spectacular blow-up after a few weeks, every few days Jim would appear, and though he did not speak to her he commanded her company. She tried to give him friendship and emotional support, but she was so burnt out it was difficult. As he was not speaking to her she never knew when he would appear or disappear.

One Sunday evening Roslyn had walked to Matrimandir after cooking dinner at the kitchen. There were a lot of people from the Society sitting on the road in front of the gate to Matrimandir which was firmly closed to them. A bunch of Aurovilians was sitting inside the gate, refusing access to the Matrimandir to the Society people, who had come to meditate there for a few minutes.

"What is happening?" Roslyn asked.

One of the Aurovilians replied, "They can't come here. They think they own Auroville."

Roslyn stupidly said, "Don't you think you are claiming to own Auroville by refusing to allow them into the Matrimandir?"

Another Aurovilian replied, "You don't understand. You go."

A van full of Indian policemen pulled up.

Several Aurovilians started shouting at Roslyn. She hastily walked way, not wanting to become involved.

Roslyn sent a note to the editors of the Auroville News to include the quotation from Mother, "Those who are for some and against others are outside the Truth." But the Community disagreed with her because Victor had told them, "You have to choose."

The virus of divisiveness had entered Auroville, and the collective ego lashed out, on one hand against the Sri Aurobindo Society, and on the other against the Aurovilians who did not conform to what the collective ego demanded.

The food-distributing agency for the community was Pour Tous. Every Aurovilian got a basket three times a week. Everyone was asked to give all they had, or at least all they could, to the community, so it could be redistributed. Everyone would have at least food, not only the people with personal money.

The Kottakarai community cut off Roslyn's basket the day after she started screaming at Jim in front of Gary. They wanted her to leave. She had nowhere to go, and four dependents, Bliss, the two Tamil boys and the old Dosama who no longer had a job because the rich people had gone back to America. Roslyn was not the only person in Auroville to have her basket cut. Suddenly the Pour Tous basket had become a political weapon. Initially everyone in Auroville got a basket three times a week. The collective ego could not bear something so pure.

Roslyn's basket was among the first to be cut, but many others followed.

One man, Jagdish, had built near Matrimandir, and was living there with several friends who worked at Matrimandir. He was accused of being a Tantric guru. Tantra was forbidden. Auroville was only for disciples of The Mother and Sri Aurobindo, not the same Sri Aurobindo who had said, "All life is Yoga," but Victor, who said that Tantrism was a threat to the Supramental transformation. First the basket was cut. One day Jagdish and his friends had gone into Pondi and came back to find their possessions sitting on the dusty road near their houses and fifty Aurovilians sitting in their houses.

They called the police.

Mother had said, "No police in Auroville."

Eventually the police came with large buses, and herded the Aurovilians - who were shouting "Om Namo Bhagavate" - into them, and took them off to jail.

The battle between Vaishnavites and Shaivites has been going on since time immemorial in India. There have always been worshipers of Vishnu, the aspect of the godhead described as the preserver, often depicted as Sleeping Vishnu, who manifests as an avatar from time to time and saves the world.

Others worship Shiva, the Godhead who destroys ignorance and evil, the god of death and transformation, the dancing god, the meditating god, the god who took in himself the poison from the oceans of chaos so the earth could live.

Like Jews and Christians, or Christians and Moslems, bloody battles have been fought time and again between sects worshipping different aspects of the deity.

For Roslyn, and many others, it was astonishing that Auroville had somehow gotten into this ancient formation.

It was explained to the community in the Auroville Notes in 1977, "It is clear: no-one's food basket is being cut off because he or she disagrees with Pour Tous (otherwise, at one time or another, everyone might be affected). It is this: we must not — actively or passively — support any claim by the Sri Aurobindo Society upon Auroville soil. If, until the situation has been resolved, we could all agree, for the time being, to abstain from relations with members of the Sri Aurobindo Society, then services could be re-established to all Aurovilians."

In this situation, if an Aurovilian was seen to smile at or speak to an old friend from the Sri Aurobindo Society in Pondicherry, his basket was immediately cut-off.

People who continued to be friendly with Vasudeva were labeled collaborators, although Vasudeva was not a member of the Sri Aurobindo Society, and had insisted that Auroville become independent of the Sri Aurobindo Society, even helping to register the Auroville Society. He had disagreed with Auroville about asking the Government of India to intercede in the battle between Auroville and the Sri Aurobindo Society.

None of this made sense to Roslyn. She had been reading novels all her life. She could not understand or grasp within the context of anything she had experienced, read or studied. what was happening. She could not believe or understand what was happening. It looked like hate. It looked like division. It looked insane. It looked like the antithesis of the Auroville Charter. It looked like a battle between the Sri Aurobindo Society and the residents of Auroville for ownership of Auroville, which is supposed to be owned by "nobody in particular". The Divine owns Auroville. Roslyn could not understand any of the sides in the stupid and wasteful battle in the context of anything she had ever envisaged as spirituality. One of the quotations she loved most from Mother was that Auroville would be a place where instead of fighting one another, people would battle ignorance, disease, poverty. She was astonished that she was suddenly an enemy of the people, and others who had been big shots in the Sri Aurobindo Society were suddenly good Aurovilians, throwing rotten tomatoes at her because she continued to greet old friends.

It was scary. Her beautiful whimsical Jim Bean, who had been moving like a flying fish a few months earlier, was now like a zombie. It was not only that he was not talking to her, but, he became so stiff. This gorgeous tall slender man who had always moved with an astonishing languid grace was moving like a robot. He looked like the tin man in The Wizard of Oz before Dorothy oiled his joints.

The community that had had so much fun, laughter and love had become angry, self -righteous, entirely male dominated. Work and worship had been synonymous with loving Mother, and performed with great joy. It became a duty, heavy handed, critical, judgmental, harsh. The word "should" appeared more and more.

Roslyn tried to shut up and be quiet, and tried to do her work in the kitchen unobtrusively. She usually cooked, took food for herself, and left, to avoid conversation that would inevitably lead to disagreement.

The community's policy was clear. Over the years there had been many individuals who had tried to give the Sri Aurobindo Society another chance. Aurovilians had tried working with them in one way or another, especially those who were most committed to being against the Sri Aurobindo Society. Some elements in the community would move faster and some slower. In Auroville there is always an individual expression and a collective one. The task is to blend the two. Can a collective judge the sincerity of an individual? No. But, it can ask him or her to restrain from actions that are clearly detrimental to the collective work or aspiration. It was clear that the collective of Auroville had the right to demand that Aurovilians suspend direct communication with the Sri Aurobindo Society. It was the right, even the duty, of the collective to be able to demand from suspected collaborators or known collaborators a clear statement from them that they would desist from further collaboration.

Auroville wanted to help hasten the evolutionary process by becoming pure from the taint of the Sri Aurobindo Society, from drugs, and from Tantra.

The morality of the day was expressed in the Auroville Notes, "As for the morality and the sentimentality of those who approve the results of the main lines of action but who refuse to dirty their hands when necessary, so much the worse for them. The time for morality and virtue is past since long... as is the time for 'grass smokers.'"

It was stressed that there was a pressing necessity for everyone in Auroville to make a choice, to choose something, which was Auroville, rather than the past, the old creation. This choice was indispensable if the community was to serve The Divine rather than something else. The choice had to be sometimes done through means that seemed idiotic or inappropriate. For example, Pour Tous, whose role was to be a cornucopia for the community, had to choose to cut off some people's food.

Some people were calling it, "Horrorville."

Auroville, conceived and dedicated to the freedom and transformation of humanity, became a laboratory of evolution in which didactic conformity, spiritual lethargy, and self-righteousness dominated.

Favorite expressions were, "He is on a power trip" or "They are on a power trip." Others were, "We must be spontaneous " and "C'est n'est pas clair."

It all meant the same thing. There was a group of people who had "paid their dues." The seven samurai who had gone to jail when the Chairman's hut in Aspiration was liberated, and the other fifty people who went to jail when the tantric guru was exorcised. These people met each week with some of the others in the community, and held a community meeting that was called the Pour Tous Meeting.

These meetings decided whose basket would be cut, who would arrange the transport to the court in Tindivanam, and would plan strategy for the day to day battle. Each occasion was filled with self-importance and drama. There was always a big photo of Mother in the room where these meetings were held. There was an atmosphere of a group of people doing something very secretive or important, like atomic scientists.

The Aurovilians were building anything anywhere, whatever they wanted, occupying all the land bought for Auroville by the Society. No one any longer paid any attention to the town plan. There were no schools. Mother was frequently quoted as having said Auroville would be a place of "Divine Anarchy."

No one had visas. All the visas were expired. A group of Aurovilians went to the Home Ministry in Delhi to try to persuade the Government of India to allow Aurovilians to have visas without the sponsorship of the Sri Aurobindo Society. The Minister agreed, but Aurovilians had to go to Cuddalore for their visas, about twenty miles south of Pondicherry.

Roslyn did not go to most of the meetings, but read about them in the Auroville Notes that she always read at the kitchen where she worked. Jim Bean took her to Cuddalore to get her visa extension. Most of the people who went to the meetings had motorcycles, and she did not even have a bicycle. Gary was riding around on her moped, and she did not have the money to maintain a machine so she let him keep it.

She walked every morning to the Matrimandir, where she would meditate on the mantra given her by The Mother in one of the four pillars representing the four aspects of The Divine Mother, Mahakali, Mahalakshmi, Mahasaraswati and Maheshwari. Jim also walked to the Matrimandir every morning from where he was staying with Dhyan. They would often meet on their perambulation of the building site. He never spoke to her. Sometimes he would give her a flower. Vasudeva also walked to Matrimandir every morning. They and the watchman were the only people there every morning at dawn..

Roslyn would walk back to her capsule, where she would then spend much of the day looking out of the opening flap of the structure.

The two nights before her birthday Jim spent with her in the forest. They woke up together on the morning of her birthday. She told him it was her birthday, and asked him to please come back that evening. He did not say anything, which she took to mean that he would come, because she felt the love between them was unchanged by the weird circumstances of their lives. He read aloud a canto of Savitri, and left. It was the same canto he had read to her at the source of the Sacramento River, Book Seven, Canto Three.

She went on the village bus to Pondicherry to visit Sri Aurobindo's room, then returned on the village bus to the forest. In the late afternoon Gary brought her a hot apple pie from the bakery. She did not cut it, but waited for Jim. Bliss came, and asked for a piece of pie. Roslyn told her she would get a piece of pie when Jim came. Finally Bliss went to sleep. By that time Roslyn was so uptight she was nearly hysterical. She was furious with Jim for leading her on, letting her believe he would be back and to wait for him. She was furious that the apple pie was cold, and that Bliss had gone to bed with nothing to eat. She was furious and unhappy and at a loss what to do.

She had no money. She worked in the early morning at Unity Kitchen, several mornings a week cooking breakfast, and several afternoons a week cooking dinner. The rest of the time she was always stitching on something, but she was not making any money. She collected twenty rupees each Saturday afternoon from the Matrimandir Office and gave it to the old woman in the watchman's hut to feed herself, the two little Tamil boys who had moved in to the forest and considered themselves part of the family.

When Jim was in the forest she fed him, although he knew she had no basket. He ate there fairly often, and occasionally brought some apples and oranges.

Usually he would appear empty handed and she would bring him food from the kitchen. Whenever she felt she might be getting herself together he would come back and she would be blown away again. She heard nothing at all from her family and friends in the USA; then suddenly she got a telegram from Frankie, "Arriving with Suzanne, next week, lots of love."

"Salvation!"

Roslyn and Jim could not speak to one another, but they both spoke to their friend Paul who always welcomed them at his house in Pondicherry any afternoon for tea at 3:15 p.m. They often met there, and Jim would address Paul with what he wanted to tell Roslyn, thereby 'communicating' without breaking his promise to Dhyan.

Jim was helping Paul start an art Boutique in Pondi. Paul had leased an old building, and they had demolished the whole inside of the structure, everything except the foundations, outside walls and roof, and created an incredible space.

Nothing like that had ever been dreamt of in Pondi in those days. There was a courtyard with a skylight. It was a shop, but it looked like an exotic, very sophisticated gallery. Under the skylight was a Zen garden, bonzais on rocks, moss, a pond. Huge sprays of flowering orchids hung in pots from the metal grill under the skylight. There were lovely arches leading into little rooms off the central courtyard, which were to be filled with gorgeous merchandise.

For months they worked on it. Whenever Jim was not with Dhyan or in the forest, he was usually there working with Paul. Roslyn was grateful that Paul had found a way to involve him in something other than caring for Dhyan. Every time she got to Pondi, which was not very often, because she seldom had two rupees for the bus, she would stop to see Paul, half looking for Jim, half curious about this gorgeous place they were creating. It looked more like a palace than a shop. The entrance opened into a court-yard then on the left was a large corner with a big beautifully carved huge round table on which danced the most stunning Ganesh Roslyn had ever seen. There were also some gorgeous books of Indian art scattered around the table, and superbly comfortable chairs. There were niches artfully inserted in the walls, filled with marvelous sculptures. The floor was polished stone. The walls had been painted a delicate shade of cream with wonderful vivid cerise and green trim. It was very exotic and everyone loved it, even if it looked, perhaps, more like a temple or an eccentric rich man's living room than a Boutique. Jim had built a small flat for Paul upstairs with a tiny balcony that looked over the garden courtyard and the shop below.

Frankie and Suzanne arrived. Roslyn was overjoyed to see them, and spent the night with them in a guesthouse in Pondicherry. They did not want to stay in Auroville. They wanted to stay in Pondi. Frankie had visited Jim once in Auroville, and thought that Auroville was just huts in mud, but he found Pondi charming.

Whenever Roslyn spent the night in Pondi she always saw Paul, and usually Jim also, at the Indian Coffee House for breakfast. Suzanne and Frankie were eager to see Jim again, and they all went to the Coffee House for breakfast.

Paul was not there, nor Jim. That was odd. Paul invariably took breakfast there every morning, as it was less than a block from his new shop. He seemed delighted with his exquisite little flat, which had a tiny cubby-hole where Jim stayed when he was in town. Paul every morning always walked around the corner down the street to the Indian Coffee House for breakfast, and sat in the table in the corner by the door.

Roslyn was certain he would like Frankie and Suzanne, so after breakfast they walked over to Paul's shop and rang the bell. A very haggard Jim Bean answered.

"Paul was not at the Coffee House, so I came by to introduce him to Frankie and Suzanne, I am sorry, I did not want to disturb you."

It was obvious from Jim's expression he did not want to see her. He looked at Frankie, "I'm sorry, but you can not meet Paul. He died last night."

Frankie asked if he could help with anything. Jim seemed grateful for his offer, but asked the ladies to please excuse them.

After months of work the shop was just ready to open. Roslyn had been happy to see one of her tapestries hanging on a wall. She hoped someone would buy it.   She had given it to Paul on consignment.

The new shop had been her last hope that she might be able to earn her living. She planned to make things in the forest and give them to Paul to sell for her. She had already given him a pile of little beaded bags. He refused to pay her in advance, but had agreed she could leave things on consignment. He was dead. The shop never opened. Everything in the shop went to the Ashram, including her little beaded bags and tapestry. She tried to get her things back, and the Ashram trustee told her she could have them if she paid him the money Paul had given her. She exclaimed, "But he didn't pay me for these things. I had given them to the store on consignment."

"Yes, but Jim Bean told us you owed Paul money."

She had, in fact, borrowed one hundred rupees from Paul. He had forgiven her the loan, but refused to help her further financially. She did not have one hundred rupees to buy back the thousands of rupees worth of stuff she had given him on consignment for the shop. Fortunately it did not develop into a full-scale disaster. Frankie was willing to give her a hundred rupees to buy her things back from the Ashram; but he did comment that he thought it was mean of Jim Bean to have mentioned that she had owed Paul money. Her sweet ice cream Jim had turned to rancid butter.

She walked up to the Matrimandir office on Saturday afternoon and was told that the community could no longer afford to give her twenty rupees a week. Nothing personal, there simply wasn't any money. She should see with the Kottakarai community about getting her basket reinstated. The people who had initially cut off her basket were gone, the authority was with someone else.

She went. She asked.

"No, no, I'm sorry, but it isn't up to me. Angela told me before she left that the community had decided that unequivocally you are no longer part of the community, and the basket is only for members of the community."

"I started this community," she said.

"That's the past. Please go," the lady's husband intervened, trying to protect his wife from Roslyn's bad vibes, which at that moment were pretty bad.

"Are you crazy Nazis?" she asked them

"Please leave," he replied, "I don't want to throw you out."

She left, shocked by the gulf, the division, which had come between her and the community.

She was horrified at what she was encountering. She screamed at The Mother, "Why did you have to leave? This could not have happened if you had not left." She felt certain that under the circumstances Mother would have helped her, maybe was helping her now, but she just could not see it.

The next morning as she was leaving Matrimandir Vasudeva approached her.

"Would you like to receive 'prosperity' from The Matrimandir Fund?"

She was amazed. Was he really offering to help her?

"Does 'Prosperity' include money?" she asked.

"I'm afraid it is not very much, only 150 rupees a month."

"I would be very grateful." she said. "You help me to think that Mother is not entirely gone from this place."

He laughed and continued to walk.

On the first of the month, each month, someone brought her 150 rupees to the forest.

She continued to work in the kitchen and meditate in Matrimandir. Jim had stopped visiting her, but her friends Frankie and Suzanne were staying in Pondi and they visited back and forth several times a week.

One day she was sitting in a restaurant in Pondicherry with Frankie and Suzanne, and Ananta staggered in.

He fell all over her, delighted to see her. He had just returned from the USA. He had left his island shortly after The Mother passed away. His mother had fallen ill, and he had taken her back to her beloved Boston so she could rest in peace with her revered ancestors. He was prostrate with grief for several years after her death, so it had taken him a while to get himself together to come back to the island. His island was a mess.

Someone had stolen his stove. The Ashram trustees had taken everything. He did not have a visa, etc. He was raving, and holding her hand as though it was the last lifeline. She invited him to join them for lunch. He was much too ill to eat anything, but he would perhaps have a beer.

Frankie and Suzanne were relieved to find some comedy in the Pondicherry sojourn. It was all very admirable, and terribly interesting, but slightly gloomy until Ananta joined the party. He was so morose it was funny, and somehow restored some equilibrium to life beyond the end of the edge.

Ananta said it would be his birthday in a few days, and invited them all to the island. Roslyn, who had been quite close to Ananta for a while, said: "Ananta, but your birthday is in March."

"The fourth day of the new moon each month is Ananta puja, my birthday. You will come?" he asked them anxiously.

"We would be delighted to come," said Suzanne sweetly.

Ananta grabbed her hand, and looked at her intensely. "I think I am in love with you."

Everyone cracked up completely.

Roslyn started to spend much of her time with Ananta on the island. Bliss did not like Ananta, and Ananta did not care much for Bliss, so usually Roslyn went alone to the island, and Frankie, or Frankie and Suzanne, would meet her there. Ananta had his servants cooking marvelous meals, but the life of the island centered on the little temple.

Every morning Ananta would go and sit in the temple for a long time, doing some esoteric practices. Several times a month the priest would come and do a big ceremony. There were mantras, fire, often musicians, sometimes fireworks, and finally prasad, which was usually a several course meal with wine and brandy. Ananta frequently had to be carried off to bed by his servants. Often Roslyn would stay overnight having missed the last bus back to the forest.

The pujas were mystical invocations of the gods. Ananta had been raised a Unitarian, and had spent long enough in Greece to speak a little Greek. He had been an initiated sannyasin in India for many years in this lifetime, and probably for many lifetimes before. During the pujas his island became a boat that traveled into long forgotten realms and invoked deities some of which have not been worshipped for centuries. At the end of each major puja the great murti of Virabadan was placed in a chariot which rode on the shoulders of two of Ananta's servants in their brilliant livery, and was taken on a tour of the island, offering prasad and mantras to the river, at the statue of Athena, the pillar of Zeus, the shrine of Varuna, and before Mother's symbol and Sri Aurobindo's symbol on a great cement lingam in a lotus pond. at the boa constrictor's cage. Everyone was beautifully dressed. The gardens were immaculate. It was totally fairytale.

Frankie and Suzanne brought their friend La Marquise de Soandso to meet Ananta. It was love at first sight.

Suzanne left for France. They had parked the twins with Frankie's mother in France before coming to India. They had received a letter that the children were ill, and Frankie's Mother was not feeling well and needed help. Frankie decided to stay on.

Frankie, Roslyn and La Marquise de Soandso were talking about a vacation in the hills, at Kodai.

The Marquise knew that Roslyn had no money, and had invited her to come with them as her guest. They mentioned it in front of Ananta. They were on the island drinking coconut milk out of coconuts through lotus stem straws. Ananta urged Frankie and Roslyn to stay where they were while he showed the Marquise his temple. Roslyn was really miffed. It was the Countess-in-the-bedroom story again.

This time, at least, she had Frankie with her, and they laughed together at Ananta and La Marquise.

The next afternoon Frankie arrived in the forest. "They have eloped!"

"Who?" Roslyn asked.

"La Marquise and Ananta. They left this morning in a taxi for Kodai. They did not take us with them."

"So let's go."

"Okay, I am ready."

Roslyn arranged for Judy to look after Bliss, and they went by bus to town and by train and bus to Kodai.

Kodai was lovely. It was a quiet village on top of a mountain, built around a lake. There was a boarding school that looked vaguely like the one Roslyn had attended in Pennsylvania. Ivy covered brick buildings behind a lovely stone wall, the campus. There was a front gate; only in Kodai there was a gurkha at the gate.

Kodai had been one of the hill stations to which the British retreated during the hot season. It was very different from any place Roslyn had seen in India. Even the poor lived in little stone houses rather than straw huts.

It was cold in Kodai. Roslyn had just made herself several new dresses out of old saris she had bought in the bazaar. She wore them one on top of the other. From the bus stand they went to look for a place to stay. Between them they had very little money. Roslyn had nothing, and Frankie had only a couple hundred rupees. He was waiting for Suzanne to send him money from France. It seemed every other place in Kodai was a hotel, or inn, or lodge, but Frankie decided they should stay with Ananta and La Marquise, because they had agreed to travel together, and that whoever had money would pay the bill.

Roslyn was quite certain that Ananta would never agree - in fact - to paying their bill, although he had agreed to the idea when they were discussing it, because he wanted someone to travel with. Obviously Ananta and La Marquise had run away from them to avoid paying their bill. Frankie insisted they would stay in the same hotel, and he would embarrass them into paying. Only, they did not know where Ananta and La Marquise were staying.

Frankie said that would be easy to find out, and asked for the best hotel in Kodai. Finally someone mentioned "The Carlton," but hastily added, "very expensive."

"Yes, yes." Frankie replied. "Where is The Carlton?"

Down the hill past the school on the lake. Frankie told Roslyn to wait in a little tea stall across the road outside the entrance to The Carlton. She sat on a little bench in front of the tea stall and ordered tea. She felt great just being out of Auroville, looking at the big trees and feeling the cool fresh air. The town was quiet and peaceful. Sitting outside the little tea-shop she could look down to the lake, a smooth clear body of water. There were some boats on the lake. The far shore was a green hill. She could see houses occasionally dotting the hillside. Some children rode by on horses.

Finally Frankie came back. "They are there," he said triumphantly. "They have two rooms in the hotel. I have taken the cottage for us. It's charming, you'll love it."

"But how will we pay for it?" She asked.

"Don't worry about that, you are on holiday, just enjoy yourself."

She was happy not to worry about it, and joyfully joined him in the cottage, which was part of the hotel, but a separate building, down on the lakefront. There was a large sun porch, a sitting room with a fireplace, a huge bedroom with six beds, and a bathroom. Frankie immediately pushed the bell that summoned a servant from the hotel, and ordered tea, toast, butter, jam, cakes, a fire, and some buckets of hot water so they could bathe before dinner.

It was glorious. Set snugly, well above the little road that circled the lake, looking over the lake, they sat and sipped their tea and took in the delightful scene.

"I wonder what they will say when we walk in for dinner?" Frankie speculated.

"Suppose they don't agree to pay for us: will we go right back?" Roslyn asked.

"We will stay as long as they do. Don't worry."

Clean, and in their best clothes, they went to the dining room for dinner. Everyone in the hotel took their meals together in the dining room, or on trays in their room. As it was off-season there were not many people in the dining room. The manager of the hotel greeted them warmly when they went in, and led them to the table next to Ananta and La Marquise, near a roaring fire in a huge fireplace. Through the wall of windows they could look out over terraces of formal gardens to the lake. It was lovely.

Frankie said, "Bonsoir."

La Marquise and Ananta ignored them.

The food was very good, and they were very hungry. Roslyn and Ananta had been friends for years and she and Frankie found it hilarious that he refused to look at her and say hello. She and Frankie were behaving outrageously to catch Ananta and La Marquise's attention. The only other guests were too far away to be bothered, and Frankie had apparently totally charmed the manager of the hotel, who seemed happy to have them as guests.

After dessert, coffee and brandy, totally replete with all good things, they went back to the cottage, a servant of the hotel walking in front of them carrying a flashlight to light their way, although the night was clear and bright. After months of sleeping on a bamboo mat on a split bamboo floor, Roslyn felt like she had died and gone to heaven when she got into the big soft bed, between the clean sheets, under a pile of blankets. She just trusted that Frankie would work out the details, like paying for the hotel. Having virtually no money, she was finding it miserable to live according to her means, and was happy to transcend into the impossible for a respite from oppressive reality.

They spent three weeks at The Carlton. They saw La Marquise and Ananta every day at lunch and dinner in the dining room, or when they were rowing on the lake, walking in the Rose garden, or in the hills. Ananta and La Marquise were spending most of the afternoon and evening in the bar. They never said a word to Frankie and Roslyn. There were several friends of Ananta's mother living in Kodai, who often dined with them. Ananta and La Marquise kept the taxi that had brought them from Pondi the whole time they were in Kodai, and never offered Roslyn and Frankie a lift, or accepted Frankie's suggestions for a day trip to the waterfalls, or into the forest, or wherever.

Ananta and La Marquise looked like a honeymoon couple. They had separate but adjoining rooms. One of Ananta's servants was staying with him. Although the servant never ate in the dining room, he always accompanied them when they went out in the car.

Ananta and La Marquise would stroll arm in arm into the dining room in the morning for breakfast. Then arm in arm they would stroll back to their rooms, after breakfast, lunch, and dinner, spending the day together, completely absorbed in one another, and never, once, acknowledging Frankie or Roslyn; although they ate at adjoining tables for three meals a day, for three weeks.

One day, Roslyn told Frankie, "I wonder what will happen today. It is Ananta's birthday, the one that only comes round once a year."

Ananta and La Marquise were there as usual for breakfast and lunch. Roslyn gave Ananta a Rose and wished him Happy Birthday. He smiled at her as though he could not remember her name, and nodded at her, vaguely acknowledging her existence.

Roslyn and Frankie went to the dining room for dinner. The dining room was always exquisite, on each table astarched white tablecloth and napkins, real silver coffee pots, fine porcelain, discreet flower arrangements, heavenly view, and delightful weather. La Marquise and Ananta had two ladies from Kodai, an Englishwoman and a lady from Boston, as their guests for dinner. The dining room was lit with candles. There was a full moon shinning over the lake.

Roslyn and Frankie entered the dining room and were shown to their table, next to Ananta and La Marquise. The rest of the dining room was nearly empty. Frankie said "Bonsoir," and was ignored.

Frankie and Roslyn were not invited to join in the libations and toasts at Ananta's table. However, they had a marvelous dinner. They were sitting, smoking cigarettes and waiting for dessert, when with a great flourish the Manager of the hotel, accompanied by two waiters in full livery, presented Ananta with a gorgeous birthday cake.

Everyone sang "For He's a Jolly Good Fellow," and "Happy Birthday." Ananta stood proudly slightly swaying, completely drunk.

Ananta said to La Marquise, "I don't know what to do."

She replied, "Make a wish and blow out the candles."

He was swaying back and forth over the cake. The wax from the candles was dripping onto the cake.

He gave a great huff and the candles were blown out.

He collapsed in his chair.

"Now you have to cut it," La Marquise said.

"I don't know how many pieces to cut!" he said in a great booming voice.

"I think four will be enough," she said.

He cut four pieces from the enormous cake. Roslyn and Frankie, at the next table, were served their pudding and coffee.

Frankie said, in a voice even louder than Ananta's, "That takes the cake!"

Roslyn convulsed with laughter at Frankie's comment. The four people at the next table ate cake, and when they had finished, three quarters of the huge cake was still there untouched.

La Marquise signaled the manager to come, clear the table, and wrap the rest of the cake in a parcel for the English lady; who, at first protested, but then said that as it was such a delicious cake, and as she was expecting guests for tea the next day, she would be happy to take it.

Again Frankie said, "That takes the cake!"

Roslyn guffawed. They walked back to the cottage.

The next morning Roslyn was idling lazily on the sun porch waiting for Frankie to go to breakfast.

Frankie came rushing in, all upset. "They've gone. I went out for a walk this morning and noticed that the car was gone. I checked at the desk, and they checked out yesterday and left early this morning.

"What about our bill?" Roslyn asked.

"They paid part of it, but we owe two hundred dollars," Frankie replied.

"What can we do?"

"Don't worry. I just spoke to an old friend of my mother's in Madras at the Theosophical Society and she agreed to telegram me the money today. It will be here tomorrow."

So they had one more day in Paradise. The promised money arrived the next morning, but then the manager informed them that their bill for the extra day was not covered by the two hundred dollars. Roslyn had a big gold chain she had bought years before, and had given to Mother to bless. She wore it constantly. There was no alternative: she took it to a bank in Kodai and pawned it. Frankie promised to give her back the money.

They went back to Pondi. Frankie decided it was time to join Suzanne and the children in France, and Roslyn went back to her capsule, Bliss, and Auroville.

It was April. Another hot season had begun.

The Bharat Nivas had been a big white elephant for years. Work began in 1971, and stopped in 1972 when the money ran out. There were two huge uncompleted buildings that were looked after by a watchman paid by the Sri Aurobindo Society. The community decided this space was needed and should be used by the community. It was decided to have an exhibition of Auroville arts in the big round building.

Roslyn contributed one of her tapestries to the exhibition. They hung all the paintings, wall hangings, etc, in the afternoon, and an Aurovilian stayed to look after everything there, with all the objets d'art in the big unfinished building. In the middle of the night the watchman came and beat him up.

The next day when everybody came to see the exhibit they heard about what happened and were universally enraged that the watchman, paid by the Sri Aurobindo Society, attacked and beat up a sleeping Aurovilian. Something needed to be done. A course of action was needed, preferably one that would not put them all back in jail.

It was decided to call a hunger strike under the Banyan tree.

Everyone was invited to participate. The Aurovilians would sit together under the Banyan, the tree at the center of Auroville, which Mother had said represented 'Unity', and fast until something happened to stop the Society on its Power Trip in Auroville.

Roslyn was not against the Sri Aurobindo Society per se, but she could not condone their having beaten up a sleeping Aurovilian. She had just finished reading "The Divine Materialization." At the end of the book it said, "If there is something you can be doing to hasten your transformation, do it!"

It was very clear.

She was not doing much sitting alone in the forest and starving. She decided to join the rest of the community under the Banyan and sit and starve with them. She walked up to the Banyan in the evening, carrying a few things in a shoulder bag, in case the hunger strike lasted a few days, wearing a long crocheted cape, which could also serve as a cover during the night and early morning. There were about eighty people on mats under the Banyan. By the next morning there were only fifty, and by the second morning there were only thirty, but those thirty people stayed there for ten days.

Jose was there with his girlfriend. After the first night she complained that the ground was too hard, and it was too damp in the morning, so he went to their house and brought a mattress for her. Even so, the next morning she complained of feeling ill, and begged him to let her go home. She would come every day to give him moral support. No one tried to coerce anyone to stay. Jose used the mattress he had brought for her. The rest of the people slept on bamboo mats under the tree. Each morning Roslyn saw Jim Bean and Vasudeva walking around the Matrimandir. She would climb up to the first concrete platform in the Matrimandir and concentrate on her mantra every morning and evening.

Several people asked her what she was doing there. They thought she was with The Society.

She was able to explain to them that she was not for The Society, but she was also not against The Society. She was for Auroville, and felt that what was being done was old. Something new was needed.

Auroville was together with itself, she believed the Society would just disappear if its true function was only a power trip.

By the third and fourth days the scene under the tree was very mellow. Some type of spiritual community was emerging. Roslyn went twice a day to the Matrimandir to concentrate on her mantra. A thin Frenchman, who called himself Shankar, did Hatha Yoga. "Savitri" and "The Agenda of The Mother" were being read individually and collectively. There was not much conversation. One person played a flute and another a guitar. The music was very charming. Everyone swept the area where he had slept each morning. Toilets and showers were available at Unity kitchen, just across the park. A lot of incense was burned. There were no arguments, no harsh words, no, loud words. For ten days thirty people lived together in the open under the tree. After five days some special vitamin tablets were received from France, and each day each participant received one, like a communion wafer.

One person passing by asked Roslyn if she was "dieting" under the tree?

She was not much interested in what people were saying. She was feeling that Auroville was really becoming a spiritual community, where people were uniting not against The Society, but were brought and held together by a deep inner connection, like love.

It was very beautiful. It was a vast and powerful peace. There was a deep commitment among the people who sat under the tree for the ten days without eating anything. Roslyn was staggered on that last day when a man came from Delhi, tall, elegant, with white hair, all dressed in white, and sat with them and asked them what they wanted.

The first person to speak was Jose. "The Sri Aurobindo Society is a bunch of crooks," he said.

Roslyn felt as if she had been punched in the stomach..

They had all been so together, so clean, so nice, so happy, but when the man from Delhi showed up, it was everybody back to where they were before they had begun the fast. What stupidity! She bundled her stuff together and took off for the forest, stopping on the way at the kitchen, gorging herself on some vegetable pie sitting on the shelf waiting to be served for dinner. She wrapped a couple of pieces in her longi for later and left.

"Is the fast over?" The kitchen workers asked.

"It is for me," she replied, chewing on and relishing the delicious food.

She had made good friends during those ten days.

Shankar had decided to move to the center, and asked Roslyn to help him make a workshop for Auroville. He promised to come and work with her. They would make beautiful things, but very inexpensive, so everyone could have beautiful things.

That summer Roslyn was cooking at the center thirteen meals a week. Another American woman managed the kitchen, purchased the food, kept it clean, but Roslyn cooked every day; often twice a day. She was also receiving a basket and the 150 rupees a month from the Matrimandir Fund.

She was really very happy again. Life was not easy, but it was not impossible. She often went into Pondi and had dinner at the little restaurant called, "Maison d'Auroville" that was run by Gary's brother. She often ran into Jim Bean there. He never spoke to her, but she loved to see him: he was so beautiful, even if he was not speaking to her or even looking at her. She flirted outrageously with Gary's brother.

With Shankar's help, by the end of the summer she was given a large unused room at Revelation for a workshop, a real room, not, a hut. Aurosarjan gave the workshop a secondhand sewing machine and sold her some cloth, but gave her credit so she could pay for it after she sold whatever she was making out of it.

She was already back from USA for two years. It had taken her two years to begin the workshop she had planned from the day she had arrived back in Auroville. It seemed that things were much more difficult without Mother in her physical body in Pondicherry.

Roslyn's old friend Ramchendran had become a tailor. She invited him to join her. He sat at the machine, and she sat on the floor, cutting and hand finishing the kaftans they had decided to make from the beautiful handloom cloth she had bought from Aurosarjan.

When she had finished a few she took them in to give to the Boutique to sell for her and to Aurosarjan for more cloth. They did not want to give her more cloth. She had not yet paid for the first lot, but they agreed that the kaftans were very nice, and gave her a few more meters of cloth, admonishing her that there would be no more until she paid for what she had taken.

At that point in time Shankar moved into the workshop with all the machines and workers from his little workshop near Aspiration. He had persuaded Sally, an American weaver, to join them and weave cloth for them.

Roslyn was very happy. The workshop was humming. They were weaving beautiful cloth that they were making into bags and kaftans, beautiful things. There were several tailors working on an order from Bangalore for cheap cotton shirts. A tailor could make four or five a day, and was paid piece rate.

Roslyn said she was not interested in money, just wanted to make beautiful things, and gave the management entirely into Shankar's hands. Roslyn came to the workshop one morning, before lunch. Shankar stopped her as she was leaving. "You can go," he said.

"What?"

"You go."

"What do you mean?" she asked.

"You go. You have nothing to do here any more."

She had a hard time not flipping out.

"Can I at least go in and get my sewing basket?"

"Yes, go take your things and go."

She walked into the workshop. No one looked at her.

She got her things together and walked up to Sally who was sitting at her loom. "How do you feel about this?" she asked Sally?

No reply.

Completely shattered she went back to the forest with her sewing basket.

The next day there was a meeting. The community quoted Mother as saying, "Matrimandir will be the soul of Auroville." The Auroville community had already refused to accept any support from The Sri Aurobindo Society. Now the community felt that they should no longer accept support from Vasudeva and The Matrimandir Fund, because Vasudeva said that Auroville should not ask the Government of India to involve itself in the battle against the Sri Aurobindo Society.

The community agreed that The Mother would provide the means to continue and complete Matrimandir. Martrimandir was the psychic being, and it should not be contaminated by contact with Vasudeva. Roslyn could not understand this at all. Mother had clearly appointed Vasudeva as Her secretary for Auroville. Jose felt that Vasudeva had hired thugs to murder him and had moved out of his house into the camp for protection.

Roslyn walked back to the forest. The Tamil children who were living there in the watchman's hut told her there was no Silence basket. She had heard about The Sunlit Path, but she must have taken a wrong turn because she felt she was on a roller-coaster ride that was absolutely nauseating.

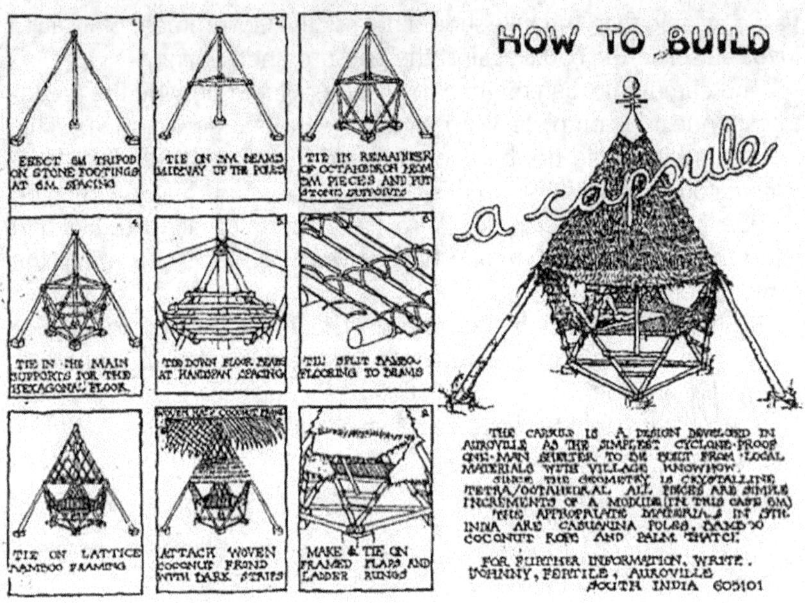

Chapter XVI

How to build a capsule

But there is a guardian power, there are Hands that save,
Calm eyes divine regard the human scene.
All the world's possibilities in man
Are waiting as the tree waits in its seed:
His past lives in him; it drives his future's pace;
His present's acts fashion his coming fate.
The unborn gods hide in his house of Life

Sri Aurobindo, Savitri

From the purified and transformed mind and will there are several modes of functioning. There is the habitual, customary action, the action a link between the higher reason and sense mind, and a kind of current understanding. If one disconnects from higher reason it fails, loses confidence it itself, falls into weakness. The stilling of the mind, running, circling, repeating thought, becoming silent, is one of the most effective disciplines of yoga.

There is a stage of dynamic meditation that is pragmatic intellectually which lives in the truth of the hour. Purified of dependence on the customary understanding, and in association with the highest mental it becomes a strong channel of the force to replace and transform the thinking mind intent on life by a greater effectuating spiritual will, the truth will of the spirit.

The mind of knowledge is seeking for the truth, but it can never be in full possession of the truth. It can only reflect the truth, and at that, only parts. It either turns partial truth into opinion or takes up and demands effectuation immediately. Its realizations are only mental realizations and no unification of truth is possible from a simple mental process. The soul must lift the mental being into the spiritual gnosis to see the very core of the supernal light and power. This gnosis contains the sum of the divine knowledge still burning in the heavens of the supreme conscious being which can link an intuitive or illumined mind to convert all thinking and willing into thought, sight, and truth, by an illumined discrimination, inspiration, revelation.

The spirit aspires for liberation from the knots of bondage of desire and ego. To be equal of mind and soul and spirit is to be universal in soul, transcendental, one in sprit with God, possessed of the highest divine nature.

Desire is observed, from below as a craving, preference, or passion. Seen from above, supported by a will of the spirit, it can become the will of the transcendent spirit who creates the universal movement of the universal spirit who supports and informs it, or of the free individual spirit who is the soul center of its multiplicity. It is one will, free in all these at once, comprehensive, harmonious, unified.

But to attempt to control or force this will brings in the ego and trouble. Effort, striving, become will of desire, craving, etc.

The ego turn is the fulcrum. It must be replaced by a oneness with the transcendental divine and with a universal being. This requires the purification of the senses, mind, breath, and body where action is persistently egoistic and separate.

(from Jim Bean's Journal. extracts from Sri Aurobindo's Synthesis of Yoga.)

Roslyn received a check from Frankie to get her necklace from the bank in Kodai. She was delighted for an excuse, and the means, to leave the gloomy forest for a few days. She ran to catch the village bus to Pondi and got to the bank just before it closed and cashed the check. She took another bus to Villupuram. From there she got the train that night to Kodai.

In the morning she redeemed her gold chain and Auroville symbol. There were enough rupees left for her to move into a very cheap lodge for a few days. Kodai was beautiful in the fall, in the rain. There was a cyclone one night, and the next morning there was no electricity. Trees had fallen everywhere. A colossal eucalyptus tree had fallen on the little tea stall opposite the entrance to The Carlton and completely squashed it.

On the days when it did not rain she wandered up into the hills, and found wonderful places to sit, and look out over the plains. It was peaceful. She could forget everything and just be absorbed in the beautiful hillside and the view of the plain far below. Thoughts and memories would assault her, and she would try to ignore them, concentrating on the beautiful world around her. It was very cold in Kodai.

One rainy morning she decided to leave Kodai and visit Panditji in Rameshwaram before going back to Auroville. She took a bus from Kodai to Madurai. In Madurai she spent half a day, while waiting for a train to Rameshwaram, visiting the big temple. It was impressive.

The next morning she arrived in Rameshwaram, and went directly to the small house Panditji used as a guesthouse for his disciples. It was a traditional Tamil house, several rooms around a central courtyard, across the street from the north wall of the great temple. She was amazed to find Joe, and all of Panditji's disciples from Auroville, there.

"Why are you all here?" she asked.

"What are you doing here?" they replied.

"I just felt like coming to Rameshwaram on my way back to Auroville."

"There is no room for you here."

"It's okay. I was planning on going back on tonight's train, but why are you all here?"

"We wanted to ask Panditji what to do about Victor and his anti-tantric pogrom."

"What did he say."

"He said, 'Victor is nice.'"

"What? After all the shit Victor has said about Panditji."

"Victor is nice. That's what Panditji said."

"Just last week I was thrown out of my workshop. My basket has been cut again. I think it is because Victor said I am a Tantric witch. What else?"

"We don't know. Panditji asked why people were giving us a hard time because we are doing practice. How do they know we are doing practice? We should not talk about our practice."

"Victor knows about my association with Panditji because he met me with Panditji."

"That's your problem, not ours. We have to get ready to go to Panditji's for puja."

"I am coming also," she said.

They looked at her, dressed in several layers of dresses made from old saris that she had been living in for a week.

"Don't you think you could clean up a bit?"

"Of course," she said. "That is why I stopped here before going to Panditji's."

She took a bath and washed most of her clothes in the antique outhouse-cum-bathroom behind the house, pumping water with a hand pump, carrying buckets into the bathroom, scrubbing some of the old dresses with a brush and banging them on the cement floor. She put on the kaftan she had made for herself in the workshop and followed the others to Panditji's for puja.

Panditji was shining.

He seemed very pleased to see Roslyn. He asked about Bliss. He asked if she was in school. Roslyn said, "No."

"Why not?" he asked.

"There are no schools in Auroville."

"You are spoiling her. You should not spoil her."

"Panditji, it is very difficult in Auroville for me now," Roslyn said.

"Yes, yes. I know. How is Dhyan?"

"I don't know. She refuses to see me. Victor told her not to see me."

"Yes, yes. Victor is nice."

"He is not nice. He is making terrible trouble for anyone associated with you."

"You should be quiet. You must learn to be very quiet."

He walked away into the puja room. He did a long and intricate ceremony, cleaning all the statues, reciting mantras, ringing bells, and offering flowers. The disciples sat with their malas silently doing japa.

Finally he came out of the puja room and distributed bananas to everyone. He was in a very good mood, laughing and joking. He invited them all to stay for lunch. They all enjoyed the delicious food his wife had prepared for them. They went back to the guesthouse after lunch so Panditji could take rest.

Roslyn told Panditji she was leaving on the afternoon train. She asked him to please do something to help her.

"Don't worry," he replied.

She got back to Auroville the next morning. She went to Unity kitchen that evening for dinner. Several people approached her and told her she was no longer welcome to take her meals there.

The community had decided to refuse any contributions from Vasudeva and Matrimandir Fund, and she was receiving rosperity from Matrimandir Fund, so she was no longer welcome in the community.

"If I refuse to take 150 rupees a month from Vasudeva, will you give me 150 rupees a month?" she asked.

"That is not the point," they replied.

"But I have an old amah and three children to look after."

"That is not our problem," they replied.

She walked back to her capsule, crushed. She had been back from the USA for more than two years. She had worked continually during that time at Unity kitchen. She had worked hard. She was no longer welcome in the kitchen. She was no longer welcome in her workshop. She did not know what to do.

She continued to walk to Matrimandir every morning and evening, but no longer felt free to stop in the kitchen. Bliss said to her, "Mama, I am not getting a proper education."

Roslyn was beside herself. She did not know what to do or where to turn.

She went to The Ashram in Pondicherry, and begged them to take Bliss in the school. They refused, saying, "Mother said The Ashram school is not for Auroville children."

She went round and around trying to get them to accept Bliss. They refused. Finally someone suggested to her that she write to the Sri Aurobindo Ashram School in New Delhi. There was a possibility she might be able to gain admission for Bliss there.

She wrote and received a very friendly reply inviting her to bring Bliss to Delhi, insisting that Roslyn stay with her there for a month. Then, if Bliss had adapted to the school, she could stay there. Roslyn begged Vasudeva for some money to take Bliss to Delhi. He finally gave her enough for the train tickets.

Roslyn had been assured that the school was an English medium school, and an international school. It was immediately apparent that the children were North-Indian, and Hindi was the language everyone used in and out of the classroom. Bliss did not know a word of Hindi. She was also way behind the other children of her age in math.

The woman in charge of the school, who had worked with The Mother in the Pondi Ashram school before she started the Delhi Ashram school, said, "That's all right, never mind."

Bliss was given a bed and a cupboard in a dormitory with fifteen other girls from eight to eighteen years old. Roslyn was given a small room. It was cold in Delhi in the winter, but there was only cold water for bathing. Roslyn wore most of her clothes with her kaftan on top, and even slept in them, for warmth. She would wash things out in the evening and hope they would dry overnight so she could wear them again the next day.

All the children wore uniforms for classes. The girls wore pleated skirts and white blouses. There was a sweater and a jacket with the winter uniform. Roslyn could not imagine how Bliss could adapt herself to the program that began in the early morning with hatha yoga for the boarding students, and concluded at 10p.m. - after study hall.   Lights out!

Bliss did not have one minute a day of free time for herself. The day began at 6:15 on the sports field with compulsory hatha yoga. Then, she had five minutes to change into school uniform. There was half an hour for breakfast. After breakfast there were fifteen minutes to make their beds and clean their rooms before assembly at 8 a.m. Then she had classes until noon. All the children ate lunch in the dining room. There were more classes after lunch until mid afternoon. The other children had two hours in the afternoon between their last class and the required participation in the sports program. Bliss had an hour with a Hindi tutor and an hour with a math tutor.

The children all ate in the dining room. The food was healthy vegetarian food, extremely bland.

For Roslyn the school looked like a prison, but she did not say anything to Bliss, who seemed able to accept it.

Roslyn had to fight with the head of the school to get permission to take Bliss out on Saturday afternoon while she was in Delhi. Finally she got permission to take the child to see a Russian ballet troupe. The children in the boarding were not allowed to leave the campus except on school excursions.

Bliss had been roaming around Auroville free as a bee for two years, but she somehow immediately adjusted to the discipline and routine of the school. By the end of the month Bliss was sufficiently comfortable in the school, and confident that she would eventually catch up with her classmates, even in math and Hindi. She did not seem to mind when Roslyn left. The expenses for the school were very minimal. The head of the school had written to Bliss's grandmother, Roslyn's mother, and she had agreed to pay for one year. She sent a letter to Roslyn saying, "I educated my children and I expect them to look after their children. I have sent money to the Delhi Ashram school for this year, but do not expect me to do that again next year."

Roslyn got the train back to Madras feeling more lost and abandoned than ever. Bliss had been her constant companion and friend, and now she would only see her twice a year, on holidays. She also would have to find the money for school fees next year somewhere.

She had to get a workshop going. She had to make money, but she did not know how to turn the situation around. She was an outcast. All the kaftans she had made in her workshop before Shankar joined her had sold, but the money had gone to the workshop, they were for Auroville, not for her. Shankar had been furious that she had made a kaftan for herself. Wasn't she part of Auroville?

Hardly anyone in Auroville would even talk to her. She had 150 rupees a month from Vasudeva, but she had the old Tamil woman, Dosama, and the two boys to feed, as well as herself. She did not have money to buy materials. She did not have a place to work, except her capsule. She did not know where she could sell anything she made, but she decided to work as hard as she could, and to make the most beautiful things she could, hoping that some law of karma yoga would do the rest.

Shunning was practiced by the community; of those who had earned the collective displeasure. It was a time of confusion. The community refused to process the visas of those people who had for one reason or another been declared 'outcast.' Most of the outcasts had originally been accepted by The Mother into Auroville, and had simply refused to stop speaking to Vasudeva. Their Pour Tous baskets had been discontinued. The community did not recommend their visas. Anyone speaking to them was in danger of becoming an outcast also.

No one spoke to Roslyn when she got back. Most of the other outcasts lived on the other side of town, and she seldom saw them. Walking to Matrimandir every morning and evening, and back to the forest, no one she passed on the way would greet her, or even look at her. If she greeted them or smiled at them they would look away, or simply through her, as though she was a ghost and they were looking at nothing when they passed her.

Months passed.

She spent most of the day sitting in her capsule embroidering on an intricate wall hanging, or, working on little beaded bags. Sometimes in the morning at Matrimandir she would see Jim Bean. Occasionally he would give her a smile or a flower, but usually he ignored her. Sometimes when she passed the kitchen there was no one there. She would dash in and grab a few pieces of bread or a few bananas.

When there was no money and no food the two Tamil boys would come to her demanding, "What I eat?"

If she had anything she gave it to them. If she did not have anything they would be angry with her. The little beaded bags she had made disappeared. She had no money to buy more materials to make more bags. If she had two rupees she would send the children to the village to bring her puris and tea from the tea stall. If she had no money the tea stall would give her credit for a few days.

She sat and embroidered the whole day, completing less than one square inch of the elaborate design each day, and then walked to Matrimandir for her evening concentration on her mantra.

She did not speak to anyone. No one spoke to her. Once a month someone brought her 150 rupees from the Matrimandir Fund. After giving money to Dosama, she would go on the village bus to Pondi and go to the Maison d"Auroville. All the people she had known since the beginning of Auroville ignored her when they saw her there. Gary's brother hung one of her tapestries behind the desk for a while, but then asked her to take it back. He did not want to get in trouble. She had hoped someone would buy it.

She was struggling. There were days each month when there was nothing to eat. She was thinner than she had been since she was sixteen years old. One day, a friend, another outcast, brought her her 150 rupees from the Matrimandir Fund. His feet and legs were covered with infected sores. She looked at her own bare feet and said, internally, to Mother, "Auroville needs shoes."

The money went to pay her tea stall bill and Dosama, and there was nothing left. Roslyn could have immediately begun running up another bill at the tea stall, but that made no sense, so she stopped eating.

She continued to walk every morning and evening to Matrimandir to concentrate on her mantra. She spent most of the day sitting in her capsule embroidering. She was not fasting; she was starving. She had no money and no food. Dosama went to several of the other houses in the community to beg for a lemon for Roslyn. They would not give even a lemon. Roslyn was taking some water from the water filter at the center kitchen one morning and was told, "You shouldn't come here. We know you come here to steal food."

She had not had anything to eat for days. She was just taking a cup of water!

She began to feel a little woozy after a couple of weeks, and smelled terrible. She also felt horrible. Her tongue was coated. She hallucinated about better days while she sat with her embroidery hoop making little stitches. She felt more alone than anyone who ever lived. She wondered how long it would take her to die of starvation.

Someone had stolen most of her clothes and bedsheets. She had two pieces of clothing. They were both a piece of yellow cloth with a hole in the middle for her head.

There were strings on the side. She tied the strings from the back piece in front and the strings on the front piece in the back. The cupboard from the storeroom had disappeared into Gary's house with her few nice things from California in it. When she asked Gary about them, he said he'd given everything in the cupboard to the Free Store.

She felt like a living ghost. The Tamil boys disappeared when it was clear there was no food. The old lady, Dosama, came every day to the capsule and complained of hunger. Roslyn ignored her. There was nothing she could do to help her. She was also hungry, but she tried not to think about it. She could not read. She spent many hours watching the little mango tree in front of her capsule growing very slowly, and imagined the mango field as it would be in a few years, full of mature fruit trees.

She wondered what had happened to the 'all for one, one for all' attitude which had bound them all together in earlier times. She wondered where were her friends who had sat with her for ten days under the Banyan only a few months before. When she would see them, they would not talk to her. No one spoke to her. She felt sick with the hopelessness of the situation.

Finally on the twenty-third day, she was walking back from Matrimandir through the Sincerity community. A red headed Australian man, Tas, who she had never met, but she had heard about, hailed her, and invited her for tea. After Shankar had thrown Roslyn out of the workshop he had invited Tas and his silver haired lady friend, Kwan Yin, to work with him. Together they had developed a new product, crocheted shoes. They had been unable to get along with Shankar so they'd left the workshop and were making the shoes in their house.

Roslyn wondered if she had come to the end of her long dark night of the soul when Tas invited her for tea. "Aren't you afraid you will be thrown out of Auroville if you give me a cup of tea?" she replied to his invitation.

"That's a bunch of bullshit," he replied.

Kwan Yin greeted her warmly. "I have wanted to talk to you for a long time. I saw you walking by here every afternoon, and finally asked Tas to invite you for tea."

"Thank you. I have not had anything to eat for twenty three days."

"Why not?"

"I don't have any money."

"This is Auroville."

"I am an outcast."

"What did you do to become an outcast?"

"I am not a member of the Victor fan club."

"Nor are we"

"Yes, but you are not outcasts."

"No. We are independent. We make shoes, and sell them. We do not eat in the Center kitchen, and we pay for our Pour Tous basket. We have heard you are a fine craftsperson and make lovely things. Would you like to work with us?"

"I would love to, but it would be trouble for you, I'm afraid."

"We can handle it."

"Do you really mean it?" Roslyn asked astonished that these two sweet young people were willing to befriend her despite the collective policy of treating her like a leper.

"Yes, why not? Come and work with us."

They talked and talked, about Auroville and other things, and drank pots of tea until late in the evening. They agreed it would be better if she continued to work in her capsule during the day, not to invite trouble from the community, but every evening, after her concentration at Matrimandir, she would stop there and they would have tea, and dinner and talk and talk and talk. Sometimes they would discuss handicraft techniques.

Auroville got another letter from Victor.

"Good news from Delhi... unexpected. It seems to me that the first thing to do is to stop all infiltration of money into Auroville through unrecognized channels. For these are the seeds of subversion and division in Auroville.

"I am particularly thinking of those who receive money from Vasudeva. It's a source of treason and division. There are possibly others that you know better than I. The Auroville Co-op should be the only source of money for Auroville.

"We must take advantage of this brief respite given to us, and establish a solid foundation. Auroville's first legislative act might be to establish a material code, giving the material conditions and qualities required for belonging to the community of Auroville, beyond the ideal and spiritual conditions set forth by Mother. If you accept these suggestions from me, it will shut the door to a number of doubtful or undesirable elements.

"It might even be good to invite these indecisive or uncertain elements to publicly state where they stand on the material points that would form Auroville's practical code. Demand an answer from them. Force them to choose. There must no longer be the least pretext for division. Don't confuse a chameleon with a penguin.

"Spiritual things can remain vague and woolly, but matter is very exact and demanding; there should be a few clearly conceived and expressed material points that no-one can slip past. That is where all the sources of division can be nipped in the bud.

"There must be a central and centralizing organ with the power to act on some generally accepted material points. These points should be recognized and accepted by Auroville's Administrators as well.

"Here are the points for a material code:

a) No personal possession.
b) No financial manipulation outside the recognized channels, and no prosperity from Vasudeva.
c) No commercial profits for personal use.
d) No activities detrimental to Auroville's unity, and no collusion with the Sri Aurobindo Society or Matrimandir Fund.
e) No drugs."

Roslyn and her friends Kwan Yin and Tas laughed when they read it in the Auroville News.

Mother had said, "There are no rules in Auroville, and as long as there are no rules there is hope."

The community called Hope was outcast because they received prosperity from Vasudeva's Matrimandir Fund.

Roslyn and Kwan Yin and Tas met each evening at Kwan Yin's little hut, and drank tea and talked. Each day they had things to show one another, things that they had made. The crocheted shoes were selling like fresh hot cakes. Sometimes customers or Aurovilians would be there in the evening and join them around the little round table drinking pots of tea and laughing.

Kwan Yin's neighbors, particularly Shankar, complained that she was receiving Roslyn in her house. He accused Kwan Yin of collaborating with the enemy and suggested that she move out of Auroville.

Roslyn decided to go to a community meeting to confront the issue.

The meeting had not yet started when Roslyn walked into the room. Shankar jumped up and said, "She goes, or I go."

Many of the other people in the meeting got up and said, "We go with him."

The Chairman of the meeting asked Roslyn to leave.

"Why?" She asked.

"Because if you do not leave everyone else will," someone said.

Shankar said, "I go." He was moving towards the door and many of the people in the room were following him. Roslyn noticed an old friend with a newly shaved head, trying to hide behind someone.

No one was looking at her. Those who were not threatening to leave were staring at the floor, out the window, anywhere but at her. They did not want to see her. They refused to speak to her.

She got up and walked out.

Jose followed her. He finally shouted to her when they were far from everyone else, "Hey, wait a minute."

She stopped.

"Don't you know why that happened?" he asked.

She nodded her head dumbly.

"We are having a revolution in Auroville," he said. "Do you know what a revolution is? Have you ever been part of a revolution before?"

She knew that what the words he was saying meant to him was entirely different to what they meant to her. She looked at him meekly, not saying anything.

"Why don't you take your fat ass and get the fuck out of here," he said, turning away from her, walking back to the meeting.

She started to cry, and wondered where had all the flowers gone?

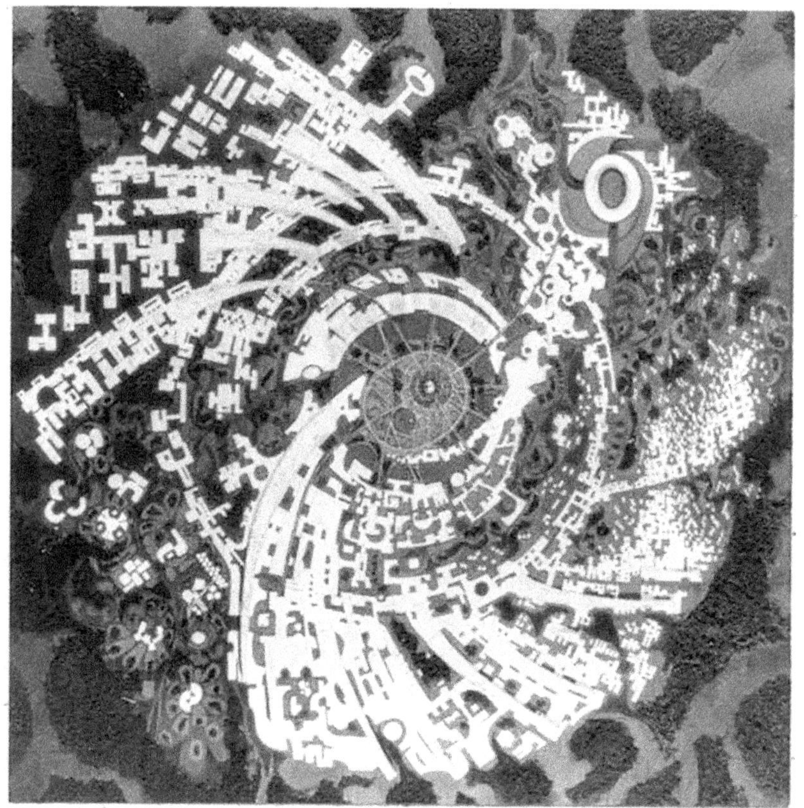

Galaxy

Yet is infinity thy spirit's goal;
Its bliss is there behind the world's face of tears.
A power is in thee that thou knowest not;
Thou art a vessel of the imprisoned spark.

Sri Aurobindo, Savitri

The way proposed by the integral yoga is a lifting up and surrendering of the whole being to the Divine. Not only do we become one with The Divine in our spiritual existence; but, we dwell too, in the Divine and The Divine in us. Our whole nature is full of the presence and changed into the divine nature; we become one spirit and consciousness and life and substance with the Divine and yet at the same time we live and move in and have delight in life.

Only in the spiritual self can we possess the complete unity, for there the individual becomes his total being and finds himself one with the universal existence and transcending divinity.

The acceptance of Nature of the instrumental ego-consciousness and the will to desire are the initial consent of the self to lapse into the lower ranges of experience in which it forgets its divine nature of being. The rejection of these things, the return to free self and the will of the divine delight, delight in being, is liberation of the spirit.

Nature's essential contribution to this in manifestation is the duality. Inertia becomes a divine calm. Aggression becomes the will of the spirit in action. Harmony becomes the self existent light of the Divine Being which is the soul of the perfect power of being and illumines, in this unity, the divine quietude and the divine will of action.

Purification and freedom are the indispensable antecedents of perfection. For the integral yoga, perfection will mean a divine spirit and a divine nature that will admit of a divine relation and action in the world and a transformation of the whole nature.

(from Jim Bean's journal. extracts from Sri Aurobindo's Synthesis of Yoga.*)*

The Matrimandir Fund suddenly stopped sending Roslyn her 150 rupees each month.

She went to Vasudeva to ask why the pittance for which she had been so ostracized by the community had suddenly been withdrawn.

He told her that it was simply like that. He also expressed to her that he sincerely hoped that money would not destroy the love between them. She was faintly surprised. They had known one another for several years. He had been the channel through whom she had sent letters to Mother for two years. He had been the intermediary between Mother and the development of Aurocreation. Roslyn always imagined he faintly disapproved of her and was surprised that he would call his affection for her 'love.'

She could accept that they were still friends although he could no longer help her financially. The two Tamil boys had been accepted by the community after the fast at the Banyan. During the fast they brought her fresh flowers every day and helped to keep the area under the Banyan clean with thirty people living there. The boys found other places to live in the community. She was alone in the forest with the old woman, Dosama. The watchman had married a young girl and moved back to the village.

A kind neighbor, a saintly man from Holland, who was trying to train all the local women in handicrafts, and build schools for all the children, Ivar, gave Dosama money every week to make him food. He had an unbelievable amount of compassion for the local people. He knew very well what things cost, and gave her enough to feed him, and herself, very modestly. She preferred to get drunk than to eat, and somehow managed to get drunk at least once every week.

Roslyn's immediate responsibility was to feed herself. This was a problem because she liked rich food, and would not eat the food Dosama cooked for Ivar. He was an ascetic. She preferred not to eat at all rather than eat that food. She did not simply want to eat; she wanted to feast!

Mother had said we should eat to live, not live to eat. Roslyn had a definite predilection to living to eat. She enjoyed a life that was 'A Moveable Feast,' when she was not starving.

She would walk to Kwan Yin and Tas's cottage in Sincerity every evening. Tas or Kwan Yin or their cobbler would cycle to Pondicherry several times a week to keep the larder full of fresh food. Roslyn cooked occasionally. Tas's neighbor, Myra, would join them around sunset every evening for tea and dinner, often with a bag of somosas from Pondi.

Kwan Yin often made some pancakes that they ate sprinkled with lemon juice and sugar. Every evening they would eat early, in the hour after sunset, and sit late around a little round table, talking, drinking tea, and enjoying being together.

After dinner Roslyn would walk home. Kwan Yin made a beautiful terraced walk for her from her house to the road. She had opened the fence, so Roslyn would not have to walk around and through the whole community to get to her house.   The nights were still and peaceful. Roslyn rarely saw anyone as she walked back to the forest until she got to the watchman's hut, where a little tiny lamp burned, a tiny flame of light, and Dosama slept on her mat. Some nights the lamp would be there, but not as bright, and no Dosama. There were even nights when there was no lamp because Dosama had not come back for more than one day. Finally Roslyn persuaded her: she had to come back every evening to light the big lanterns in the capsule, because Roslyn could not light them herself without getting her fingers dirty. She promised Dosama twenty rupees a week for kerosene, which made the old lady very happy. Water had to be carried from the hand pump, near the old storeroom, over two hundred meters away.

Months passed.

The young man who used to bring Roslyn 150 rupees a month from Vasudeva visited and told her, Matrimandir Fund would like to help her. They would put a new hand pump on the well in the forest, build her a small temporary workshop, and give her a cupboard so she could start her workshop. They would expect her to contribute regularly part of her profit to Matrimandir when she became successful.

Kwan Yin also needed a workshop, because she had workers and customers swarming all over her one room hut all day long. She planned to open a wall and build another room on the back of her hut for a workshop, but there was not enough money.

They had talked about possibly building a small workshop in the forest, but there was no money.   The little crocheted shoes sold like fresh hot bread locally, but with only three workers they made just three pairs a day. However, that produced enough money for the four of them to eat dinner and drink tea in the evening. The materials were expensive. There were wages every week. Kwan Yin and Tas had started to build another room on their hut by knocking down a wall. There were too many other things to do and no money to build. Eventually there was a pile of bricks and a pile of sand.

Roslyn was very happy to accept the offer from Vasudeva of a workshop hut.

The new workshop building was finished just when Bliss came for a week vacation. Roslyn made a huge feast for Tas, Kwan Yin and Bliss with the money she had received to pay Bliss's school fees.

Bliss went back to school. The school wrote to Roslyn's mother to please send her payments directly to the school. She replied that she was not sending any more money. If they wanted money they should approach Roslyn.

Kwan Yin and Tas were both young Australians. They had visited Auroville in the early seventies. At the time they thought it looked like a good idea, but were on their way out of India after a three-week holiday.

They thought about it. They talked about it, and finally decided to come back. A friend in Australia had a small catamaran he wanted someone to sail to Bali so it would be there on the beach for him when he flew in for his holiday. They volunteered, and spent 27 days at sea.

It was amazing. They had to navigate across the ocean. Kwan Yin said, "I'd never done anything like that before." Roslyn was astonished at the spirit of adventure and discovery in that story.

Every day Kwan Yin and Roslyn were making beautiful things. Roslyn admired the evolution of Kwan Yin's work, and the aspiration for perfection and consciousness in matter. Roslyn made Kwan Yin a beaded belt to express her admiration. Kwan Yin gave Roslyn a pair of shoes. It had been years since she had shoes.

Bliss's grandmother invited her for a visit to USA to see her great-grandmother. Roslyn went to Delhi to put Bliss on the plane. She dressed Bliss's hair in French braids. While she was in Delhi she went into a shop called National Leather on Connaught Square. They tried to buy the bag she was carrying, off her shoulder. She did not want to give it to them. She agreed to make for them six of her little beaded bags. They refused to give her any advance. They promised her they would pay when they received the bags. They promised to reorder a larger quantity. They bargained with her about the price, until the price they agreed to pay barely covered the cost of the materials, but it was an order, and a potential customer.

She got back to Auroville hopeful that this could lead to something that would make it possible for her to support herself and Bliss financially. She borrowed money from Kwan Yin to make the bags. She had silver buttons with the Auroville symbol made for them in the silver bazaar. She stitched from dawn till dusk for weeks, until finally they were ready. She mailed them by Registered post with a return receipt.

She received the receipt so she knew they had received the bags. When she did not hear from them after one week she wrote to them. After several weeks she wrote to them again. They never responded. They never paid for the bags. Months later she saw one of the bags slung across the shoulder of a tourist in Pondicherry. She went up to him and asked where he had gotten it. He replied, "In Delhi, on Connaught Square."

She asked him how much he had paid for it, and was astonished to hear that it was ten times the amount they had agreed to pay her. She wrote to them again. No reply!.

Meanwhile the whole scene had gone crazy again.

Kwan Yin was having an affair with a Canadian man who had long blonde hair and played the guitar. Tas flipped out. Half the walls had been taken down from the hut as the preliminary step to building another room. Instead of more space it had somehow become less space. It was very surrealistic to sit there in the evening, the roof half off, the house completely open on one side, like being on stage.

For some reason Tas also flipped out at Myra and beat her up. Roslyn did not pay much attention to what was going on there, because she was too busy working on her bags. She made a couple for the Boutique d'Auroville in Pondicherry, and was delighted that they had sold immediately. If she worked from dawn till dark seven days a week she could finish two bags. If she could also sell two bags she had enough money to pay for her materials, give Dosama money for kerosene, and go to Pondi once a week to see if anything had sold. She could see and feel that Kwan Yin, Tas and Myra were into something else. Sometimes she was too tired to join them, or they were out when she walked past their houses after meditating at Matrimandir.

She was still enjoying their evenings together. They were not meeting as regularly as they had before she went to Delhi. Although Tas had beaten up Myra, she continued to join them on their last evening. No one knew that would be the last evening they would sit around the little round table drinking tea. Myra's big black eye was shining brightly. The house was in chaos. They were all very merry and laughed a lot. Roslyn stayed with them till late, because Tas seemed very angry at Kwan Yin and she tried to mollify him by joking about the intensity of the drama of the moment among them.

The next morning Roslyn walked up to the house and there was nobody there. Half the roof and the back wall were still open. She went to Myra's.

"What happened."

"I don't really know. It seems that Tas went completely crazy and flipped out and nearly strangled Kwan Yin. I heard her screaming and walked into the middle of it. I started screaming, and tried to force him to let her go, but I was afraid he would turn on me again, so I was shouting for help. Then Shankar came and stopped him from killing Kwan Yin. Her face was blue. I think they've taken him to a mental hospital. I don't know where she is."

"Was she okay."

"Yea. Yea, it took her a couple of minutes to get her breath, but she is okay - just shocked. She is definitely afraid of him and does not want to be with him any more."

"What are they going to do?"

"I don't know."

The next evening Roslyn walked up to Kwan Yin's, and Kwan Yin was there. She looking decidedly the worse for wear.

Kwan Yin welcomed her, and invited her to have some tea and pancakes. "How are you? How is Tas?" Roslyn asked.

"I called his father and he will come and take him to Australia. I am taking him to Madras tomorrow morning to meet the plane. He is under sedation. I am afraid of him. I guess I am okay, but for a moment there it looked like the end of the road. I couldn't breathe. He was choking me. My eyes were open and I couldn't see anything. I totally lost it."

"I think it sounds as if he lost it."

"I am afraid he might escape from the hospital and come back here. Can I come with you to the forest for the night."

"Sure."

"What is going to happen to the workshop?"

"I don't know."

They ate and went back to the forest, carefully closing the door of the house, although the whole back wall was open.

The next morning Kwan Yin went back to her house and took a taxi to the hospital, got Tas, and went to Madras to meet his father. She spent the night with them in a hotel, helping his father arrange Tas's exit permit and plane ticket so he could take him back to Australia. He had had a history of mental illness, but this was his first relapse in several years, since he met Kwan Yin.

She got back to Auroville the next evening completely exhausted from the heavy emotional scenes, the trauma of nearly being murdered, the trauma of being separated from her partner of several years, to find someone else in her house, Shankar.

He blocked her way in at the door. "The community has decided you should not be here, so you go."

"You're crazy," she said to him. Wondering why she was suddenly surrounded with lunatics.

"No. You go."

"What about my things?"

Myra came out from behind Shankar, wearing dark glasses in the house in the evening to cover her black eye. "We put all your personal things in the Free Store, and all the workshop stuff I took to Revelation where I am running the workshop. Sorry, Kwan Yin."

Kwan Yin was flabbergasted. "How can you do this?"

Myra withdrew into the house. Shankar looked at Kwan Yin and said, "You go!"

She went to the forest, to Roslyn, who let her sleep on Bliss's mattress on the ledge under the sleeping loft where Roslyn slept.

They could not believe what had happened. They could not imagine how Myra had walked off with the workshop, but there it was.

Kwan Yin went in the morning to the Free Store to reclaim a few of her things. She did not have very many things, but Roslyn did not have a pot to cook in. They made a little fireplace out of six bricks, two on each side, two on the back, in the new workshop, and used fuel from the forest. Kwan Yin had one pot, a kettle, a teapot and cups that she retrieved from the Free Store. Roslyn had one woman whom she had trained in beadwork and embroidery. She had been working with her intermittently, when she had enough money to pay her the pittance she asked. Her friend, Ramchendran the tailor, had always said that he was willing to quit his job elsewhere anytime she could afford to hire him.

It was amazing that this workshop they had been building should be so ephemeral that it could just slip out of their hands because Kwan Yin went to Madras for one day. They had a product that Kwan Yin had spent over a year developing and a market. Crocheted shoes. The shoes were gorgeous. It had taken over a year to train the workers. Kwan Yin had sat and worked with them from eight in the morning until five in the afternoon every day. Myra could not make a pair of shoes if her life depended on it: how could she just take the workshop? Roslyn was amazed. She could not imagine what Mother and Sri Aurobindo were doing creating such untoward situations, but it did not feel like a disaster.

In the afternoon Kwan Yin's cobbler and women came and told her that they did not want to work with Myra. They wanted to work in the forest with Roslyn and Kwan Yin. The next day Myra (still wearing dark glasses) came and asked if they would let her please keep the workers for another two days to complete the order she was finishing for Findhorn. She would be willing then to let them go.

"What about the tools and materials?" Roslyn asked.

"If the workers want to work for you, I cannot stop them."

"Would you please get out of here?" Kwan Yin asked. Myra beat a hasty retreat.

Kwan Yin went and ascertained that Andre at La Boutique was still willing to handle their business. He said, "Sure, why not?"

Kwan Yin took an advance from him and went off to Kodaikanal for a rest.

Roslyn was in the forest with five workers who expected to be paid regularly. Andre sent her a message, "Thirty pairs, full cash advance, please send someone to pick up the money. Deliver the shoes as soon as possible. Good luck!"

She went with the cobbler and the tailor to pick up the money. She gave them half the money to go to Madras for materials.

The workshop was up and running.

Roslyn was absolutely at the end of her resources. She had only two dresses and one pair of pants. The dress she wore most of the time was the piece of yellow cloth with a hole in the middle for the head. It just covered her knees, and was a barely adequate piece of clothing.

When Kwan Yin got back from Kodai she took Roslyn's kaftan and pants and copied them in striped cotton. Roslyn thought it looked like prison garb, but they were at least decent. Kwan Yin insisted that the yellow tent could not be worn even during workshop hours. The workers were surprisingly well dressed. The ladies wore bright saris that seemed to always be clean, and even ironed. The men wore sports shirts and longis.

Roslyn had in her sleeping loft a little table covered with a piece from one of Mother's saris, on which there were some sacred objects, and a small vase for flowers that each day had fresh flowers. There was also an incense holder where she burned incense each morning and evening. The table was always covered with a patina of fine ashes from the incense.

Roslyn got up every morning before six, with the call to prayer from the mosque in the nearby village. The sun would not have come up and the morning would be silent except for the birds. She would wash at the hand pump and walk to Matrimandir. As she was walking back from Matrimandir the sun would come up over the horizon and the village radio would play Bande Mataram.

By the time she got back to the little workshop hut, where she and Kwan Yin were living and working with their workers all day long, everyday, Kwan Yin would be up and the kettle would be on the fire for the first pot of tea of the day would be in the teapot under the tea cozy. Kwan Yin slept on a ledge under the sleeping loft. There were no walls in the workshop. They were both living and working in the workshop. Roslyn had moved into the loft to give the capsule to Kwan Yin. Kwan Yin was afraid to sleep alone at night in the mango field. She preferred to sleep on the ledge in the workshop, with Roslyn just above in the loft.

Kwan Yin was so upset after the incident with Tas that, if Roslyn was out when the sun set, she would start crying, and continue to cry until Roslyn got home. It reminded Roslyn of Bliss as an infant.

By seven thirty every morning they were working on laying out the materials, and planning the work for each worker. Each worker had different skills, and it was coordinating the skills that produced the beauty in the lovely things they were making. At eight the workers came. There were initially five, but quickly the number grew to ten, fifteen, and within one year, sixty-five. Roslyn sat in one cane chair across from Kwan Yin, who sat in the other, at the little round table Kwan Yin had salvaged from the Free Store. Roslyn was usually working on beaded bags; Kwan Yin usually worked on shoes.

Kwan Yin did not want to be bothered with workers. She was busy making beautiful things with her hands, and making the place more beautiful. She built an exquisite, simple structure, a beautiful round wall from woven casurina branches. She found stones in the canyon that she used for a floor, cementing them together with earth. She put together a pile of big stones and set two large clay pots of water and a cup. A bathroom! A place to bathe. It became suddenly possible for Roslyn to wash during daylight without being visible to anyone who was passing through the forest. Roslyn had practically become accustomed to bathing in her yellow dress - opening the strings at the side and just washing herself under the cloth, or at sunrise before anyone else was awake.

Kwan Yin and Roslyn talked and laughed together endlessly over pot after pot of tea, about everything and anything. Auroville was a favorite topic of conversation. There were not as many orders for custom made shoes as there had been at Kwan Yin's little workshop in Sincerity. However, business was brisk. They would no sooner finish one order than another would come. Shoes, bags, everything they made was selling locally and abroad through La Boutique d'Auroville. They had one export order after another.

They were in South India where labor is cheap but shoes and bags sell for very little money.

They were dependent on export sales, and the manager of the Boutique provided them with a continuous stream of export customers.

Nothing had become something, and it was selling. There was a cash flow. Everything they made was selling. They were growing steadily. The ladies would come walking into the forest every morning, smiling, saying "Good morning." A few minutes later the cobbler and tailor would come on their cycles. They were skilled, and shared their skills with one another.

Kwan Yin dyed their thread for the shoes every color of the rainbow. On dyeing days the trees in the forest would be decked with hanks of bright colored thread. The thread was then spun into balls and crocheted into shoes. The shoes were bright and fanciful. Kwan Yin wanted to make beaded shoes.

The bags developed; a whole line, including a handbag, a six pocket bag; and a shoulder bag. The bags were unique because they were hand-stitched with leather lacing. Some were beaded with mandalas on the flaps. They sold slowly, but one bag brought in as much cash as six pairs of shoes.

It was miraculous that the cash flow that began the day the workshop moved into the forest never stopped. It looked as if it was the beginning of economic prosperity. They spent the money as fast as it came in. They would go into Pondi on the village bus occasionally, and come back by auto-rickshaw after having dinner in town. Kwan Yin went regularly to Madras to buy materials. She always went by taxi.

They made themselves new clothes. When the bill came for the school fees they were able to pay it. The workers were happy and well paid. The circumstances were decidedly more comfortable. They heard that Auroville needed money to pay for the cow food. They had bought a cow for milk for tea for themselves and the workshop. They had enough money to contribute something to Auroville every week. They gave it to the community representative of the financial cooperative.

Their relationship with the Auroville community was very marginal. No one spoke to them. They did not receive a basket from Pour Tous.

They did not eat in the community kitchens. They did not go to meetings. Few people came to see them. But they received bread from the bakery.

One afternoon, instead of their half loaf of bread, they received a note from the bakery asking Roslyn to appear before a meeting with the Auroville Council the next afternoon. She had vague hopes that it would be an opportunity to reintegrate with the community.

Roslyn dressed in her best clothes; a gray tunic made from a beautiful piece of cloth from Guatemala, and black pants. Around her neck she was wearing a gossamer scarf that had belonged to The Mother. She had bought the scarf from The Ashram in Pondicherry. It was pale blue with tiny silver six pointed stars woven through it. It was as fine as a spider's web. She had made herself a pair of shoes in the same colors as the tunic and scarf, embellished with tiny silver stars.

She walked up to the Matrimandir office where the meeting was to be held. She suspected they might ask her to pay for the bread she and Kwan Yin were receiving from the bakery.

The others had already assembled when she arrived. There were ten people there. In the middle of the room was a large picture of Mother. She walked in and sat down. A hush fell over the others. Then one of them asked her, "Why are you here?"

One of the others got up and went and sat directly in front of the photo of Mother and was chanting quietly, "You go. You go. You go."

Roslyn was stunned by the hostility.

She did not know what to say. What could she say? She felt as though she had come from a different planet to these people, in her fine clothes.

She should have worn her old yellow tent.

They were all wearing tee shirts and shorts. Some of them were not very clean. Most of them had dirty feet. They all wore rubber flip-flops. She looked like an enemy of the revolution.

Finally she replied, "I received a note asking me to come here today."

One of the French people replied, "Yes, we know you received a note telling you to come here today, but why are you still in Auroville. You have been told to leave."

Roslyn was dumbfounded by their animosity. Most of them had come to Auroville after 1973.

"I have Mother's permission to live in Auroville," she replied.

Through the whole interchange the man sitting in front of Mother's photo never stopped his chant, "You go. You go."

Then one Frenchman, dressed entirely in black, with his black curly hair pulled back in a long ponytail, said, "Zere is only one question. Do you support Vasudeva?"

She was thunderstruck. She had affection and respect for Vasudeva, but she did not "support" him, nor did he support her. The group waited impatiently for her reply. Finally she said, "I support Auroville."

The chairperson closed the topic at that point and said, "This meeting can not make a decision on this. It will have to come up at the next general community meeting." Roslyn was dismissed.

A few days later Roslyn and Kwan Yin walked to the Matrimandir office for the general meeting, dressed in their brightest and prettiest clothes. They walked up to the door of the meeting room. Myra glared at them. "You are not welcome here."

The others agreed to refuse them admittance to the meeting. They were asked to wait outside. Many of their friends were in the meeting. Boy had been dismissed as Dhyan's attendant, and had started visiting Kwan Yin often. He could not look at her when the chairperson told her to 'Please wait outside.' He did not say anything to challenge the decision of the meeting that they were not welcome to participate in the process. Roslyn was amazed that people who had been her friends for years sat there like dummies and allowed the chairperson to refuse to allow them into the meeting.

She sat for a while with Kwan Yin listening to the meeting. The first topic on the agenda was the cow food bill. Cooper Swamy refused to extend further credit. Could the farms grow enough cow food for the Auroville cows? There was a discussion that concluded with a consensus that cow food was a priority.

Roslyn got up and left to walk back to the forest. A couple of hours later Kwan Yin arrived in tears.

There was a pot of tea ready under the tea cozy. Kwan Yin sat down and sobbed. Roslyn tried to concentrate on the beadwork she was doing.

Finally Kwan Yin stopped crying and offered to pour the tea. Roslyn set aside her work. They sipped their tea for a few moments. Kwan Yin burst into tears again. "Why do they hate you so much?"

"Do they hate me?" Roslyn mused. "What happened at the meeting after I left?"

"There was a long discussion about whether Pour Tous should provide special baskets for children. Everyone agreed; children need better food. Then there was a long discussion about what should be included in the children's basket. They finally decided to give the children raisins. Then someone suggested that the diet is so sparse that it would be good if everyone got raisins. Then the meeting agreed that everyone should get 100 grams of raisins from Pour Tous." Kwan Yin started laughing as she related that part of the meeting. She was not ready to question the entire process, but she could see that it was, at least in part, ridiculous.

She went on with her story. "Then they started talking about us. What did you do to Auroluigi? He got up and said that you are the personal emissary of the Dark Force in Auroville?"

"Who is Auroluigi?" Roslyn asked.

"He is Miriam's new boyfriend. He spoke against you for at least five minutes. He said that Victor told the community years ago that you are a tantric witch. Why are you still here? You should leave Auroville immediately. The community must insist you leave."

Kwan Yin continued, "It was beginning to sound like they were going to come down here en masse and run you out of town!"

"We don't have running water nor electricity. I don't think anyone is going to throw us out of here, because no-one else would want to live here." Roslyn replied, having somewhat lost her fear of them confronting her face to face. She could not imagine anyone would throw her out of the forest. There was not even a single tree there when she had gone there in 1976, and now in 1980 there was a forest and a fruit garden (thanks to Jim Bean). And there was a workshop that was supporting several village families. Nothing they were doing was harmful to Auroville or to others. Roslyn could not imagine how the Divine would allow anyone to throw her out of the forest.

Kwan Yin said, "I think they are afraid to face you. They decided not to come as a mob and throw us out, only to shun us for one year. No one in Auroville is to have anything to do with us for one year. The Boutique may not handle our products. The community will not recommend our visas. No bread from the bakery. No one is to talk to us or smile at us." She burst into sobs.

"How could they do that?"

"After several people spoke against you very reasonably and dispassionately, finally Dennis said, 'We cannot judge these people. Let us simply withdraw all rights to any Auroville services for a year, then we can see.' We will lose our visas within a year. It is a neat way to get rid of us without throwing us out," she spoke through her sobs.

"What does Boy say about all this?" Roslyn asked.

"He walked me home up to the forest, then said 'Goodbye,' got on his cycle, and rode off."

"Well, you always know who your friends are when they ride off into the sunset during a crisis," Roslyn commented.

Kwan Yin replied with more tears. Finally Kwan Yin got on her cycle and went off to visit Boy.

Roslyn sat on her cane chair in the light of the lantern and watched darkness fall.

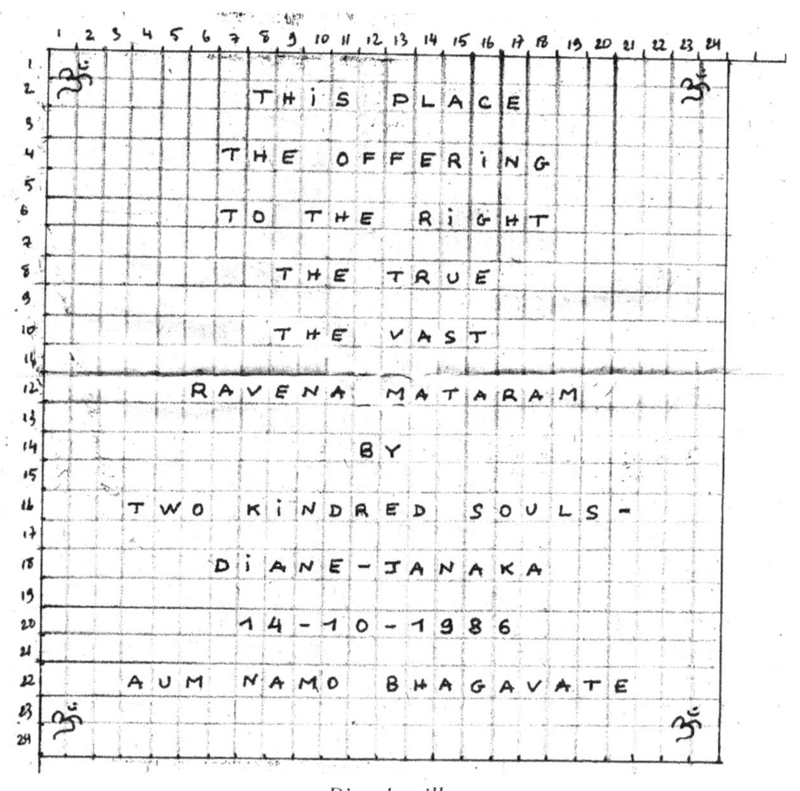

THIS PLACE
THE OFFERING
TO THE RIGHT
THE TRUE
THE VAST
RAVENA MATARAM
BY
TWO KINDRED SOULS -
DIANE - JANAKA
14 - 10 - 1986
AUM NAMO BHAGAVATE

Diane's will

The Ideal must be Nature's common truth,
The body illumined with the indwelling God,
The heart and mind feel one with all that is,
A conscious soul live in a conscious world.

Sri Aurobindo, Savitri

The self is one in all.

Raise all the active parts of the human nature to that highest condition of their power and capacity. The Divine power must be called in to replace our individual effort. The mental must be transfomed into the gnostic being: this, is effected, by breaking beyond the mental limits. Stride upward into the next higher plane or region of our being hidden from us at present by the shining lid of the mental reflections; and, a conversion of all that we are into the terms of this greater consciousness. The change will be effected; by bringing in the law of the gnostic purusha and bliss, into the physical consciousness from above downward. Whatever desire will remain will be divine desire.

The whole gnostic evolution opens the being to bliss.

(from Jim Bean's Journal extracts from Sri Aurobindo's Synthesis of Yoga.*)*

Kwan Yin did not come back until morning.

Roslyn woke up ill. Her back hurt. Her front hurt. Her head hurt. Her feet hurt. She could barely move. She decided to move out of the workshop and back into the capsule in the mango field. She suggested to Kwan Yin that she could move off the ledge into the sleeping loft. The workers helped them move.

Roslyn managed to walk through the forest to the mango field. There she collapsed. She had so much pain she could not sit up. Kwan Yin came to her with a note from Andre at Boutique d'Auroville.

"Please come and remove your things from the Boutique this evening. They are already packed and in the storeroom. Some people threatened to come and remove them by throwing them in the street, so I packed everything and put it in the storeroom for you. Love."

Roslyn could not bear to think about it. She was in such agony she could not sit up. She did not want anything except that the pain should go away. She did not care much what Kwan Yin did with the workshop and business.

Kwan Yin went by bus with Boy to Pondi.

Dosama and the workers were there to look after Roslyn.

The next morning Kwan Yin came again to visit her.

"How are you?" she asked.

Roslyn had such acute pain it was impossible to sit up.

Kwan Yin gave her a letter in the distinctive blue envelope used by their big Australian customer. "Maybe this will make you feel better, Andre gave it to me yesterday."

Roslyn read the letter. At the bottom of the letter it said, "Check enclosed."

"What happened to the check."

"Andre gave me 18,000 rupees."

It was more money than they had ever had.

"He agreed to continue to handle our export orders, but I should only go in to the export office at night, and never in to the Boutique. You should never be seen in the office or the Boutique."

"I don't care."

"Lorelei has copied our shoes and hers are already in the Boutique for five rupees a pair less than ours. Do you think that might have had anything to do with what is happening to us?"

"I don't know, but I think all this money is Mother's reply to the community's action against us," Roslyn said.

"Do you mind if I go with Boy to Madras tomorrow to buy materials?"

Kwan Yin asked.

"I don't mind."

"Will you be all right alone?"

"I'm sick. I just want to be alone."

"Do you need anything?"

"I'll call you if I do."

"Do you mind if Boy stays with me in the workshop?"

"That's why I moved out."

Kwan Yin left with her bag full of rupees, and Roslyn wondered if the terrible pain she was suffering was physical or emotional. Whatever it was she could not deal with it. She could not move. She did not want to talk or eat. She only wanted to sleep to escape the pain.

Kwan Yin went to Madras for materials and came back. She went to Andre to deliver some shoes for an export order, and there were another 18,000 rupees for them.

She came back and asked Roslyn what she wanted to do with the money.

Roslyn could only respond, "I don't care. Do what you want."

Kwan Yin asked if she should get a taxi to take Roslyn to a doctor.

Roslyn told her she could not walk from the capsule to the road to get into the taxi. She could not even sit up. She asked Kwan Yin to visit occasionally, but to please let her rest. She would ask if she wanted or needed anything.

Kwan Yin looked after the workers and the work, and spent her evenings and nights with Boy. Roslyn was sick in bed in her capsule for weeks.

Kwan Yin blamed Roslyn for their being outcast. She rarely visited her, although she would send a servant to the capsule several times a day to see if she needed anything.

Roslyn was too sick to read. Her insides felt like they had been rent with an axe. She could hardly move. She had no appetite. It was Christmas. Bliss came for a few days break from school.

Roslyn was very happy to see her little girl, but she wasn't able to be very good company because she was still so ill.

Bliss took off on her cycle to seek out her old friends and playmates.

It was Christmas eve. Bliss went with her friends to Unity kitchen for the Auroville Christmas party. She came back to the capsule after a short time.

"Momma, is there anything to eat here?"

The food cupboard in the workshop was full to bursting with good things to eat that Kwan Yin had bought for Roslyn.

"There is plenty of food in the food safe. Are you hungry?"

The child burst into tears. "I went to the Center with my friends. The people refused to give me anything to eat. One Frenchman came and said to me, 'You go.' So I left."

Roslyn called Dosama, who came and took Bliss over to the workshop and helped her get some food.

Roslyn might have described her life in Auroville since returning from California as going from bad to terrible to worse. She was glad that Bliss's break was only for a few days. She hated it that the child had been subjected to the collective lunacy. Roslyn was lying on her mattress, barely able to sit up to use the piss pot.

The next morning Bliss went off on her cycle to play. In the evening she came back with a beautiful fragrant flower. "Here momma, Jim Bean gave me this flower for you. He heard you were sick."

Roslyn took the flower and put it on her pillow.

"Did you have a nice day?" she asked the child.

"Yes, everybody was very nice to me today. All the kids went to a Christmas party at the playground and the 'burgermeister' invited us all for cake. It was fun."

The trauma of the night before seemed forgotten.

Bliss slept with Roslyn in the capsule. In the morning Roslyn was feeling a little better. She asked Dosama to bring some water, and after weeks of lying in bed tried to wash herself. She still was not able to stand up for more than a very short time; and she walked with terrible pain, but she had gotten out of bed and washed her body and her hair.

Each day she felt a little better. Bliss went back to school. After five weeks Roslyn was finally well enough to walk from the capsule to the workshop. More workers had been hired. Money and orders were still pouring in. Kwan Yin suggested that Roslyn move back into the workshop so she and Boy could use the capsule.

Roslyn was happy to move back to the workshop. The next morning Kwan Yin came into the workshop in tears. "My bicycle is gone."

She had parked her locked cycle under the capsule when she slept. In the morning it was gone. Roslyn raged at the workers and threatened to send everyone home if the cycle was not returned, and sent two of the workers out to look for it.

A couple of hours later the boys came back with a wrecked cycle frame. The tires were gone, the pedals were gone, the handlebar was gone, the carrier was gone. There was only a brutalized twisted frame.

Roslyn and Kwan Yin looked at it and felt sick. The cycle had been violently vandalized.

Kwan Yin asked Roslyn, "Do you think that is a message to us?"

After looking at that brutalised bicycle frame there was no way Kwan Yin was going to spend a night alone in the capsule. She did not want to move back onto the ledge in the workshop. There was not even a wall to protect her from whatever might pass in the night. She decided to go to live with Boy in his little house in the corner of the vegetable garden. It was very small, but exquisite. Boy was delighted to have such a beautiful roommate and companion, who was also making money. Boy had no money, but he had a great way about him. People loved him and loved to be around him, and with beautiful Kwan Yin they would only love him more.

He was happy that he had been chosen as consort.

Roslyn was making enough money from her export sales not to have to charge Aurovilians for their shoes. Mother had said, "No exchange of money in Auroville." She rarely left the forest. She was there in the workshop with the workers, always working on something, organising something, doing something. She enjoyed working with her workers. Together they made some beautiful things. She had a few friends who visited her, and some people came for shoes.

She and Kwan Yin were amused to make and give shoes to the same people who had sat in the meeting and not said a word when they were declared outcast.

People came. Gave their orders. Took their free shoes, and perhaps a cup of tea, but if Kwan Yin passed them on the road or met them in a restaurant in Pondi they did not acknowledge her. She was very unhappy with the situation. One day she went into "Maison d'Auroville," an Aurovilian restaurant, in Pondicherry, open to the public. She sat down and asked for a cup of tea.

Several Aurovilians were there. They approached her and told her to leave and take her bad vibes out of the restaurant.

She had only asked for a cup of tea in a restaurant, looking like a beautiful silver butterfly. What were they projecting on her? She left the restaurant in tears and cried for days. She wanted to leave Auroville, but she did not want to leave Boy.

Boy told Kwan Yin that he had overheard a conversation between his friend who looked after the vegetable garden and some of the Frenchies. The Frenchies said they wanted to throw Roslyn out of the forest, and were willing to resort to violence if necessary. His friend had replied, "Over my dead body."

An old friend of Kwan Yin who was living in Germany wrote and offered her a ticket to come for a visit. She accepted the ticket and made plans to leave for a few months. Kwan Yin's tears were driving Roslyn crazy.

Boy came and suggested to Roslyn that if she gave some of the money they were making to Auroville, people would probably change their attitude towards her.

She was in the process of building a new workshop. They had already over thirty workers, and no place for more workers in the existing workshop. She was building a large space with three large interconnected huts with a little flagstone patio in the center. There was a storeroom loft in one hut and a sleeping loft in another. It was a large casurina, bamboo and coconut palm roof. There were no walls. For the foundation and floor she used lime, rather than cement, mixed with broken bricks and pebbles.

Boy told her that everyone in Auroville knew how much money she was making, and everyone was angry with her because she was not giving any of it to the community.

"They don't want anything from me. They won't accept anything from me." She said.

"Try. Just put some money in an envelope every week and Kwan Yin can give it to the community's representative to the co-op meeting."

"Fine. How much do you want me to give?" She asked.

"Whatever you can afford."

She put some money in an envelope and gave it to Kwan Yin. Kwan Yin gave it to the co-op rep. He accepted it and gave it to the community each week as part of the donation from the Kottakarai community.

Some uneventful weeks passed. Kwan Yin spent more and more time with Boy and less and less time in the forest. Roslyn had a friend, a young Frenchman, Zuzu, from Dijon, who visied her nearly evening. They spent hours talking about esoteric lore, reading Sri Aurobindo, and playing backgammon. They were friends. He was hopelessly in love with someone who was hopelessly in love with someone else. Roslyn was still hopelessly in love with Jim Bean.

Zuzu would inevitably come to the forest after the meeting on Thursday and give Roslyn a report on what momentous decisions had been reached each week. They laughed a lot together.

One Thursday evening he came and burst into tears when he walked in. He collapsed on one of the cane chairs, sobbing. He could not speak. He could not stop crying. His hands were shaking.

It was too much. Roslyn turned from him and went to the fire to give him a chance to compose himself, while she made another pot of tea.

She filled the tea pot, took the milk and sugar out of the food cupboard and put them on the table. She took two clean cups off the shelf, and put one in front of her chair and one in front of him.

She poured them each a cup of tea.

He had gotten his sobs under control and was sniffling, wiping his face with a corner of his longi.

"I'm sorry," he groaned, looking at her through swollen eyes.

"Can you tell me what is happening?" she asked.

He got up and went outside for a moment to take a few deep breaths, then came back.

He sat down and looked at her and said, sobbing, "They even took the child."

"What child?"

"Selvam," he said, bursting into tears.

Roslyn knew Selvam was a little Tamil boy who had adopted Zuzu and moved into his house. He had refused to go back to his family in the village.

"Please Zuzu, what are you talking about? Why would anyone take Selvam? How could anyone take Selvam? He is so devoted to you he won't even go visit his parents."

"They have taken everything from me! Don't you understand?'

He was sobbing, and she was bewildered.

"Please Zuzu, tell me what happened in the meeting."

He brought himself under control, and them looked at her and said, "Why? Why do they hate you so much?"

Even without more words she was beginning to get the idea about what had happened, but she couldn't believe it. It was impossible to imagine that the community would throw Zuzu out and take his house, and all the assets he had created and the child he was looking after, because he was her friend.

He took a sip of tea. "I do not believe what happened today in the meeting."

She tried to hide behind her teacup, afraid of what was coming.

"I was just sitting there. I never say a word in the meeting. I like to go to the meeting. I identify with the community and the collective process, and I like to participate as an observer. Sometimes I don't agree with what is happening, but it is still interesting. Usually there is something to laugh about. I get a lot out of it.

"I don't like some of the people and they don't like me, but it doesn't matter. We are all in Auroville together. We are here for the Supramental Transformation, not for 'I like... I don't like'. I did not like what they did to you and Kwan Yin, but we are only at the beginning of something. I could not imagine they would attack me! I am French. I have given them a lot of money. I cannot believe they could do something like that."

"What did they do?" she asked.

"They said I am not Aurovilian, and must go out from Auroville. I was just sitting there. They were talking about the cow food bill again, and suddenly my neighbor, Paul, attacked me. He told them he had seen me coming here. He said I am a spy and a snake and should not be allowed in the meeting or in Auroville, and that he was willing to look after Selvam, my house, everything, for Auroville.

"I tried to reply and they all suddenly turned on me and started chanting, 'You go!'

"I screamed at them, 'what about my house? What about the boy?'

"They said, 'Auroville will look after everything. You go.'"

"I could not help it. I started to cry. This is the third house I have built in Auroville, the second well I have put in. With help from my parents I have just put a new roof on my house, and bought a new pump. Not again!"

He was weeping and screaming and Roslyn could say nothing.

"I asked them why they hate you so much. I told them you give them money every week. They said it is a lie; anyway it is not a question of money. You are against Auroville. You should leave Auroville, and I am not welcome in Auroville, because anyone who talks to you is not Aurovilian and has no place here."

Roslyn was overwhelmed by a sense of helplessness. She could not believe that there was so much active animosity towards her. She could not imagine what she might have done to have engendered all that animosity.

"How can they hate me so much? What have I done?"

"I came to ask if I can stay here for a few days. I have to move out of my house immediately. My neighbor threatened to burn it down with me in it if I stay there another night. May I stay in the loft in the workshop for a few days?"

"Of course," she agreed.

"I have no money at the moment. My parents have sent money but it has not arrived."

"That isn't a problem here at the moment. The workshop is making money."

Despite the shock, they were quite happy in the forest for the next few days. Kwan Yin was busy getting ready to go to Europe. Roslyn had agreed to buy a ticket for Boy so he could go with her. Kwan Yin was shipping boxes of shoes ahead so she would have something when they landed in Europe. Roslyn was happy to have Zuzu in the forest as a companion.

In the evening after the workers left they would play Go and drink tea for hours in the evening.

A few days later Boy brought back the thousand rupees Roslyn had contributed to the community that week. It had been offered to the coop as part of the donation from the Kottakarai community. At the meeting someone mentioned Zuzu's remark that Roslyn was giving money to the community. The Kottakarai representative admitted; that the thousand rupees he had just put on the table; had actually been given by Roslyn. Someone threw the wad of notes on the floor. "Take it back. We don't want her money!"

Roslyn felt she was between a rock and a hard place. Kwan Yin came and told her that Andre had said that somehow the others had discovered he was still handling her export, and so they had taken his export license, because it was only for Auroville, and they had taken the Boutique from him.

Zuzu went for a walk. He passed his neighbor, who shouted at him, "You are not allowed to walk on Auroville roads. You have been thrown out of Auroville. Get out of Auroville."

It was too much for him. His money had arrived in the bank. He bought a plane ticket and went to France.

Zuzu was gone. Kwan Yin and Boy were leaving. Roslyn had a product, a workshop, customers, but no friends, and no place to display and sell her products, no exporter.

At 6 a.m. on July 1st Kwan Yin and Boy left for Europe. Roslyn was alone.

Entrance to Janaka House

Then kindling the gold tongue of sacrifice,
Calling the powers of a bright hemisphere,
We shall shed the discredit of our mortal state,
Make the abysm a road for Heaven's descent,
Acquaint our depths with the supernal Ray,
And cleave the darkness with the mystic Fire.

Sri Aurobindo, Savitri

A perfect equality of our spirit and nature is a means by which we can move back from the troubled and ignorant outer consciousness into the inner kingdom of heaven and possess the spirit's eternal kingdoms of greatness, joy and peace. They can be reached by calm, impersonal and equal self-identification with all beings, and an understanding of all energies.

"Abandon all dharmas and take refuge in Me alone:
I will deliver thee from all
sin and evil. Do not grieve."
Equality is the very sign of liberation.

By renouncing the egoistic sense of desire and possession, the soul enjoys divinely its self and the universe. The function of the prana is enjoyment, but the real enjoyment of existence is an inward spiritual Ananda, not vital, nor mental, degraded by predominance of physical mind, but universal, profound, a massed concentration of spiritual bliss, possessed in calm ecstasy of self and all existence. Possession is prana's function, but the result is not dependent on the outward seizings making us subject to what we seize.

By equality of the heart we get away from the troubled desire soul on the surface, open the gates of this profounder being, bring out its responses and impose their true divine values on all that solicits our emotional being.

The ordinary mental standards will be exceeded on the basis of this dynamic equality. The eye of will must look beyond to a purity of divine being, a motive of divine will power guided by divine knowledge of which perfected nature will be the engine.

There is a passive or negative equality that liberates us from the lower nature and admits us to the calm peace of the divine being. There is an equality of receptivity that fronts impassively the impacts and phenomenon of existence and negates the dualities of the appearances and reactions that they impose on us.

Instead of seeking to protect itself or shun or escape impacts, the soul may confront and teach itself to bear with perseverance, fortitude, endurance, blows. What was before unbearable becomes easy to endure. Conscious nature divides in two parts. There is still the mental and emotional nature of customary reactions, but there is also the higher will and reason that observes and is untouched. This power comes by endurance and mastery and separation and rejection of the lower nature. It is necessary to get rid of normal reactions and remold all modes of experience by the strength of the spirit.

(from *Jim Bean's Journal extracts from Sri Aurobindo's* Synthesis of Yoga.)

Kwan Yin and Boy left at dawn on the first of July in their taxi to the Madras airport, to catch their plane to Germany. Roslyn was bewildered at how she should face the day, and finally - out of despair - offered in her heart and mind the situation to Mother and Sri Aurobindo. She considered sending the workers home, but the work she was doing represented four years of solid effort. She decided to sit it out.

At 10 a.m., a blonde bearded man came to Roslyn's forest with a petition for her to sign to be presented to the Supreme Court of India. The petition said that the Auroville Act which had been passed by Parliament, taking the administrative responsibility of Auroville from the Sri Aurobindo Society and giving it to Government of India, was illegal under the Constitution of India, because Auroville was a spiritual, not a political endeavor.

She did not know whether she wanted to sign it or not. Mother had said clearly that Auroville could belong to no individual, group or nation, but Roslyn wanted nothing at all to do with the political battles.

The blonde man tried to explain to her that it was not only politics, but it would destroy the possibility to realize Mother's Dream if the Government of India took over Auroville. Everyone would be affected in many ways. Spiritual anarchy would be replaced with bureaucracy.

She had to agree with him, but she did not want to put herself out there to take more hate from the segment of the Auroville community that considered a Government takeover an answer to their prayers.

Roslyn tried to stall signing, by asking the blonde man about himself, "Who are you?"

"My name is Robert Goodman. I am a disciple of The Mother and Sri Aurobindo, although I have only recently come to Auroville."

He looked very young, perhaps in his early thirties, but he had the demeanor of a much older person. He seemed to be terribly serious.

She asked him what he wanted to do in Auroville.

He replied that he had bought several plots of land in the Auroville area and was already beginning building a community with some of his friends from Europe. By profession he was a jeweler and a business man. He owned shops in Europe and had set up a small factory in Pondicherry for cutting gems.

She asked him if he would buy some crocheted shoes for his shops.

He said they were not a good item for Germany, because it was too cold and wet there to wear crocheted shoes.

"Even in the summer?" she asked.

"Some years there isn't any summer," he replied. "Is there some other way I can help you?"

"I have no place in Pondi to sell my products, because they refuse to accept anything I make in Boutique d'Auroville, and my exporter refuses to export any longer for me."

"I can help you. We are opening a shop in Pondi, and we have an export license."

"Yes, but you want me to sign this petition. I don't want any more trouble. I am afraid," she said.

"What is your situation now?" he asked.

"The situation is that I am an outcast. I have no money. I have a workshop that employs forty-five people. We have export customers who order shoes from us regularly, but our exporter has said he will not accept any more orders for us, and can not continue to export our goods. I have no access to new customers because my goods are not displayed anywhere where anyone could see them. Aurosarjan has copied my shoes, and they are on sale in the Boutique and exported by the Boutique. My business is dead. What can I do? All these people are dependent on me."

"I can help you. We have an export license in the name of 'Aurodevi'. We would be happy to export for you. We will also have a showroom in Pondi."

It was a miracle, an answer to her prayers. Roslyn signed the petition and asked him to immediately send two telegrams to her export customers asking them to send their orders and payments to Aurodevi.

After a few days she received a reply from one of her customers. He had already sent the check to Boutique d'Auroville, but would in future send his payments to Aurodevi. She never heard from the other customer again, and he had been ordering 15,000 rupees worth of crocheted shoes each month. Years later she found out that he continued to order shoes from Boutique d'Auroville because they were five rupees a pair cheaper than her shoes.

She sent a note to Andre asking him to send the money to export her Australian customer's shoes to Aurodevi, who would be looking after her export in the future. Members of Vasudeva's family were involved in the Aurodevi enterprise. Vasudeva was a hate object in Auroville because he objected to involving the Government of India in the administration of Auroville. He had hoped that the community could establish an autonomous administration free from the Sri Aurobindo Society without the intervention of the Government of India. Mother had said; no individual, group, nation, or organization could run Auroville.

She had imagined Auroville as a 'Divine anarchy.'

By the time the money arrived from Australia Roslyn had not been able to pay her workers for two weeks. The workshop had nearly run out of material. They were making children's shoes out of scraps. It was an order for five hundred pairs of shoes, but Aurodevi received only half the money she would normally have been paid for 500 pairs of shoes. Andre claimed the other half of the money as commission for all the shoes he had exported for Roslyn, on which he had charged no commission.

She had to be grateful that he had paid her at all, because he had lost his Boutique and export license because he had exported for her. Half the money did not cover the cost of manufacturing the shoes.

Aurodevi hired a business manager/accountant for her to look after the business, Mr. Madhavan. She had to pay him 1,200 rupees a month. He handled the money when it came in, and arranged for bank loans when it did not. He would come to the forest every Saturday afternoon with a bag of money, in neat little envelopes. Each envelope had the name of a worker on it, and the wages were in the envelopes. Roslyn received an envelope each week with two hundred rupees in it.

Roslyn and her workers worked together six days each week from eight in the morning until four thirty in the afternoon. They were making beautiful things. The major product was crocheted shoes. There was also a line of beaded hand-stitched bags, vests and belts. They were making everything except money. The cash flow that had started abruptly in December suddenly dried up.

The Australian customer, Rob, sent a letter of credit for the August and September orders. The letter was written in such a way that Roslyn had to produce shipping documents for a thousand pairs of shoes and then wait for thirty days for payment. She had to produce fifteen hundred pairs of shoes without any money! She had no savings, no cash in hand, because she had used all the money to pay Bliss's school fees, to build a new workshop, for Kwan Yin and Boy, and to contribute to the Auroville community. She was already in debt on the production of the July order.

Madhavan managed to secure a bank loan for sixty per cent of the value of the letter of credit for twenty two per cent interest.

They produced the shoes and shipped the shoes. It was very tight. Roslyn wrote to Rob begging him to please send a cash advance by bank draft for the October order. He sent a bank draft, but it was unsigned and not negotiable. There was no more credit to be had.

There were forty thousand rupees of debts. They were again back to making baby shoes from scraps. There was no money to pay the wages. There were sixty-five workers.

Finally another letter of credit arrived, with the same terms as the first letter of credit, for the October and November order. Madhavan negotiated another loan, the workers were paid, and production continued. Out of her two hundred rupees a week Roslyn had to pay Dosama, because she was not working in the workshop, although she made tea for all the workers twice a day. Roslyn was making half as much as Madhavan, and less than the tailor and chief cobbler. She was at work every day from seven in the morning when she went to the workshop to arrange all the work for the day. The workers arrived at eight o'clock. She finished cleaning up after the workers left usually by 5 p.m. each afternoon.

Once or twice a month she would go into Pondi on the late afternoon bus and check in the office or at the Boutique to see if there was any mail or money, and have supper in a rooftop restaurant under the stars. Occasionally she would visit Sri Aurobindo's Samadhi and sit in that peaceful garden for some minutes.

Several times a month Ananta would send one of his workers to bring her in an auto-rickshaw to the island. He did a special puja four times a month that was the work he had been given by Mother. He did worship to Zeus, Athena, Poseidon, Apollo, and other gods who have not been worshipped in living memory. Two Brahmin priests came for the pujas. They lit a fire and said mantras in front of his little temple. Often there were musicians and fireworks. After each puja the statue of Shiva and the photos of Mother and Sri Aurobindo were carried around to the various shrines on the island, and rites of offering, homage and prayer were observed. There was always a big dinner after the puja. Ananta provided the transport for Roslyn from the forest to the island. Occasionally he would demand that she should travel by bus. Then she would not go to see him for several weeks. Then he would send an auto-rickshaw or a taxi for her, and they would have a joyful reunion.

They had a very happy relationship. His little house was much more comfortable than her capsule. His servants were good cooks. He had a record player and all the records from the old musical comedies. She often stayed overnight. Occasionally, on a weekend she would stay on the island for two nights. One time she returned to the forest to find someone had stolen her bedcovers, and most of her clothes, although she had hired a watchman to look after the capsule and the workshop in her absence.. Another time the sewing machine was stolen. All the materials and shoes were in a big locked cupboard. When they stole her mattress she could only be grateful that they did not also steal her little puja table. She became afraid to stay away overnight.

Each time it was a battle with Ananta, who wanted her to stay with him because he was very lonely on his island. She would make him buy her clothes, glasses, and other things she needed. His reward would be that she would say on the island for one or two nights in the other room, and allow his servants to wait on her hand and foot. She also helped him with his correspondence, because he was usually too drunk to write legibly.

She tried to get him to give or lend her money when she was in trouble. He refused to give her a single paise. He would buy her the most expensive silk for clothes. He would pay for taxis. But, no money!!

The end of November came. Madhavan still had not been able to get the bank to encash the first letter of credit. The bank in Pondi refused to pay because the bank in Madras said the letter of credit was void because the shoes had been transshipped through Singapore rather than directly to Australia. There are no direct flights from Madras to Australia.

Meanwhile two thousand pairs of shoes had been produced and shipped and none had been paid for. Roslyn almost had a heart attack when she heard that the bank was not accepting the letters of credit. She was sending letters and telegrams to Rob, and getting no reply.

At last at the beginning of December she got a letter and telegram saying he would be coming at the end of December. He promised to straighten everything out with the bank and see that she received payment for all the shoes she had shipped to him. He also ordered 650 pairs of shoes for December, included a small advance, and promised full payment when he arrived.

Roslyn was over 100,000 rupees in debt, and she had to borrow more money to produce another six hundred and fifty pairs of shoes to keep her sixty-five workers working, to maintain the production cycle. Roslyn found herself working harder and harder producing more and more shoes. The only reward she had for making all those shoes was more debts and responsibilities. She did not know if it was more stressful to be deeply in debt with sixty-five dependent families, or just be broke with her own dependents. She wondered, if there was any truth in karma yoga, how had she merited such consistently difficult karma?

She would get up every morning before dawn. She was usually awake when the call to prayer, sung from the mosque in the nearby village, resounded in the deep silence of early morning before dawn, when the only other beings awake were a few birds. The silence was pristine.

Roslyn would walk across the mango field to the hand pump. There were no walls around her hand pump, but there was no one else awake or around at that hour of the morning. There was a screen of living bamboo around the pump. The sky would be full of the rich promise of dawn.

After her bath she would walk to Matrimandir. There were no houses between her capsule and Matrimandir along the road. The Matrimandir was about two and a half kilometers from her capsule. It was very surrealistic to walk in the silent morning and see no one else. Finally she would come to the great evolving mass of concrete that was Matrimandir, slowly rising from the earth or coming down out of the sky. Often she would see Jim Bean walking around Matrimandir. He seemed not to see her. He would walk right by her without even glancing at her. Vasudeva was also often walking around Matrimandir at that hour of dawn. Roslyn sometimes felt they were the only people in Auroville at that hour of the day, and they had nothing at all to say to one another, nothing at all in common, except the habit of walking around Matrimandir at dawn.

Usually as she was walking back to the forest Roslyn would hear the horn of the village bus and Bande Mataram being played by All India Radio over the village loudspeaker. When she got back to the forest Dosama would be sitting by her fire near her little hut at the top of the tope, and would greet Roslyn with a warm smile. Roslyn would return the greeting and go to the workshop.

There she would begin work checking the finished work from the day before, which the workers left on the workbench when they finished in the afternoon, and putting it into the cupboard. Then she would decide on the work for the day and lay out the materials on the table for the workers. After that she would go and sit in her cane chair by her little round table and work on her accounts and correspondence. Often by the time the workers arrived she was in her hammock with a good book.

The workers would start arriving a 7:50 a.m. The young girl who was at the bottom of the workshop hierarchy came a few minutes before the others to sweep the workshop every morning, and draw a kolam* in front of the entrance. She also brought the milk, she purchased each morning in the village. The milk was an essential part of the morning ritual.

Two liters of fresh milk came every day. The milk had to be boiled. Most of Roslyn's milk was used for curd, which the next day was strained through a cloth and served as cheese with bread to the workers with their afternoon tea.   She prepared her simple meals on the little fireplace of six bricks set in a U where she also dyed the thread. She took heart from Mother, who had cautioned sadhaks, "Rely only on the Divine."

At eight each morning the workers would arrive. Usually Roslyn was in the hammock waiting for her tea. The ladies always looked beautiful in their brightly colored saris. They seemed impervious to the tornadoes and twists of fate that were constantly blowing Roslyn away. They arrived beautifully dressed, their long hair neatly combed, and wished Roslyn a 'good morning.' She would get up and give them their orders for the day, the colors, sizes and designs. The cobblers and tailor always arrived, a minute or two after the ladies. They were inevitably cheerful, and occasionally one of them would bring Roslyn a flower. She would return their greetings and give them their work for the day. Each worker had found a place to sit in the workshop that became his or her place. Roslyn had not had enough money to finish the floor, so the floor was only a foundation of lime mixed with rubble. The workers sat on cushions on bamboo mats. They sat there quietly, with a half-hour for tea between 10 and 10:30 a.m. and 3 and 3:30 p.m., and an hour for lunch between twelve and one. They sat and worked from eight in the morning until four-thirty in the afternoon six days a week. They did not say a word of complaint if at the end of the week Roslyn had no money for them. Roslyn loved them for their steadfastness, and was horribly embarrassed that she was unable to always meet her commitments to them.

She dreamed about shoes when she slept. She dreamed about paying customers. Kwan Yin and Boy were ordering shoes and bags, but they weren't sending any money. She hoped and prayed every day for at least enough money to pay the workers each week. Sometimes she was three weeks behind on the wages. She could actually see that the tailor was getting thinner. She could see the other workers, who were already thin, becoming nearly skeletal. She was grateful to the workers that they continued to support her by coming to work, and having patience even though they were not being paid regularly, but it was a horror. They all worked all day, every day. The shoes were being shipped as fast as they could produce them, and for five months they had received no money.

Finally Rob arrived in Madras, hale and hearty. He went to the bank that had, for months, refused to honor the letter of credit. Suddenly the cash was on the counter. He also paid cash for the shoes he had ordered for December and ordered 1,000 pairs of shoes for January and 1,000 pairs of shoes for February. He promised to send an advance on the January/February order as soon as he got back to Australia.

The debts were all paid, plus the interest. Roslyn was dismayed that after all the debts were paid, plus the interest, and material purchased for the January order, there was barely enough money to pay Bliss's school fees. There was not even enough left over for her to repair the roof of the capsule.

Rob and Madhavan got along with one another like a house on fire. For the few days Rob was there, there were taxis, dinners in the best restaurants in Pondi, and good times. Roslyn was hopeful when Rob the Robber left, that he had understood her financial situation, and would see to it in future that she was promptly paid for the shoes he had ordered. He admitted that he was making a great deal of money on the shoes. He was selling them for five times what he was paying her and they were selling like hot cakes. She imagined that it would be easy for him to see that it was to his advantage to maintain her and the workshop by keeping his agreements with them. She hoped she would not again be inundated with debts, and would start making some profit from the huge orders he was placing.

By the third week of January, when there still was no money from him, she had to ask Madhavan to take another bank loan. She received a letter and a telegram confirming the January order for 1,000 pairs of shoes, and the February order for 1,000 pairs of shoes, and promising the check was in the mail. The check did not arrive, so she tried to take another bank loan, but there was no letter of credit for collateral, and the bank refused to lend her money.

She had received a small order from Europe for children's shoes, and a small order from Bloomingdale's in New York City, which helped her purchase the materials for the 1,000 pairs Rob had ordered for February, but there was once again no money to pay the workers.

On the last day of February she got a telegram, cancelling the March order, ordering 500 pairs of shoes for April, and promising that the check was in the mail.

Roslyn wrote to her mother asking if she would help with Bliss's school fees. She received no reply. Some weeks later she received a letter from the Administrator of the Delhi school with a letter from her mother enclosed, and a note, "Why is she writing like this to me again? She had already written this to me last year. Please send Rs.5,000 immediately for this term's fees." The letter from her Mother was addressed to the school: "I educated my children, and I do not feel any responsibility to help them educate their children."

Roslyn ran into Joe in Pondicherry, and he told her that Panditji had passed away a few days before. She had not been to see him in two years, but she felt diminished by his passing.

Roslyn had no materials for the workers. She had not paid the workers for three weeks. She had no credit. She had no market for all the shoes she was able to produce. She had to close. She had to close the workshop owing the workers three-week's wages. She had to send them all home without paying them what she owed them.

She begged Madhavan to try to borrow money for them at any rate of interest. He said it was impossible. She had no collateral. She had shipped two thousand pairs of shoes and she had no collateral?

"How could you ship two thousand pairs of shoes without any collateral?" she asked him.

"Rob and I made an agreement, so he would not have to pay so much duty. I agreed to ship the shoes as tourist parcels."

"That's incredible. Why am I paying you?" she screamed at him? He just turned his back on her and walked away.

She went to Robert Goodman and asked him what kind of people he had connected her to.

He replied that they were doing a service for her, exporting for her when Auroville had refused to handle her exports. He told her that they all felt that she had behaved very badly by getting angry. In future, they would take 25% commission on all her income.

It was a nightmare. Some of her workers were very nice, and patient about not being paid, but some were furious, shouting at her, threatening to beat her up. She was all alone in the workshop in the forest, and desperate and helpless.

An old friend from Australia came and took 100 pairs of shoes and promised to pay for them within a month. She never paid. The ex-wife of another old Australian friend took fifty pairs and promised to pay for them within a few weeks. She never paid. There was a check from Kwan Yin and Boy with an order for fifty pairs of shoes. The check barely covered the postage to send them the shoes. A Swiss lady took a hundred pairs of shoes and promised to pay for them, and paid promptly. An Italian ordered 100 pairs to be shipped through the bank. This is supposedly an infallible system. He should have had to pay the bank before he could pick up the shoes, but somehow he got the bank to give him the documents without any money. It was only months later that Roslyn was paid, and could finally pay the school fees.

It was hell. She eventually managed to pay off and fire fifty of her sixty five workers, but she still had to find the money and materials to keep fifteen people working..

At the beginning of April she got another telegram from Rob cancelling the April and May orders, promising re-orders in June for June, July and August. Meanwhile he'd never paid anything for the two thousand pairs of shoes she had shipped him in January and February.

Madhavan demanded a large advance for his daughter's wedding. Roslyn tried to refuse, but then he disappeared along with most of the money the Swiss lady had sent.

Old customers, new customers, acquaintances and strangers drifted into the forest. She sold them one pair of shoes, five pairs of shoes, ten pairs of shoes, a bag, or whatever they wanted. There was an Italian girl married to an Englishman who came through every few months and bought thousands of rupees worth of shoes and bags for cash. She would take them to Goa, Kodaikanal or Katmandu and sell them.

The Aurodevi Boutique was a nightmare. She was in Pondicherry, and did not have any money for the village bus back to the forest, and they refused to give her a one-rupee advance. She had gone to the Boutique and asked for an advance. The lady in charge told her she would be paid for her sales less their commission at the beginning of the month. There was no money for advances during the month. She finally agreed to give Roslyn a rupee advance, for the bus, but had to admonish her not to come again until the second Friday of the month for her payments. And, to please not come asking for handouts during the month.

Roslyn forgot about exporters. She had been working with Aurodevi for eight months, and they were claiming she owed them money, although she had given then thousands of pairs of shoes on export orders for which she was never paid. Finally Robert Goodman came to see her and offered her five thousand rupees for all the shoes they had shipped which she had not been paid for.

She protested. "I have given you over 200,000 rupees worth of shoes."

"Yes, yes, I know, but we have not received any of those payments. We want to conclude our business with you."

"What happens when you are paid for the shoes?" she asked.

"If we get paid for the shoes, we will, of course, keep the money."

"I cannot accept 5,000 rupees as payment for over 200,000 rupees worth of shoes," she pleaded.

"Okay, so we give you nothing."

"Won't you pay me when you receive the payment?"

"Yes, of course, but if we don't receive any payments we will not give or lend you any money, and if we do receive any payments we will take twenty five per cent commission."

"I think that is a better deal than 5,000 rupees, but I have no money for myself or the workshop."

"That is your problem."

"I guess so," she said, looking at him, wondering how he had ever convinced her to do business with them.

She said, "Aurodevi, I should have guessed when you told me the name of your company that you would put me through hell."

He just looked at her, then said, "Don't bother coming by to see if anything has arrived, if money comes we will send you a message."

She could not even look at him as he got on his motorcycle and rode off.

After that when someone asked her to send them shoes she made parcels and mailed them from the Post Office as insured parcels. She could only insure them for two hundred and fifty rupees because they were being posted as gifts or tourist parcels, which can only have a maximum value of two hundred and fifty rupees. The actual value of each parcel was usually several thousand rupees.

Roslyn found that she had spent five years creating an enterprise that was a profound trauma.

She was completely bewildered by what had happened to her. She was spending several days a week dying thread for Ivar so there would be at least some cash flow. She would dye hundreds of kilos of thread each week, standing day after day over two fires. Two big pots of boiling colors sat on the bricks surrounding the fire. She would stand over the fire from morning to evening, working with two village girls, mixing the thread with forceps so the dye would be evenly distributed on the thread, or Ivar would make her do it again before he paid her. Her clothes were all spattered with color. Her hands were often a very strange color. She hated dyeing, but it was a dependable cash source.

Ivar brought her customers, but they were all very tough business people who were willing to pay such low prices for the shoes and bags that the only reason to go on working was to pay the worker's wages. The roof on Roslyn's capsule was full of holes. When it rained, she got wet. There was no money to fix it. Finally she moved into one of the lofts in the workshop, because the roof was in better condition, and it was no longer used as a working space because most of the workers were gone.

The people who had signed Robert Goodman's petition against the takeover of Auroville by the Government of India were called 'Neutrals.' These people were considered to be traitors by the majority of Aurovilians. There were only about 35 of them, as against nearly 700 in the rest of Auroville. Robert Goodman organised them into a group to protect their visas, and other essential interests. There was also at least a minimum of friendship among them, because they were all in the same boat. They were all subject to continual abuse by the community. There was not much sweetness and light among them. They were all very unhappy, but committed to Auroville and to living in Auroville.

One of them, a Japanese American, who was born in the American concentration camps for Japanese Americans during World War II, was nearly persuaded to leave when a gang of the children attacked him. They threw stones at him and shouted at him to get out. They did not want Japs in Auroville. He was shocked, as were all the other Neutrals, to learn that that kind of hate and prejudice was acceptable in Auroville. When he went to the parents of the children to tell them what had happened, the parents said that the children were right: he should leave Auroville. He was one of the first people accepted by Mother into the Auroville community. He was horrified. The other Neutrals were the only people who agreed with him that such an attack was shocking, the rest of Auroville seemed to consider it wonderful that the children were trying to help purge Auroville of undesirable elements.

On November 5th, 1982 the Supreme Court of India declared that the Auroville Act, passed by the Parliament of India, placing Auroville under the management of an Administrator, appointed by the Government's Department of Education, for three to five years, did not contravene the Indian Constitution, should be immediately enforced.

The Administrator was already in place in Auroville awaiting the decision of the court. The Sri Aurobindo Society had claimed that Auroville was a religious organisation and protected by the Constitution of India. Vasudeva had presented to the Supreme Court the petition of the 'Neutrals' asking that the Act be considered void because Mother had said that Auroville was not to be managed by any group or nation.

Many people in Auroville considered this proof that the Neutrals were siding with the Society against Auroville. They could not understand what Mother meant when she said, "Those who are for some and against others are outside the Truth."

Misunderstanding was rampant. There was great rejoicing in Auroville over the Supreme Court decision. Bliss was visiting for a few days because a group of children from the Delhi school had come to Pondicherry to visit the Ashram.

The Administrator had prepared a paper to be distributed to every Aurovilian declaring that the assets, land, plantations, buildings, businesses, were all relateable to Auroville and under the management of the Government of India. Everything that had been achieved in the fourteen years since Auroville had begun as an offering to Mother and Sri Aurobindo was to be offered to the Government of India, through its Administrator, who would decide how the assets would be maintained in the future and by whom.

For the most part he appointed the same people responsible for handling the assets who had been handling them previously; however, in some cases he appointed extra co-executives, in others he just dismissed the management and appointed new management. He took Vasudeva's daughter's workshop and gave it to an Italian man. Roslyn was worried that he would give her workshop, forest, and mango grove to someone else, when she received a paper from asking her to sign that all the assets she had created were the property of Auroville and under the management of the Administrator appointed by the Government of India.

One of the Neutrals had gotten a copy of Victor's recent letter to Auroville, and had given it to Roslyn to read:

"The power of sincerity alone should oblige the undesirable elements to go away or change. And I find that in a certain measure we have succeeded, for eight years ago Auroville was a sort of muddy soup where all sorts of people - more or less unconscious and more or less desirable - floundered about. The mongooses embraced the snakes and allowed themselves to be bitten in the name of "human unity" - but was it a unity of poison or a unity of truth? And then there were a certain number of slugs who were neither of one side nor the other and who simply let their trail of sticky spiritual saliva enhance the situation, trying to take the place of the other two sides - I don't know which is preferable, saliva or venom, and if the three united to make another soup, at the end of a few generations of Aurovilian, towards the year 2000, or after the flood, would that make an ideal Auroville?

"I myself find that our enemies have helped us a great deal for eight years; there has been a blessed progression in the consciousness of Aurovilians - they've begun to open their eyes, to see clearly, to put each thing more or less in place; we know who is the Lion and who the Chameleon. It's an enormous progress. The undesirables have helped us to see what is desirable - to know what we want in fact; a hotch-potch of cats and slugs, or something else? Now, eight years later, do you want to start the experience of the hotch-potch of cats and slugs again, to see if that will make for human unity at the end? 'Take out the fangs of the snake' did you say? Well, try it!

"For a few thousand years different prophets and avatars have been coming to try that very thing. But, all the same, after all this sad story, the human race has begun to see a little more clearly and to let itself be persuaded a little less by the devil - which is to say that everything is more or less unmasked, laid bare; we see the little devils crawl about publically; on the way they've had to let go of their false spiritual auras and their false moustaches - we know who is what. That's the real progress of the Earth; it's not that she had swallowed and transformed the undesirables, it is that she's reached the point where she begins to know or guess the only thing Desirable. Apocalypse, that does not only mean to 'reveal,' it means 'lay bare.' The clothes fall off, the clothes of the serpent, chameleon or baboon, and we know who is there. We are what we are and nothing else. And if you are not, misfortune to you.

"So we are in this situation in Auroville, in which the masks have more or less fallen. It is Auroville's immense progress. Now, what are you going to do with these 'unmasked' ones? Be Neutral? But it is not Neutrality. It tell you it's a hotch-potch of cats and slugs! Chase them away? But we're not the Gestapo! Then what?

"Well, it seems to me that this necessary, very necessary, cleaning can be done in a simple way: Aurovilians can come to agreement on a number of material points, like, for example, no personal profit, no personal money, a single cooperative center which gives out the necessities and receives donations. Then automatically, you would see a number of small slugs and medium-sized snakes saying No! And the sorting out would be done. Those who don't want to follow the law of Auroville have only to go elsewhere and make their own law. The all-important thing is to know what you want. Define a few simple material points that would make up the practical code of Auroville. Then either one accepts it or one doesn't. One cannot do his small business or distribute money to right and left and sow corruption at the same time. You must know if you want to let things contaminate and go bad in the name of ':human brotherhood' or if you want to make some order in your house and keep it clean.

"It is simple.

"It is clear.

"It is a question of smell.

"We must not confuse those who aspire with those who strangle us to make us aspire - if we are strangled, there's nobody left to aspire and nobody left to remember."

This letter, coming to her the same day as the demand of the Administrator to hand over her assets, terrified Roslyn. Robert Goodman had brought the letter to her and warned her that the new Executive Council had decided to throw all the Neutrals out of Auroville.

She showed him the paper she had received from the Administrator and said, "If I sign this they do not have to come and throw me out, he can just give this place to anyone."

"Yes, but you have to sign it," he replied.

"You mean, I'm damned if I do and I'm damned if I don't," she said.

"Yes, something like that. Don't worry, maybe the Administrator will let you stay here."

She went to Pondi on the village bus in the evening and asked Vasudeva whether she had to sign the paper from the Administrator, handing over her assets to the Government of India. He told her to sign and pray.

She took an auto-rickshaw back to Auroville, stopped at the Administrator's house and gave him the paper, and asked him what he would do with it. He explained to her it was just a formality, but as there was some objection to her presence in Auroville, he would have to appoint a co-executive to help her manage her assets. She had been through hell creating that workshop, and he was blithely going to appoint a co-executive. The Administrator seemed determined to appoint new management for the assets controlled by Neutrals, to use the opportunity of takeover to resolve the conflict in Auroville with a minimum of fuss. He seemed to think that if he got rid of the Neutrals there would be no problems in Auroville.

She felt quite sick after speaking to him. She got back to the forest very late. Invariably in the evening she would sit in front of her puja table, light a candle and some incense, and repeat the mantras Panditji and Mother had given her several hundred times, but that night she was too tired when she got back to the forest. She simply went to sleep.

Roslyn had put all that she had into creating the little workshop in the forest, but she knew that did not make it hers. In Auroville, nothing belongs to anybody in particular. She had signed the paper saying that the assets she had created were relateable to Auroville, because she was completely committed to the ideals of Auroville. She knew that one of her neighbors wanted her forest for firewood for his pottery, but she hoped that he would not be appointed as her co-executive.

She went to sleep hoping that if having signed the paper was going to cost her her workshop, that whoever took the workshop would give her a plane ticket to San Francisco.

She was completely exhausted. It was the first evening in years she went to bed without meditating, thanking The Divine that nothing worse had happened that day. Bliss was spending the night with her friends in the children's community, Ami.

She was sleeping. She was dreaming wonderful dreams of old friends who had refused to even speak to her for several years, talking with her. There was a strange sweet smell. She was awake, but had not opened her eyes.

POW! SMASH!!!

Someone had knocked out her teeth!!!

She did not open her eyes to try to see who it was, but put her hands over them to protect them from the rain of ringing blows with a blunt instrument that followed.

Whack! Whack! Whack!

The blows fell on her hands, arms, head, in a seemingly never-ending horror of torment, beyond her wildest dreams.

She let go all resistance, and lay there unmoving. She felt hands, not too gently, remove the thick gold chain she wore around her neck that had been blessed by The Mother. She felt the attackers move away from her on the split bamboo floor of her sleeping loft.

She waited several minutes before she opened her eyes.

They were gone. The night was very still. In the distance she could hear a car starting. There were never any cars on the road next to the forest in the night, there were almost no cars ever on that road during the day.

She lay there for a few minutes until she realised she was soaked in her own blood. It had been an unusually cool evening. She had worn to bed a beautiful woollen dress Ananta had given her. It was completely soaked in blood. The bed sheets, the pillows, everything was soaked in blood. She slowly opened her eye. She sat up. She did not have much pain, but her hands were already swollen to twice their normal size, and she could hardly move them. She turned up the light on the lantern on the puja table near her bed. Her bag with the wages for the workers and their Deevali bonus was still there under the puja table. Her watch was lying on the table. It was 3 a.m.

She put her hands on her face. It seeemed to be a mess. She put her fingers in her mouth and pulled out a molar. The teeth she still had were shaky in her gums, the others were gone.

She did not cry. The worst of the pain was the horror of the hatred she had somehow engendered. She could not imagine any justification for such brutality. It was like nothing she had ever seen or heard of, or might have imagined in her wildest dreams. It was unimaginable that this could happen in Auroville.

She had heard from others that they had been beaten up, but none of them bore the kind of scars she would bear from that day. Her face had been cut to ribbons. Her teeth had been knocked out. Her arms and hands were broken and bruised. Fortunately her attacker had smashed a nerve, so although one side of her face was actually paralyzed, she could feel no pain.

She decided she needed to go to her neighbors for help. In recent years, some nice people had built little houses on the outskirts of the tope. They had not been unfriendly, and occasionally visited her in the forest. She never visited them, because if she was seen in their house they might get thrown out of Auroville.

At three in the morning she was not worried that someone might see her, and she could not just lie there in pools of her blood and hope that everything would come right.

She went to the neighbor, and timidly knocked on the door.

She heard Melanie call, "Who is there?"

"Roslyn," she replied, having great difficulty pronouncing her name.

Melanie opened the door, holding a lantern in her hand. She took one look at Roslyn and gasped, "Hero," she called to her partner, "Come quick! Roslyn has been hurt!"

Roslyn nearly collapsed with gratitude that there was still some compassion in the world, but she held herself together.

"What happened? Come in! Sit down. Let me bathe your face. How can I help you?" Melanie said, falling all over herself to be nice.

Hero climbed down the ladder from the sleeping loft, looked at Roslyn, and said, "Oh, my God, what happened?"

"I don't know what happened. Someone attacked me when I was sleeping."

"Unbelievable. How can we help?"

"What should I do?"

"You need to get to a doctor. I will take you on the motorcycle. Let's wait a little bit, until the sky gets a bit lighter."

"Would you go and get me my bag and some clean clothes?"

"Sure. I will take you to the Ashram Nursing Home."

"Yes, I guess that is the best. They have always been very nice to me there."

They set off on the motorcycle in the first light of early morning. The only other motorcycle they passed between the forest and Pondi was Robert Goodman, driving in the opposite direction. Roslyn recognized him, signalled for him to stop.

He stopped and was aghast when she dropped the scarf that covered the worst of her injuries.

He asked where she was going, and told her he would come to see her there. He promised to do everything he could to help her.

They arrived at the Nursing Home at dawn. They rang the bell. They waited. They rang the bell again.

A nurse opened the door. She looked at Roslyn and said, "Come," and taking her bags, led her very gently upstairs to an immaculate bed.

The nurse put her things in the little cupboard next to the bed, gave her a painkiller, made her as comfortable as possible, brought her an extra pillow, and promised to call the doctor.

Roslyn collapsed and slept.

She woke about an hour later feeling like she was in a refrigerator.

She went to the bathroom, then sat on her bed, mindlessly started repeating the mantras which had become an instant source of solace, and freedom from outrageous circumstances.

She was cold, so she put on most of the clean clothes she had brought with her and stripped the bed covers from the other, empty cots in the room. She tried to snuggle down in the bed, but was too uncomfortable, in too much pain, and then the whole horror of what had happened came back. The nurse was asking if she would like something to eat or drink. The young American doctor who was practising homeopathy came in with the nurse, and gave her some little placebos which instantly ameliorated the shock; either that, or it was his charm.

He stayed with her for a while, and asked her what had happened. People from Auroville and The Ashram who had somehow heard what had happened were coming. People who had not said a word to her for years suddenly turned up at her bedside. She felt that some of them came as voyeurs. Others came in with friendship. Her tailor came, looked at her face, and burst into tears.

It was the doctor's birthday. The doctor was an Ashramite. Mother always made a big thing about birthdays. Even today, in the Ashram, everyone is permitted to meditate in Sri Aurobindo's room on his own birthday. For most devotees of Sri Aurobindo it is the highlight of the day, and perhaps the year. It was Dr. Sen's birthday. Instead of sitting in the room of his beloved guru he was in his clinic, trying to repair Roslyn.

He assembled a team of doctors, and prepared the surgery. He did a four-hour operation. He offered Roslyn the option of being put to sleep, in which case they would have to put a tube in her throat to help her breathe, or to stay awake and not move throughout the operation. She chose to remain awake.

There was a large picture of Mother and Sri Aurobindo in the operating theatre. Roslyn concentrated on the mantra The Mother had given her and let the doctors do whatever they wanted to do. It was already obvious to her that her face had been irrevocably smashed.

Bliss came to see her and told her that she would not go back to Delhi to school. "Moma, you need me," the child said.

Roslyn felt terrible. The child was not old enough to leave school, and the only schools in Auroville were for little children.

"Don't worry," Bliss said. "I can go to Kodai School next year, if you are okay."

Roslyn was too exhausted to try to explain that Kodai was six times more expensive than the Delhi school. It was closer to Auroville, however. Roslyn hated being so far from Bliss, and she had never won an argument with Bliss, but she asked, "What about your things?"

"They can send them to me with the next bunch of kids they send to Pondi to visit the Ashram. I don't have much, mostly school uniforms, which I've outgrown."

"I can't tell you what to do, but I hope it is not a mistake."

"Don't worry Moma. I want to be here with you for a while."

Roslyn was very grateful to the child.

Robert Goodman came and promised to pay all Roslyn's medical and dental bills. Then he added as an afterthought, "By the way, I would like to bring someone to see you this afternoon."

"I'm not really up to seeing people." She said.

"Don't worry, we will only stay one or two minutes."

She did not bother to reply.

Auroville was much in the India news. The Supreme Court decision was headlines. In the afternoon Robert Goodman came to the Nursing Home with a photographer from a Bombay newspaper. The doctor saw them entering the Nursing Home and stopped them in the waiting room. He went up to Roslyn and asked her if she wanted to be photographed for the newspapers.

She replied, "No, certainly not!"

The doctor went back down and told the photographer that Roslyn had refused to see him.

Robert Goodman argued with him, "But this morning she agreed that we should come."

The doctor refused to allow the photographer to go upstairs.

Robert Goodman left with his photographer friend, angry with Roslyn and the doctor, and refused to pay any of the bills when they were submitted to him.

The next morning Roslyn looked in a mirror for the first time since her face was smashed.

It was unbelievable. Her whole face was swollen, and most of it was black and blue. The doctor had used black thread to stitch up her upper lip and left cheek. She looked too horrible to be human. She was very grateful to the doctor that he had protected her privacy. She felt so ugly that it would be impossible for her to do anything but hide in the forest for the rest of her life.

Reading Savitri under the Banyan

XX

But first, the spirit's ascent we must achieve
Out of the chasm from which our nature rose.
The soul must soar, sovereign, above the form,
And climb to summits beyond mind's half-sleep;
Our hearts we must inform with heavenly strength,
Surpass the animal with the occult god.

Sri Aurobindo, Savitri

There needs to be an impartial indifference, and luminous impassivity, an inhibiting rejection, a habit of disassociation and desuetude, for the mind is voluntarily bound by the petty joys and troubles of life and in reality these can have no inner hold on it if the soul simply chooses to cast off its habit of helpless determination by external influences. There remains a split between the lower and outward mind still subservient to the habitual touches and the higher reason and will that stands back to live in the indifferent calm of the spirit. Calm becomes inexpungable, watches as one might a child. The inner mind does not regard this as its own, and the outer mind comes to do likewise. In the presence of an all pervading power of wide tranquillity and peace the deep undisturbed exceeding happiness of the touch of the eternal and infinite fixes the soul in delight, in the single and infinite Ananda of the spirit. It observes as a spectator of a play.

Finally one must submit to the will of God, the supreme Purusha. All else falls away, only one thing of importance remains, to approach God, or to be in touch or tune with the universal and infinite existence, or to be united with the Divine. When this happens the lower mind is swallowed up in love, joy, delight in the divine and everything with the equal peace and bliss of that union.

Once we turn to the full consciousness of self, of God, we can then put a true divine value on things and receive and act on them with the calm joy, knowledge, seeing will of the spirit. This requires the knowledge of unity. To see all things as oneself and to see all things in God and God in all things, and achieve, the will of equal acceptance of all as part of the Self, movements of one energy, and an equal delight in all the cosmic manifestations of the Divine.

There must be an identification of myself with self of the universe, a vision and a feeling of oneness with all creatures, a perception of all forces and energies and results as a movement of this energy of my self and therefore intimately my own. Not ego, which must be silenced, eliminated, cast away, but of greater impersonal or universal self with which I am now one.

For my personality is now only one center of action of that universal self, but a center intimately in relation-unison with all other personalities and also with all these other things which are to us only impersonal objects and forces. In fact they are also powers of the one impersonal person ego, self, spirit.

(from Jim Bean's Journal extracts from Sri Aurobindo's Synthesis of Yoga.*)*

After two weeks in the Nursing Home Roslyn felt she was ready to return to the forest and the workshop. She had to go back. She had nowhere else to go. She could not afford to stay longer in the Nursing Home. She had to sell shoes. She felt she had to supervise the production. She still had fifteen workers.

The tailor had mentioned that his brother was sleeping in the workshop at night, so there was a watchman on the site. She should not worry about thieves. He had agreed to remain there as night watchman, for which she was grateful. The only problem was, it meant another person she would have to pay each week.

Bliss had moved in with the other teenagers in Ami, a community of kids. She seemed happy. She had told Roslyn that she had had enough of The Delhi Ashram school and wanted to go to the Kodaikanal International School in Kodai, which was not so far away, and used the American system of education rather than the Indian system. She had heard that in Kodai the teachers were not allowed to hit the kids. Although no one ever hit her in Delhi, she did not like it when the teachers hit the students for not calling them 'Sir,' or not 'mugging up.'

Roslyn was shocked to hear that the teachers hit the children in a school that claimed to be 'The Mother's International School,' but could not imagine where she would find the money for school fees in Kodai. She could not argue with Bliss, who was completely certain about what she was doing. Bliss had written to Kodai and asked for an application, and had given it to Roslyn to fill in..

Before going back to Auroville Roslyn decided to walk to The Samadhi in The Ashram to pay her respects at the tomb of Mother and Sri Aurobindo, and enjoy the wonderful peace she always found while sitting in that courtyard. As she was walking down the street, about to turn in to The Ashram gate, she saw Jim Bean riding by on his bicycle.

She looked at him and felt something flash between them. He looked at her. Her face was still swollen, and black and blue. Her eyes were surrounded by big black and blue circles. She was badly scarred, and most of her upper teeth were gone. He fell off his cycle. Careful not to look at her again, he picked himself and his cycle up and rode off. She walked into the courtyard, amused that what had happened to her had startled him so severely that he fell off his bicycle. He had been riding that cycle everywhere, every day for years, and no-one had ever seen him fall off. She nearly forgot the incident the moment it happened. He had not spoken to her for years, and it did not seem likely that would ever change. She had to look after herself.

She knew that she needed help, so she sat at The Samadhi and asked The Mother and Sri Aurobindo to look after her and Bliss. Years before she might have included Auroville and others in her request, but she did not know what Auroville was anymore. It was called by some observers of what was happening there, from the relatively safe vantage point of Pondicherry, 'Horrorville.'

She did not know if she was going back to Horrorville or to Auroville. She just prayed for the strength to do whatever Mother and Sri Aurobindo wanted and needed her to do. She could not understand what was happening in Auroville.

She had to go back. It was like having fallen off; a horse you have to get right back on. She had to accept what had happened, and believe that even though she could not see the light at the end of the tunnel she had been crawling though for six years, it was there. All the horrors were merely a test of faith, but she had learned that if she passed a test in the yoga, she was always given a harder test.

The only way out is to go through, she tried to tell herself. She ignored the temptation to go to Madras and ask the Consul to repatriate her to the United States. She had not heard from Frankie for years. Saschwa had visited earlier in the year for a few weeks, and had taken a load of shoes and bags with him to the USA that he promised to sell for her and send money. She had not heard a word from him. She had no address to write to him. She did not feel she had anywhere to go in the United States. She was not certain that there was anyone there who would receive her, although Kwan Yin and Boy were there living in the bus in front of the Peacock Court. She would hear from them occasionally. Sometimes they would send her a small order. Occasionally they would include a small check to cover some of the money they owed her and the workshop.

She went back to the forest, because although a member of the community had offered to take it and manage it for Auroville, the Administrator had not given it outright to him, but appointed him as her co-executive. The Administrator insisted that she would be able to continue to live and work there; and, the new co-executive would help her manage her business and the forest for Auroville.

The day after she got back from the forest someone came with a note from her co-executive. "Please give Sunder twenty big trees for the roof of his house." A week later there was a note, "Please give Sundaranaikum twenty trees for the roof of the new temple in Bharatipuram." Her co-executive came and talked with her about her accounts, and agreed to let her carry on without interference if she would give him a thousand rupees a month.

She kept trying to roll with the punches, and protect as much of herself as she could. She agreed to the remittance, but insisted he should stop giving away the trees. Reluctantly he agreed. He had planned to take about half the trees for fuel for his pottery. She threatened to go to The Administrator to complain. She had paid all the expenses of watching and cultivating the forest and mango tope for six years. She had not cultivated the trees for fuel for his pottery. If he wanted the trees for fuel he would have to buy them. He asked her why he should pay for it. He was her co-executive. The trees did not belong to her. They belonged to Auroville. They were his trees also. She threatened to complain to The Administrator. Finally he desisted, and agreed to not cut any more trees as long as she gave him 1,000 rupees each month, paid all the bills, and saw to it that proper accounts were submitted to the Administrator. He did not want her to drop in at his house, because she was still an outcast, and he wanted no problems from the rest of the community. Exhausted, she gave in and agreed to everything, but became upset each time he broke the agreement by sending people to cut trees.

Old and new acquaintances somehow heard about her work and came to the forest. She lived and ran the workshop on what she sold there. It was very tough. Often there was no money for wages for three weeks. The Administrator demanded accounts, a stock book, receipts, vouchers, a day-book. She heard from Kodai School. They would accept Bliss if she would send them a ten thousand rupee advance by the end of the month. She had no money. She could see that the advance was only the beginning of four years of very high school fees.

She wrote back asking about scholarships.

They replied that for the first term it would be impossible for them to award a scholarship. After that, if Bliss had a high grade average, and was recommended by her teachers, she would perhaps be awarded a scholarship grant covering part of the fees.

She wrote back asking that they charge her the local rate rather than the foreign rate because she had been a resident in India for thirteen years. They wrote back saying that would not be possible, as she was a foreign passport holder. They reminded her that if the advance was not forthcoming Bliss would forfeit her place. There were many more applicants than places available in the school.

Bliss said, "It's okay Moma, I don't mind not going to school. I am having a good time in Auroville."

Roslyn looked at her in horror. The child was only thirteen. The teenage community where Bliss was living was one of the scandals of Auroville. There were loud rock and roll parties several nights a week, and mythical quantities of beer and booze were consumed.

Roslyn went to Aurelec, a company of outcasts in Auroville, successful business people who were not even Neutrals. They were simply outcast because they were self sufficient and did not persecute Neutrals. Financially they helped maintain the health service and the electrical service rather than giving their money to the community to use as it saw fit. They made computers. They immediately lent her 10,000 rupees.

She was surprised to receive a letter from her mother with a check. Her grandmother had passed away, and had left Roslyn several thousand dollars, check enclosed. The letter went on to clearly state that Roslyn had no further claim at all on the family, and should expect no further remittances. Her mother concluded the letter by suggesting she put the money in the bank..

She was sad that her grandmother had died. She had been her last friend in the family. She had been the only family member who had given her any financial support for ten years. It was not much, but it was something. She had the security every year of knowing she would receive a gift of several thousand rupees, which was always very welcome. She understood that even that little comfort was gone. She was entirely on her own now. It was sink or swim. She had not only herself and the workers and their families to care for, but also of course Bliss. Roslyn was happy to be able to give Bliss something, because the child was very independent. Bliss understood that to receive the opportunity of a high school education was a privilege. Bliss told Roslyn, "I like to learn things."

Roslyn was able to respect that, and wanted to encourage Bliss to learn as much as she could about whatever interested her. Roslyn was awed by Bliss, who spoke French, Tamil and Hindi, and was her best and most wonderful friend. Roslyn understood the challenge, and hoped that she would be up to the task. It was her karma to complete that task. It was like a fairy tale. Roslyn still hoped and prayed that there was a Divine purpose for all the trials and difficulties punctuated by descents of Divine Grace.

Roslyn was grateful to her grandmother for having left her several thousand dollars. It was more money than she had ever had at one time in her life. It was enough to repay Aurelec. It was enough to pay her debts, buy a motorcycle, and fix the roof on her capsule. She felt that the banks had enough money. She preferred to gamble once again on Auroville, on herself, and on her workshop, with the money. In the bank it would not grow fast enough to pay the school fees. It was not even enough for one term.

Day by day, week by week, month by month, she struggled to find markets and make and sell enough stuff to continue buying materials and paying the workers. It was tough, but after a few months she noticed that a perceptible cash flow seemed to have established itself. Week after week, a miracle would occur, and enough stuff would sell for her to pay the wages.

By the time Bliss left for school Roslyn felt she had a fighting chance to earn enough during the term to pay the fees. The school had been offensively explicit that if Roslyn fell behind in paying the fees, Bliss would be immediately sent down.

Roslyn imagined that her life would have been easier if she had run away and joined the circus and become a tightrope walker. The situation seemed impossible. She had no outlet for local sales. She had no exporter. People were thrown out of Auroville for talking to her. But she did not feel entirely hopeless. She felt it was a challenging situation where she was being forced to rely on The Divine.

Having her teeth knocked out did not hurt nearly as much as having been abandoned by her true love, Jim Bean. She felt the whole situation was somehow comical. She was powerless, and people were still attacking her verbally. Jim Bean still looked away when he passed her on the street, but he gave Bliss a beautiful leather bound copy of Savitri with her name inscribed in gold on the cover and fifty rupees for her birthday.

Roslyn made beautiful things. The quality of the handicrafts produced in her workshop was completely different from anything else being produced in Auroville. She was still working in the workshop with her own hands eight to ten hours a day. She had a talented group of craftspeople whose abilities complemented one another. She had a cupboard of beautiful leather garments, bags, shoes and accessories.

She had stopped giving goods on credit, and demanded payment for any goods before they left the workshop. This was difficult, but rewarding. Sometimes there would even be a check in the mail with an order from an old customer or Kwan Yin and Boy.

One morning, early, she went off to visit a friend, a fellow Neutral. Roslyn's friend Helen had a big house with eight bedrooms and five bathrooms, and a studio. She lived there with her daughter, and often had guests. It was one of the most beautiful and well-maintained houses in Auroville, and everyone had tried to take it away from her. Roslyn and Helen would often sit on the terrace and laugh at the latest rumor that a mob of fifty Aurovilians had threatened to descend and take the house, or that the Administrator wanted the house. They laughed, but it was not very amusing. Helen lived with a deep anxiety for herself and her daughter, their personal safety, and the house, their home. For a long time the Administrator refused to sign the necessary recommendation for her visa, feeling he would be more comfortable in that house than the two bedroom two bathroom house the community had given him.

Helen was very upset about this, because she could not imagine how she could stay in India without a visa, and no-one in Auroville got a visa at that time from the Government of India without a recommendation from the Administrator. The Government of India was managing Auroville, and the community of Auroville had no authority, because even a person accepted by the community would not be allowed to remain in India without a visa. It was the same problem Auroville had faced with The Society.

Helen was not an accepted member of the community; she was a Neutral. She and Roslyn were one another's moral support system. They tried to laugh about everything that was happening to them as Neutrals. Helen would have left fifty times, but for her daughter, who had met and remembered The Mother. Her daughter was completely committed to Her Dream, Auroville, and refused to even consider leaving. Helen's friendship with Roslyn was like water in the desert for both of them. Neither of them had anyone else they could rely on for friendly emotional support, except their daughters, who were also having a difficult time as children of Neutrals. When Helen went to visit Roslyn in the hospital, all she could say was, "Oh God!!"

They really liked one another, and tried to be there for one another. They were both in an uncomfortable and difficult situation.

One morning, after the workers came and everyone had settled down to the work for the day, Roslyn took off on her nearly new Crusader motorcycle to visit Helen, who was freaking out because she and her daughter could not get a visa. The Administrator would not recommend her visa, even though she and her daughter had been accepted by The Mother, and had lived in Auroville since 1971.

Helen had gone to Germany for several years to work and earn money, but her daughter had refused to leave Auroville, and remained in Auroville with Helen's ex-husband, who was also a Neutral. He had a small farm with cows and chickens, and sold milk, butter, eggs and vegetables. He had worked at the Matrimandir for many years, but he refused to stop speaking to Vasudeva, so he was no longer welcome at Matrimandir.

Helen was sitting at the table outside the kitchen, on the patio of her big house, surrounded by orchids and other exotic plants, eating her breakfast. The house looked like a dream from the future. Helen was a maniac about beauty and order. The house was always well looked after. The painters were there every summer. It looked like new, although she had lived there for years. She used the room that had originally been designed for a TV studio for a tailoring studio, and made beautiful clothes. She had designed costumes for the cinema in Germany, and was a great couturier. There was usually a pile of beautiful cloth or clothes on the kitchen table, so she nearly always used the table on the patio as her dining room. The table was laid for two.

Roslyn sat down at the unoccupied place.

"That is for my guest," Helen said.

"Who is your guest?"

"A French lady, a friend of Mr. Lala, who is now the head of The International Advisory Council."

"How did she come here?" Roslyn asked.

"Robert Goodman wrote to Mr. Lala about The Neutrals, and he sent her here to find out what is happening."

Just then Roslyn's old friend Yvonne Le Mieux swept out onto the patio. She was wearing a gorgeous tiger print peignoir and gown, in the softest, most clinging mutely glowing material.   Her face was like a shining moon, and her platinum hair, even at breakfast, looked as if she had just walked out of a beauty parlor. She was looking wonderfully glamorous.

She introduced herself to Roslyn. Helen got up and went into the kitchen for another place mat, plate, cup, silver and a napkin for Roslyn.

Roslyn had mentioned Yvonne to Helen in her stories about the amazing, interesting people who used to visit Auroville and Pondicherry in the golden olden days when Mother was there.

Roslyn introduced herself to Yvonne. "You don't remember me?"

Yvonne stared at her.

"We met several times about ten years ago. You shared a taxi from the airport with my sister. You had dinner with my father and me at the Grand Hotel d'Europe."

Yvonne said, "You have changed a great deal." She looked slightly aghast a Roslyn's scars and missing teeth.

"But you look exactly the same," Roslyn said.

"Do you really think so?" Yvonne asked.

"No, you are more beautiful now," Roslyn said.

"And you, perhaps you are not as beautiful, but you are very interesting. Are you a Neutral? Mr. Lala sent me to Auroville to find out what is the problem. What happened to your face?"

"Someone came into my hut and tried to kill me while I was sleeping one night."

"Was it The Society?"

"I have no idea who it was."

"But why don't you get false teeth?"

"I tried with a dentist in Pondi. It was hopeless."

"But there is an excellent dentist in Auroville. He was the best dentist in Paris before he came here."

"He won't do anything for me. I am a Neutral."

"Wasn't your father a dentist? Didn't he contribute a complete dental unit to Auroville? Isn't this the equipment Francois is using?"

"Probably."

"I cannot believe this." Yvonne said.

"It is okay.   I am getting used to it. But I wish they would stop attacking us." Roslyn said.

"I cannot believe this. I am having tea with Francois this afternoon, and I will take you to see him tomorrow morning." Yvonne said.

Just then Robert Goodman pulled up on his motorcycle. Yvonne greeted him and agreed to meet the entire Neutral Group the next day in the afternoon in a nearby garden.

Helen offered Robert Goodman tea. He declined. He was on his way to work and was already late. He invited Yvonne to spend the day, or any part of the day, or evening with him.

She, very graciously, declined. She was having lunch next door, at the burgermeister's, and would be going to tea with the dentist. She had been invited to another house nearby for dinner.

He wished her a good day, excused himself and drove off on his motorcycle, leaving behind a trail of dust and noise.

Roslyn looked at Yvonne. "You are very popular."

"You brought me to Auroville the first time I came to Auroville. I remember; it was in the taxi from the airport with your sister. I had been coming to Pondicherry for several years to see The Mother, but that was the first time I had come to Auroville. I think perhaps the trees have grown better than the people."

"There were no trees then," Roslyn said, turning to Helen to include her in the conversation.

"Yes, I know," Helen said.

"Where are you living? What do you do?" Yvonne asked Roslyn.

"I live in a forest and have a workshop."

"What do you make in your workshop?" Yvonne asked.

Roslyn was carrying a bag she had made. She was also wearing shoes and a dress she had made. "I made everything I am wearing and this bag," she replied, handing the dainty little beaded bag to Yvonne.

"That is very interesting. I would like to see your workshop." Yvonne said.

"What are you doing after breakfast?" Roslyn asked.

"I am free until lunchtime." Yvonne replied.

"Then come with me to the forest and I will bring you back before noon."

"How can we go? I have not ordered a car for this morning," Yvonne said.

"No problem, we can go on my motorcycle. I would be happy to be your chauffeur while you are in Auroville."

"Wonderful. Just give me a minute to change my clothes," Yvonne said, setting down her teacup and gracefully wiping her fingers with her napkin.

She went into the house to change her clothes.

Helen looked at Roslyn, "So that is your friend."

"Yes."

"Amazing. She seems very sympathetic."

"How did she happen to come here?"

"She came in a taxi from the airport. Robert had arranged with Mr. Lala that she could stay here, in a Neutral house. You know she has many friends in the rest of the community. She has visited Auroville often over the years, and persuaded Mr. Lala to give several grants to Auroville for sustainable energy projects and environment regeneration."

Yvonne reappeared. It had taken her only minutes to change, but she looked as though she had spent hours in front of a mirror. Every platinum hair was in place, and shining, drawn back into a perfect chignon.   She was wearing white silk slacks, and although she must have been in her sixties, she looked very gorgeous and sexy. Her fingernails and toenails were exactly the same shade of orange as her beautifully tailored silk shirt. Her sandals were exquisite. She was carrying a white shoulder bag.

"That's a gorgeous bag." Roslyn commented.

Yvonne grinned at her. "It should be, it was made by Hermes."

They all laughed at that.

She called Roslyn's motorcycle 'Ganesh' because the day before she had celebrated Ganesh puja in Bombay. Ganesh was the god known as the remover of obstacles. The Ganesh motorcycle would remove the obstacle for Yvonne of how to move around in Auroville. She got on behind Roslyn, admitting she had never been on a motorcycle in her life.

Roslyn was a confident driver. Bernie had given her a motorcycle when she was 12 years old that she could not drive on the roads because she did not have a driver's license. She used to ride on the paths in the forest behind their house in Pennsylvania. She loved the freedom of mobility that the motorcycle gave her.

Roslyn and Yvonne spent a wonderful morning together at the workshop. Yvonne was interested in everything. She insisted on being introduced to each of the workers. She was pleased at the way Roslyn merged their skills to create something beautiful. A bag was cut by the cobbler, stitched by the tailor, and then ornamented by the bead lady. She was impressed at the simplicity and sincerity of the work. She loved Roslyn's bathroom. It was very clean, and she liked that very much. The workers were all clean, well dressed, and in good humor. The work they were doing was unique, and very fine. The workshop, the bathroom, everything had been built by hand of casurina and bamboo tied together with rope. The roof was hand-woven, coconut, fronds.   Yvonne mentioned that she had a friend with a shop in the Taj in Bombay. She bought several bags, and promised to show them to her friend who could become a regular customer. She said the craftsmanship was superb, and the designs elegant.

Roslyn felt her whole life was vindicated because this person bought several of the most attractive pieces. She felt she had taken a step on the path Mother had pointed out to her when she said, "Auroville will be known through the arts."

Roslyn took Yvonne back to Helen's, and agreed to pick her up the next morning and go with her to the dentist.

The next morning Roslyn went to pick up Yvonne.

Yvonne came out already dressed and ready to go. "Are you ready?" She asked Roslyn.

"Yes, of course. Did you speak with Francois?"

"I told him I wanted an appointment this morning for an Aurovilian who needed urgent dental treatment. He told me to come at 8:30. Do you know where the Dental Clinic is?"

"I think so."

They took off again on Ganesh. Roslyn went a little too far, past the Dental Clinic, and drove into another community a bit farther down the road.

"No, no. I am sure this is not it. This is 'Le Jardin de Mere,'" Yvonne said.

Roslyn had never been there because she had heard that some of the most virulent anti-Neutrals lived in 'Le Jardin de Mere.' She did not want to stop. She just wanted to turn around and get out, but Yvonne stopped her. "No, stop. I have friends here. Mr. Lala is helping this community and has funded the windmill, the community kitchen, and organic gardens here. They can give us directions to the Dental Clinic." Roslyn turned off the engine and Yvonne got off the bike. She said to Roslyn, "Come, come."

They walked down the path from the parking space, through the garden towards the community kitchen.

Yvonne pointed at the building, and was telling Roslyn that Mr. Lala had given the community a grant to build this new kitchen with a big solar oven on the roof.

Two men walked out of the kitchen. Two men whom Roslyn had never met, nor exchanged a single word with in her life.

The shorter one said, "Hello Yvonne.   I'm sorry, but your friend is not welcome here."

Yvonne said, "Bonjour, Jacques. May I have a glass of water?"

"You may have a glass of water, but your friend may not."

Yvonne was shocked.   She said, " Is this Auroville? Where is the Dental Clinic?"

"Go back to the road and turn left. It is the second turn off to your left down the road," the larger man answered. He looked at Roslyn and asked, "Do you understand?"

The shorter fellow said to Yvonne, "You know you are always welcome here."

Yvonne turned away without saying another word, and Roslyn followed her back to the motorcycle that was parked near the entrance of the compound. They rode down the road to the Dental Clinic. Roslyn parked her bike and followed Yvonne into the little clinic.

Francois greeted Yvonne warmly, looked at Roslyn, and said, "Please, you wait outside."

Roslyn went out and sat at the little table near the door and picked up a magazine. She could hear Yvonne and Francois talking. They spoke mostly in French. Then she heard Yvonne exclaim in English, "Fine. I fly tonight to Bombay and tell Mr. Lala Auroville is finished!"

The dentist was shaking his head and saying, "No, no. I don't want to make trouble for Auroville."

Then they started speaking more quietly again with one another, mostly in French.

A few minutes later the dentist came to the door and invited Roslyn into the clinic. He told her to please take her shoes off and sit in the dental chair.

He covered his nose and mouth with a surgical mask as through he was afraid of catching a terrible disease from her. He told her to open her mouth. He put on a light and took a little mirror and looked into her mouth. He then told her to close her mouth and please wait outside.

He spoke for several minutes to Yvonne through the closed door. Then he went out to speak to Roslyn.

"Yes, I can do something, but not now. Not immediately. You must wait until I call you."

"I don't mind waiting," Roslyn said.

"Oh," the dentist added as a little addendum, "When I call you, you must give me five thousand rupees before I will start the work. Okay?"

Roslyn was shocked. Hadn't he ever heard of professional courtesy? She tried not to communicate her reaction, because he was the only person in the area who could repair some of the damage to her face, but 5,000 rupees was an enormous sum of money. Where would she get that much money to spend on herself? She felt that he would use the lack of money as an excuse not to do the work. She tried to assure him that she would be happy to pay him for the work, and decided she would have to find the money somewhere.

She thanked him, and he promised he would call her. She rode off with Yvonne. They were both shaken by the two encounters; that illuminated to Yvonne about what it meant to be a Neutral in Auroville in 1983.

Yvonne asked Roslyn to take her to the bank. She wanted to change some money so she could make a guest contribution to Helen. They drove to the bank. It was in the same part of the developing town as the Dental Clinic.

Standing in front of the bank was a friend of Yvonne's from Brazil. They had flown together once from Mexico City to Paris.

Christina was the child of some Germans who had migrated to South America at the end of the second world war. She had fallen in love with marijuana and rock n'roll. She left home before she was eighteen. She had traveled all over South and Central America and was on her way to Europe looking for something.

She and Yvonne had talked to one another nearly non-stop through the ten-hour flight. Yvonne told Christina about Auroville. When they arrived in Paris, Christina admitted she had no place to go in Europe. Yvonne bought her a ticket to Madras and gave her the names of some of her friends in Auroville.

Christina had been in Auroville for several years, and had married a Frenchman who had been in Auroville since 1969. They lived in the fancy section of the city of the future, a community where they live by the slogan, 'good fences make good neighbors.' There are high fences or walls between the villas in that part of town. Some even have gates with gurkhas posted at them, even in the middle of the day. They had a workshop producing garments for export, and were doing very well.

Christine greeted Yvonne warmly, and ignored Roslyn. She invited Yvonne to go with her to her workshop. Yvonne said she was with Roslyn. Christine said, "That's all right, she can go. You can come with me on my motorcycle."

Yvonne turned away from Christine; her face was wet with tears. She wiped her eyes and walked into the bank.

As they were driving from the bank back to Helen's house, Yvonne said to Roslyn, "Who does she think she is?"

In the afternoon Roslyn met Yvonne again at the meeting with the rest of the Neutrals. There were about forty people there, some of them Tamil.

Yvonne sat between Robert Goodman and the lady of the house, an American who had been beaten up by villagers and her arm broken in a boundary dispute. She had come from California, met Mother, gone back to California, sold her property, come back to Auroville, and built a very simple house, using durable materials. Most of her energy went into her garden, which was marvelous. It had peacocks strutting on the lawns, but Clarissa was complaining about them to Yvonne, "They also get into the lettuce and spinach."

She had a herb garden, a vegetable garden, a few acres of cow grass, a small dairy, and was living with Helen's ex-husband, another Neutral, apparently very happily.

There was a parrot sitting in a cage behind Yvonne and Clarissa.

Clarissa was telling Yvonne, "Whatever is happening in Auroville, whatever has happened to me, I have never doubted The Mother."

"When the villagers attacked me and broke my arm, instead of struggling I just relaxed and started calling Mother. It was miraculous. The very instant I let go and started to call Her they let me go and went away."

"What can I do for you? How can I help?" Yvonne asked.

The parrot in the cage behind her started cawing, "Mother! Mother! Mother!"

Everyone started laughing.

Helen asked Yvonne if she could ask the Administrator why he had refused to recommend her visa and her daughter's visa.

Yvonne agreed, and listened to what else they had to say.

She agreed to go with a few of the Neutrals the next afternoon to see the burgermeister and discuss the situation with him.

They all met at the burgermeister's house in the late afternoon. Yvonne had called the burgermeister to make an appointment. He invited her to come for tea. She told him she would bring a few friends.

When they arrived they saw he was busy on the tennis court. He didn't look at them or smile, or acknowledge them in any way. The whole area in front of his house had been turned into a sports ground for the community. There were tennis courts, a volleyball court, badminton court, basketball court, a field for running, ball games, etc., and jungle gyms where every afternoon all the children of the community, and many of the adults, came for some hours of supervised play.

They watched the play for some minutes. The burgermeister did not even look at them. Yvonne said, "Perhaps he wants us to wait for him in his house. They went to the front door of his house. His sister was there.

"Hello Yvonne." She said.

"Hello Marianne." Yvonne replied.

"Come in. But your friends cannot come in."

Robert Goodman, Roslyn and several other Neutrals were with Yvonne.

"Why do you welcome me, and not them?" Yvonne asked.

"The community has decided that we do not receive these people in our house. This is not my house, this is my brother's house, and I cannot let them come in here because the community has decided that no-one should allow them in any Auroville house."

"The tea party that never was," Roslyn muttered under her breath to Yvonne.

Yvonne asked Marianne, "Is this your house?"

"No, it's my brother's. He will be here soon." Marianne was standing alone in the shining spacious entry hall.

The burgermeister's mother suddenly appeared.

She came to the door, "Yvonne, come, come. Roslyn, come, come. Look Marianne. Here is Roslyn. I have not seen her for a long time. Come. Come." She was a regal old German lady who had lived through two world wars.

Marianne said, "We cannot invite them in; the community has decided that we cannot invite these people into our houses."

Her mother turned to Yvonne, Roslyn and the other Neutrals, "Come, come, the burgerneister will be here soon to speak with you. We will sit on the terrace, not in the house. Yes, Marianne, we will not sit in the house. Don't worry."

Marianne said, "I will make tea."

The old woman, Omma, said, "That would be very nice." She led everyone through the house and out onto a terrace with a lotus pond full of large gold fish and tiger fish. There was a table and comfortable chairs. There were enough chairs for everyone.

"Omma asked Robert Goodman, "What do you want Robert Goodman?"

Robert Goodman said, "I want to be an Aurovilian."

Omma said, "Ya, this is good.. You wait, drink tea, the burgermeister comes."

She turned to Yvonne and started talking in French, a language, that no-one else there, understood, while Marianne served tea.

Finally the burgermeister came and said, "Don't worry, everything is all right. There is a group in the community that has taken up the work of reintegrating the Neutrals into the community, only it has been decided that we cannot accept you as a group. If you apply separately to join Auroville, each of you will have the opportunity to re-join the community.

"There will be a meeting soon. We will call you. Meanwhile, to begin with you should all stop speaking to Vasudeva."

There was some more discussion.

Eventually Yvonne said, "Excuse me, I must go, my car will be waiting. I am moving to Pondicherry tonight."

Everyone said a friendly goodbye, and the party was over.

Yvonne invited Roslyn to have lunch with her at the Grand Hotel in the morning. She suggested she should come a bit early so they could go to the Samadhi and visit some shops.

Roslyn got into Pondi the next morning by 10 o'clock. Yvonne was waiting for her on the dining room/terrace of the Grand Hotel.

"Would you like a tea, or coffee, or something?" Yvonne asked.

"No. Thank you."

"Then we go?"

They went first to The Ashram. They were sitting there quietly at the tomb. Suddenly Roslyn looked up, and there was Jim Bean looking at her. She had not seen him in months. She had heard that he had taken Dhyan to Bangalore for treatment from a famous healer there who had a reputation for miraculous cures. Roslyn could see in Jim's face that there had been no miraculous cure, although she had heard rumors that Dhyan was standing and walking.

Jim turned away from her, and she knew they were only rumors.

She took Yvonne into the bazaar for shopping.

"Who was that very good looking man?" Yvonne asked.

"That was Jim Bean. He looks after Dhyan, who had fallen from Matrimandir."

"Yes, I remember hearing about that? How is she?"

"I don't know. I think she has become a bit of a recluse. I don't know anyone who had seen her in the past several years."

"That is very strange. Let's go to Boutique d'Auroville." Yvonne suggested.

Roslyn said, "I can't go in there."

Yvonne said, "Come, let's go. All those people are my friends."

They got to Boutique d'Auroville. The big guy from Le Jardin de Mere was sitting there at the desk by the entrance. He looked at Roslyn. "You are not welcome here."

Yvonne spoke to him in French. Several other French people from Auroville were there. Roslyn knew enough French to understand that Yvonne was trying to tell them that not only should she be allowed into the shop, but her products also should be in the shop. They told her that Roslyn would be given an opportunity to join Auroville and become part of the process, but until then, nothing was possible.

They went back to the Grand Hotel for lunch.

"What can I do?" Yvonne asked. "I can do nothing. Just remember what the parrot said, 'Mother, Mother, Mother.' Just call Mother. What else can we do?"

Roslyn told her that she had thoroughly enjoyed the days they had spent together.

Yvonne assured her that the pleasure had been mutual, and gave her a box of Roger Gallet soap.

Roslyn rode home in a happy daze. She stopped at her friend Helen's to talk about the amazing deus ex machina that had miraculously appeared. Helen was slightly less enthusiastic. "Let's see what happens," she said.

Roslyn drove through the sports ground on her way back to the forest. All the guys playing basketball stopped their game and waved to her. None of them had spoken to her or acknowledged her existence for years. She took it as a sign of things to come. She hoped the days of outcasts in Auroville were over.

Chapter XXI

With His Holiness at Forecomers

There is an Influence from a Light above,
There are thoughts remote, and sealed eternities:
A mystic motive drives the stars and suns.
The world is other than we now think and see,
Our lives a deeper mystery than we have dreamed:
Our minds are starters in the race to God,
Our souls deputed selves of the Supreme.

Sri Aurobindo, Savitri

A difficulty is that we vibrate to the movements of others. Eventually there comes a delight in meeting and feeling and surmounting all troubles, obstacles and difficulties until they are eliminated by their own transformation. The whole being lives in a final power, the universal calm and joy, the seeing delight and will of the spirit in itself and its manifestation.

For the power of feeling, beyond pleasure, pain, indifference, the vital being has to be liberated from desire and its inequalities, and accept and turn into pure enjoyment the rasa with which the understanding greets the Self.

For the power of knowledge, beyond ignorance, error and knowledge, everything must be accepted. Cling to nothing. Be repelled by nothing, however imperfect, or however subversive, of fixed notions. Allow nothing to lay hold to the detriment of the free working of Truth Spirit. Only with this equality can we rise to the Supramental power of will, immoral, amoral, moral. All must be transformed into the freedom of the divine will in action.

The equal will need not feel sorrow, remorse or discouragement over its stumblings, if these reactions occur in the habitual mentality, it will only see how far they indicate an imperfection and the thing to be corrected, and so get beyond them to a calm and equal guidance.

The stumblings are steps to the goal.

(from Jim Bean's notes on Sri Aurobindo's Synthesis of Yoga)

Roslyn was suddenly back in the mainstream of Auroville. Some of the Neutrals stopped speaking to her because she accepted to be accepted before they were all accepted. She did not feel like sitting Boddhisatva-like waiting for all the other Neutrals to enter the mainstream. She was happy to no longer be an outcast and public object of derision.

She was formally accepted by the Entry Group for a year of probation as a Newcomer. In her case they waived the Newcomer contribution, however. They insisted her unit become part of the Auroville Handicraft Trust.

After her probationary year they told her she had been accepted.

"Accepted into what?" she asked.

"Auroville," they replied.

"You have no right to accept me in Auroville. I was accepted by Mother 14 years ago."

"If you really feel like that then we do not accept you," they said, intimidating her to be quiet..

She backed down, "Okay, thank you for accepting me in the name of the dictatorship of the proletariat. I feel like an artist who has somehow survived the cultural revolution."

"Watch out."

She took care to maintain a low profile. She was aware that although she had been formally 'accepted', the general attitude towards her had not changed. The people who had not liked her still did not like her, and the children who had been taught to fear her continued to fear her.

She went to the Handicraft Trust, which accepted her workshop as part of her co-executive's unit and told her she could have her own unit after a year of probation. They told her she could not use the profit from the workshop to pay Bliss's school fees. If she made any money it was for Auroville, not for Bliss's school fees. They refused to give her five thousand rupees for the dentist.

It was clear for her that as long as there was no-one else to pay Bliss's school fees it was her sacred task to do so. She felt as if she had joined the fascist party. She simply started cooking her books so she could pay the school fees. Some compassionate people in Auroville helped her to pay the dentist. It was two years before the dentist finally gave her her denture. It had been made in France. After he gave it to her he invited her into his office.

She was gushing with gratitude and delight.

The dentist looked at her shyly and said, "I think I owe you some money."

Roslyn was astonished. She was way behind, and needed money desperately for school fees. "Yes," he said. "I cannot charge you anything for my work, I can only take from you the lab charges in Paris that came to just fifteen hundred rupees, because they do not charge Auroville for the work they do; they only charge us for the materials they use. They are friends of Auroville."

"That is very generous. I would just give you the money, because I am so delighted with my teeth, but I need the money for my daughter's school fees. I would like to take two thousand rupees, and offer you the other fifteen hundred as a donation to the Dental Clinic."

"Thank you," he replied, with an open face full of friendship and affection.

Roslyn was delighted that she not only had new teeth, but also some money to send to the school.

She felt as if she was skateboarding on the edge of the edge, but somehow surviving.

She was happy and busy and making beautiful things for markets all over the world. She sold shoes to Dominci in Rome, Henri Bendle in New York, Origins in Santa Fe, and other stores; as well as to individuals, who marketed them for her. She was still making custom shoes, as well as fulfilling orders for local sales and export. She had customers from Bombay and Delhi. She had never charged any Aurovilian for a pair of shoes, until her co-executive, whose family had received at least eight pairs of free shoes that year, gave her a bill for one hundred and fifty rupees when she asked for three cups from his pottery. She was shocked.

He had not actually taken the one thousand rupees a month remittance, because he could see from her books that she was not making any money, but he could not give her a free cup from his pottery.

After that she decided to charge him and his family for anything they took from the workshop.

She finally went to a meeting. It was a terrible meeting. The topic was coming to a consensus to outcast James Walker, an American poet who called the police when the community tore his house down in Fraternity, when he tried to move back into it. He had lived elsewhere in Auroville, had visited France, and had not lived in the house for a couple of years. He had been a disciple of Panditji.

Roslyn spoke saying she did not think it was good for the collective process to brand individuals as outcasts and shun them. It was a very harsh way to deal with non-conformity. The meeting ignored her remarks. Everyone else agreed that James Walker would be outcast and shunned thenceforth and forever more, and the topic would be discussed again the following week.

Roslyn was astonished at the process.

It went on week by week.

Finally the hard liners left the meeting — because they could not understand why the meeting continued to discuss the question.

The main question for the community, then, which occasionally they got into, was what did the Auroville community want to happen when the Auroville Act expired? The Auroville Act had been passed by Parliament in 1981. It had taken the management of the assets of Auroville from The Sri Aurobindo Society for three to five years and placed it under the management of the Department of Education of the Government of India. The Sri Aurobindo Society had contested the Act. The question went to the Supreme Court of India. The Supreme Court ratified the Act of Parliament in November 1982. Unless there was another Act of Parliament when the Act expired, the management of Auroville would go back to the Sri Aurobindo Society. No-one wanted that. In 1985 Parliament agreed to a two year extension on the Act to give the community a further opportunity to clarify its wishes on the topic.

Someone came from Canada with the idea of a land trust. Auroville was not to be owned, but stewarded by willing servitors of The Divine Consciousness. There would be a supervisory body, appointed by perhaps the Government of India, with the responsibility to see that Auroville evolved towards the realization of the goals of The Charter.

To become more credible Auroville needed to define criteria for membership, and have a master plan for development. A group was formed to coordinate the development of Auroville, that had been entirely spontaneous and haphazard for the past ten years. The group called itself Auroville Resource Center, and was guided by the ideal of coordinating the development of the town, taking into account the wishes of the greenworkers, developers, architects and builders.

The 'green' people of Auroville who had built the forests were mostly idealists who rode bicycles rather than motorcycles to conserve fossil fuels.

The people who were thinking of Auroville as a concrete town mostly lived in Europe ten or eleven months of the year. The chief architect had built a machete of his dream in his office in Paris. The plan was like an exploding spiral galaxy. For a few this was clearly the 'master plan' for the city. Others felt that his plan was completely inappropriate for the environment, and were aware of an ecological global crisis that would effect development.

Auroville was growing; some harmonization process was needed to coordinate development, roads, utilities, etc, and to have a databank of existing development.

Roslyn was happy working with the Auroville Resource Center. She found that the existing development patterns on the map, and the spontaneous development of the town over the previous ten years, exactly coincided with the architect's plan. Workshops had flourished in the industrial zone, schools in the cultural zone, homes in the residential zone, and the only building in the International Zone was Bharat Nivas, the pavilion of India.

Bharat Nivas had become a complete living building. It was the center for all kinds of activities, from food processing to art to administration. Roslyn had always thought of it as Sri Aurobindo's building, and The Matrimandir as the Mother's building.

The community agreed to support ARC, and anyone wanting to build was to ask permission.

It was at an ARC meeting that Roslyn heard that Jim Bean had purchased a big plot of land and wanted to build a house. The land was at the southernmost point of Auroville, at the edge of the green belt. He was given permission to build, but as it was in the green belt he was requested to use only sustainable energy.

Roslyn wondered why he was building a house. The only person she knew of who was admitted to Dhyan's presence was a masseur, Devaji. When she asked him about Dhyan, he had said she was making progress. When she asked him if Dhyan was walking he replied, "Not yet."

It had been eight years since Dhyan's accident. For several years Jim Bean had been Dhyan's only attendant. Boy had been dismissed for disco dancing with one of Jim's old girl friends from New York who had come for a visit. Jim had completely ignored her, but Boy had befriended her and took her to the rock n'roll parties. Dhyan felt his disco dancing was harmful to the atmosphere she was trying to maintain, and dismissed him as an attendant.

He had told Roslyn that Jim was not allowed to smoke, drink alcohol, or eat in restaurants.

She asked, "What if he breaks a rule? What will she do? She can't throw him out. She would have no-one to look after her?"

"I don't know," Boy said. "I have heard they have a suicide pact."

Roslyn was horrified. "That is the most stupid thing I have ever heard."

"Maybe it isn't true, I just heard it from Gary's brother."

Roslyn wondered if Dhyan was improving to the point that Jim imagined they might live a normal life, so he was building a house for them. She could not imagine what he was thinking. Why didn't he take Dhyan to the West and consult some doctors there? Roslyn felt Dhyan did not need a house, so much as she needed to be able to stand on her own two feet, but she could not object to the group giving Jim permission to build.

Roslyn was still in love with Jim. After he moved out of the forest she had had a few casual affairs. She simply had not found another man who could enchant her, blow her mind, take her into the invisible realms that felt like home, where she had dwelt with Jim, so she became unavailable for emotional relationships. She lived alone. She loved The Divine. The Divine Loved her. She loved Jim Bean. He apparently did not love her. She often ran into him in the office, on the street, on the road. He would pass her on his motorcycle and look away from her, careful not to even give her a smile or nod of acknowledgment. Even though he never spoke to her, and usually did not even look at her, it was still a thrill to see him. She could feel him approaching. It was as though her heart would light up and the light would extend to beyond her extremities, then he would appear. She wished that there was someone else who could do that to her, but there wasn't; or if there was she had not found him, or her.

She hardly ever thought about Jim Bean and Dhyan. There was nothing she could do for them, and they apparently wanted no contact with her, so she completely forgot them for days and weeks on end. Then there would be the flash, and Jim would pass by or be standing there, not far away, and she wondered how the beautiful connection between them had become so twisted. They could not even say hello to one another, although there was an enormous empathy between them.

The only thing Roslyn could do was pray that Dhyan would walk, so Jim would be free to speak to her again.

Dhyan was not walking, but Jim was building a house for her. Someone sent Roslyn an article about computers being used to simulate the damaged nerve in the spinal chord, making it possible for some terminally paralyzed people to walk.

She passed the article on to Devaji. Jim did not take Dhyan to the

West, but started building his house. At one point he sent a note to ARC complaining about the high energy power lines that were running through the canyon near his house. Another time he sent a note complaining that he had heard the land across the canyon was being turned into an airport.

The airport was coming. There was nothing anyone could do about it. The face of Auroville and Pondicherry was changing.

Roslyn was completely bored with the day-in-day-out routine of the workshop. She enjoyed working for the community and with others in ARC, and then in the Auroville Trust administration.

She enjoyed working with other people who could read and write. She was still enchanted with the overall fantasy of Auroville. Whatever her personal path had been, she felt blessed that she had been able to use her life as a participant in the great adventure of Auroville.

She gave part of the forest to a Persian woman, and another part of the forest to a group that wanted to build a 'healing community.'

She sold enough shoes to pay Bliss's school fees, and worked in the administrative offices three or four days a week. She was still friendly with Helen, who had also been accepted by the main stream. The other Neutrals hardly spoke to them, and most of the others did not speak to them either.

Roslyn was happy. She did not care if this or that was not what she wanted. Her life was challenging, interesting, and purposeful. She was bored with Helen's woeful complaints that someone wasn't nice to her or someone else was cheating her. Some people were not nice to Roslyn, but that was their problem, not hers. Some people cheated her. She tried to avoid those people.

The forest was beautiful. She had carefully cultivated the trees. There was a carpet of wild flowers. All the roofs had been repaired and thatched. The school fees were paid. She would get up in the morning and meditate. She would prepare the work for the workers, assign it to the workers when they came, then go off to the office. She would return at mid-day, and often after checking the work go back out to a meeting.

In the evening there were movies, videos and cultural programs several times a week.

Suddenly she was not feeling well. For several years her health had been surprisingly good. She was visiting her neighbor, and complained that for several days she had not been feeling well; nothing specific, just not well, malaise. Her neighbor's boyfriend mentioned, "That's funny.

Something is wrong with Jim Bean. It isn't clear, maybe it is something with his leg, he had a terrible infected sore, but he can't walk."

The next morning Roslyn was feeling better, and did not want to think about Jim Bean, though she hoped that he was also feeling better.

For several days she heard nothing more.

One afternoon, at the end of a meeting, Didier, a Frenchman, came into the meeting, and asked to speak. He had been helping Jim to build the house. He had always been a close friend of Dhyan. He was a passionate follower of Victor.

He said, "Jim Bean is not well. I have been helping him build the house. I need people to help me to take care of Jim and Dhyan." There was an immediate show of hands, of people who would be willing to help. "Please you can stay after the meeting to speak with me."

The meeting was adjourned.

Roslyn stayed with the others. Didier looked at her and said, "Please, you go."

"Would you please tell Jim and Dhyan that I would do anything I could for them," she said.

"Please, you go."

"If he is so ill, why don't you take him to a hospital or Nursing Home?" She asked.

"Please go," he said. Several of the others also enjoined her to go. She left.

A few days later a friend who lived near where Jim was building dropped by her workshop in the evening for a cup of tea.

"You know Jim is sick."

"Yes, I'd heard," Roslyn replied.

"Geoff said, ' Jim Bean is dying,'" her friend said.

"Who is looking after him?" Roslyn asked.

"Some of your neighbors from the healing community, and several others from Auroville are attending him and Dhyan, but they refuse to see any doctors. I think there is a masseuse from The Ashram who visits them. Several doctors and homeopaths have gone offering to help, and were not admitted. Mari came out from The Ashram. She has a reputation for being a 'great' homeopath. Everyone knows how close she was to Mother. She was not allowed to see them. There is a strange aura of secrecy around the whole scene."

"What is happening with the house?" Roslyn asked.

"Work is going on. It is enormous. It is completely out of place there in the forest. I wish we had been there when the community gave them permission to build there. I would have protested. It is not the place for such a huge house."

"Jim Bean cannot die. Who will look after Dhyan?" Roslyn asked.

"I am certain the community will look after her," her friend replied.

Roslyn noticed that Dhyan's daughter Aura was living next door with the Persian lady.

Several weeks later Roslyn was feeling ill. She found she had worms. One of her neighbors from the healing community dropped by.

"Hi. How are you?" her neighbor asked.

"Not so well." Roslyn replied. "I have worms."

Her neighbor cracked up with laughter.

"What is funny about that?" Roslyn asked.

"Jim Bean vomited a big worm yesterday, I cannot believe how connected you two are."

"He vomited a big worm, and still won't see a doctor?" Roslyn asked in horror.

"It's okay. We are giving him some worm medicine," her neighbor replied.

"How can you do that? Are you doctors? How do you know what medicine he needs?"

"Don't be so stupid. He just needs some ordinary worm medicine. He doesn't want a doctor; maybe he doesn't need a doctor. Don't be so dramatic."

Roslyn felt she had to do something. She was dreaming about Jim often, and did not feel comfortable with the fact that he was not receiving any professional medical help although he was terribly ill. She went to visit his neighbors.

"Hello," she said, appearing at their kitchen door early one morning while they were still at breakfast.

"Hi, come in. What can we do for you?" they asked.

"I have come about Jim Bean," she said.

"Yes, what about him?"

"I have heard he is ill and will not see a doctor. I am thinking about writing to his sister."

"Don't do that."

"Why not?"

"We just typed a letter for him yesterday to his father, asking for more money to finish the house."

"Why did you have to type a letter for him?"

"His right side is paralyzed. He can't write."

"Are you crazy? If you don't call a doctor, and take a doctor to him, now, this week, I will surely write to his sister."

"I don't think it is any of your business," the neighbor replied.

"There is a young doctor who has just graduated, named Shiva, living at Ami. Maybe you can persuade Jim to see him."

"Okay, we'll try, but please don't write to his family."

Roslyn was tempted to go to where Jim was lying, according to rumor surrounded by flies, and grab him and taking him to a Nursing Home. However, she was afraid that he would die of shock if she went to him, or that he would get angry and refuse to go with her, so she wrote a note to Dhyan and Jim asking if she might visit.

She did not receive any reply to her note, but Dr. Shiva was called to examine Jim.

Several days later she asked Dr. Shiva what happened when he went to see Jim and Dhyan.

He told her that he had been specifically told not to speak about it with her, but he wanted to talk to her anyhow. She had to promise not to say a word to anyone that he had spoken to her.

"Don't worry. Who can I talk to?"

"It is a very strange scene. She was sitting in a chair weeping and he was lying on the bed. I had only to take one look at him to see that he had apparently had a stroke. The right side of his face was paralyzed.

"Jim opened his eyes and said, 'Please don't touch me.'

"I asked if I might take his pulse.

"He extended his wrist to me.

"I checked his pulse and blood pressure, and told him he needed to be moved immediately to a hospital. He had suffered a stroke, and needed medical help and supervision to prevent further strokes.

"He just thanked me for coming. I was dismissed, and there was nothing more I could do or say. So I went out, but the attendant told me to wait.

"He came back to me about an hour later and told me that Dhyan did not want to move John to a hospital at the moment. She had written to Victor for advice. She asked the attendants to please stay with them and wait with them for Victor's reply. The attendants had agreed to stay on and wait for the reply from Victor. He thanked me for waiting and offered me some money, which I refused. I don't know what to do," he said.

Roslyn felt very sober and chilled at the end of this recitation. She was afraid to write to Jim's sister. She did not know where to turn. She went to Joe, who had always remained friendly with Jim, and begged him to go and see Jim and take him to a nursing home or hospital.

Joe went three times, but the attendants each time refused to allow him to see Jim. He got a note from Dhyan saying , "We will invite you to see us as soon as Jim is better. Please be patient."

Joe had lived in Pondicherry from 1967 to 1973 as a member of The Ashram. He had met Mother, who had healed herself repeatedly from seemingly terminal illnesses for twenty-five years. He could not imagine that young, handsome, healthy, wealthy, humorous, delightful, charming Jim Bean could simply sicken and die. It was a preposterous concept.

Roslyn was having more and more dreams involving Jim Bean.

She would go to bed after a full day in the workshop, and rushing around Auroville. In the middle of the night she would be wakened by a horrible dream of Jim Bean lying in a bed gasping, "Help! Help! Help!"

She had written to Kwan Yin and Boy and asked them to tell Gary, who was in California, to please return, as he was the one person allowed to see Jim and Dhyan.

Kwan Yin and Boy arrived, but they said it would be a few weeks before Gary would arrive, because he had a good job and needed more money.

Finally Gary arrived.

Although Roslyn had not spoken to him in years she went to him the day after he got back.

"Hello Gary."

"Hi Roz."

"You know that Jim is sick," she said.

"Yes, I already went there yesterday when I got back. Didier would not let me it. He brought me a note from Dhyan, a very sweet note, telling me she would call me when Jim was better."

Roslyn left wondering what she could do. Knowing that Jim needed help. She was afraid that he would get angry and have a heart attack if she just barged in there. She felt that he had sacrificed ten years of his life so everyone should give Dhyan respect, and it would be disrespectful of her to go in there without Dhyan's permission, unless she could get his permission.

Night after night she was woken up by dreams of Jim screaming, "Help! Help! Help!"

She finally went to Didier.

She said, "I'm sorry, excuse me, but although I have not spoke to Jim for nine years, and I have my own life and have nothing to do with him, I am having these terrible dreams every night and hear him calling, 'Help!' Would you please tell him that I would gladly do anything I can for him. What can I do? How can I help?'

"He is not calling 'Help!' You go. Everything is fine."

Roslyn accepted what he said, and attributed her dreams to some part of her still holding on to Jim Bean, not something emanating from Jim himself. She made a determined effort to forget about Jim, and meditated half the night, to sleep only when she was too tired to dream, but the dreams continued.

Some days later after a meeting she overheard Mariana speaking to someone.

"I went to see Dhyan and Jim this morning. She was very sweet, as always, but he was lying there looking like he was in a coma. His face looked like white wax. He looks like he might be dead, but Dhyan said he was getting better."

Roslyn gave her neighbor a note for Dhyan asking for permission to visit Jim

Her neighbor brought a rely, "'When Jim is better you may visit him,' Dhyan said. Now you can forget about it. Don't disturb them." Her neighbor said.

Roslyn burst into tears, because the words said one thing but she felt they were actually saying something else.

A few days later she was sitting in her hammock reading Ruud Lohman's book, "A House for the Third Millennium", when her worker came in and said to her, "Jim Bean dead."

She could not believe it. It was suddenly as though the life force started to flow out of her body. She went to her neighbors, and they took her hands and told her it was true, Jim had died that morning in the Nursing Home in Pondi.

"In the Nursing Home? When did he go to the Nursing Home?"

"Yesterday."

"How did that happen?"

"Jim hasn't eaten anything for a long time. He had big open sores. He could hardly breathe. With each breathe he was gasping, 'Help!'

"Finally Dhyan and the attendants decided to call Dr. Chatterjee, the Auroville homeopath, but Dr. Chatterjee is out of station and I am looking after her patients, so I went.

"I went there in the morning on my scooter," Eleanor said.

"Dhyan was looking wonderful, and Jim was lying on the bed gasping,

'Help!'

"I knew there was nothing I could do. I am a self educated homeopath. I could tell from half way across the room that he required more help than I could offer him. I said, 'This man needs a doctor and a hospital.'

"I touched his arm. His skin was completely dehydrated."

"I asked the attendant to go call The Ashram doctor and ask him to come, and to explain that it was an emergency.

"An hour later Dr. Sen was there. He was horrified. He said, 'If you had called me two weeks ago I might have been able to save him, but now, only Mother can help him.' He insisted on taking Jim with him in his car. One of the attendants went with him. I think Gary was there with him when he died."

Roslyn said, "Thank you for telling me what happened."

She went back to the forest. She wrote a note to Dhyan, "I share your grief. If I can help you in any way I am your friend." She got no reply. She sat in her hammock, and continued reading Ruud's essays on Matrimandir. She decided she would go in the morning and pay her final respects to Jim's body.

In the morning the workers told her that Dhyan had died during the night by taking poison.

The Inner Chamber

xxii

In this investiture of fleshly life
A soul, that is a spark of God, survives,
And sometimes it breaks through the sordid screen,
And kindles a fire that makes us half-divine,
In our body's cells there sits a hidden Power
That sees the unseen and plans eternity;
Our smallest parts have roof for deepest needs;
There too the golden Messengers can come:

Sri Aurobindo, Savitri

All energies and actions are seen as proceeding from the one Existence and their perversions as imperfections inevitable in the developing movement, and of powers that were needed for that movement. It will therefore have charity for all imperfections, even while pressing steadily towards a universal perfection. This equality will open the nature to the guidance of the divine and universal will and make it ready for that Supramental action in which the power of the soul in us is harmoniously full of and one with the power of the Supreme Spirit.

Endurance is only mastery of possession of universal energy. Impartiality is impartial acceptance striving to transform all. Resignation should be full surrender into embracing oneness till all is acknowledged as Divine.

Equality is the spiritual way of replying to life or rather of embracing it and compelling it to become a perfect form of action of the self and spirit.

It is the first secret of the soul's mastery of existence. To be equal, not to be overborne by any stress of desire is the first condition of real self-mastery; self-empire is its basis.

A mere mental equality, however great it may be, is hampered by the tendency of quiescence. It is only the spirit that is capable of sublime undisturbed rapidity of will as well as an unlimited patience. It can accept the smallest work in the narrowest circle of the cosmos, but it can work too upon the whirl of chaos with an understanding and creative force. It has detachment because it is above all. It has that intimate acceptance for it is yet one with all.

(from Jim Bean's Journal extracts from Sri Aurobindo's Synthesis of Yoga)

The deaths of Jim Bean and Dhyan did not apparently seem to affect Roslyn's life. She felt the only way to salvation for herself and Auroville was perhaps Matrimandir. If that big mess in the middle of Auroville would become something that somehow held Mother and Sri Aurobindo's Force, the force for the Supramental Transformation, then it might perhaps justify somehow the sacrifice. For her it had to be like the concrete materialization of what Sri Aurobindo had written about, and what Mother had worked for all Her life. Roslyn was having trouble remaining certain what was happening in Auroville was Mother and Sri Aurobindo's yoga. Another friend, a brilliant person of only forty-eight, had died a few months before Jim and Dhyan. He had chosen to ignore the fact that the community had declared her an outcast. He would often drop by for tea in the afternoon, usually with his small son. Sometimes he would bring her a Rose from the Matrimandir Rose Garden or a stone he had found on the way. He was so respected by everyone that no one harrassed him for visiting her. He had a marvelous sense of humor. He had worked on the Matrimandir every day from the beginning, and always did the most difficult and physically demanding work, as well as night watch, writing, looking after the administration of Matrimandir, and looking after his son. Roslyn thought he was one of the nicest people she had ever met. She had been amazed when he visited her after she had just finished thatching her roof, and looked longingly at her roof and said, "That is what I need."

"What do you mean?"

"There is an old keet roof on our house, full of holes."

"Why don't you fix it?"

"No money."

"Can't Auroville give you the money?"

"They say there is no money."

Roslyn could not believe what she was hearing. He was the most saintly and respected member of the community, and the community claimed not to have the funds to repair his roof? Roslyn would have given the money, but she did not have it.

And then, a few weeks later, he was dead. They said he had a heart attack, but Roslyn felt he was so frustrated that he could not put a roof over his family's head that he dropped dead. She wondered when would the Auroville community realize that something must be terribly wrong if the most beautiful and intelligent men of the community were dying before they are fifty.

Roslyn could not imagine how Auroville was being administered if the community could not provide a decent roof for this saintly man who had spent so many years in concentrated service. The news of his death was a terrible shock.

He had left behind the small book of essays, "A House for the Third Millennium," that she had been reading when her worker had come and told her that Jim Bean was dead.

Matrimandir was for Roslyn the symbol of the sacrifice of Jim Bean's life, Dhyan's life and Ruud's life. She sought strength in the essays to believe that the sacrifice was worthy of those lives.

She reread what Mother had said, "The solution is to go deep within oneself and find the place where all the differences combine to constitute the essential and eternal Unity." Roslyn looked within herself to try to find that place of unity, to assuage her anger at these deaths. She tried to imagine what the Inner Chamber would be, white, still. A big twelve-sided room with a white ceiling, white marble walls, and a thick white rug on the floor. In the center of the room there would be an enormous crystal ball. A single ray of light from the sun would pass through the crystal, through a hole in the floor of the chamber and descend to a pool of water at the bottom of Matrimandir.

Roslyn felt the little book of essays had been given to her at that moment to help her find her way through what was happening. Something Mother said resounded, "It is not difficult to distinguish the voice of the Divine: one cannot make a mistake. You need not be very far on the path to be able to recognize it; you must listen to the small still peaceful voice that speaks in the silence of your heart. I forgot one thing: to hear it, you must be absolutely sincere. For if you are not sincere, you will begin by deceiving yourself and you will hear nothing at all except the voice of your own ego, and then you will most assuredly commit (thinking that is the real small voice) the most awful stupidities. But if you are sincere, the way is sure. It is not even a voice, not even a sensation, it is something extremely subtle - a slight indication..."

Roslyn hated herself for not having believed in her self and in her impulses to wrest Jim from the clutch of Dhyan's attendants.

On the surface their deaths did not seem to change her life. She was living in her capsule, making and selling crocheted shoes, and trying to keep Bliss's school fees paid. She was invited to a Thanksgiving feast in Madras and went in a van full of Aurovilians. Sitting across from her was Gary. They did not say a word to one another for several hours, then he said to her, "Aura wants the house."

Roslyn looked at him, "I don't want that house."

Gary gook a crumpled little piece of poor quality paper out of his wallet and showed it to Roslyn. A magic square had been painstakingly drawn on the paper based on the number 24 by Dhyan. There was the symbol Om in each corner, painstakingly, lovingly drawn. Very gently these words were placed in the square,

"This place
The offering
To the right
The true
The vast

Ravena Mataram

by

two kindred souls

AUM NAMO BHAGAVATE"

Roslyn looked at the little scrap of paper and said to him, "Well, at least she got that right."

"She wrote it after she ate the thorny balls of poisonous dattora that killed her."

"Well, it looks as though she achieved something, although she fell on her face and brought the rest of us toppling with her."

Gary went on talking. Roslyn and Gary had never been on intimate speaking terms, but he perhaps wanted to unburden himself. "I was there in the Nursing Home when Jim died."

"I did not quite get that part. How did he get to the Nursing Home?"

"The doctor from The Ashram arrived in a car and took him in the car to the Nursing Home the day before he died. The doctor was screaming at everyone because Jim was absolutely dehydrated. 'It is too late!' he raged. 'What can I do?'"

"So how did he die?" She asked.

"I don't know. I had been told to go there as he needed an attendant and everyone was busy with Dhyan. I went there; he was hooked up to drips, etc. A nurse came in and asked me to leave, she was going to wash him. I was in the corridor. She came out and told me he was gone. I couldn't believe it. I went into the room. I don't want to remember - and cannot forget - the expression on his face."

Roslyn looked away from Gary and said to the person sitting there, "Are we really going all the way to Madras just for lunch?"

The person next to her laughed.

It was an amazing lunch. Turkeys had been flown in from the USA with cranberry sauce, lettuce, celery, sweet potatoes, pecan pie. Roslyn was able to forget about Auroville, shoes, death, workers, and everything else, and completely enjoyed the feast. They ate for five hours. Completely drugged with good food she sat in the van back to Auroville glad that she had gone to Madras for lunch, and homesick for the USA.

Bliss was waiting for her at the capsule. She had just arrived home on vacation from school. Roslyn had brought for her, a small tiffin, full of tidbits from the feast. They were very happy to be reunited.

The days passed swiftly. Bliss went back to school for her last term, and Roslyn made shoes and tried to sell them. Several American colleges offered Bliss a full scholarship. It was clear she would be going to the USA when she graduated. Roslyn had no dollars to give her, but the child was determined to go to college in the USA. She went, and at the end of her first year of college she visited Roslyn for a month.

Roslyn was amazed by Bliss. She had gone to college in the USA with $100, and had worked and studied for a year. She then came to visit with gifts in her suitcase. Roslyn was grateful that her daughter was an unbelievably nice person with a lot of self -discipline.

Then Bliss left for her summer job not knowing when she would get back to India. Roslyn was working in the administration of Auroville as well as in her workshop, so she was very busy. She was handling the maintenance fund for the community and was amazed at how little money most people were living on, and how little was available..

One day Roslyn got a letter from Frankie which ended mysteriously with, "Maybe I will see you soon."

The next day she was sitting in the workshop drinking tea and a taxi drove into the forest.

Roslyn could not believe it when Frankie and She got out of the taxi.

They all hugged one another. Roslyn surprised herself at how happy she was to see them. She had not been happy for so long, it was a strange sensation, another state of consciousness. She had been so lonely, and had not been able to even look at her emotional being because she was fully occupied with her responsibilities to the community and her workers.

Frankie and She joined her at her little wobbly table drinking tea and talked about Suzanne and the boys, and Bliss. They invited her to come and stay with them in town. They were staying at the Grand Hotel d'Europe. They were going to be in Pondi for a few days, then fly to Bangalore to see Sai Baba.

She did not go with them to town for the night, but agreed to meet them the next day for lunch.

After lunch they were sitting together on the terrace upstairs in comfortable teak and rattan chairs overlooking a garden full of flowers. Frankie asked about Jim Bean.

Suddenly all the tears she had not shed were pouring down Roslyn's face. She shared with them what she knew about what had happened.

They suggested it might be interesting to see the house.

Roslyn replied, "I never want to see that house again."

She said, "You know, I knew his parents. When I was married to Harold his parents used to play croquet with them. I was invited once for tea in their house in Georgetown."

"What were they like?" Roslyn asked.

"They seemed very stuffy. Jim must have been a shock for them."

"I heard that when his mother heard he had died she collapsed and died." Roslyn said.

"That's a terrible story," Frankie said. "Who could have imagined that ending from those divine weeks of peaches, champagne and Roses?" He looked at Roslyn who had stopped crying. "You must remember the good times."

Roslyn started crying again.

She leaned over and patted her hand. "Cheer up."

Roslyn said, "I can't imagine what's come over me, I never cry."

Frankie said, "Well I guess this is another dimension to our relationship; we have certainly laughed together, so now we have also cried together."

She said to Roslyn, "We actually stopped in Pondi because I am looking for a companion. Would you be interested in coming to California and living in my Gatehouse for a while?"

Roslyn accepted immediately, delighted to be leaving Auroville, India, and going to the USA, where she would be closer to Bliss. She needed to find someone to look after the forest, the workshop, the maintenance fund, and the orchard. It would take a few weeks, but she was ready to leave Auroville, forever.

She chose April 24th to fly, because Mother had come back to India on April 24th and stayed for the rest of her life. Roslyn hoped the magic would work for her in the other direction, and that she would never return to India.

Roslyn could not imagine how she would get along with She, who was too much like H. Rider Haggard's Goddess for her to feel complacent about what was coming. Roslyn had managed to sell enough shoes to pay for her ticket and had a hundred dollars in cash. She had agreed that if Roslyn paid her ticket to California, she would pay her ticket back to India. Roslyn spent her hundred dollars during her stopover in Singapore, mostly on chocolate. She eventually ended up sending all the chocolates to Auroville with a friend from Bidonville.

Roslyn landed in San Francisco and felt like she had come home. Frankie and some of his friends holding a big bouquet of scraggly flowers were there to meet her. They got into the big old American gas-guzzling car and whizzed through San Francisco. The next thing Roslyn was aware of was being on the glorious Golden Gate Bridge. Suzanne was in France nursing her ailing father, and Frankie was on his way to Mexico to spend some time on the beach looking at the sunset.

She let herself in and re-lit the stove. She put a pile of cushions together in the window seat and had a happy meditation.

She slept until the phone rang. It was She.

"Are you ready for lunch?"

"Yes. Should I come down?"

"No, I'll pick you up on my way out. We are going out for lunch. Is there any place in particular you would like to go?"

"No, give me five minutes to get dressed."

"Okay."

There went the afternoon: lunch, a nap, tea, scrabble, and then preparing dinner and watching TV, or having friends over to play mah jong. The days flew by through sylvan forests, to wonderful hot-springs, a lark. Halcyon days.

One day She came up to The Gatehouse, looked around, and fussed that the strings on the cushion covers had not been tied properly.

Roslyn was gushing about how beautiful she found The Gatehouse, and how comfortable.

She said, taking Roslyn's hand, "I think we are going to get along."

Roslyn said, "I hope so."

She loved her house. It was exquisite in every detail, though an enormous labor of love to maintain.

Her kitchen was certainly a masterpiece in fantasy. There was a curved wall of windows overlooking a herb garden with a nook, a huge window seat and big round table enclosed by a red plush banquette surrounded by windows facing east. Roslyn loved to sit there with She in the morning, comfortable and cozy in the early hours watching the garden wake up, sometimes opening the windows to feel the crisp air or tang of rain.

They sat across from one another or next to one another at that table and talked. Both of them had been living alone for ten years or more. Suddenly after all those years of silence there was someone there to listen to and talk to. They became nearly inseparable. Roslyn slept in The Gatehouse and She slept in her bedroom, but they spent many hours every day together, and it seemed there were not enough hours in the day for them to be together. They were very happy.

She's daughter-in-law saw this and had a fit. She told She that she was being taken advantage of. Roslyn was a bad person. She should not let herself get involved like that, etc.

She started shouting at Roslyn. "Why don't you go back to India?"

Roslyn was not ready to go back to India, so she said, "I'll go to India if you come with me."

She laughed and said, "Okay, we'll go next winter for three weeks."

Three weeks sounded about right to Roslyn for India.

They went, and She fell in love with Auroville. She was not well, and unhappy in California, for months after they returned. Roslyn loved California. She loved the cold air and the hot baths. California cuisine, and strawberries fresh from the garden, made her happy and healthy. Running around with She to concerts, shopping in San Francisco, going to workshops. It was all paradise.

She's son and daughter-in-law refused to come for Christmas because Roslyn was still living there.

One night Roslyn had a dream. Jim Bean told her to come and live in his house. She did not want to go back to Auroville. That morning when she was meditating she saw Mother, and Mother told her it was time for her to go back to Auroville. She did not want to go back to Auroville. A few minutes later the phone rang. She was on the other end of the line. "I think it is time for you to go to India."

Roslyn knew she had to go, but she did not want to leave her friend. She promised to come and visit, or to call her back if she needed her. They parted in tears.

The Mother - February 21, 1973

xxiii

The light now distant, shall grow native here.
The strength that visits us our comrade power;
The Ineffable shall find a secret voice,
The Imperishable burn through Matter's screen,
Making this mortal body godhead's robe.
The Spirit's greatness is our timeless source,
And it shall be our crown in endless Time.

Sri Autobindo, Savitri

First there is freedom from all preferences, and even acceptance of God's workings within and around him. To be equal is to be infinite and universal; to live in the spirit, not mental or vital.

Then there will be an undisturbed calm.

Even then it is necessary to remain on the watch from above the purusha, ready to repel even the least indication of disturbance. When one sees something disturbing coming, try to find the source and deflect the inward motions of egoistic claim, vital desire, before they damage the will, spiritualized intelligence or soul unity with the Master. God is within us, and the world, the Supreme self, the universal spirit.

If we see unity everywhere, if we recognize that all comes by the divine will, see God in all, in our enemies or rather our opponents in the game of life, in all energies, forces and happening...

The Integral Yoga founds itself on a conception of the spiritual being as an omnipresent existence. The fullness of which comes not essentially by a transference to other worlds or a cosmic self-extinction, but by a growth out of what we now are phenomenally into the consciousness of the omnipresent reality which we always are in the essence of our being.

These three elements, a union with the supreme Divine, unity with the universal self, and a Supramental life action from this transcendent origin and through this universality, but still with the individual as the soul-channel and natural instrument, constitute the essence of the integral divine perfection of the human being.

(from Jim Bean's notes on Sri Aurobindo's 'Synthesis of Yoga')

Roslyn arrived at Madras by plane. Her cobbler met her at the airport with a note from her neighbors that said, "There is no place in Auroville for you."

She cringed. She felt that she was walking back into the battlefield, and she had no armor, no weapons, nothing except The Divine. She immediately went inside herself and called The Mother asking, "Is this true?"

Roslyn went into a trance, and the three- hour journey seemed to take three minutes.

Again she saw Jim Bean's ghost telling her to go to the house he had built. She rejected that idea. She went to Silence. All the buildings she had built there were full. No one offered her a space. Someone asked her to please fix the roof in the building where he was staying. Roslyn replied, "I have no place to stay myself. You're living here; you fix the roof."

She went around to all the guesthouses, and all were full. It was February, the peak of the 'season.' Finally she went to Jim Bean's house, which was also a guesthouse, but it was all the way out on the edge of town. It was dirty, empty and depressing. It had the atmosphere of a bus station. The caretaker lived in a hut nearby. He agreed to give Roslyn a room for two thousand rupees a month. There was a kitchen in the house. She could use it. The house had been rented for the next five years to a program in environmental education, so she would have to leave within a couple of months because groups of thirty to fifty trainees would come. Then there would be wall-to-wall mattresses all over the house. The trainees in these programs were all men, poor farmers from all over South India.

He did not imagine she would be happy to stay in the house in such circumstances.

Roslyn hoped to be going back to the USA in a couple of months. She asked him, "Does it have to be so dirty?"

He replied, "You are coming from America. You are back in India. If you don't like it, leave."

At that point in her life she had nowhere else to go, so she shut up. She rented her room, and began to clean the house. She was only a guest. She was told by the caretaker the servant would wash her clothes, but Roslyn was not to tell the servant what to do or complain that the bathroom was not clean. If she was not happy she could leave.

The five-year contract was mysteriously cancelled, so she didn't have to move out, after four months, but she had to put up with whatever guests the caretaker imposed on the house. Then his hut burned down, and someone gave him a house elsewhere in Auroville. The others in the community agreed she should have the house.

The house was standing in the middle of a garden, near the edge of a vast forest, near the edge of a canyon which had been a world class site of erosion when Auroville began.

There had not been a tree to be seen there in 1968, and the monsoon waters rushed down into the canyon, turning the ocean red with the topsoil from Auroville being carried out to the sea. The first Aurovilians saw this and immediately became concerned with the work of building dams and planting trees to try to save the topsoil.

It was hard work, digging holes in the hot sun, and protecting young trees from marauding goats from the village. Twenty-five years later the land is a fertile area, surrounded by hundreds of acres of blooming forest. Roslyn would go for a walk with her dog every morning and enjoy the new flowers in the garden every day. It was so beautiful it boggled the imagination. The house was of a noble proportion, rising majestically in the park around it, discretely from the front, but wide open on the back with a terrace that looked out over forever.

It was a beautiful house. There was a courtyard, with a garden, in the middle of the house and a lotus pond on the terrace with goldfish.

In the storeroom cupboard she found a copy of the Prayer of St. Francis of Assissi written out by Jim Bean and framed. Roslyn felt this was to be the purpose Jim had ascribed for the house.

"Lord, make me the instrument of Your peace,
Where there is malice may I bring pardon;
Where there is discord may I bring harmony;
Where there is error may I bring truth;
Where there is doubt may I bring faith;
Where there is despair may I bring hope;
Where there is darkness may I bring Your light;
Where there is sadness may I bring joy;
O, Master, may I seek not so much to be comforted as to comfort,
To be understood as to understand,
To be loved as to love,
For it is in giving that we receive,
It is in losing ourselves that we shall find them,

It is in forgiving that we shall be forgiven,
It is in dying that we shall rise up to eternal life.
.....Amen..."

She felt it was an honor to look after the house. Although guests brought money, she was not desperately in need of money. She was sending Roslyn a small allowance from California. Roslyn had enough money to live in the house, and to make the house as beautiful as possible, as a repository of Auroville arts and crafts, which is something she felt Jim would have done.

The house was a wonderful place for concerts, so occasionally there were concerts there, parties with dinners and dances on the terrace under the moon - like a clock by which one reads the hours of the night.

Roslyn realized for herself there was nothing to do but to be happy and grateful. But she was in Auroville, and she was still alive, so she tried to participate also in the collective process. She did not want to release her ego to do battle with other egos. She was so happy and grateful she wanted to try to be a person living in Auroville, as a willing servitor of the Divine Consciousness.

She did not want anything. Everything she needed had been given to her in abundance. If she really needed anything more she could always ask Bliss, who was a perfect and devoted child and always extremely generous to her mother.

Roslyn loved Matrimandir. She was walking up the ramp early one morning. It was Auroville's birthday. The outer skin of the structure had not yet been put up, and the inner chamber was seemingly suspended at the top of a great concrete geodesic dome. The hundreds of interweaving triangles were a three dimensional Shri Chakra in her vision that morning. Through the openings in the triangles as she was ascending the ramp she saw the bonfire being lit and sparks rising to heaven. She had to stop and watch. It was so beautiful it took her breath away. She was so grateful to The Mother and Sri Aurobindo to have been given the opportunity to do something with her life, and to have been vouchsafed such a glorious vision. She was content to know she was able to participate in creating the very beautiful thing, Auroville, a gift of Mother and Sri Aurobindo to their children, the new Garden of Eden; though it sometimes appeared more like Hieronymous Bosch's Garden of Earthly Delights than the innocent garden of Eden. When Mother spoke about the people living in Auroville in the early days to Vasudeva, she kept saying, "They are behaving like dogs and cats."

It did not matter. The power of The Dream of The Divine Mother and the power of the soul or psychic being in every individual had been more powerful than the sum of individual weaknesses, faults, ego trips, etc. Of course, although perhaps individuals made mistakes, they were not made out of malice, but out of confusion. It seems there is one law in this Garden of Eden, which Mother had given as a mantra of behavior for the first three Aurovilians who were living at 'Peace', in the center of Auroville. They were squabbling and someone had written to Mother about it. Mother's reply was... "Goodwill towards all, goodwill from all, is the basis of peace and harmony."

People keep saying that Auroville will be the place of the fulfillment of Mother's 'Dream.'

That seems impossible if one looks at the story in terms of the personalities, but if one stands back and looks at the material result it seems very inspiring. It grows more and more beautiful as people of goodwill from all over the world, all ages and all walks of life, gather in this little corner of South India.

A place that was desolate and barren thirty-five years ago is in process of becoming an enormous garden. An area where there was 100% illiteracy thirty-five years ago now has achieved literacy for at least half the indigenous people.

Roslyn looked around and could see that Auroville had started to become an actual embodiment of a true human unity. Each person was playing their part, but somehow none of them had done anything. Somehow, everything; had been done by Mother and Sri Aurobindo. It was a model of social evolution towards a global society where, obviously, poverty must be eradicated. There must be adequate food, shelter, medical care and educational opportunities for everyone, and slowly, slowly, Auroville, without even perhaps consciously trying to reach that point, was getting there.

To have died for this, is not, to have died for nought.

Death is a part of life, but as it already takes up much more time than life, it is important to remember that it is essential to live and participate in life. The challenge for everyone in this age is to serve a future humanity.

Roslyn was constantly amazed at the inspiring and interesting work she was being given in Auroville, such as organizing international conferences and exhibitions on the evolution of consciousness. She felt she had somehow been reborn, and was beginning a new life, looking towards the future.

The high point of the International Seminar was a meeting under the Banyan Tree at dusk. The place was aglow with the light of hundreds of candles, and as the sun set the moon was rising behind the Matrimandir, and a tape played. The Mother speaking, in April 1964, after having been silent for weeks. "There is no pain, there is no death, there is only love."

The End